Lecture Notes in Computer Science 15723

Founding Editors

Gerhard Goos
Juris Hartmanis

Editorial Board Members

Elisa Bertino, *Purdue University, West Lafayette, IN, USA*
Wen Gao, *Peking University, Beijing, China*
Bernhard Steffen, *TU Dortmund University, Dortmund, Germany*
Moti Yung, *Columbia University, New York, NY, USA*

The series Lecture Notes in Computer Science (LNCS), including its subseries Lecture Notes in Artificial Intelligence (LNAI) and Lecture Notes in Bioinformatics (LNBI), has established itself as a medium for the publication of new developments in computer science and information technology research, teaching, and education.

LNCS enjoys close cooperation with the computer science R & D community, the series counts many renowned academics among its volume editors and paper authors, and collaborates with prestigious societies. Its mission is to serve this international community by providing an invaluable service, mainly focused on the publication of conference and workshop proceedings and postproceedings. LNCS commenced publication in 1973.

Sabine Graf · Angelos Markos
Editors

Generative Systems and Intelligent Tutoring Systems

21st International Conference, ITS 2025
Alexandroupolis, Greece, June 2–6, 2025
Proceedings, Part I

Editors
Sabine Graf
Athabasca University
Edmonton, AB, Canada

Angelos Markos
Democritus University of Thrace
Alexandroupolis, Greece

ISSN 0302-9743　　　　　　ISSN 1611-3349 (electronic)
Lecture Notes in Computer Science
ISBN 978-3-031-98280-4　　　ISBN 978-3-031-98281-1 (eBook)
https://doi.org/10.1007/978-3-031-98281-1

© The Editor(s) (if applicable) and The Author(s), under exclusive license
to Springer Nature Switzerland AG 2026

This work is subject to copyright. All rights are solely and exclusively licensed by the Publisher, whether the whole or part of the material is concerned, specifically the rights of translation, reprinting, reuse of illustrations, recitation, broadcasting, reproduction on microfilms or in any other physical way, and transmission or information storage and retrieval, electronic adaptation, computer software, or by similar or dissimilar methodology now known or hereafter developed.
The use of general descriptive names, registered names, trademarks, service marks, etc. in this publication does not imply, even in the absence of a specific statement, that such names are exempt from the relevant protective laws and regulations and therefore free for general use.
The publisher, the authors and the editors are safe to assume that the advice and information in this book are believed to be true and accurate at the date of publication. Neither the publisher nor the authors or the editors give a warranty, expressed or implied, with respect to the material contained herein or for any errors or omissions that may have been made. The publisher remains neutral with regard to jurisdictional claims in published maps and institutional affiliations.

This Springer imprint is published by the registered company Springer Nature Switzerland AG
The registered company address is: Gewerbestrasse 11, 6330 Cham, Switzerland

If disposing of this product, please recycle the paper.

Preface

The 21st International Conference on Intelligent Tutoring Systems (ITS 2025) was held in Alexandroupolis, Greece, from June 3 to June 6, 2025.

Given the recent advances in generative artificial intelligence, ITS 2025 evolved to focus on Artificial Intelligence (AI) especially related to GENERATIVE SYSTEMS, including different areas such as education and health care. Generative systems use different techniques, architectures, and methods with a particular focus on machine learning and deep learning to generate texts, images, solutions, and environments. At ITS 2025, we looked into how AI and particularly generative systems can enhance human intelligence and support people whether it is in education, well-being, or any other area.

The conference supported eight distinct tracks to which papers were submitted. Each track included (but was not limited to) a list of topics of interest which can be found below.

Conference tracks

T1: Generative Tutoring Systems

The goal of this track was to show how new techniques inspired by artificial intelligence and new methods in education can improve learning and teaching and generate the capacity for knowledge acquisition. The topics of this track were related to intelligent and generative tutoring systems, including generative learning strategies, distance education, learning analytics for tutoring systems, deep learning and machine learning for tutoring systems, online and distance learning, generative learner models, emotion recognition, human-machine interaction, case-based reasoning, cognitive modeling, open learning, authoring systems, cultural learning, and adaptive learning.

T2: Generative Systems in Healthcare Informatics

The goal of this track was to show the progress of AI tools for increasing the propagation of healthcare techniques and their efficiency. Health informatics provides the means to improve the prediction, analysis, and treatment of diseases and the control of patients over their own care. The topics of this track were related to intelligent and generative systems in health informatics, including AI and telemedicine, medical image processing, virtual systems for healthcare, learning analytics in medicine, progress of AI for nonpharmacological Alzheimer's treatments, predictive modeling of healthcare, intelligent tutoring systems in medicine, machine learning and deep learning in healthcare, AI in medical education, AI in public health, home management of healthcare, neurofeedback techniques, games for healthcare, virtual reality (VR) and augmented reality (AR), robotics for healthcare and rehabilitation, VR/AR and AI for medical applications, ambient assistant living, biomedical signals, human-computer interaction in healthcare systems, ambient intelligence applications, AI for assisting medical diagnosis, mobility and behavioral analysis, and physiological signals monitoring and analysis.

T3: Generative Systems in Human Interaction, Games, and Virtual Reality

The goal of this track was to show the progress of interactive games, virtual reality applications, and supporting human interaction using artificial and generative intelligence techniques. Intelligent games can adapt to the characteristics of the player and can be used to enhance learning, skills, memory, cognitive capacities, brain-computer interaction, and strategic decisions. They can be used in various applications (education, healthcare, group management, decision support systems, industry control). Similarly, virtual reality applications can enormously benefit from the use of artificial intelligence and generative systems. In addition, this track looked into human interactions and how such interactions can be enhanced by AI and generative techniques. The topics of this track were focused on research related to intelligent games, the use of AI in VR as well as in human interaction, including Brain-Computer Interaction (BCI), game design, intelligent immersive games, multi-agent systems, educational games, social games, generative simulations, theory of games, reinforcement learning in games, virtual and generative reality, simulation training, emotions recognition, neurofeedback games, generative scenario design, human interaction with games, multimedia technologies in games, fuzzy systems in games, artificial intelligence in games, and intelligent games content generation.

T4: Neural Networks and Data Mining

This track was a crucible for innovation, where the latest techniques in neural networks and data mining intersect with the rich, untapped data of educational environments, aiming to revolutionize the pedagogical landscape and pave the way for a future where intelligent tutoring systems are as nuanced and insightful as the educators they seek to augment. The topics of this track were all related to neural networks or data mining, including supervised machine learning, genetic algorithms, Markovian regulation, smart sensor networks, determinate regulation, games and strategies, fuzzy systems, web information processing, applications of data mining in social sciences, data-driven reasoning, deep learning and statistical methods for data mining, big data mining, algorithms for data mining, ethical data analytics, and data mining for recommendation.

T5: Generative Systems and Metaverse

This track was dedicated to exploring the innovative synthesis of generative algorithms and the boundless educational landscapes within virtual environments. We delved into how generative AI is revolutionizing personalized learning experiences, creating dynamic content, and fostering engaging educational models that are as limitless as the Metaverse itself. Participants gained insights into the latest advancements, discussed the integration of AI-driven pedagogies in virtual spaces, and engaged with groundbreaking research that shapes the future of learning. Here, educators, technologists, and researchers came together to craft the nexus of next-generation learning platforms—where intelligence generation meets the expanse of the Metaverse, setting a new paradigm in digital education. The topics of this track were related to intelligent/generative systems and the Metaverse, including technology and creativity around the Metaverse, gaming and interactivity, mixed reality and virtual worlds, social and digital identity, extended reality, digital art, social communication, applications of the Metaverse in health, global Metaverse, industrial Metaverse, digital twins, and simulation optimization and decision making.

T6: Security, Privacy, and Ethics in Generative Systems

As we step into an era where AI's capabilities to generate content are nearly indistinguishable from human output, we must also navigate the complex web of security challenges, privacy concerns, and ethical dilemmas that accompany these advancements. This track offered a multidisciplinary forum for examining the safeguarding of digital identities, the protection of intellectual property, and the moral imperatives guiding AI interactions in educational settings. Experts, scholars, and practitioners from around the globe converged to share their wisdom, debate best practices, and forge strategies to ensure that artificial and generative intelligence develops in a manner that is secure, respects privacy, and adheres to the highest ethical standards. Together, we charted the course for responsible stewardship of AI technologies that enhance learning while honoring the trust placed in them by educators and learners alike. The topics of this track were related to security, privacy, and ethics in intelligent and generative systems, including commercial security; data privacy and security; web security; applied cryptography; authentication, identity management, and biometrics; electronic payments; culture of ethics; business and human rights; diversity and inclusion in teaching and learning; environmental ethics; machine learning and security; cloud computing and data outsourcing security; mobile payments; security in games; security of peer-to-peer networks; security metrics; sustainability; language-based security; security and privacy for the Internet of things; and socio-technical security.

T7: Generative Systems for Applied Natural Language Processing

This track was dedicated to unearthing and showcasing the transformative power of intelligent and generative models that are reshaping the way we interact with language in computational settings. It served as a beacon for those who are leveraging these advancements to build sophisticated tutoring systems capable of understanding, generating, and personalizing language-based interactions. The topics of this track were related to AI and generative systems for applied natural language processing, including language modeling, domain ontologies, computational linguistics, cognitive semantics, text mining, translation, question answering, dialogue systems, information retrieval, speech recognition and synthesis, discourse, machine translation, and lexical semantics.

T8: Generative Systems for Autonomous Robots and Learning

Artificial and generative intelligence with robots includes a variety of new criteria that provide more human characteristics to robots. Such elements concern emotions, mood, and facial expressions which lead to more realistic interactions with humans. They transform robots into useful human-like companions. The topics of this track were related to autonomous robots and learning using artificial and generative intelligence, including emotional robots, voice recognition, intelligent agents, cognitive robots, planning and goal reasoning, entertainment robotics, intelligent systems and robotics, applications of autonomous intelligent robots, sensors and vision systems for robots, generative exploration in hazardous situations, extraction of environment maps, robots in medicine, teaching robots, large language models (LLMs) for motion planning, LLMs for path planning and navigation, generative systems for simultaneous localization and mapping, generative systems for path planning, social robots, social navigation, human-robot interaction, and robots for health care and rehabilitation.

The call for scientific papers solicited works presenting substantive new research results in using AI and generative AI, advanced computer technologies, and interdisciplinary research for enabling, supporting, and enhancing human learning.

The international Program Committee consisted of 66 leading members (30 senior and 36 regular) of the Intelligent Tutoring Systems and AI communities, assisted by additional external reviewers.

Research papers came from 22 countries and were reviewed by four reviewers through a double-blind process. ITS 2025 retained the strict and high standards in the review process that have been established during the previous years, and which have rendered it a top-flight, rather selective, and high-quality conference. This year, from 67 submissions, 21 papers were accepted as full papers, whereas 27 papers were accepted as short papers and 5 as posters. This led to an acceptance rate of 31%. We believe that the selected full papers describe some very significant research and the short papers demonstrate some very interesting new ideas.

The management of the review process and the preparation of the proceedings was handled through the EasyChair platform.

ITS 2025 had two outstanding Invited Speakers in the plenary sessions: Angelos Sifaleras (University of Macedonia, Greece), a renowned figure in Operations Research, Optimization, and Metaheuristics, and Elvira Popescu (University of Craiova, Romania), a globally recognized researcher in educational technology, adaptation, and personalization as well as social learning environments. Both are leaders in different specialized areas of the ITS field.

Moreover, ITS 2025 hosted one workshop under the title "Breaking Barriers with Generative Intelligence (BBGI 2025)" and a panel with the title "Trustworthy and Explainable AI in Education".

In addition to the contributors mentioned above, we would like to thank all the authors, the members of the Program Committees of all tracks, the external reviewers, and the Steering Committee members as well as the Hosting Institution of the Conference, the Democritus University of Thrace, Greece.

We finally would like to acknowledge that ITS 2025 was held under the auspices of the Institute of Intelligent Systems (IIS) and was organized by Neoanalysis Ltd., under the guidance of Kitty Panourgia, the Organization Chair and her team.

May 2025

Sabine Graf
Angelos Markos

Organization

Conference Committee

General Conference Chair

Antonios Gasteratos — Democritus University of Thrace, Greece

Program Committee Chairs

Sabine Graf — Athabasca University, Canada
Angelos Markos — Democritus University of Thrace, Greece

Program Advising Chairs

Fuhua Oscar Lin — Athabasca University, Canada
Angelos Sifaleras — University of Macedonia, Greece

Organization Committee

Organization Chair

Kitty Panourgia — Neoanalysis Ltd., Greece

Organization Members

Kostantina Traka — Neoanalysis Ltd., Greece
Paula Dona — Neoanalysis Ltd., Greece
Isaak Tselepis — Neoanalysis Ltd., Greece

Program Committees

Senior Program Committee

Roger Azevedo	University of Central Florida, USA
Emmanuel Blanchard	Le Mans University, France
Benedict Du Boulay	University of Sussex, UK
Bert Bredeweg	University of Amsterdam, The Netherlands
Stefano A. Cerri	LIRMM, University of Montpellier, France
Maiga Chang	Athabasca University, Canada
Alexandra I. Cristea	Durham University, UK
Michel Desmarais	Polytechnique Montréal, Canada
Claude Frasson	University of Montreal, Canada
Yugo Hayashi	Ritsumeikan University, Japan
Wu-Yuin Hwang	National Dong-Hwa University, Taiwan
Seiji Isotani	Harvard University, USA
Lewis Johnson	Alelo Inc., USA
Charalampos Karagiannidis	Aristotle University of Thessaloniki, Greece
Kinshuk	University of North Texas, USA
Milos Kravcik	Educational Technology Lab, Germany
Amruth Kumar	Ramapo College of New Jersey, USA
Fuhua Oscar Lin	Athabasca University, Canada
Alessandro Micarelli	Roma Tre University, Italy
Riichiro Mizoguchi	Japan Advanced Institute of Science and Technology, Japan
Roger Nkambou	Université du Québec à Montréal, Canada
Elvira Popescu	University of Craiova, Romania
Demetrios Sampson	University of Piraeus, Greece
Filippo Sciarrone	Universitas Mercatorum, Italy
Angelo Sifaleras	University of Macedonia, Greece
Marco Temperini	Sapienza University of Rome, Italy
Stefan Trausan-Matu	Politehnica University of Bucharest, Romania
Christos Troussas	University of West Attica, Greece
Julita Vassileva	University of Saskatchewan, Canada
Panagiotis Vlamos	Ionian University, Greece

Program Committee

Mohammed Abdel Razek	Al-Azhar University, Egypt
Galia Angelova	Bulgarian Academy of Sciences, Bulgaria
Renu Balyan	SUNY Old Westbury, USA

Maria Lucia Barron-Estrada   Instituto Tecnológico de Culiacán, Mexico
Azza Basiouni   Liwa College, UAE
Hamdi Ben Abdessalem   University of Chicoutimi, Canada
Chih-Yueh Chou   Yuan Ze University, Taiwan
Evandro Costa   Federal University of Alagoas, Brazil
Diego Dermeval   Federal University of Alagoas, Brazil
Ali Akber Dewan   Athabasca University, Canada
Davide Fossati   Emory University, USA
Reva Freedman   Northern Illinois University, USA
Ashok Goel   Georgia Institute of Technology, USA
Xiaoqing Gu   East China Normal University, China
Ella Haig   University of Portsmouth, UK
Srecko Joksimovic   University of South Australia, Australia
Mizue Kayama   Shinshu University, Japan
Mohammad Khalil   University of Bergen, Norway
Georgia Koloniari   University of Macedonia, Greece
Shaozi Li   Xiamen University, China
Carla Limongelli   Roma Tre University, Italy
Pin-Chuan Lin   Mount Saint Vincent University, Canada
Chao-Lin Liu   National Central University, Taiwan
Mirko Marras   University of Cagliari, Italy
Tassos Mikropoulos   University of Ioannina, Greece
Wolfgang Mueller   University of Education Weingarten, Germany
Kuo-Liang Ou   National Hsin-chu University of Education, Taiwan
Sasha Poquet   Technical University of Munich, Germany
Valéry Psyché   Université TÉLUQ, Canada
Ricardo Queirós   Agostinho Neto University, Angola
Traian Rebedea   University Politehnica of Bucharest, Romania
Ange Tato   Laval University, Canada
Radu Vasiu   Politehnica University of Timisoara, Romania
Riina Vuorikari   World Bank Group, Belgium
Dunwei Wen   Athabasca University, Canada
Stelios Xinogalos   University of Macedonia, Greece

Additional Reviewers

Amani Alrobai   Durham University, UK
Fareeda Almutairi   Princess Nourah University, Saudi Arabia
Víctor Manuel Bátiz Beltrán   Instituto Tecnológico de Culiacán, Mexico
Jason Bernard   Athabasca University, Canada

Jayson Brown — Georgia Institute of Technology, USA
Jeanette Luu — Georgia Institute of Technology, USA
Zhifei Hu — Durham University, UK
Cherie Lum — Georgia Institute of Technology, USA
Travis Taylor — Georgia Institute of Technology, USA

Steering Committee

Chair

Claude Frasson — University of Montreal, Canada

Members

Stefano A. Cerri — LIRMM, University of Montpellier, France
Maiga Chang — Athabasca University, Canada
Amruth Kumar — Ramapo College of New Jersey, USA
Yugo Hayashi — Ritsumeikan University, Japan
Isabel Fernandez-Castro — University of the Basque Country, Spain
Guy Gouarderes — University of Pau and the Adour Region, France
Sabine Graf — Athabasca University, Canada
Alan Lesgold — University of Pittsburgh, USA
James Lester — North Carolina State University, USA
Oscar Fuhua Lin — Athabasca University, Canada
Angelos Markos — Democritus University of Thrace, Greece
Alessandro Micarelli — Roma Tre University, Italy
Roger Nkambou — Université du Québec à Montréal, Canada
Giorgos Papadourakis — Hellenic Mediterranean University, Greece
Elvira Popescu — University of Craiova, Romania
Angelos Sifaleras — University of Macedonia, Greece
Elliot Soloway — University of Michigan, USA
John Stamper — Carnegie Mellon University, USA
Daniel Suthers — University of Hawaii, USA
Stefan Trausan-Matu — University Politehnica of Bucharest, Romania
Christos Troussas — University of West Attica, Greece

Advisory Committee

Members

Luigia Carlucci Aiello	Sapienza University of Roma, Italy
Kinshuk	University of North Texas, USA
Demetrios Sampson	University of Piraeus, Greece

Abstracts of Invited Talks

Technology-Enhanced Peer Assessment in Education: Exploring Solutions and Trends

Elvira Popescu

Computers and Information Technology Department, University of Craiova, Craiova, Romania
elvira.popescu@edu.ucv.ro

Abstract. Peer assessment, also known as peer review or peer evaluation, is increasingly popular in education, especially in collaborative learning settings. It involves students evaluating each other's work, offering feedback, and sometimes assigning grades. This process benefits both the reviewer and the recipient of the review, by enhancing understanding, critical thinking, self-confidence, and engagement. While it offers more detailed and timely feedback than instructors often can, especially in large classes, challenges such as fairness, reliability, and student resistance can arise. Despite these drawbacks, peer assessment promotes greater student interaction, responsibility, and motivation through active involvement in the learning process. This has led to the development of technology-supported peer assessment systems, which have evolved in complexity and functionality over the past two decades. Various platforms have been proposed in the literature, each tailored to specific instructional settings, learning activities, disciplines, or artifact types. We present an overview of these systems, highlighting the current state-of-the-art along with the key challenges and existing gaps in the field. We also introduce an innovative general-purpose peer assessment platform called LearnEval, developed by our research group over the past several years. We conclude by outlining emerging research trends, particularly in relation to the rise of Generative Artificial Intelligence.

Keywords. Peer assessment · Peer review · Peer feedback · Educational platforms · Emerging technologies · Generative Artificial Intelligence

Towards a Manufacturing as a Service Framework: Decentralized Value Chains with Embedded Volume and Variety Dynamics

Angelo Sifaleras

Department of Applied Informatics, School of Information Sciences, University of Macedonia,
156 Egnatia Street, 54636 Thessaloniki, Greece
sifalera@uom.gr

Abstract. This presentation explores the Manufacturing as a Service (MaaS) model through the Tec4MaaSEs (T4M) initiative. It introduces a framework where manufacturing and production procedures are offered as on-demand services by leveraging advanced Industry 4.0 and Industry 5.0 technologies to establish a sustainable and flexible network of distributed value chains. Central to this approach is a highly adaptable Digital Twin (DT) architecture that adjusts to changes in supply and demand, fostering collaboration and optimization across varied manufacturing situations and among different stakeholders. The effectiveness of the proposed approach is tested in three distinct real-world value networks, each exhibiting unique volume and variety characteristics. The T4M MaaS Platform supports adaptability and boosts performance under different supply and demand circumstances. This initiative underscores the significant impact of the volume-variety principle in designing MaaS ecosystems and offers practical insights to enhance collaboration, resilience, and sustainable industry methods.

Keywords. Smart manufacturing · Industry 4.0 · Digital Twins · Digital Transformation · Circular and Resilient Value Networks · Explainable AI

Acknowledgments. This research was funded by the European Health and Digital Executive Agency, Project: 101138517, Tec4MaaSEs, HORIZON-CL4-2023-TWIN-TRANSITION-01.

Contents – Part I

Generative Tutoring Systems

Leveraging Large Language Models for a Swahili Mathematics ITS
in Tanzania: Designing Effective Prompts 3
   Edger P. Rutatola, Koen Stroeken, and Tony Belpaeme

Ensemble Stacking Case-Based Reasoning and a Stochastic Recommender
Algorithm with the Hawkes Process Applied to ITS AI-VT 17
   Daniel Soto-Forero, Marie-Laure Betbeder, and Julien Henriet

From Struggle (06-2024) to Mastery (02-2025) LLMs Conquer Advanced
Algorithm Exams and Pave the Way for Editorial Generation 32
   Adrian Marius Dumitran, Theodor-Pierre Moroianu,
   and Vasile Paul Alexe

An Approach to Organizing Intelligent Tutoring Systems
with Customizable Decision-Making Logic 47
   Viktor Uglev

Enhancing Pilot Training and Decision-Making Using Ontologies:
A Cognitive Assistance Approach 59
   Guy Carlos Tamkodjou Tchio, Roger Nkambou, Valéry Psyché,
   and Ange Adrienne Nyamen Tato

Enhancing Intelligent Tutor for Program Element Scope Training: Lessons
Learned 74
   Nikita Moskalenko, Andrey Sidor, and Oleg Sychev

Mapping AI Tools in Education: A Topic Modeling Analysis of Cognitive,
Metacognitive, and Affective Insights 88
   Michael Pin-Chuan Lin, Arita Li Liu, Saeed Saffari, Daniel Chang,
   and Jeeho Ryoo

Unravelling Emotional Nuances: A Cross-Linguistic Analysis of Sentiment
Differences in Multilingual Movie Versions 102
   Adam Wynn, Jingyun Wang, and Xiaoyan Li

A Method and Semi-automated AI Tool Supporting Tutors in Preparing
Audio-Tactile Exercises for Blind Students 116
   Mateusz Kawulok, Michał Maćkowski, and Maria Rosiak

AI-Powered Tutoring for Novice Programmers: Supporting Students
Throughout Project Development 131
   Juan Diego Lugo Sánchez, Brena Marques Ribeiro, Rubén Manrique,
   and Kelly Garcés

Language Models for Educational Question Generation: Practical
Challenges, Personalization Opportunities, and Parameter Optimization 144
   Jason Bernard and Sabine Graf

A Negotiation and Explainable Approach to Automatically Reduce
Cognitive Conflicts and Enhance Learner Model Accuracy in an Intelligent
Tutoring System for Propositional Logic 159
   Evandro Costa, Emanuele Silva, Priscylla Silva, Marlos Silva,
   Leandro da Silva, and Dante Costa

Scaling Effective Characteristics of ITSs: A Preliminary Analysis
of LLM-Based Personalized Feedback 171
   Rachel Van Campenhout, Jeffrey S. Dittel, and Benny G. Johnson

Leveraging LLMs for Bayesian and Deep Knowledge Tracing
in the Logic-Muse Intelligent Tutoring System 182
   Ange Tato and Roger Nkambou

AI-Generated Code Detection: An Examination of Current Tools
in Education 192
   Juan Esteban Cuellar Argotty and Ruben Manrique

Manchita: An AI-Powered Gamified Learning Environment 202
   Nicolás Klopstock, Ernesto José Duarte, Edier Becerra,
   and Rubén Manrique

An Educational Virtual World System with Gamification Features
and LLM Guided NPCs 213
   Ariadni Barmpari, Eleni Voyiatzaki, and Ioannis Hatzilygeroudis

Using Minigames to Teach Computer Architecture 224
   Reva Freedman, Ian Sullivan, Annalise Brockmann, and Minhaz Patel

Evaluating an AI-Driven Chatbot Tutor for Enhancing Introductory
Programming Learning 235
   Pablo Alejandro Guatibonza Briceño, Daniel Osorio Cárdenas,
   Rubén Manrique Piramanrique, Edgar Eduardo Rosales Rosero,
   and Mario Eduardo Sánchez Puccini

A Comprehensive Survey and Taxonomy on Large Language Model-Based
Knowledge Tracing 246
   Sunwoo Park and Hyeoncheol Kim

Improving Feedback Generation in a Drawing-Based ITS 259
   *Islam Barchouch, Nathalie Girard, Eric Anquetil, Laura Leconte,
and Eric Jamet*

A Unified Ontological Approach for Modeling Domain Theory
and Procedures: Applications, Issues and Prospects 270
   Marc-Antoine Courtemanche, Roger Nkambou, and Psyché Valéry

Designing an AI Coaching System for Interactive Video-Based Skill
Learning 281
   *Cherie Lum, Erin Deye, Grace Brazil, Tim Bydlon, Shashank Verma,
Rochan Madhusudhana, Rahul Dass, and Ashok Goel*

Large Language Models Performance in Propositional Logic Proofs:
Solving and Evaluating Argument Validity 292
   *Evandro de Barros Costa, Jean Felipe Duarte Tenório,
Alison Bruno Martires Soares, Rian Américo Brito da Silva,
Wallace Lins Casado de Sousa, Davi Silva de Melo Lins,
and Dante de Araújo Costa*

Generative AI Agents for Instructional Co-design: A Sequential
Agent-Based Approach Using a Low-Code/No-Code Platform 301
   *Dimitrios Tolis, Stylianos Mystakidis, Ioannis Hatzilygeroudis,
and Konstantinos Siozopoulos*

Author Index 307

Contents – Part II

Generative systems in Healthcare Informatics

Efficient Attention-Guided CNN for Alzheimer's Disease Prediction 3
   Rahma Kadri, Bassem Bouaziz, Mohamed Tmar, and Faiez Gargouri

LLMs for Question-Answer and Synthetic Data Generation and Evaluation 17
   Renu Balyan, Kayla Thompson, and Francisco Iacobelli

Assessing the Potential of AI-Generated Assessments in Medical
Education: A Study on Diagnostic Microbiology Using Copilot and Gemini ... 32
   Azza Mohamed and Ray Al-Barazie

Generative Systems in Human Computer Interaction, Games and Virtual Reality

Impact of Experience on Cognitive Load and Physiological Responses
in Aviation Pilots 47
   Amin Bonyad, Hamdi Ben Abdessalem, and Claude Frasson

Virtual Reality Application for Enhanced Cognitive Rehabilitation
and Occupational Therapy 64
   Michail Kosmidis, Ioannis Kansizoglou, Vasiliki Balaska,
   Athanasios Psomoulis, Daniel Bratanov, and Antonios Gasteratos

Neural Networks and Data Mining

Automatic Piecewise Linear Regression for Predicting Student Learning
Satisfaction 73
   Haemin Choi and Gayathri Nadarajan

Counterfactual Fairness Evaluation of Machine Learning Models
on Educational Datasets 88
   Woojin Kim and Hyeoncheol Kim

Performance of Neural Networks for Recognizing Images of UML Class,
Sequence and State Diagrams 104
   Irina-Gabriela Nedelcu, Stefan Alexandru Mocanu, Daniela Saru,
   Simona Iuliana Caramihai, and Anca Daniela Ionita

Multidisciplinary Educational Assessment Model Using Genetic
Algorithms 114
    Doru Anastasiu Popescu, Michalis Stefanidakis, Anna Sotiropoulou,
    Nicolae Bold, and Ion Alexandru Popescu

Model Decomposition of Multi-dimensional Workflows to Petri Nets
for Well-Handledness Verification 125
    Therese Nuelle Roca and Jasmine A. Malinao

Two-Level Imbalance Mitigation (TLIM): A Dual-Strategy Approach
for Multi-class Error Classification in Programming Education 137
    Sunwoo Park and Hyeoncheol Kim

Advanced Machine Learning and Data Mining Techniques for Fault
Diagnosis in Industrial Applications 152
    Vasileios I. Vlachou, Theoklitos S. Karakatsanis,
    Dimitrios E. Efstathiou, Eftychios I. Vlachou, Stavros D. Vologiannidis,
    and Antonios C. Gasteratos

Neuromorphic Knowledge Representation: SNN-Based Relational
Inference and Explainability in Knowledge Graphs 159
    Gaganpreet Jhajj, Jerry Ryan David Gustafson, Raymond Morland,
    Carlos Enrique Gutierrez, Michael Pin-Chuan Lin,
    M. Ali Akber Dewan, and Fuhua Lin

Generative Systems and Metaverse

Gamified Team Programming in MUVEs: Effects on Student Engagement
and Achievement 169
    Yeonju Jang, Seongyune Choi, Heeseok Jung, and Hyeoncheol Kim

Heat of the Moment: Exploring the Influence of Stress and Workload
on Facial Temperature Dynamics 181
    Amin Bonyad, Hamdi Ben Abdessalem, and Claude Frasson

Security, Privacy, and Ethics in Generative Systems

Person Identification with Arrhythmic and Normal ECG Signals Using
Hybrid Machine Learning and Deep Learning Models 197
    Sihem Hamza and Yassine Ben Ayed

Generative Systems for Applied Natural Language Processing

LLaVA-Docent-V2: Improving Data Quality and Pedagogical Data Generation to Train Large Multimodal Models for Art Appreciation Education 213
    Unggi Lee, Yoorim Son, Jaeyoon Shin, Gyuri Byun, Yunseo Lee, Junbo Koh, Minji Jeon, and Hyeoncheol Kim

Multi-domain Evaluation of Auto-paraphrase Generation at Paragraph-Level: Insights for Education and Plagiarism Detection 229
    Arwa Al Saqaabi, Craig Stewart, Eleni Akrida, and Alexandra I. Cristea

Towards a Smarter Homophone Correction Tool: A Case Study in Khmer Writing 244
    Seanghort Born, Madeth May, Claudine Piau-Toffolon, and Sébastien Iksal

ES-KT-24: A Multimodal Knowledge Tracing Benchmark Dataset with Educational Game Playing Video and Synthetic Text Generation 259
    Dohee Kim, Unggi Lee, Sookbun Lee, Jiyeong Bae, Taekyung Ahn, Jaekwon Park, Gunho Lee, and Hyeoncheol Kim

A Predictive Model for Story Points Leveraging Features Like Readability and Sentiment from User Story Description 274
    Giseldo da Silva Neo, J. Antão B. Moura, Alana Viana Borges da Silva Neo, and Evandro de Barros Costa

Generative Systems for Autonomous Robots and Learning

Echo-Teddy: Preliminary Design and Development of Large Language Model-Based Social Robot for Autistic Students 287
    Unggi Lee, Hansung Kim, Juhong Eom, Hyeonseo Jeong, Seungyeon Lee, Gyuri Byun, Yunseo Lee, Minji Kang, Gospel Kim, Jihoi Na, Jewoong Moon, and Hyeoncheol Kim

Humanized TASC: Tag-Less and Automated Stock Counting in Smart Warehouses 302
    Sarantis Antoniou, Vasiliki Balaska, Ioannis Kansizoglou, Symeon Symeonidis, Theoklitos Karakatsanis, and Antonios Gasteratos

Real-Time Adaptive Navigation for AVs via Hybrid Deep Learning 313
Leila Haj Meftah and Sirine Mnejja

Author Index 325

Generative Tutoring Systems

Leveraging Large Language Models for a Swahili Mathematics ITS in Tanzania: Designing Effective Prompts

Edger P. Rutatola[1,2](✉), Koen Stroeken[3], and Tony Belpaeme[1]

[1] IDLab-AIRO, Ghent University – imec, Ghent, Belgium
Edger.Rutatola@ugent.be
[2] Department of Computing Science Studies, Faculty of Science and Technology, Mzumbe University, Morogoro, Tanzania
[3] CARAM, Ghent University, Ghent, Belgium
https://airo.ugent.be/, https://research.flw.ugent.be/en/caram

Abstract. The advancement of Large Language Models (LLMs) has significantly enhanced intelligent tutoring systems, enabling them to engage learners through natural dialogues. This interaction boosts learner engagement but presents challenges for low-resource languages, such as Swahili – Tanzania's national language. By design, LLMs rely on patterns learned during training to predict subsequent words, making them more suited for conversational tasks than factual computations and reasoning tasks, such as solving mathematics problems. This study investigates the suitability of GPT-4 in generating Swahili-language mathematics content for teaching geometry to primary school students, assessing both contextual and factual accuracy. Using nine varied prompts, we generated 621 different topic introductions, which were evaluated by primary school mathematics teachers. Results reveal that GPT-4 can generate contextually relevant content but struggles with complex mathematical computations. Additionally, the prompt variations provided valuable insights into designing effective prompts for similar tasks.

Keywords: GPT-4 · Large Language Models · mathematics education · intelligent tutoring systems · prompt engineering · Swahili

1 Introduction

The United Republic of Tanzania (URT) has Swahili and English as official languages, with most of the population being more conversant in Swahili [15]. These two languages also serve as the medium of instruction in primary schools, with the Swahili language being used in the majority of public (state-owned) schools. At the same time, English is dominant in private schools [17]. Furthermore, as of 2022, 89.2% of the primary schools in the country were public schools [19].

A look into the results of the URT's national primary school leaving examination (PSLE), the passing of which is a requisite to joining secondary education, reveals a significant failure in the mathematics subject. Specifically, 46.72% and 51.17% of the students failed in mathematics in 2022 and 2023, respectively [3]. This is, in part, caused by acute poor teacher-student ratios which limit personalisation, pupils' engagement, and overall class management [18,20].

One of the ways to ensure pupils' inclusion, engagement, and personalisation in the learning process —despite the class size— is through the use of intelligent tutoring systems. Globally, following the advancement and increased accessibility of technology, different intelligent tutoring systems are being developed and adopted [4,14]. While these systems are effective, they used to lack in interaction with learners through robust conversations, which has been shown to enhance their engagement [24].

Recently, leveraging Large Language Models (LLMs) has proven to be one of the more effective ways to make intelligent tutoring systems more interactive, autonomous, and engaging [5]. Among the various LLMs available today, OpenAI's ChatGPT stands out as the most popular, thanks to its open accessibility and wide-ranging capabilities [8]. By the time of conducting this research, GPT-4 was OpenAI's most current model. Furthermore, the quality of the content produced by LLMs greatly depends on the availability of training data. Even powerful LLMs such as GPT-3.5 and GPT-4 underperform when dealing with low-resource languages [23]. Unfortunately, Swahili only contributes to about 0.009% of GPT's training data, making it a low-resource language [10].

Several studies highlight ChatGPT's ability to perform adequately in providing professional content in low-resource languages. For example, a study by Maginga et al. [16] evaluating GPT's performance as a Swahili agricultural extension tool reports 89% of content correctness and 69% of good language use. While this holds promise, it would be naive to just assume that a similar level of correctness would be achieved in subjects like mathematics, which require step-by-step problem solving rather than the simple prediction of the next word. In addition to factual correctness, the resourcefulness of a language—culture, to an extension—leads to biases and affects the contextual correctness of the generated content by an LLM [1] . Contextual correctness is equally important, especially in teaching and learning, as the contextual correctness and relevance of examples given are crucial to understanding and retention.

These limitations further complicate the use of LLMs in education, underscoring the need for careful prompt engineering. Although powerful, LLMs depend heavily on prompts to guide the content they produce [28]. In addition, LLM APIs charge per token, which includes both the prompt and the output [21]. This makes it essential to obtain the desired content with as few trials as possible, highlighting the importance of effective prompt design. One approach is few-shot prompting, where examples of the desired output are incorporated into the prompt [6]. Although often effective, few-shot prompting can be inefficient and less ideal in dynamic learning environments that demand heterogeneous outputs [7]. Also, approaches such as Chain-of-Thought prompting have proven effective for tasks that require step-by-step reasoning [11,27], but it remains important to consider issues like contextual correctness and relevance. Hence, there is a need for prompt design techniques that are both effective and efficient, incorporating only the necessary components to yield correct and relevant outputs.

Therefore, three research questions are addressed in this paper, which are: (1) Can GPT-4 generate Swahili content with contextually relevant examples to help a Tanzanian pupil understand mathematics concepts?, (2) can GPT-4 correctly and clearly handle the step-by-step mathematical calculations to enable a pupil to understand the process?, and (3) in teaching mathematics in the Swahili language, how does the variation of the prompts improve the quality of content generated?

2 Methodology

2.1 Study Design

The study was conducted in the United Republic of Tanzania. Being the domain experts, and based on our research questions, primary school mathematics teachers were the main respondents. We involved teachers from both private and public schools so as to fully capture the contextual diversification. Moreover, we sought data from both groups to be able to compare the results and shed more light on the disparities between high- and low-resource languages in LLMs.

We chose geometry as the topic of intervention, focusing on the calculations of areas and perimeters of various geometrical shapes. This selection allowed us to incorporate problems of varying complexity, enabling us to effectively evaluate the content generated by GPT-4. To that end, we formulated 16 sub-topics: (1) perimeter of a square; (2) area of a square; (3) perimeter of a rectangle; (4) area of a rectangle; (5) circumference of a circle with a diameter that is divisible by 7; (6) circumference of a circle with a diameter that is not divisible by 7; (7) circumference of a circle with a radius that is divisible by 7; (8) circumference of a circle with a radius that is not divisible by 7; (9) area of a circle with a diameter that is divisible by 7; (10) area of a circle with a diameter that is not divisible by 7; (11) area of a circle with a radius that is divisible by 7; (12) area of a circle with a radius that is not divisible by 7; (13) surface area of a cylinder closed on one side, having a diameter that is divisible by 7; (14) surface area of a cylinder closed on one side, having a diameter that is not divisible by 7; (15) surface area of a cylinder closed on one side, having a radius that is divisible by 7; and (16) surface area of a cylinder closed on one side, having a radius that is not divisible by 7.

Perimeter and area of rectangles and squares were assumed to be simple topics as their calculations only involve basic additions and multiplications. Area and circumference of circles were categorised as having medium complexity and interesting diversity, as they involve fractions (if radius/diameter is a factor of 7, thus $\pi = \frac{22}{7}$) or decimals (if radius/diameter is not a factor of 7, thus $\pi = 3.14$). Lastly, the surface area of a cylinder closed on one side was labelled as complex, because it involves relatively more complex calculations and needs attentive step-by-step solving.

2.2 The Application

We created a comma-separated values (.csv) file with the following details for each topic, in both English and Swahili as separate columns: (1) the name of the shape (2) the calculation to be done (area or perimeter); (3) the formula for the calculation; and (4) the full name of the topic. We then created a Python script containing an API call to the GPT-4 model. Though GPT-4 is not specifically known for its mathematical precision, our decision to have it handle the computations was motivated by its demonstrated ability to accurately understand and solve relatively complex math problems compared to other models [22]. Additionally, GPT-4 has proven capable of comprehending and solving undergraduate-level math [11]. Given the simpler level of math in our study and the need for dialogue-based explanations, GPT-4 was the most suitable choice. The script loaded the CSV file in each runtime and consequently requested GPT-4 to generate introductory content for each topic. To set the context, we defined some variables (in both English and Swahili, where applicable) such as the model's name and role (Zuhura and teacher, respectively); the pupil's name and age; the country, Tanzania; and the languages, English and Swahili, to be used in the generated output as specified in the respective prompt. We also provided a flattering persona for the model:

> You are a helpful and knowledgeable mathematics tutor, who performs calculations accurately, and explains concepts clearly, step by step, and in an easy way.

Nine (9) different prompts were designed to generate the content, as elaborated in the supplementary material[1]. In a nutshell, the variations in the prompts were as follows: an English prompt demanding an English response (prompt 1); a Swahili version of prompt 1 demanding a Swahili response (prompt 2); an English prompt (same as prompt 1) requiring an answer in Swahili (prompt 3); an English prompt demanding a Swahili response, but it has a custom dictionary attached for correct contextual translations of some words (prompt 4); a Swahili version of prompt 4 (prompt 5); prompt 4, but this time we also added the correct formula for the calculations (prompt 6); a Swahili version of prompt 6 (prompt 7); prompt 6, with the addition of the expected correct answer (prompt 8); and, a Swahili version of prompt 8 (prompt 9). Thus, for each topic, nine different introductions were generated based on each prompt. Moreover, the script rendered the introductions in a PDF file, with each topic having an independent file.

For dynamic examples, the dimensions of the figures were randomly generated in the script, with defined floor and ceiling values. Only when a value needed to be perfectly divisible by 7 was that criterion added to the random number generator. Furthermore, we utilised the Matplotlib library to generate illustrations of these figures, including their dimension labels, and incorporated them into the PDF files for their respective topics.

---

[1] Annex 1 The Prompts: https://drive.google.com/drive/folders/1djgFY-_TSpN1AY-qoaEOJYK7CkgqyAG-?usp=drive_link.

2.3 Data Collection

The study employed a mixed-methods approach, combining qualitative and quantitative data collection. A total of 621 topic introductions generated by the system were evaluated. Ten primary school mathematics teachers qualitatively assessed the content's relevance, correctness, and contextual appropriateness for teaching. Each teacher reviewed and annotated six to seven documents (5463 topic introductions).

For the second research question, the 621 contents were categorised into four groups: (1) correct flow, wrong answer; (2) correct answer, wrong flow; (3) correct flow and answer; and (4) wrong flow and answer. These results were quantitatively recorded and analysed.

2.4 Data Analysis

The qualitative results from the teachers were thematically analysed. We manually coded their feedback and grouped them into common themes. Moreover, the teachers' demographic information and our quantitative evaluation of the content were both descriptively analysed.

3 Results

3.1 Teachers Demographic Information

Seven of the ten teachers worked in public schools (teaching in Swahili), while the rest were in private schools (teaching in English). 60% were aged 20–30, with 20% in both the 31–40 and 41–50 age groups. Five teachers had less than 5 years of experience, two had 6–10 years, and three had over 10 years, providing insights from both new and experienced educators. Regarding AI and LLM awareness, nine responded: six had heard of it but never used it, two had used it, and one was unaware of AI. This highlights AI's novelty in Tanzanian education.

3.2 Qualitative Evaluation of the Content by the Teachers

Theme1: Contextual Appropriateness and Relevance. In general, all teachers agreed that the provided examples were appropriate for classroom learning. Nothing unethical or culturally inappropriate was noted in all the evaluated content. Moreover, the examples used were deemed contextually relevant, as they were drawn from the pupils' everyday encounters, making learning easier. Some quotes to commend the appropriateness and relevance of the introductions are:

> The introduction has prepared the child appropriately for the lesson. The mention of a garden and circular fields makes the lesson real (Topic: circumference of a circle).

> Appropriate examples have been used, for example, a book's surface (Topic: area of a rectangle).

Nevertheless, it is important to note that three (3) teachers pointed out that the introductions were too wordy. One of the teachers even gave an introduction a perfect score just because it was short and straightforward.

Theme 2: Contextual Correctness. The introductions were appropriate and relevant but lacked contextual correctness. For example, the model used pizza to explain the area and circumference of circles. While pizza is familiar in many places, it is considered a luxury in Tanzania and unfamiliar to most public school pupils, as noted by five public school teachers. However, private school teachers approved of the example, highlighting cultural and lifestyle differences between public and private school pupils, which are likely to impact learning.

A notable issue was the incorrect use of SI units. In Prompt 3, *"cm"* (centimetre) was used instead of the correct Swahili form, *"sm"* (sentimita). Additionally, seven teachers noted that in Swahili, the SI unit precedes the number, e.g., *sm 5* for 5 cm.

Theme 3: Factual Correctness. (**1**) **In the examples:** The model mostly provided relevant examples, such as soda cans, buckets, and cooking pots for cylinders; gardens, tables, walls, and books for rectangles and squares; and wheels, plates, clocks, and coins for circles. However, some errors occurred, such as using running around a football pitch to explain a circle's circumference. A teacher who identified this error stated:

> An example given states that knowing the circumference of a circle can help you determine the distance you have to run around a football pitch. Though this is a good example to understand the concept of circumference, a football pitch is not a circle.

Five teachers observed that some examples used the amount of paint needed to explain areas and perimeters, but they noted that paint quantity (measured in litres or cubic centimetres/metres) is typically associated with volume calculations, not areas or perimeters.

(**2**) **In the calculations:** The model performed well in calculations for certain topics, handled some adequately, and struggled with others. Specifics for this are presented in Sect. 3.3. However, some teachers noted incorrect formulas, inaccurate calculations, and correct but not best use of equations. Incorrect equations were mainly observed in the calculations of the surface area of cylinders, where the two correct formulas are "$A = \pi r^2 + 2\pi rh$" or "$A = \frac{\pi d^2}{4} + \pi dh$", given radius or diameter, respectively. The model often used these wrong equations, e.g. "$A = \pi r(r+h)$", which expands to "$A = \pi r^2 + \pi rh$"; and "$A = \pi r^2 h$", which calculates volume. This was remedied in prompts 6–9, by explicitly providing the correct formulas in the prompts.

Inaccuracies were observed in calculations involving fractions and decimals, particularly when using π. More complex calculations, such as for cylinders, increased the likelihood of errors. In some cases, the model avoided calculations altogether, as shown below (translated from Swahili):

Now, let us take an example of a cylinder with a diameter of 7 cm and a height of 17 cm.
Remember, $\pi = \frac{22}{7}$.
We will use this formula: $A = \frac{\pi d^2}{4} + \pi dh$
Step one is to take the diameter (d) and substitute it into the formula. This will be $(\frac{22}{7} \times 7^2 \div 4)$.
Step two, take the height (h) and the diameter (d) and substitute them into the formula. This will be $(\frac{22}{7} \times 7 \times 17)$.
Then, add the results from the first and second steps to get the final answer.
This is a simple formula and should always be used. Remember, practice makes perfect.

Teachers noted that students are expected to use the equation corresponding to the given radius or diameter in class. However, the model often disregarded this, using correct but mismatched formulas, as emphasized by four teachers. The model showed a preference for formulas with radius, unless instructed otherwise. In hindsight, this might be because of being tasked to teach the pupil the simplest formula for the task. Computations with radius are simpler, especially for areas, as they do not involve division. For example, $A = \pi r^2$ is simpler than $A = \frac{\pi d^2}{4}$. This issue was addressed in prompts 69, where the correct formulas were incorporated. We also observed that the language of instruction, i.e. English in Prompt 1 and Swahili in the rest, did not impact the correctness of the calculations.

Theme 4: Teaching Methods. **(1) Use of Examples:** Unanimously, teachers agreed that the model used sufficient examples that enhance learning. This was commended as good practice because it draws students to learning and stimulates them to think.

(2) Pupils' Engagement: The model was praised for its examples but sometimes failed to engage pupils. Teachers suggested various engagement strategies, including: asking questions to assess prior knowledge (2 teachers), measuring objects related to the topic (5 teachers), confirming understanding (5 teachers), and having pupils solve arithmetic problems (1 teacher). Overall, all teachers emphasised the importance of pupil engagement, with one suggesting using a flipped classroom approach:

> The introductions are one-sided. The teacher should not be the only source of knowledge in class. We believe that the pupils also have something to offer, so they should be given a chance.

(3) Teaching Aids: The model sometimes relied on imagined scenarios (e.g., football pitch, garden, pizza). Teachers stressed that effective learning requires examples of items readily available in class, such as books, tables, or walls. For topics involving uncommon objects, teachers either prepare them beforehand or ask students to bring items like buckets or soda cans, which serve as effective teaching aids.

(4) **Step-by-Step Approach:** This aspect drew significant attention from teachers. In many instances, the model failed to explain the meaning and importance of each equation component, as noted by five teachers. A common example was the lack of explanation about π, its relation to diameter and circumference, and its role in calculations. Students were told its value and asked to memorise it and related equations. Additionally, six teachers observed that the model often skipped step-by-step demonstrations of arithmetic computations, e.g.:

> Now, let's calculate the surface area step by step:
> First, we calculate the curved surface area:
> $\pi \times diameter \times height = 3.14 \times 18cm \times 20cm = 1130.4cm^2$ Next, we calculate the area of the base:
> $\pi \times (radius)^2 = 3.14 \times (9cm)^2 = 3.14 \times 81cm^2 = 254.34cm^2$
> Finally, we add these two areas together:
> $1130.4cm^2 + 254.34cm^2 = 1384.74cm^2$
> So, the surface area of the drum is $1384.74cm^2$.
> That's the area you would need to cover if you were to paint the outside of the drum!

On the same note, one teacher further stressed that the math could have been easier if the model had simplified the fractions step-by-step:

> Where the radius or diameter is divisible by 7, we normally use the π in fraction form ($\frac{22}{7}$). Then, we show the pupils how they can simplify the calculations by simplifying the fractions. The simplification was not explained in the calculations.

(5) **Psychological Engagement:** Teachers praised the model for preparing pupils' mindsets and building their confidence by emphasizing the subject's simplicity and approachability.

3.3 Topic Evaluation

This section evaluates GPT-4's mathematical correctness in its solutions. As shown in Fig. 1, the model excelled in simple topics (e.g., area and perimeter of squares and rectangles) and performed satisfactorily in medium-complexity topics (e.g., area and circumference of circles). However, it struggled with complex topics, such as the surface area of a cylinder.

We further analysed the introductions, categorising them into four groups: correct flow, wrong answer; correct answer, wrong flow; correct answer and flow; and wrong answer and flow. As shown in Fig. 2, the most common cause of mathematical errors was the model failing to find the correct answer despite following the right flow. It rarely produced correct answers with the wrong flow. Notably, for the surface area of cylinders, the model often got both the flow and answer wrong, consistent with Sect. 3.2 (Theme 3), where it was observed that incorrect formulas were repeatedly used unless explicitly provided in the prompt.

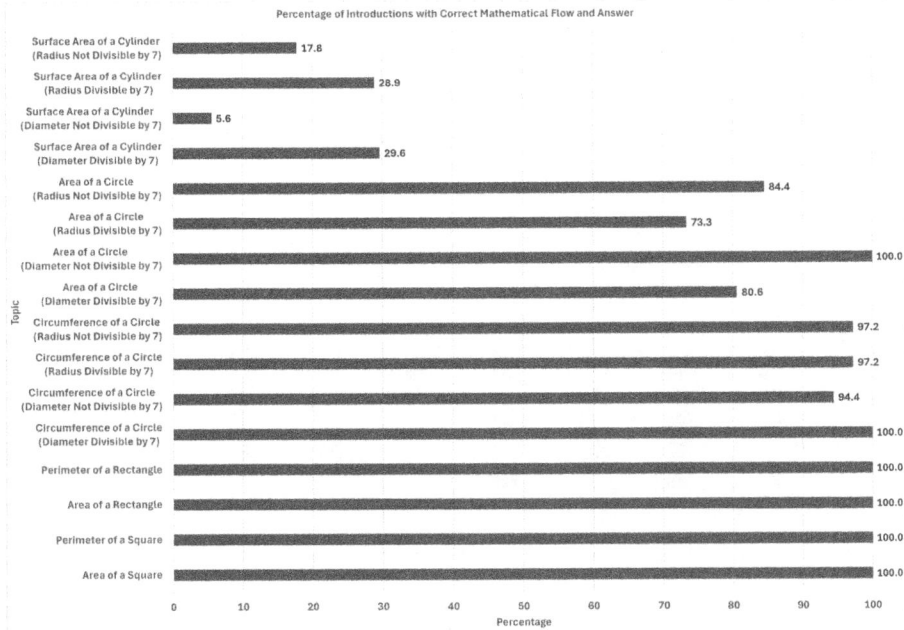

Fig. 1. Correctness of tutoring per topic

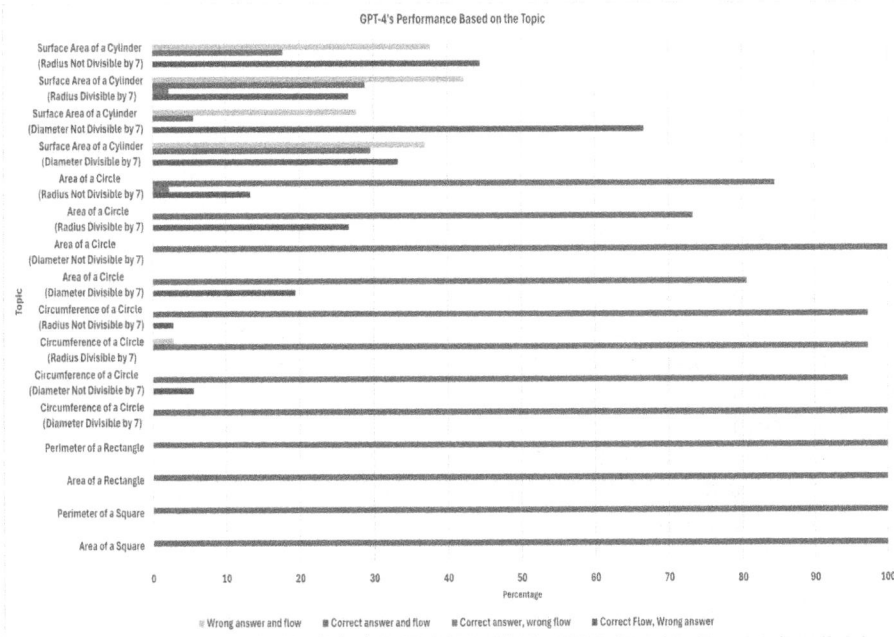

Fig. 2. Breakdown of failures per topic

3.4 Prompt Evaluations

We quantitatively assessed how often each prompt produced mathematically correct computations, including flow and answers, as shown in Fig. 3. While no prompt was 100% accurate, prompts 8 and 9 performed best, with prompts 3 and 5 performing worst.

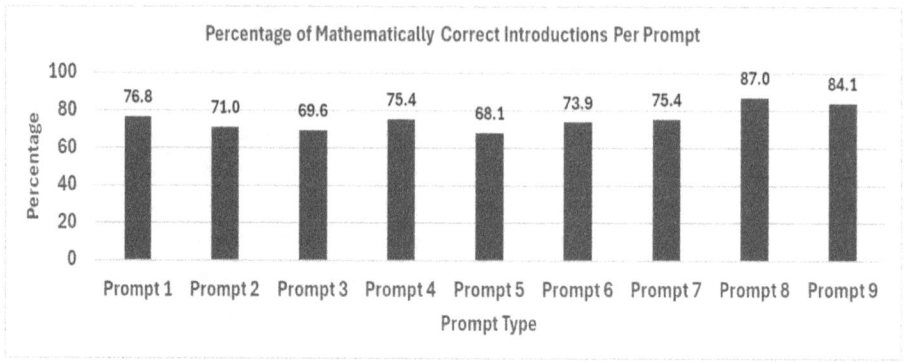

Fig. 3. Evaluation of prompts

4 Discussion

Our domain experts value **effective teaching methods** above all: encouraging active learner engagement, using demonstrations and examples effectively, offering step-by-step problem-solving, and offering encouragement for learners. These align with recommendations on wider effective teaching strategies [12, 26]. Unsurprisingly, our domain experts believe that AI-generated content should incorporate these attributes for ITSs to be effective.

Furthermore, our findings demonstrate that, though not primarily developed to solve math, **GPT-4 for now can only handle simple mathematical computations**. This is directly tied to its nature as an LLM, where it simply generates content by predicting the next best word based on the patterns in the data it has been trained on. Thus, if the math calls for a simple calculation such as $Perimeter = 2 \times (Length + Width)$, it will get it right as it has encountered such addition and multiplication patterns in its training data. Unfortunately, when it comes to more complex math involving multi-step reasoning, such as the surface area of a cylinder, the accuracy declines as its predictive nature fails. To mitigate this, external libraries have to be engaged. This confirms the findings in the study by [25], where several GPT models were tested with mathematical modelling tasks of varying complexity. The future availability of neurosymbolic LLMs is expected to remedy this [9].

Additionally, our findings demonstrate that the **resourcefulness of a language and culture significantly impacts the output of LLMs**. This was evident in the cultural bias found in some of the generated examples. For instance, the model used 'pizza' to illustrate the area and circumference of circles – a concept that, while familiar globally, was considered unfamiliar and even luxurious to most public school pupils in Tanzania. This aligns with the study by [1], which similarly highlights ChatGPT's limitations in cultural relevance and contextual awareness in a low-resource context.

The study by Frieder et al. [11] shows that **prompt engineering** and specifically "chain-of-thought prompting" (e.g. telling the model to solve a problem step by step) improves (Chat-)GPT's performance in solving math. This was also observed in our study, where the later prompt versions (prompts 8 and 9), which had the correct formula and the expected answer, performed better than the rest. However, in teaching the pupils, getting the context right is also as important. Therefore, our study highlights the crucial details that need to be included in the prompts for both factual and contextual correctness, as described in Table 1.

Table 1. Prompt parameters

Detail	Relevance	Description/Comments
Model's name and role	Contextual	Provides the model's persona for it to engage with the learner
Learner's name and age	Contextual	To enable the model to personalise the interactions to the leaner
Learner's purpose	Contextual	To inform the model of the nature of the interactions (e.g. educational)
The locale	Contextual	Could range from the country, region/city, to a more specific setting like a classroom. This enables the model to provide more specific and relevant examples.
Examples to be used	Contextual and Factual	Should be both, the things available in the learning environment that the learner can interact with (for engagement) and the things they encounter in their daily surroundings.
Custom dictionary	Contextual and Factual	Contains a few contextual translations of terms the model is likely to get wrong. Might be included as a key-value pair.
The formula to be used	Factual	To reduce the chances for errors and confusion for the learner
The expected correct answer	Factual	For dynamicity, it can be computed by a script. This enables the model to fact-check itself.
Step-by-step approach	Factual	To increase the chances of the model systematically arriving at the correct answer. Might also involve a call to an external library to handle this.
Words limit	Contextual	To ensure that the output is not unnecessarily too wordy
An example of the desired output	Contextual	To prevent the errors, such as 35cm instead of $sm35$.
Level and means of engagement	Contextual	If needed, explain how and to what extent the model should engage the learner.

The inclusion of this information will solve most of the contextual and factual issues observed in Sects. 3.2 and 3.3. Moreover, it should be noted that the custom dictionary is unnecessary if the expected output is in English. Furthermore, in three out of four cases, the versions with Swahili prompts requiring Swahili responses were outperformed by their counterparts having English prompts requiring Swahili responses. This could be because the model comprehends English instructions better than Swahili, demonstrating the gap in language resources ploughed into LLM training [2,13]. Nevertheless, for a more robust application, these parameters could be filled in by the user in a well-designed form, making each interaction unique.

5 Conclusion and Limitations

The study answers the three research questions set. Firstly, yes, although not 100% accurate, GPT-4 can generate Swahili content with contextually relevant examples to help a Tanzanian primary school pupil understand mathematical concepts. As accuracy is of utmost importance in learning, we offer prompt engineering advice to increase factual and contextual correctness. The second research question has more than just a yes or no answer. Though GPT-4 correctly handled the math for simple and moderately complex topics, it underperformed on more complex problems. Moreover, while it demonstrated a step-by-step approach in its reasoning, it did not fully implement that in the calculations, where it simply provided the answers to computations without showing the underlying work out. Finally, the variation of the prompts improves both the contextual and factual quality of the content generated. Adding more contextual information enriches the relevance of the output, while incorporating solution-related specifics, such as formulas and expected answers, enhances mathematical accuracy. Therefore, while GPT-4 holds a significant promise in Swahili-based mathematics tutoring, prompt engineering is yet crucial for its effectiveness.

Our study has several limitations that may have influenced the findings and their generalisability. For instance, we focused solely on GPT-4. Experimenting with other LLMs might yield different results. Moreover, we only engaged teachers as domain experts, but other stakeholders, such as pupils might also provide valuable insights. Finally, our study was limited to geometry, and therefore more research focusing on other mathematics topics of varying complexity should be done to comprehensively understand the model's capabilities.

Acknowledgments. We are sincerely grateful to all the teachers who offered their valuable time to participate in the study. Their insights are highly treasured. Furthermore, we are extremely thankful to VLIR-UOS for funding the entire study.

Disclosure of Interests. The authors have no competing interests to declare that are relevant to the content of this article.

References

1. Ahmad, I.S., Dudy, S., Ramachandranpillai, R., Church, K.: Are generative language models multicultural? a study on hausa culture and emotions using ChatGPT. In: Proceedings of the 2nd Workshop on Cross-Cultural Considerations in NLP, pp. 98–106. Association for Computational Linguistics (Aug 2024). https://doi.org/10.18653/v1/2024.c3nlp-1.8,
2. Bang, Y., Cahyawijaya, S., et al.: A multitask, multilingual, multimodal evaluation of ChatGPT on reasoning, hallucination, and interactivity, vol. 1, pp. 675–718. Long Papers (2023). https://doi.org/10.48550/arXiv.2302.04023
3. Baraza la Mitihani la Tanzania: Taarifa ya Matokeo ya Mtihani wa Kumaliza Elimu ya Msingi (PSLE) Uliofanyika Septemba, 2023 (2023). https://www.moe.go.tz/sites/default/files/PRESS%20PSLE%202023%20final_231123_121622_1.pdf
4. Belpaeme, T., Kennedy, J., Ramachandran, A., Scassellati, B., Tanaka, F.: Social robots for education: a review. Sci. Robot **3**, 5954 (2018). http://robotics.sciencemag.org/
5. Cao, C.: Scaffolding CS1 Courses with a Large Language Model-Powered Intelligent Tutoring System.,pp. 229–232. Association for Computing Machinery (Mar 2023). https://doi.org/10.1145/3581754.3584111
6. Chaaben, M.B., Burgueño, L., Sahraoui, H.: Towards using few-shot prompt learning for automating model completion. In: Proceedings - International Conference on Software Engineering, pp. 7–12. IEEE Computer Society (5 2023). https://doi.org/10.1109/ICSE-NIER58687.2023.00008, https://ieeexplore.ieee.org/abstract/document/10173909
7. Chang, K., Xu, S., Wang, C., Luo, Y., Liu, X., Xiao, T., Zhu, J.: Efficient Prompting Methods for Large Language Models: A Survey. In: IEEE International Conference on Program Comprehension, vol. 2022, pp. 36–47. IEEE Computer Society (March 2024). arxiv:2404.01077
8. Coello, C.E.A., Alimam, M.N., Kouatly, R.: Effectiveness of ChatGPT in coding: a comparative analysis of popular large language models. Digital **4**, 114–125 (2024). https://doi.org/10.3390/digital4010005
9. Colelough, B.C., Regli, W.: Neuro-Symbolic AI in 2024: A Systematic Review. arXiv preprint arXiv:2501.05435 (2025)
10. Common Crawl Foundation: Statistics of Common Crawl Monthly Archives: Distribution of Languages (2024). https://commoncrawl.github.io/cc-crawl-statistics/plots/languages
11. Frieder, S., et al.: Mathematical Capabilities of ChatGPT (2023). https://ghosts.friederrr.org
12. Ghafar, Z.N., Sawalmeh, M.H.M.: The influence of effective teaching on elementary school students: a review paper. J. Learn. Develop. Stud. **3**, 10–14 (2023). https://doi.org/10.32996/jlds
13. Hendy, A., Abdelrehim, M., et al.: How Good Are GPT Models at Machine Translation? A Comprehensive Evaluation arxiv:2302.09210 (Feb 2023)
14. Kulik, J.A., Fletcher, J.D.: Effectiveness of intelligent tutoring systems: a meta-analytic review. Rev. Educ. Res. **86**, 42–78 (3 2016). https://doi.org/10.3102/0034654315581420
15. Lupogo, I.: Language of instruction: a challenge for secondary schools and tertiary institutions in implementing VET in Tanzania. J. Educ. Policy Entrepreneurial Res. **1**, 26–30 (2014). http://www.iiste.org/Journals/index.php/JEPER

16. Maginga, T.J., Kutuku, S.J., Hamza, H.M., Mulokozi, G.G., Nsenga, J.: MkulimaGPT: Equitable AI Use Via a swahili chatbot for maize farming system in Tanzania. African J. Agricult. Food Sci. **7**, 172–188 (2024). https://doi.org/10.52589/AJAFS-VERNTB5I
17. Mapunda, G., Gibson, H.: On the suitability of Swahili for early schooling in remote rural Tanzania: do policy and practice align? J. British Acad. **10**, 141–168 (2022). https://doi.org/10.5871/jba/010s4.141
18. Mazana, M.Y., Montero, C.S., Casmir, R.O.: Assessing students' performance in mathematics in tanzania: the teacher's perspective. Inter. Electr. J. Mathem. Educ. **15**, em0589 (2020). https://doi.org/10.29333/iejme/7994
19. National Bureau of Statistics: Tanzania in Figures (2022). https://www.nbs.go.tz/index.php/en/tanzania-in-figures/891-tanzania-in-figures-2022
20. Ndijuye, L.G.: Early learning attainments of children of naturalized citizens of refugee backgrounds in the sub-Saharan region: evidence from Tanzania. Child Developm. Perspectives **17**, 67–73 (3 2023). https://doi.org/10.1111/cdep.12479
21. Petrov, A., Malfa, L., Torr, P.H.S., Bibi, A.: Language Model Tokenizers Introduce Unfairness Between Languages (2023). https://proceedings.neurips.cc/paper_files/paper/2023/file/74bb24dca8334adce292883b4b651eda-Paper-Conference.pdf
22. Plevris, V., Papazafeiropoulos, G., Rios, A.J.: Chatbots Put to the test in math and logic problems: a comparison and assessment of ChatGPT-3.5, ChatGPT-4, and Google Bard. AI (Switzerland) **4**, 949–969 (2023). https://doi.org/10.3390/ai4040048
23. Robinson, N.R., Ogayo, P., Mortensen, D.R., Neubig, G.: ChatGPT MT: Competitive for High- (but not Low-) Resource Languages (Sep 2023). arxiv:2309.07423
24. Schmucker, R., Xia, M., Azaria, A., Mitchell, T.: Ruffle&Riley: Towards the Automated Induction of Conversational Tutoring Systems (2023). https://gaied.org/neurips2023/files/38/38_paper.pdf
25. Spreitzer, C., Straser, O., Zehetmeier, S., Maaå, K.: Mathematical modelling abilities of artificial intelligence tools: the case of ChatGPT. Educ. Sci. **14** (2024). https://doi.org/10.3390/educsci14070698
26. Telaumbanua, F., et al.: psychological encouragement for high school students in preparation for online learning during Covid-19. Middle European Sci. Bull. **14** (2021)
27. Wei, J., et al.: Chain-of-thought prompting elicits reasoning in large language models. In: Proceedings of the 36th International Conference on Neural Information Processing Systems. Curran Associates Inc. arxiv:2201.11903 (Dec 2022)
28. White, J., et al.: A Prompt Pattern Catalog to Enhance Prompt Engineering with ChatGPT arxiv:2302.11382 (Feb 2023)

Ensemble Stacking Case-Based Reasoning and a Stochastic Recommender Algorithm with the Hawkes Process Applied to ITS AI-VT

Daniel Soto-Forero[✉], Marie-Laure Betbeder, and Julien Henriet

DISC, Université Marie et Louis Pasteur, CNRS, institut FEMTO-ST, 16 Route de Gray, Besançon 25000, France
{daniel.soto_forero,marie-laure.betbeder,julien.henriet}@univ-fcomte.fr

Abstract. This paper presents a recommender algorithm integrating a multi-agent ensemble case-based reasoning (ESCBR-SMA), a Thompson sampling-based (TS) recommender system, and a Hawkes process. The final integrated algorithm is applied to improve the real-time adaptation of an Intelligent Tutoring System called AI-VT. We have compared the static recommendation algorithm (ESCBR-SMA with TS) and the dynamic recommendation algorithm (ESCBR-SMA, TS with the Hawkes process) by evaluating the knowledge acquisition evolution of each learner. The metrics used allow us to determine the stability of prediction and change in the probability distributions for each learner and each level of complexity. The results show that the integration between stochastic adaptation, the prediction with the case-based reasoning paradigm, and the Hawkes process allows reinforcement of knowledge as well as a more realistic estimation of the recommendation for each case independently.

Keywords: Case-Based Reasoning · Stacking · Regression · Ensemble Methods · Stochastic Recommender · Intelligent Tutoring System · Machine Learning

1 Introduction

The AI-VT (Artificial Intelligence - Virtual Trainer) system is an Intelligent Training System (ITS) created to assist learners in understanding and acquiring knowledge in various domains. The system is generic and aims to identify learner weaknesses and adapt the exercises accordingly to improve their learning indicators in a personalized way regardless of the course content or domain of study. The system uses a database of questions associated with multiple skills depending on the domain. These questions are organized according to the level of complexity estimated for the learner.

There are different classifications of an ITS, one of which is that an ITS is composed of four elements: an expert model, a student model, pedagogic knowledge, and an interface. These components interact with each other to make the system dynamic and capable of modeling the learner in various scenarios to build a personalized curriculum [3]. Another possible classification is one that divides an ITS into three logical layers: a presentation layer (user interface), an e-learning system layer (course enrollment and management, user profile and activities, teaching or learning assessment and feedback, user communication, and collaboration), and a data layer (collected, stored, and used education data) [17]. In any case, this kind of system allows the development of individual learning education, which is much more effective than classroom learning [9].

One of the main modules of an ITS is the recommender system, which aims to find weaknesses and adapt the platform locally or globally to facilitate the learning process and knowledge acquisition. This module is very important because it allows adaptation of the system and customization of the contents and exercises according to the needs and results of each learner. The effectiveness of the system in the acquisition of knowledge and adaptation to different types of learning depends on this module [17]. It is therefore necessary to find techniques and algorithms that can exploit the available data and explore the learning options dynamically, thereby improving the overall performance of the ITS.

The contributions of this paper are:

- Forgetting curve simulation in the learning process using the stochastic Hawkes process.
- Integration of case-based reasoning, multi-agent systems, and the Hawkes process in a recommender algorithm.
- Verification of the progression, stability, and precision of the proposed stochastic recommendation algorithm using simulated-student database and heterogeneous real student database.

This paper is organized as follows: Section 2 presents a background of definitions and concepts. Section 3 contains the related works about case-based reasoning, ensemble techniques, Thompson sampling, and regression. The proposed algorithm is explained in Sect. 4. Section 5 shows the experimental description, the results, and the discussion. Lastly, the conclusions and future work are discussed in Sect. 6.

2 Background

This section introduces the concepts and definitions necessary to understand the proposed algorithm as well as fundamental models and metrics. The first fundamental paradigm used in this work is case-based reasoning (CBR), which is used to exploit historically acquired knowledge and accumulated experience with respect to a specific problem. This paradigm is used to generate emergent solutions for a new problem using a knowledge database. The main idea is to search for similar past situations and use the experience to solve new problems.

CBR is especially useful when the underlying causes of a problem are not well understood. CBR defines a cycle of four steps to propose a solution [18].

The proposed recommendation algorithm associated with AI-VT is based on the reinforcement learning paradigm. Reinforcement learning is a machine learning technique that allows, through actions and rewards, improvement of the system's knowledge about a specific task [1]. The algorithm used for adaptation is a reinforcement learning algorithm called Thompson Sampling that, through an initial probability distribution (an a priori distribution) and a set of predefined update rules, can adapt and improve the initial estimates of a specific analyzed process [22]. The initial probability distribution is generally set up as a specific distribution of the Beta family of distributions (Eq. 1) with initial predetermined values for α and β [21,30].

$$Beta(\theta|\alpha,\beta) = \frac{\Gamma(\alpha+\beta)}{\Gamma(\alpha)\Gamma(\beta)} \theta^{\alpha-1}(1-\theta)^{\beta-1} \qquad (1)$$

where Gamma function Γ is formally defined as Eq. 2.

$$\Gamma(x) = \int_0^\infty t^{x-1} e^{-t} dt \qquad (2)$$

Using the explicit Γ definition and a double variable replacement, the family of beta distributions can be written as in Eq. 3. The metrics used in this paper are written based on this equation.

$$Beta(\theta|\alpha,\beta) = \frac{\theta^{\alpha-1}(1-\theta)^{\beta-1}}{\int_0^1 t^{\alpha-1}(1-t)^{\beta-1} dt} \qquad (3)$$

The forgetting curve is an important component of human learning, and for Intelligent Tutoring Systems (ITS), it is a good indicator to evaluate the long-term retention of knowledge and to adapt the system content [32]. Generally, the forgetting curve is modeled using a decreasing exponential function associated with time [25].

In this paper, we use the Hawkes process to simulate the forgetting curve. The Hawkes process is a class of self-exciting point processes whose jump rate is determined by their history. They are usually considered continuous-time processes but can also be used with discrete-time processes. Formally, the Hawkes process can be described as shown in Eq. 4 by an intensity function μ and an excitation function ϕ, depending on time t and history events t_i [24].

$$\lambda(t) = \mu(t) + \sum_{t_i < t} \phi(t - t_i) \qquad (4)$$

The prediction used in the proposed algorithm is based on the work of Soto et al. [28]. It is a case-based reasoning stacking algorithm that implements two levels of integration. Globally, it uses the stacking strategy to run multiple algorithms to search for information in a dataset and generate solutions to different generic problems. In addition, there is an evaluation stage that allows the selection of the most optimal solution for a given problem according to an adaptive metric defined for regression problems. We decided to implement the stacking-based algorithm because it is an ensemble method based on Stein's paradox since it combines the points of view of different estimators to the case-based reasoning retrieve and reuse stages [19].

3 Related Works

To improve the learner experience, an ITS adapts the contents to the needs and knowledge of each learner to enable each one of them to advance in their knowledge acquisition and achieve their learning objectives. This identification and adaptation are generally made with new artificial intelligence techniques such as neural networks, Support Vector Machines (SVM), decision trees, Naive Bayes [2], or long short-term memory networks (LSTM) [29]. Other techniques have been employed to enhance the ITS functionalities, such as the work of Arnau-Gonzalez et al. [4] that allows natural language interaction with the system, implementing a conversational agent through the artificial intelligence-driven natural language understanding (NLU) using the Rasa framework. The results show good cooperation between the NLU and the ITS in producing consistent dialogue and identifying user intents with high precision.

An application of reinforcement learning can be found in the work of Mao et al. [20], where a reinforcement learning-based two-sided recommender system (RTR) is proposed to personalize a quiz, selecting the relevant questions for each learner by considering different parameters such as knowledge level, question type, and question difficulty. The reward for each question is calculated with a learner preferences evaluation. To test and compare the model, a simulation was performed with random selection and greedy selection. The results using the cumulative reward are better with the RTR after 10 and 30 steps.

The integration of historical data and insights gained through an ITS application enhances the effectiveness of artificial intelligence algorithms, facilitating better system adaptation as demonstrated by the method proposed by Li et al. [16], which leverages knowledge graphs (KG) to incorporate the structural information of knowledge concepts. By doing so, it enables an Intelligent Tutoring System (ITS) to select questions that are more informative and representative. The method is composed of two main elements. The first one obtains previous information from the learner and proposes a list of possible questions to be followed in the learning sequence. The second one is in charge of evaluating each one of the proposals predicting of the learner's performance so that it can proceed to select the question that potentially gives a higher performance. The model was tested with two public datasets: ASSISTments 2009-201 and Eedi 2020. The results demonstrate that the system can recommend correct exercises to the learners, improving their performance.

The use of information to predict learner performance can contribute to system adaptation by anticipating possible changes and evaluating possible adaptations before proposing them to learners. The work of Clemente et al. [8] infers information about the progress of the learners and a flexible and adaptable ontology based on competencies to detect and correct weaknesses, and to adapt the recommender system. To create the ontology, some criteria and key points have been defined. The global architecture has been divided into two models. The first one contains the information about the learner, and the second one has the system recommender rules. In general, the effects of adaptation and personalization of an ITS on learning and knowledge acquisition are positive. As an example, we can look at the work of Badier et al. [5], where a mobile recommendation application has been implemented to adapt the navigation and pedagogical resources according to the results and interests of each learner using a three-module architecture. In this case, the metrics used measure the use of the application rather than the performance of the learners to evaluate whether the recommendations provided by the proposed model allow greater interaction of the learner with the application. If the interactions with the application increase, it means that the learners work longer as demonstrated by the results obtained. The authors can then conclude a positive effect on learners. Prediction with case-based reasoning is possible given the implicit analogical reasoning process. The analogical process is able to work with a small number of instances to handle context or to allow creativity. The principle of the analogical process is that similar situations have similar outcomes [6]. In the work of Louvros et al. [18], case-based reasoning is used to predict the real-time survivability of ships. The proposed model combines machine learning predictions and case-based reasoning in similar cases, where the machine learning gets a prediction based on the case-based reasoning results. The goal is to predict the evolution of ship damage scenarios in real time. Chun et al. [7] also predicts stock prices with an adaptation of case-based reasoning to retrieve neighboring cases using graphical pattern identification. In this case, data are represented as a time series, thus demonstrating that the reasoning from cases is adapted to this type of representation for the retrieve phase where the model gets acceptable results.

Another application appears in Pei et al. [23] leveraging the good performance of case-based reasoning for predicting the hazard grade of coal spontaneous combustion. The complete model integrates the reasoning from cases with principal components analysis (PCA) and fuzzy clustering (FM), obtaining good prediction results and improving the computational efficiency of the calculations.

In general, recommender systems are used in various fields, ranging from the sciences to online product stores. This type of system facilitates decision-making and allows in some way to customize content and/or products, as can be seen in the works mentioned below. Iftikhar et al. [13] modeled a recommender system with the Markov Decision Process (MDP). The complete model is composed of multiple stages that seek to reorganize the information of the user evaluations for different products according to a bi-cluster representation and thus identify user preferences and decide on personalized recommendations. The model obtains information from multiple users on all products and can use this information to tailor recommendations to specific preferences. The results show that the proposed algorithm achieved a better start state that yields an optimal policy to achieve the goal. However, a common obstacle with recommender systems is the cold-start problem, which consists of generating recommendations without historical data or with little initial data. To try to solve that problem, reinforcement learning is generally used, as can be seen in the work of Giannikis et al. [12], where reinforcement learning has been used successfully and has obtained better results than some of the more popular AI paradigms. A reinforcement learning algorithm widely used in recommender systems for its ability to work with data whose level of uncertainty is high and that also provides acceptable solutions in cold-start cases is Thompson Sampling. Zhu and Van Roy [34], propose a recommender system based on an epistemic neural coupling with TS to solve a recommender problem defined as a contextual bandit problem. TS is also used because it is a good algorithm for exploring the research space and keeping the computational cost at a minimum. The experiments with two databases in comparison with other algorithms present better scalability. Also, Ghoorchian et al. [11] integrate the Thompson Sampling strategy after a random projection to reduce the dimensionality, because high dimension can reduce the TS accuracy. By posing the recommendation problem also as a multi-armed bandit problem, the model was compared with other recommendation algorithms on three different databases and showed an average gain in computation time and cumulative reward. Another work with TS applied to a recommender system is Eide et al. [10], which proposes a dynamic sequential recommender system based on Thompson Sampling. The model changes the recommendations over time according to the evolution of user data preferences, demonstrating that TS applied sequentially allows for increasing the diversity of the search space exploration and improvement of the specific learning algorithm. Since the recommendation in ITS is also highly variable per learner and dynamic over time, using a TS-based algorithm is a good strategy. This has been seen in previous works, including the work of Soto et al. [26], which serve as the model presented in this paper. That model uses the Beta probability distributions family to estimate learner knowledge and adapt an ITS to each learner. The basic Thompson sampling model has been mixed with the stratification sampling, and the information is updated in a correlated manner to get better estimations of a learner level in each complexity level and to avoid the Simpson's paradox.

The dynamics of the Hawkes process are useful to some tasks because they improve the results and allow simulation of real-life situations. The work of Zhang et al. [33] uses the Hawkes process to predict user preferences in a spaciotemporal context based on historical sequential data to improve the recommendations. The proposed approach outperforms the baseline. In the case of simulation, the work of Lamprinakou and Gandy [15] uses the Hawkes process with stratification to make an epidemic model more realistic. The model produces dynamics very similar to the spreading of a real epidemic, so it is possible to characterize behavior and make predictions to improve prevention measures.

4 Proposed Algorithm

The proposed algorithm is an integration of stochastic adaptation (Thompson Sampling based), ensemble case-based reasoning (ESCBR-SMA), and the Hawkes process. In this case, the recommender algorithm produces an adaptation according to learner grades, the ESCBR-SMA performs a prediction to validate the generated adaptation, and the Hawkes process simulates the forgetting curve in the learning process.

The idea of unification is to obtain information from the local point of view where a recommendation is obtained using only the information of individual learners (Thompson Sampling-based model), the global prediction (where the information is obtained from all learners who have similar results through a collaborative filter with CBR), and the dynamic learning process with the Hawkes process. The algorithm architecture is shown in Fig. 1, where it can be seen that TS and CBR are executed in parallel and independently with the information extracted from the same database. Once the results of each algorithm are obtained, the results are unified through a weighting function, and the distribution of probabilities are updated dynamically according to past events and the selected complexity level. The final recommendation is the one that maximizes Expression 7. Consolidating the two global results allows mitigation of the effect of Simpson's paradox [31].

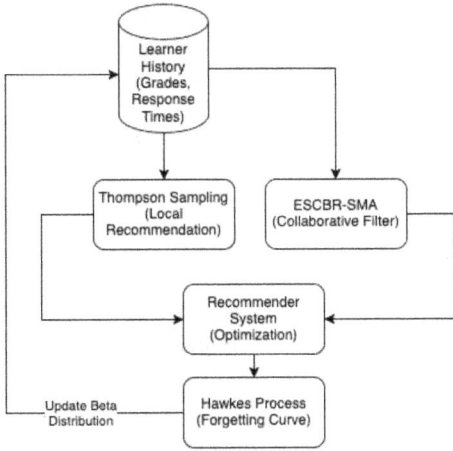

Fig. 1. Proposed Algorithm Architecture

The first step is the adaptation with Thompson Sampling and the ECBR-SMA prediction. Then the decision is made and sent to the learner. The recommender system obtains a probability value for all the complexity levels for the learner, and the ECBR-SMA evaluates the proposition with a prediction for each complexity level. Table 1 shows the variables and parameters for the proposed algorithm and the employed metrics.

Table 1. Parameters (p), variables (v), and functions (f) of the proposed algorithm and metrics

ID	Type	Description	Domain
α	p	Beta distribution parameter	$[1, \infty] \in \mathbb{R}$
β	p	Beta distribution parameter	$[1, \infty] \in \mathbb{R}$
t	p	Time defined as iterations	$\mathbb{N}$
c	p	Complexity level	$\mathbb{N}$
x_c	p	Mean grades for complexity level c	$\mathbb{R}$
y_c	p	Number of questions for complexity level c	$\mathbb{N}$
n_c	v	Normalized probability value for complexity level c	$[0, 1] \in \mathbb{R}$
TS_c	v	Thompson sampling reward for a complexity level c	$[0, 1] \in \mathbb{R}$
TSN_c	v	Normalization of TS_c with others complexity levels	$[0, 1] \in \mathbb{R}$
$ESCBR_c$	v	Grade prediction for a complexity level c	$\mathbb{R}_+$
p_c	f	Probability density function for complexity level c	$\mathbb{R}_+$
r	f	Recommender metric function	$[0, 1] \in \mathbb{R}$

The integration is made in three steps. The first step is to get random values for each c complexity level using the probability distributions generated with the TS (Eq. 5). Once all the probability values corresponding to all the levels of complexity have been obtained, the normalization of all of them is calculated as shown in Eq. 6. The normalization values serve as priority parameters for the predictions made by the ESCBR-SMA as calculated in Eq. 7.

$$TS_c = rand(Beta(\alpha_c, \beta_c)) \tag{5}$$

$$TSN_c = \frac{TS_c}{\sum_{i=0}^{4} TS_i} \tag{6}$$

$$n_c = argmax_c(TSN_c * ESCBR_c) \tag{7}$$

With the final values calculated for each level of complexity, the level of complexity that has the highest value is proposed as the final recommendation (Eq. 7).

After the complexity-level selection, all the distributions of probability are updated according to the Hawkes process (Eq. 4) for each α and β parameter using the constant defined intensity function (Eqs. 8 and 9) and the excitation function (Eq. 10), which generates the dynamic evolution of the Beta probability distributions, thus simulating the forgetting curve.

$$\mu_{\alpha,c}(t) = \begin{cases} 2, & c = 0 \\ 1, & 1 \leq c \leq 4 \end{cases} \quad (8)$$

$$\mu_{\beta,c}(t) = \begin{cases} 1, & c = 0 \\ 3, & c = 1 \\ 5, & c = 2 \\ 7, & c = 3 \\ 9, & c = 4 \end{cases} \quad (9)$$

$$\phi_h(t) = (10)(0.02)e^{-0.02t} \quad (10)$$

Then, Eq. 11 shows the complete definition for all α, and Eq. 12 shows the definition for β parameters.

$$\lambda_\alpha(t) = \mu_{\alpha,c}(t) + \sum_{t_i < t} \phi_h(t - t_i) \quad (11)$$

$$\lambda_\beta(t) = \mu_{\beta,c}(t) + \sum_{t_i < t} \phi_h(t - t_i) \quad (12)$$

Finally, Eq. 13 describes the distribution of probability for each complexity level c.

$$P_c(x, \lambda_\alpha(t), \lambda_\beta(t)) = \frac{x^{\lambda_\alpha(t)}(1-x)^{\lambda_\beta(t)}}{\int_0^1 u^{\lambda_\alpha(t)}(1-u)^{\lambda_\beta(t)} du} \quad (13)$$

5 Results and Discussion

5.1 Recommender System with a Real-Student Database (TS with Hawkes)

The TS recommender system has been tested with an adapted dataset extracted from real data of student interactions with a virtual learning environment for different courses [14]. The total of learners is 23,366. In this database, there are the learner grades in different courses and multiple evaluation types. For this test, the database format is adapted to the AI-VT structure (grades, response times and complexity levels). The complexity levels are divided into five stages and calculated with the weight percentage defined in the dataset. Figure 2 was generated after 100 executions of the algorithm and shows that despite the stochasticity, the algorithm is stable because the global variance in all the complexity levels is low according to the total number of learners and the total number of recommendations.

The algorithm recommends more low-complexity levels with Hawkes because the knowledge tends to decrease with time. The algorithm force to reinforce the learner knowledge in all complexity levels and since the initial configuration gives a higher probability to the lower levels, the algorithm tends to repeat the more accessible levels needed to reach the higher levels.

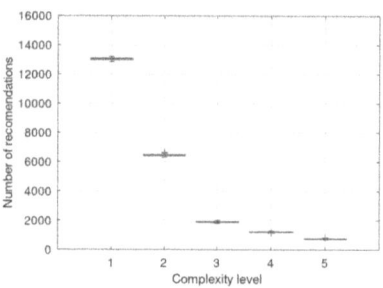 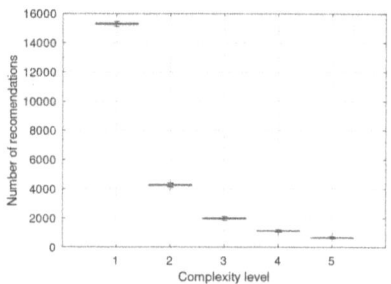

Fig. 2. Number of recommendations per complexity level (left: static learning process, right: dynamic learning process with the Hawkes process)

5.2 Simulated Database (ESCBR, TS with Hawkes)

The simulated database is generated using a log-normal distribution of probability to simulate grades of 1,000 learners in five complexity levels, each one with fifteen questions. The generator simulates more complexity by reducing the mean distribution and increasing the variability.

The comparison is according to Eq. 14, which calculates the relation between the grades mean x_c and the number of questions y_c for each complexity level c.

$$r(x_c, y_c) = e^{-2(x_c + y_c - 1)^2} \tag{14}$$

A specific scenario was defined without initial data (grades and answer times), i.e., a cold start. Table 2 shows the numerical results after 10,000 executions (1,000 learners) for TS and TS-Hawkes in the evaluated scenario. Even with the changes in each complexity level, the total change is only 3.7% in eight questions. Comparative results with others scenarios, a deterministic model and BKT (Bayesian Tracing Model) model was executed and can be consulted in our previous work Soto et al. [27].

Table 2. ESCBR-TS and ESCBR-TS-Hawkes Metric comparison

	r_{C0}	r_{C1}	r_{C2}	r_{C3}	r_{C4}	Total	Percent
TS	0.951	0.812	0.675	0.605	0.563	3.606	72.12
TS-Hawkes	0.941	0.718	0.643	0.576	0.545	3.423	68.46

The variance evolution (Fig. 3) shows that with the Hawkes process, the values are maintained around the initial configuration, which allows greater adaptability to the dynamic changes in knowledge that occur in the learning process. Since the Beta probability distribution converges rapidly to a single value, as more values are obtained, the variance is smaller. If there is a change in the convergence value, the distribution requires more data to converge to the new

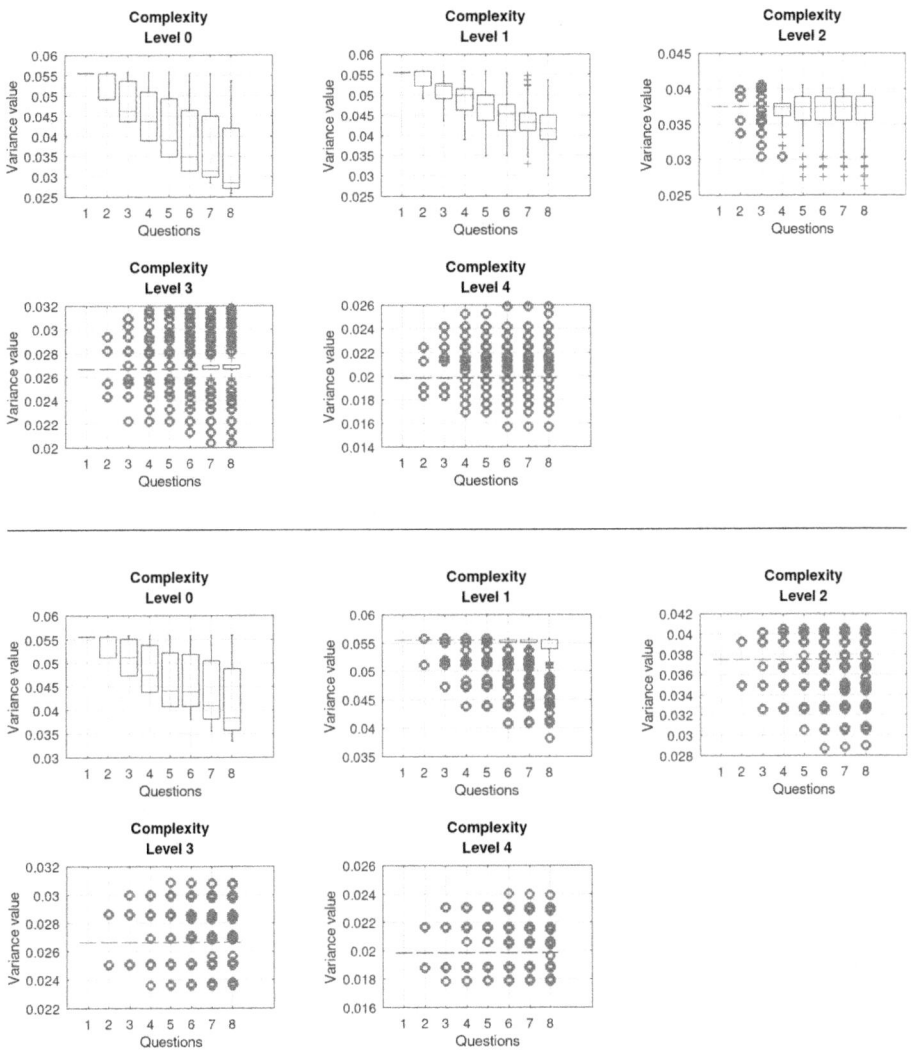

Fig. 3. Variance evolution for Beta distribution of probability and all complexity levels (Top: static learning process. Bottom: dynamic learning process with Hawkes process)

value, since the changes in the mean are proportional to the value of the variance with a constant step of change for the parameters. In the case of modeling the learning process, it is preferable to maintain a relatively high variance value to facilitate adaptation to unforeseen changes, that is the main contribution of the Hawkes process to Thompson Sampling for modeling the knowledge evolution.

6 Conclusion

This paper presents an integrated algorithm based on previously developed models: a recommender system based on a Thompson sampling algorithm, an ensemble regression model based on case-based reasoning, and a forgetting curve simulation using the Hawkes process. The integrated algorithm is applied to an ITS called AI-VT. The results show that the integration allows obtaining similar results but with a more realistic process giving the possibility of better personalization of the system and facilitating knowledge acquisition.

The advantages of the proposed model are: i) It allows the generation of personalized recommendations for each learner with relatively little historical data; ii) Since multiple points of view (different algorithms) on the same problem and with the same database are integrated based on Stein's paradox, the risk of falling into Simpson paradoxes is reduced; iii) The two models with the Hawkes process is more realistic and dynamic in the global learning process.

As future work, it is proposed to integrate into the model other variables obtained with complementary artificial intelligence algorithms such as video analysis, audio analysis, and even the analysis of data obtained from learners throughout the learning process. It would also be beneficial to evaluate the learners performance and progression according to proposed recommendations as well as analyze the model with different parametric configurations in order to determine which are the most appropriate configurations and how each variable influences the global behavior of the executed algorithms in the final result.

References

1. Abel, D., Barreto, A., Van Roy, B., Precup, D., van Hasselt, H.P., Singh, S.: A definition of continual reinforcement learning. In: Oh, A., Naumann, T., Globerson, A., Saenko, K., Hardt, M., Levine, S. (eds.) Advances in Neural Information Processing Systems, vol. 36, pp. 50377–50407. Curran Associates, Inc. (2023)
2. Ahmed, E.: Student performance prediction using machine learning algorithms. Appli. Comput. Intell. Soft Comput. **2024**(1), 4067721 (2024). https://doi.org/10.1155/2024/4067721
3. Alrakhawi, H.A., Jamiat, N., Abu-Naser, S.S.: Intelligent tutoring systems in education: a systematic review of usage, tools, effects and evaluation. J. Theor. Appl. Inf. Technol. **2023**(4), 4067721 (2023)
4. Arnau-González, P., Arevalillo-Herráez, M., Luise, R., Arnau, D.: A methodological approach to enable natural language interaction in an intelligent tutoring system. Comput. Speech Lang. **81**, 101516 (2023) https://doi.org/10.1016/j.csl.2023.101516, https://www.sciencedirect.com/science/article/pii/S0885230823000359
5. Badier, A., Lefort, M., Lefevre, M.: Comprendre les usages et effets d'un système de recommandations pédagogiques en contexte d'apprentissage non-formel. In: EIAH 2023. Brest, France (Jun 2023). https://hal.science/hal-04092828
6. Badra, F., Lesot, M.J.: Case-based prediction – a survey. Int. J. Approximate Reasoning **158**, 108920 (2023). https://doi.org/10.1016/j.ijar.2023.108920, https://www.sciencedirect.com/science/article/pii/S0888613X23000440

7. Chun, S.H., Jang, J.W.: A new trend pattern-matching method of interactive case-based reasoning for stock price predictions. Sustainability **14**(3) (2022). https://doi.org/10.3390/su14031366, https://www.mdpi.com/2071-1050/14/3/1366
8. Clemente, J., Yago, H., de Pedro-Carracedo, J., Bueno, J.: A proposal for an adaptive recommender system based on competences and ontologies. Expert Syst. Appl. **208**, 118171 (2022). https://doi.org/10.1016/j.eswa.2022.118171, https://www.sciencedirect.com/science/article/pii/S0957417422013392
9. Desmarais, M.C., Baker, R.S.J.d.: A review of recent advances in learner and skill modeling in intelligent learning environments. User Model. User-Adapted Interact. **22**(1), 9–38 (2012). https://doi.org/10.1007/s11257-011-9106-8
10. Eide, S., Leslie, D.S., Frigessi, A.: Dynamic slate recommendation with gated recurrent units and thompson sampling **36** (2022). https://doi.org/10.1007/s10618-022-00849-w
11. Ghoorchian, S., Kortukov, E., Maghsudi, S.: Non-stationary linear bandits with dimensionality reduction for large-scale recommender systems. IEEE Open J. Signal Process. **5**, 548–558 (2024). https://doi.org/10.1109/OJSP.2024.3386490
12. Giannikis, S., Frasincar, F., Boekestijn, D.: Reinforcement learning for addressing the cold-user problem in recommender systems. Knowl.-Based Syst. **294**, 111752 (2024) https://doi.org/10.1016/j.knosys.2024.111752, https://www.sciencedirect.com/science/article/pii/S0950705124003873
13. Iftikhar, A., Ghazanfar, M.A., Ayub, M., Ali Alahmari, S., Qazi, N., Wall, J.: A reinforcement learning recommender system using bi-clustering and markov decision process. Expert Syst. Appl. **237**, 121541 (2024). https://doi.org/10.1016/j.eswa.2023.121541, https://www.sciencedirect.com/science/article/pii/S0957417423020432
14. Kuzilek, J., Hlosta, M., Zdrahal, Z.: Open university learning analytics dataset. Scie. Data **4**(1), 170171 (2017). https://doi.org/10.1038/sdata.2017.171
15. Lamprinakou, S., Gandy, A.: Stratified epidemic model using a latent marked hawkes process. Math. Biosci. **375**, 109260 (2024). https://doi.org/10.1016/j.mbs.2024.109260, https://www.sciencedirect.com/science/article/pii/S0025556424001202
16. Li, L., Wang, Z.: Knowledge graph-enhanced intelligent tutoring system based on exercise representativeness and informativeness. Int. J. Intell. Syst. **2023**(1), 2578286 (2023). https://doi.org/10.1155/2023/2578286
17. Liu, M., Yu, D.: Towards intelligent e-learning systems. Educ. Inf. Technol. **28**(7), 7845–7876 (2023). https://doi.org/10.1007/s10639-022-11479-6
18. Louvros, P., Stefanidis, F., Boulougouris, E., Komianos, A., Vassalos, D.: Machine learning and case-based reasoning for real-time onboard prediction of the survivability of ships. J. Marine Sci. Eng. **11**(5) (2023). https://doi.org/10.3390/jmse11050890, https://www.mdpi.com/2077-1312/11/5/890
19. Malladi, R.K.: Application of supervised machine learning techniques to forecast the covid-19 u.s. recession and stock market crash. Comput. Econ. **63**(3), 1021–1045 (2024). https://doi.org/10.1007/s10614-022-10333-8
20. Mao, K., Dong, Q., Wang, Y., Honga, D.: An exploratory approach to intelligent quiz question recommendation. Proc. Comput. Sci. **207**, 4065–4074 (2022). https://doi.org/10.1016/j.procs.2022.09.469, https://www.sciencedirect.com/science/article/pii/S1877050922013631, knowledge-Based and Intelligent Information and Engineering Systems: Proceedings of the 26th International Conference KES2022

21. Nguyen, A.: Dynamic metaheuristic selection via thompson sampling for online optimization. Appl. Soft Comput. **158**, 111566 (2024). https://doi.org/10.1016/j.asoc.2024.111566, https://www.sciencedirect.com/science/article/pii/S1568494624003405
22. Ou, T., Cummings, R., Avella Medina, M.: Thompson sampling itself is differentially private. In: Dasgupta, S., Mandt, S., Li, Y. (eds.) Proceedings of The 27th International Conference on Artificial Intelligence and Statistics. Proceedings of Machine Learning Research, vol. 238, pp. 1576–1584. PMLR (02–04 2024), https://proceedings.mlr.press/v238/ou24a.html
23. Pei, Q., Jia, Z., Liu, J., Wang, Y., Wang, J., Zhang, Y.: Prediction of coal spontaneous combustion hazard grades based on fuzzy clustered case-based reasoning. Fire **7**(4) (2024). https://doi.org/10.3390/fire7040107, https://www.mdpi.com/2571-6255/7/4/107
24. Seol, Y.: Non-markovian inverse hawkes processes. Mathematics **10**(9) (2022). https://doi.org/10.3390/math10091413, https://www.mdpi.com/2227-7390/10/9/1413
25. Shah, D.P., Jagtap, N.M., Shah, S.S., Nimkar, A.V.: Spaced repetition for slow learners. In: 2020 IEEE Bombay Section Signature Conference (IBSSC), pp. 146–151 (2020). https://doi.org/10.1109/IBSSC51096.2020.9332189
26. Soto-Forero, D., Ackermann, S., Betbeder, M.L., Henriet, J.: Automatic real-time adaptation of training session difficulty using rules and reinforcement learning in the ai-vt its. Inter. J. Mod. Educ. Comput. Sci. (IJMECS) **16**, 56–71 (2024). https://doi.org/10.5815/ijmecs.2024.03.05, https://www.mecs-press.org/ijmecs/ijmecs-v16-n3/v16n3-5.html
27. Soto-Forero, D., Ackermann, S., Betbeder, M.L., Henriet, J.: The intelligent tutoring system ai-vt with case-based reasoning and real time recommender models. In: Recio-Garcia, J.A., Orozco-del Castillo, M.G., Bridge, D. (eds.) Case-Based Reasoning Research and Development, pp. 191–205. Springer Nature Switzerland, Cham (2024). https://doi.org/10.1007/978-3-031-63646-2_13
28. Soto-Forero, D., Betbeder, M.L., Henriet, J.: Ensemble stacking case-based reasoning for regression. In: Recio-Garcia, J.A., Orozco-del Castillo, M.G., Bridge, D. (eds.) Case-Based Reasoning Research and Development, pp. 159–174. Springer Nature Switzerland, Cham (2024). https://doi.org/10.1007/978-3-031-63646-2_11
29. Subha, R., Gayathri, N., Sasireka, S., Sathiyabanu, R., Santhiyaa, B., Varshini, B.: Intelligent tutoring systems using long short-term memory networks and bayesian knowledge tracing. In: 2024 5th International Conference on Mobile Computing and Sustainable Informatics (ICMCSI), pp. 24–29 (2024). https://doi.org/10.1109/ICMCSI61536.2024.00010
30. Uguina, A.R., Gomez, J.F., Panadero, J., Martínez-Gavara, A., Juan, A.A.: A learnheuristic algorithm based on thompson sampling for the heterogeneous and dynamic team orienteering problem. Mathematics **12**(11) (2024). https://doi.org/10.3390/math12111758, https://www.mdpi.com/2227-7390/12/11/1758
31. Xu, S., Ge, Y., Li, Y., Fu, Z., Chen, X., Zhang, Y.: Causal collaborative filtering. In: Proceedings of the 2023 ACM SIGIR International Conference on Theory of Information Retrieval, ICTIR 2023, pp. 235–245. Association for Computing Machinery, New York (2023). https://doi.org/10.1145/3578337.3605122,
32. Zaidi, A., Caines, A., Moore, R., Buttery, P., Rice, A.: Adaptive forgetting curves for spaced repetition language learning. In: Bittencourt, I.I., Cukurova, M., Muldner, K., Luckin, R., Millán, E. (eds.) Artificial Intelligence in Education, pp. 358–363. Springer International Publishing, Cham (2020). https://doi.org/10.1007/978-3-030-52240-7_65

33. Zhang, X., et al.: Multivariate hawkes spatio-temporal point process with attention for point of interest recommendation. Neurocomputing **619**, 129161 (2025) https://doi.org/10.1016/j.neucom.2024.129161, https://www.sciencedirect.com/science/article/pii/S0925231224019325
34. Zhu, Z., Van Roy, B.: Scalable neural contextual bandit for recommender systems. In: Proceedings of the 32nd ACM International Conference on Information and Knowledge Management, CIKM 2023. pp. 3636–3646. Association for Computing Machinery, New York (2023). https://doi.org/10.1145/3583780.3615048

From Struggle (06-2024) to Mastery (02-2025) LLMs Conquer Advanced Algorithm Exams and Pave the Way for Editorial Generation

Adrian Marius Dumitran[1,3], Theodor-Pierre Moroianu[2], and Vasile Paul Alexe[1(✉)]

[1] University of Bucharest, Bucharest, Romania
marius.dumitran@unibuc.ro, vasile-paul.alexe@g.unibuc.ro
[2] ETH, Zurich, Switzerland
theodor-pierre.moroianu@my.fmi.unibuc.ro
[3] Softbinator Technologies, Bucharest, Romania

Abstract. This paper presents a comprehensive evaluation of the performance of state-of-the-art Large Language Models (LLMs) on challenging university-level algorithms exams. By testing multiple models on both a Romanian exam and its high-quality English translation, we analyze LLMs' problem-solving capabilities, consistency, and multilingual performance. Our empirical study reveals that the most recent models not only achieve scores comparable to top-performing students but also demonstrate robust reasoning skills on complex, multi-step algorithmic challenges, even though difficulties remain with graph-based tasks. Building on these findings, we explore the potential of LLMs to support educational environments through the generation of high-quality editorial content, offering instructors a powerful tool to enhance student feedback. The insights and best practices discussed herein pave the way for further integration of generative AI in advanced algorithm education.

Keywords: Generative Tutoring Systems · Large Language Models (LLMs) · Generative Learning Strategies · Learning Analytics for Tutoring Systems · Human-Machine Interaction · Editorial Generation

1 Introduction

Recent breakthroughs in large language models (LLMs) have dramatically expanded their capabilities across various domains. Historically, although LLMs excelled in many areas, their performance on advanced algorithm problems was limited. Over the past year, however, significant improvements have been made, enabling newer models to solve complex algorithmic challenges with remarkable accuracy. This is highlighted very clearly in this 2025 paper about OpenAi's o3 model, which reaches extraordinary levels in competitive programming [6].

In this paper, we conduct an in-depth analysis of these advancements within the context of a university-level advanced algorithms exam. Our empirical results reveal that models older than six months tend to perform in the bottom 40% of the ranking, whereas recent models from January–February 2025 consistently rank within the top 15%, with the new o3-mini even achieving top 5% status. We show these improvements in Sect. 3, where we focus on evaluating LLM performance as exam solvers in real-world scenarios. We also highlight areas where LLMs still underperform compared to average students.

Additionally, we explore two promising applications of LLM technology in educational settings. First, we present a human-in-the-loop approach for generating detailed grading schemes, enabling instructors to efficiently grade student work. Second, we examine how LLMs can assist in generating high-quality editorial content, providing clear and actionable feedback to students. We also offer a free-to-use framework for this task.

2 Related Work

Our work builds upon research at the intersection of Large Language Models (LLMs), algorithmic problem-solving, and educational applications. LLMs are increasingly being explored for their ability to tackle complex tasks, as evidenced by their application in competitive programming environments [6].

The use of LLMs in education is a rapidly developing area, with studies investigating their potential for grading and assessment [10,11] and automatic feedback generation [7]. Recent efforts, like that of [20], also focus on improving automated grading systems with LLMs, addressing issues such as rubric generation, scoring consistency, and introducing "Grade-Like-a-Human" systems that mimic human evaluation through multi-agent approaches. The impact of LLMs on education is also being broadly considered, examining both opportunities and challenges for various stakeholders [9].

This work differs from existing research by focusing on advanced STEM content in a real-world exam setting, evaluating grading consistency and performance on the content on Romanian algorithmic exams and by providing a novel dataset in the low-resource Romanian language, with a similar study being done by Anton, A. et al. [13] for Brazilian exams and by Dumitran, A. M. et al. [3] on Romanian competitive programming.

3 LLMs as Exam Solvers: An Empirical Evaluation

We start by conducting a thorough evaluation of their problem-solving capabilities in the context of a challenging computer science exam, composed of 11 algorithmic problems. This exam, which we release as a publicly available dataset [4], covers advanced algorithms with a focus on graphs and was originally administered in Romanian. This chapter details our methodology and presents the results of this evaluation, focusing on the performance of a diverse range of state-of-the-art LLMs.

3.1 Methodology

We evaluate a broad range of LLMs to assess their exam-solving abilities. Our selection includes models with diverse architectures and training methods. We prioritize those accessible via user interfaces–mimicking a typical instructor's approach–while also including deprecated models to illustrate that older models are ineffective as tutoring partners.

Models were selected from the ChatBot Arena LLM Leaderboard [2], choosing a few from each family. From the OpenAI UI [15], we evaluated `GPT-4 Legacy`, `GPT-4o`, `o1`, `o3-mini` (Jan 31, 2025), and `o3-mini-high` (Jan 31, 2025). From Google AI Studio [8], we assessed `Gemini 2.0 Flash` (Feb 2025), `Gemini 1.5 Pro`, `Gemini 2.0 Pro Experimental` (Feb 2025), and `Gemini 2.0 Flash Thinking Experimental` (Jan 2025), as well as the open-source `Gemma 2-27B`. Using the *Together AI* platform [17], we also evaluated `DeepSeekR1`, `Qwen2.5Max` (Jan 2025), `Claude Sonnet 3.5`, and models from Meta, namely `Llama3.3-70B`, `Llama-3.1-405B`, `Mistral 7B Inst-v0.3`, and `Mixtral 22x8 Inst-v0.1`. In this paper, we will refer to each LLM by its model name without including its brand. Thus, 'OpenAi's o3-mini' will be referred to simply as 'o3-mini', and 'Claude Sonnet 3.5' as 'Sonnet 3.5'.

For most models, we use their official user interfaces with default settings and a simple, neutral prompt, reflecting an "out-of-the-box" usage scenario.

The exam, originally in Romanian, is also translated into high-quality English. Crucially, the LLMs are instructed to solve the entire exam in a single interaction, i.e. one-shot, rather than addressing each of the 11 problems individually. This design choice is made to evaluate the models' ability to manage long contexts and maintain coherence across a complex, multi-part task – a key requirement for real-world exam solving. All LLM responses are scored by the course instructor, ensuring consistency and fairness with the grades received by the students who took the exam.

3.2 New Models Triumph Where Old Ones Fail

Leading-edge LLMs' performance on the advanced algorithms exam is strongly correlated with the models' release dates. As shown in Fig. 1, models released within the last four months such as OpenAI's `o3-mini` and Google's `Gemini2.0 Flash` consistently score above 80 and 70 points (top 5% and 15% respectively) on our evaluation exam. In contrast, older models often score below 40.

The older models struggle not only with intricate algorithmic problems but also with processing the extensive context of the exam. This suggests that handling larger and more complex context windows is a key differentiator between newer and older LLMs. Although isolated exceptions exist, the overall trend strongly indicates that recent LLM development has crossed a critical threshold, making them effective tools for challenging educational assessments in advanced computer science topics. Consequently, this period represents a crucial juncture for investigating the potential of LLMs in advanced algorithm courses, as recent breakthroughs have dramatically enhanced their applicability.

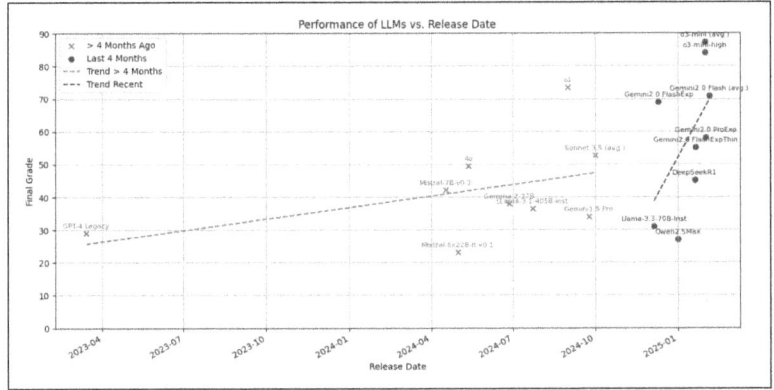

Fig. 1. LLM Performance on Advanced Algorithms Exam vs. Release Date. Models are grouped by release date: more than four months ago (red line, crosses) and within the last four months (blue line, circles) (Color figure online)

It is also important to mention that neither `DeepSeekR1` nor the new `Qwen 2.5 Pro` perform well; both fail the exam and rank in the bottom half. Additionally, high server load hindered `DeepSeekR1`'s usability via both the UI and API.

3.3 Consistency Analysis of LLMs in Exam Grading

As our goal is to assess LLMs for tutoring we examine their consistency in solving the exam's problems. For this experiment we select the models obtaining good results in our initial study: we are not interested in using as a tutor an LLM that is consistently wrong. This subsection examines the consistency of LLMs in grading exams by evaluating three representative models: `o3-mini`, `Gemini 2.0 Flash`, and `Sonnet 3.5`. Consistency is measured by the standard deviation (SD) of their final grades across multiple runs – a lower SD indicates higher consistency.

Our methodology for measuring the consistency of the 3 models is the following:

– We ask each model to solve the exam in 5 different sessions.
– We grade each solution independently.
– For each model we compute the mean and SD of its 5 solutions.

The consistency results can be seen in the Table 1.

We observe that `o3-mini` and `Gemini 2.0 Flash` exhibit significantly higher consistency, as evidenced by their low standard deviations (2.41 and 2.70, respectively), compared to Sonnet 3.5, which shows substantial variability with an SD of 16.95. A further analysis reveals that the scores of `Sonnet 3.5` are quite similar in 4 of the runs at around 50 points, but one of the runs scores an excellent 77 points, like a black swan situation.

Table 1. Final grade consistency across multiple runs

Model	Runs	Final Grade Mean	Final Grade SD
o3-mini	5	86.60	2.41
Gemini 2.0 Flash	5	69.90	2.70
Sonnet 3.5	5	53.70	16.95

3.4 Collaborative Solving

LLMs are trained on different datasets and thus show varying strengths. While the o3-mini model generally performs well, the Gemini family of models excels in theoretical tasks and competitive programming. We explore whether combining multiple solutions could yield a more effective solver.

We run two experiments, in which models are tasked with solving the exam:

- **RunAvg**: Each LLM is provided with its own previous answers (from 3 different runs).
- **RunAvgAll**: Each LLM is provided with three solutions from different LLMs (including DeepSeekR1 to ensure diversity).

Table 2 shows the difference between the scores obtained using these strategies and the mean individual scores.

Table 2. Impact of RunAvg and RunAvgAll prompting strategies on scores

Model	RunAvg (Total)	RunAvgAll (Total)
o3-mini	0.67	−0.33
Gemini 2.0 Flash	−2.40	12.10
Sonnet 3.5	−8.67	13.83
DeepSeekR1	0.50	15.00

The *RunAvg* strategy shows little change, as self-reinforcement tends to maintain standard behavior. The only substantial difference is observed for Sonnet 3.5, where the score converges towards its mean, effectively reducing the impact of its outlier-level performance.

In contrast, the *RunAvgAll* strategy resulted in a substantial increase for Gemini 2.0 Flash, Sonnet 3.5, and DeepSeekR1, and a minor decrease for o3-mini. This outcome is understandable since the first models benefit from exposure to the better solutions of o3-mini, whereas o3-mini only gained access to lower-quality results.

Notably, o3-mini is able to leverage Gemini 2.0 Flash's solution to optimally solve one of the problems (by employing a *BFS 0-1* algorithm instead of Dijkstra's), although its max-flow solution suffered, preventing overall improvement.

3.5 Comparison of LLM Scores and Student Performance

In this section, we compare the performance of various Large Language Models (LLMs) with student exam results. The distribution of student grades is presented in Fig. 2, where we also highlight the scores of different LLMs for a direct comparison.

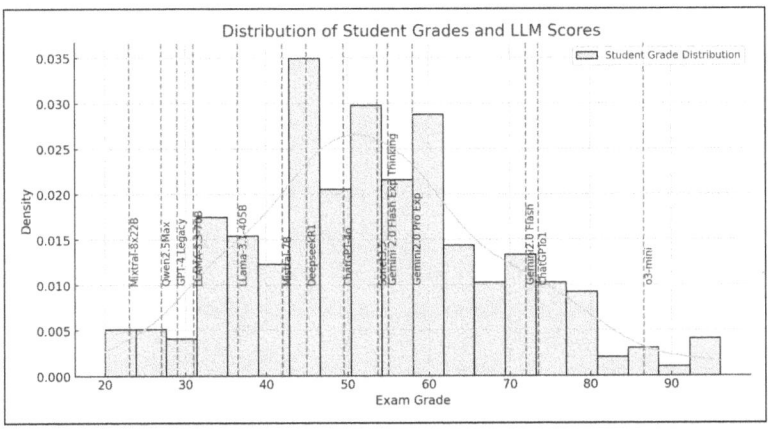

Fig. 2. Distribution of student grades with LLM scores highlighted

From the figure, we observe that `o3-mini` and `Gemini2.0 Flash` perform well, achieving scores that place them among the top percentiles of student performance. In contrast, models such as `Mixtral-8x22B` and `GPT-4 Legacy` rank lower.

Table 3. LLM Average Grades and Percentiles (Top Models on Left, Weaker on Right)

Top Half			Bottom Half		
Model	Grade	Percentile	Model	Grade	Percentile
o3-mini	86.60	98	4o	49.50	40
o3-mini-high	84.00	97	DeepSeekR1	45.00	28
o1	73.50	89	Gemma 2-27B	38.00	17
Gemini2.0Flash	72.30	88	LLama3.1-405B-Inst	36.50	15
Gemini2.0FlashExp	69.00	83	GPT-4 Legacy	29.00	4
Gemini2.0ProExp	58.00	64	Qwen2.5Max	27.00	4
Sonnet 3.5	53.70	53	Mixtral-8x22B-Inst	23.00	2

Table 3 shows each LLM's standing within the student grade distribution, sorted by percentile ranking.

It is worth mentioning that around 5% of the student cohort has previously participated in the National Olympiad in Computer Science, and the results obtained by *o3-mini* places it not only top 3% of the class but also, likely, top 1% nationwide in computer science.

3.6 LLMs VS Students Task Analysis

We compare the results obtained by LLMs and students for each problem. The exam subjects are found in Appendix A (Table 4).

Table 4. Comparison of Student and LLM Performance

Problem	Student Avg	LLM Avg	Difference
Problem 1	4.11	1.21	**2.91**
Problem 2	4.21	3.59	0.62
Problem 3	6.06	3.38	**2.68**
Problem 4	4.30	3.21	1.09
Problem 5	2.43	2.59	−0.16
Problem 6	4.34	2.76	1.58
Problem 7	1.67	2.94	−1.28
Problem 8	7.68	2.82	**4.85**
Problem 9	4.78	7.53	−2.75
Problem 10	1.96	4.32	−2.36
Problem 11	5.04	8.29	−3.26

It is very interesting to note that the problems where LLMs perform significantly worse (such as Problems 1 and 3) are those that require visual analysis of a graph rather than the application of a typical algorithm.

In Fig. 3, two such tasks are illustrated. While human students can easily solve visual tasks like these – where one needs to, for example, visualize a bipartite graph or analyze the structure of a graph, LLMs face notable challenges.

For instance, in Problem 1 most LLMs fail to correctly identify a valid solution. Below are a few sample outputs from various LLMs for this task:

- 4o outputs a long text, followed by:
    "It seems that no sufficiently large bipartite component exists in the graph. The structure of the graph includes odd-length cycles that prevent direct bipartiteness. If you want, I can modify the graph by removing minimal edges to make it bipartite."
- DeepSeekR1 outputs an invalid solution:
    "A = {4, 9}, B = {5, 8, 7}."

As one can see from the drawing, vertices 8 and 7 are neighbors; thus, the solution is not only non-maximal but also invalid.

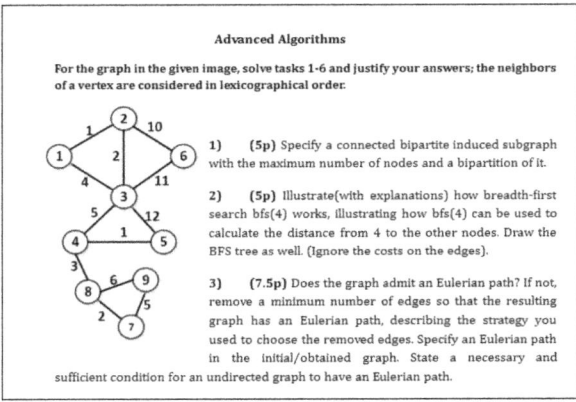

Fig. 3. Examples of visual tasks from Problems 1 and 3 that challenge LLMs

- Gemini2.0 Flash (one of the best models):
  • Set 1 (Color 0): {1, 4, 7, 9}
  • Set 2 (Color 1): {2, 3, 8}
  Again, this solution is not valid.
- o3-mini offers a valid solution:
  • Red: $\{3, 8\}$
  • Blue: $\{1, 4, 6, 7\}$

Problem 3 poses a similar challenge by asking for the minimal number of edges that must be removed from a given graph to allow for an Eulerian path. In this case, some of the newer thinking models–such as DeepSeek and Gemini2.0 Flash Experimental Thinking attempt backtracking but ultimately fail, often stalling after reaching the maximum number of output tokens.

Additionally, applying max-flow algorithms to a graph also seems to pose a challenge for LLMs (problem 8).

On the other hand, LLMs demonstrate strong performance in proving theoretical exercises (problems 7 and 9), applying string algorithms to concrete examples (exercise 10), and problem-solving (problem 11).

3.7 Romanian vs. English Performance

We evaluate each model on the same advanced algorithms exam in both Romanian and its English translation. We define the performance difference as the following:

$$\Delta = \text{Grade}_{\text{En}} - \text{Grade}_{\text{Ro}},$$

Note that a positive Δ indicates a higher score on the English version.

Table 5 shows each model's release date, grades for the Romanian and English versions of the exam, and their delta. Models are sorted by release date and grouped (A vs. B) to highlight trends in more recent versus older systems. For models tested multiple times we present the average. Overall, newer models (Group A) exhibit a small statistically unimportant difference in favor of Romanian (−0.69), while older models (Group B) see larger gains in English (+9.0).

Table 5. Performance Comparison with Grouping (First 12 vs. Last 6)

Model	Release Date	Grade (Ro)	Grade (En)	Diff.	Group
Gemini2.0 ProExp	2025-02	72.5	58.0	−14.5	A
Gemini2.0 Flash (avg.)	2025-02-05	61.0	70.8	+9.8	A
o3-mini (avg.)	2025-01-31	81.7	87.3	+5.7	A
o3-mini-high	2025-01-31	83.0	84.0	+1.0	A
Qwen2.5Max	2025-01	34.0	27.0	−7.0	A
Gemini2.0 FlashExpThin	2025-01-21	61.0	55.0	−6.0	A
DeepSeekR1	2025-01-20	46.5	45.0	−1.5	A
Gemini2.0 FlashExp	2024-12-11	68.5	69.0	+0.5	A
Llama-3.3-70B-Inst	2024-12-06	30.0	31.0	+1.0	A
Sonnet 3.5 (avg.)	2024-10	50.0	52.7	+2.7	A
Gemini1.5 Pro	2024-09-24	40.0	34.0	−6.0	A
o1	2024-09	67.5	73.5	+6.0	A
Group A Averages	After 09-2024	**58.0**	**57.3**	**−0.69**	
LLama-3.1-405B-Inst	2024-07-23	34.0	36.5	+2.5	B
Gemma 2-27B	2024-06-27	27.0	38.0	+11.0	B
4o	2024-05-13	22.0	49.5	+27.5	B
Mixtral-8x22B-It-v0.1	2024-05	27.0	23.0	-4.0	B
Mistral-7B-v0.3	2024-04-17	23.0	42.0	+19.0	B
GPT-4 Legacy	2023-03-14	31.0	29.0	-2.0	B
Group B Averages	Before 09-2024	**27.3**	**36.3**	**+9.0**	

Notably, older models like `4o` and `Mistral-7B-v0.3` show a strong bias toward English, reflecting potentially unbalanced multilingual data. Meanwhile, recent models such as `o3-mini`, `o3-mini-high` and `Gemini2.0 FlashExp` have much smaller gaps, pointing to improved multilingual training.

4 LLM-Assisted Grading Schemes and Editorial Generation

4.1 Grading Scheme Via Human-AI Collaboration

We develop a grading scheme through a Human-AI collaboration between the course instructors and the top-performing LLM solvers, `o3-mini` and `Gemini`

`Flash 2.0`. The process involves providing the LLMs with brief descriptions of solutions and prompting them to expand these into a comprehensive grading scheme, with instructors refining and correcting any errors along the way.

The result is an exceptionally detailed grading scheme, which can be found within the dataset on GitHub [5]. The grading scheme is far more extensive than a typical one, as instructors would rarely have the time or energy to create such a thorough evaluation framework manually.

4.2 Web-Based Platform

To showcase the practicality of our technique, we design and implement a web-based application, the design of which is presented in Fig. 4, and whose user interface can be seen in Fig. 5. For pricing reasons, our platform only supports `Gemini2.0 Flash` and `Mistral large`, which the users can freely pick when submitting a request.

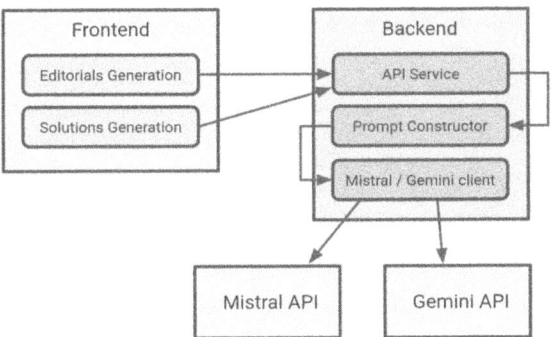

Fig. 4. Design of our application

The application aims at being a tool tailored to professors and students work speeding up their editorial / grading scheme creation, respectively their learning experience, and is based on the observation that modern LLMs are sufficiently good and consistent for generating one-shot useful solutions, explanations and editorials for complex tasks. While it is currently more focused towards computer science, it can be easily modified to support a wide range of disciplines. 2 potential use-cases of the platform are:

- **Editorial generation**: A history professor composed a written exam in German on the history of the Roman Empire, with the language choice made arbitrarily. After preparing a model solution outlining the expected answers, she uploaded both the exam questions and her solution to the platform.
  The system automatically generated a comprehensive editorial featuring step-by-step reasoning and detailed explanations for each exercise. Finding one explanation somewhat ambiguous, she added an instruction requesting a more in-depth analysis for that exercise and regenerated the editorial.

- **Solution generation**: A student received a geography assignment, but failed to come up with the right answers. He opens the framework, uploads the assignment's statement to the platform, provides its current ideas and explains what he approaches he tried, and the platform automatically generates a solution to the assignment.

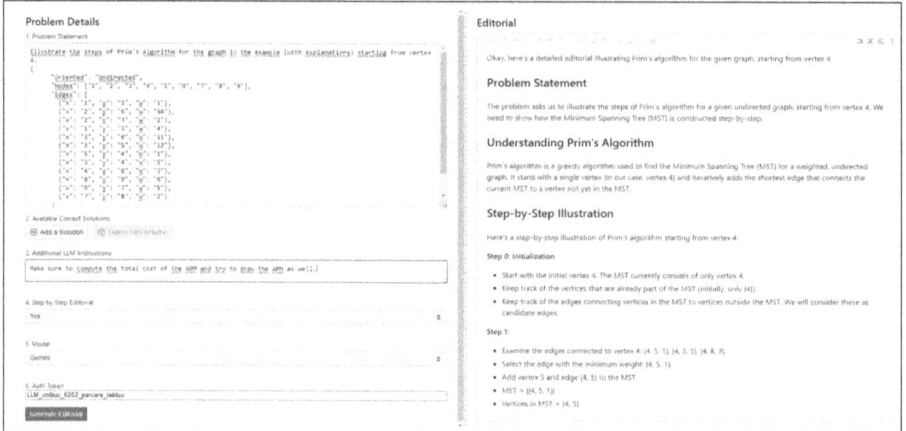

Fig. 5. Framework for generating solutions to a problem

The platform [14] is not a commercial product, and is currently only intended to be used for research purposes, mainly due to a lack of authentication mechanisms. Exposing an unprotected application querying LLMs to the internet can incur unexpected costs due to an abusive usage of our API: attackers can use techniques such as [12] for bypassing our prompts and run arbitrary queries at our expense. To prevent this, we define an *auth token*, which is stored in the browser's local storage (i.e. only needs to be entered once), which acts like a pre-shared secret between the researchers using the application and the backend hosting it.

As one can see in Fig. 4, the application is made out of two main components. The frontend is implemented in *React* and heavily relies on the *BlueprintJS* ui library. The backend is implemented in *Python* and interacts with the frontend with the help of *FastAPI* and with the *Mistral* and *Gemini* APIs using their specific *Python* module. For the purpose of this article, the most relevant part however is the prompt engineering [19]. This was done in an iterative process, by adding and tweaking existing prompts to make the LLMs behave in an expected, useful and consistent manner. Our prompts add on average 2000 additional characters to the LLM inference requests we make to *Gemini 2.0 Flash* and *Mistral large*, and we offer users the possibility to insert additional prompts.

5 Conclusion

In this study, we have explored the progress of state-of-the-art Large Language Models (LLMs) in tackling complex, university-level algorithm exams. Our empirical evaluation places models such as `o3-mini` and `Gemini2.0 Flash` on-par with top-performing students, showcasing their robust reasoning skills and consistency across multi-step algorithmic challenges.

Our consistency analysis provides a metric demonstrating a strong correlation between LLM consistency and performance on algorithmic tasks, indicating that improved models exhibit greater consistency. Modern LLMs, excelling in both theoretical exercises and practical applications, can support educational environments by generating high-quality editorial content. The consistency and performance of these models make them valuable tools for instructors and students, offering detailed grading schemes and actionable feedback to enhance learning.

6 Future Work

Our study reveals remaining challenges in LLMs, particularly in handling graph-based tasks and ensuring grading fairness and accuracy. Future research should address these limitations, exploring multimodal capabilities for seamless interpretation of visual and textual data to unlock LLMs' full potential for interactive and effective learning experiences.

Rapid advances in LLMs unlock exciting applications, particularly in automated essay scoring (AES), a field previously limited by models' grasp of complex tasks. While AES has evolved considerably since its introduction [1,16,18], few studies examine LLM potential in advanced STEM grading. Future work should analyze LLM effectiveness in these contexts, overcoming challenges in processing graph-rich exams and handling low-resource languages. This requires improvements in OCR, specialized digital exam capture, or future LLMs with robust multimodal image interpretation. Addressing these challenges will be crucial for harnessing LLMs in advanced STEM assessment.

Another promising direction is the development of specialized feedback loops that utilize LLM-generated editorial content to provide detailed, step-by-step explanations for complex algorithmic problems. This approach could help students better understand advanced concepts and identify common pitfalls. Finally, conducting controlled studies to measure the impact of such editorial feedback on student learning outcomes in advanced algorithms courses will be essential for validating these techniques and establishing best practices for generative tutoring systems.

Another promising research direction emerging from this work is the use of collaborative LLMs to tackle tasks where individual models consistently struggle, as discussed in Subsect. 3.4.

Acknowledgments. The authors gratefully acknowledge Softbinator Technologies for their support of this research.

A Advanced Algorithms Exam Statement

Advanced Algorithms

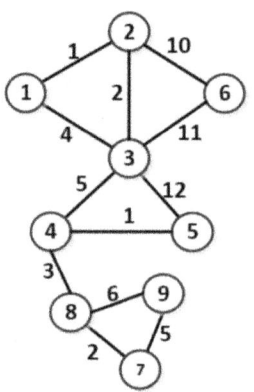

Fig. 6. Graph representations for Exercises 1-6.

For the graph given below, solve tasks 1–6 and justify your answers; the neighbors of a vertex are considered in lexicographical order (Fig. 6).

1. **(5p)** Specify a connected bipartite induced subgraph with the maximum number of nodes and a bipartition of it.
2. **(5p)** Illustrate (with explanations) how breadth-first search bfs(4) works, showing how bfs(4) can be used to calculate the distance from 4 to the other nodes. Draw the BFS tree as well.
3. **(7.5p)** Determine whether the graph admits an Eulerian path. If not, remove a minimum number of edges so that the resulting graph has an Eulerian path, describing the strategy you used to choose the removed edges. Specify an Eulerian path in the initial/obtained graph. State a necessary and sufficient condition for an undirected graph to have an Eulerian path.
4. **(7.5p)** Describe an efficient algorithm for determining the critical nodes of an undirected graph and exemplify (with explanations) the algorithm for the graph in the image.
5. **(5p)** Describe the Floyd-Warshall algorithm for determining distances in a weighted undirected graph with n vertices, detailing the following scheme:

```
Initialize the distance matrix D with the cost matrix.
for j ← 1 to n do
    for i ← 1 to n do
        for k ← 1 to n do
            ...
```

Write which values are modified in the matrix for the graph in the example at stages $j = 1$, $j = 2$, and $j = 3$ (with explanations).
6. **(5p)** Illustrate the steps of Prim's algorithm for the graph in the example (with explanations) starting from vertex 4.
7. **(5p)** Is the following algorithm for determining a minimum spanning tree of a connected weighted graph $G = (V, E, w)$ correct? Justify (without appealing to the functioning of other algorithms in the justification; the used results must be demonstrated and it must be explained how they were used):

```
T = (V, E = < empty set>)   -- initially V contains all the
vertices and contains no edge.
for i = 1 to |V|-1
    Choose the connected component C of T that contains vertex i.
    Choose an edge of minimum cost e with one end in C and
    the other not in C and add e to T.
```

8. **(12.5p)** Illustrate the steps of the Ford-Fulkerson algorithm for this network starting from the indicated flow and choosing at each step an s-t f-unsaturated path of minimum length (the Edmonds-Karp algorithm). Indicate a minimum cut (s-t cut) in the network (the vertices in the bipartition, the direct arcs, the reverse arcs, and how it is determined by the algorithm) and determine the capacity of this cut. Justify the answers.

9. **(15p)**
    (a) Show that a graph with $n > 2$ nodes that satisfies the condition $d(x) \geq \frac{n}{2}$ for any node x is connected.
    (b) Give an example of a non-Hamiltonian graph in which there are two distinct non-adjacent nodes with the sum of degrees $\geq n$.
    (c) Show that if a graph G with $n \geq 2$ nodes has $m \geq \binom{n-1}{2} + 2$ edges, then G is Hamiltonian.

10. **(7.5p)** Briefly describe the algorithm for determining the maximum length of a common subsequence of two words. Illustrate the algorithm for the words *cerceta* and *retea* by writing the matrix with the values of the subproblems and explaining how they were calculated.

11. **(15p)** A team of explorers has discovered an old map of an underground mine renowned for a rare and valuable crystal. The mine is composed of a series of chambers interconnected by unidirectional tunnels. For our experienced explorers, the tunnels can be traversed without any effort. However, some of the chambers have collapsed, and to cross them, they need to use dynamite. The team's goal is to get from the entrance chamber to the chamber containing the rare crystal using as little dynamite as possible. Write an algorithm of optimal complexity that determines if there is a path for the explorers and, if there is, determines the path. (7.5p for explaining the solution and 7.5p for complexity analysis)

References

1. Attali, Y., Burstein, J.: Automated essay scoring with e-rater® v. 2. J. Technol. Learn. Assessment **4**(3) (2006)
2. Chiang, W.L., et al.: Chatbot arena: an open platform for evaluating LLMs by human preference (2024), arXiv:2403.04132 [cs.CL]. https://lmarena.ai/?leaderboard
3. Dumitran, A.M., Badea, A.C., Muscalu, S.G.: Evaluating the performance of large language models in competitive programming: a multi-year, multi-grade analysis (2024). https://doi.org/10.48550/arXiv.2409.09054, arXiv:2409.09054 [cs.AI]

4. Dumitran, A.M., Moroianu, T.P., Alexe, V.P.: Advanced algorithms exam dataset (June 2024). https://github.com/marius135/ExameneAF2025 (2024), gitHub repository. Accessed 15 Feb 2025
5. Dumitran, A.M., Moroianu, T.P., Alexe, V.P.: Comprehensive grading scheme dataset. https://github.com/marius135/ExameneAF2025 (2025), Accessed 22 April 2025
6. El-Kishky, A., et al.: Competitive programming with large reasoning models (2025). https://doi.org/10.48550/arXiv.2502.06807
7. Furuhashi, M., et al.: Automatic feedback generation for short answer questions using answer diagnostic graphs. In: Proceedings of the 16th International Conference on Education and New Learning Technologies (EDULEARN25) (2025). https://doi.org/10.48550/arXiv.2501.15777, in Press. Available at
8. Google: Google AI studio. https://aistudio.google.com/ (2024), Accessed 15 Feb 2025
9. Kasneci, E., et al.: ChatGPT for good? on opportunities and challenges of large language models for education. Learn. Individ. Differ. **103**, 102274 (2023). https://doi.org/10.1016/j.lindif.2023.102274
10. Lee, G.G., Latif, E., Wu, X., Liu, N., Zhai, X.: Applying large language models and chain-of-thought for automatic scoring. Comput. Educ. Artifi. Intell. **6**, 100213 (2024). https://doi.org/10.1016/j.caeai.2024.100213
11. Lee, S., Cai, Y., Meng, D., Wang, Z., Wu, Y.: Unleashing large language models' proficiency in zero-shot essay scoring. In: Findings of the Association for Computational Linguistics: EMNLP 2024, pp. 181–198. Association for Computational Linguistics (2024)
12. Liu, Y., Deng, G., Li, Y., Wang, K., Wang, Z., Wang, X.: Prompt injection attack against LLM-integrated applications (2023), arXiv:2306.05499 [cs.CR]
13. Locatelli, M.S., et al.: Examining the behavior of llm architectures within the framework of standardized national exams in brazil (2024), arxiv:2408.05035
14. Moroianu, T.P.: LLM editorial generation framework. https://llm.moroianu.work/generate-editorials (2025), Accessed Feb 2025
15. OpenAI: Chatgpt (2023). https://chatgpt.com/ last accessed 15 Feb 2025
16. Page, E.B.: The imminence of grading essays by computer. Phi Delta Kappan **47**(5), 238–243 (1966)
17. Together AI: The AI acceleration cloud (2024). https://www.together.ai/ Accessed 15 Feb 2025
18. Wang, W., Chen, Z., Yan, G.: Transformer-based automated essay scoring with discourse-aware attention. In: Proceedings of the 28th International Conference on Computational Linguistics (COLING 2020), pp. 6276–6287. International Committee on Computational Linguistics, Barcelona, Spain (Online) (2020)
19. White, J., et al.: A prompt pattern catalog to enhance prompt engineering with chatgpt (2023), arXiv:2302.11382 [cs.SE]
20. Xie, W., Niu, J., Xue, C.J., Guan, N.: Grade like a human: rethinking automated assessment with large language models (2024). https://doi.org/10.48550/arXiv.2405.19694

An Approach to Organizing Intelligent Tutoring Systems with Customizable Decision-Making Logic

Viktor Uglev[1,2]

[1] Siberian Federal University, Zheleznogorsk, Russia
vauglev@sfu-kras.ru
[2] Russian State University for the Humanities, Moscow, Russia
uglev.va@rggu.ru

Abstract. The problem of updating the logic of ITS operation when introducing innovative functions and adapting to the requirements of a particular educational institution (localization) is considered. Arguments in favor of multi-stage decision-making based on the model of P.K. Anokhin are given. The architectural solution of such ITS is proposed and the stages of generalization of processed data from the digital educational footprint are described. The possibilities of using the mechanism of recommender systems and fuzzy logic for reconfiguring the logic of decision-making are discussed. By the example of using the mechanism of competency development assessment and course individualization, the process of changing the logic to fit the new functionality of the system is shown. The results of implementation in the ITS are demonstrated for an experimental ITS used in the educational process of the master's degree program at the Siberian Federal University.

Keywords: Intelligent Tutoring Systems · decision-making · recommender systems · knowledge base · afferent synthesis

1 Introduction

The development, implementation and support of the *Intelligent Tutoring Systems* (ITS) in educational institutions and online platforms require a special approach to the process of making informed decisions by an intelligent scheduler (solver). This determines both the level of trust of the learner in the tutoring system [2] and the ability to pass any inspection held by the supervisory/accrediting body (e.g., AMBA, ENAEE, AKKORK, etc.) or participate in the official handling of disputes (appeals).

The logic of decision-making and argumentation of the decisions to a human learner should be based on the knowledge of a human teacher, a human methodologist, and a human tutor. This determines the presence of the *knowledge base* (KB) block. However, some of this knowledge should be constantly updated due to one of the following reasons:

- emergence of new pedagogical theories (decision-making logic) that promise to improve the quality of e-learning;
- emergence of new algorithms (data preprocessing and generalization logic) that will improve the effectiveness of decision-making;
- emergence of experimental methods that require verification during the real educational process;
- expansion of the list of parameters recorded by the ITS related to the learning situation and the learner model (their inclusion in the decision-making logic of previously developed fragments of the knowledge base);
- changes in the requirements of the regulatory framework of the educational institution or supervisory bodies that it is desirable to take into account (e.g., introduction of new standards for assigning marks);
- presence of specific approaches in the scientific school of the institution, for which the ITS is localized;
- commitment of individual teachers to a specific setting of the parameters of the tutoring system for assessing student performance in their own courses;
- adding data to the statistics of decisions that affect the quality of subsequent generalization of certain parameters (e.g., when implementing the fuzzification mechanism).

The need to update the content of the knowledge base often has a cumulative effect and requires a serious modification of the software part. It should be taken into account that in addition to the knowledge that the ITS scheduler operates with, it records and analyzes the current situation to make adequate decisions, and also takes into account the dynamics (change history) of the indicators. All this is stored in the *digital educational footprint* (DEF), which is recorded by the ITS and forms the *learner model*.

There are instances when the logic of decision-making on a set of available data and knowledge from the knowledge base shall be modified with the least changes in the ITS itself. This will require a special approach to coordinating the work of the ITS subsystems, one of the options of which we will propose below.

2 Existing Solutions

The decision-making procedure in the ITS since Skinner's time [12] has been focused on event-driven reactions to the learner's actions. In most cases, these reactions are of a planned nature: enrolling in a course, moving between elements of didactic material, solving a task or an entire test (following the planned curriculum). When difficulty or need for clarification arises, the learner can initiate a request for prompting or clarification, or revisit the course elements. The "learner action - system response" scheme works here. In some cases, the reverse sequence applies, when the tutoring system records the frequency and time parameters of the learning situation and can initiate events in relation to the course settings: reminders, a clarifying dialogue, opening or closing access to an element of the learning environment or interface (see Fig. 1). The consequence of any of the trajectories of interaction between the learner and the tutoring system is adding data from the digital educational footprint to the log, and, possibly, modification of the learner model, reaction of the interface part of the learning environment, and transition to a subsequent dialogue.

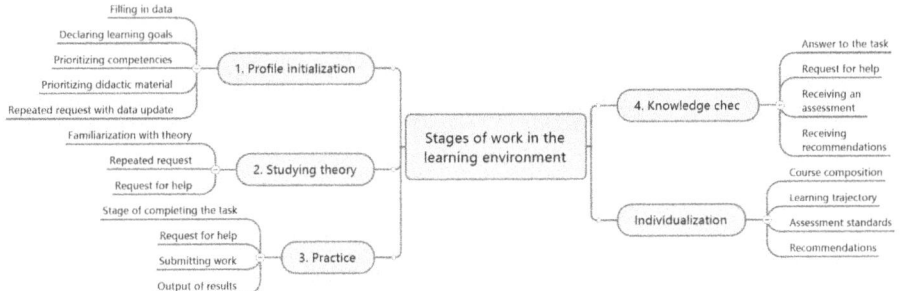

Fig. 1. Events in the ITS that initiate major decisions on the scheduler side

The process of e-learning (development of pedagogical impact) corresponds to the cybernetic approach [18], where the learner is the object of control. Recording the initial data (primarily the DEF contents) and transferring them to the scheduler can be described by the black box model: the specifics of the decision-making algorithms in each ITS are implemented in accordance with the internal logic, i.e. the KB content and algorithms [3,13]. From a technical point of view, the stages of data processing by the scheduler can be expressed in the following sequence: loading variables → statistical preprocessing (if necessary) → distribution of variables by arguments/inputs into analytical functions → KB fragments → evaluation of the values of each input (if necessary) → decision-making procedure → output preprocessing (e.g., defuzzification of values) → recording of explanatory arguments → reaction corresponding to the decision (including synthesis of the dialogue form). Therefore, acceptable modification of the system's decision-making logic (without major changes to the code) is carried out through the mechanisms listed in Table 1. Each of them, individually and in combination, enable to increase the flexibility of ITS decision-making.

It follows from the table that in methods #1 and #3 most ITSs limit themselves to connecting third-party modules via standard APIs (e.g., Moodle [6]) or service their systems in "closed" mode even if they have advanced knowledge management modules (e.g., [11]). Standard mechanisms for changing the logic without consulting the developers are usually "not welcome". This is understandable: it is easy to introduce errors into the decision-making mechanism, and then the logic of assessing the learner model cannot be used correctly when explaining decisions. It should be added that in addition to the learner model in developed ITSs there is a model of a study course (methodologist), a teacher model and a tutor model, each of which has its own fragment in the KB and should influence the logic of decision-making.

Table 1. Methods for adapting decision-making logic in tutoring systems

Method	Nature of the modification
1. Modification of knowledge only in the KB	KB update
2. Updating the scheduler module (open source)	ITS rebuild
3. Switching between templates	Using presets
4. Changing settings	Expanding the number of variables, selecting external event handlers
5. Automatic connection of external extensions/libraries (dll)	Loading of new algorithms via API
6. Providing overloaded functions for each event	Loading of new algorithms

Based on the established practice of using ITS, we will propose an approach to modifying the logic of its operation on the example of the experimental ITS AESU. For this purpose, we will describe the logic of data processing sequence (Sect. 3), practical results of its use in the process of updating the ITS functioning (Sect. 4), as well as an architectural solution for organizing the tutoring system (Sect. 5).

3 Method

Decision-making according to the cybernetic scheme was best reflected by P.K. Anokhin in his work on the *theory of functional systems*. His model of afferent synthesis [1] assumes that the following aspects should be simultaneously taken into account:

- goal-setting (A, taken from questionnaires);
- situational afferentation (X, taken from the DEF);
- memory (Kb, all models of participants of the educational process in the form of KB and data on the dynamics of indicators X').

This model leaves out of consideration the decision-making process F itself, which involves identifying alternatives and describing the logic of decision-making (formalizing the principle of optimality), i.e. a group of related sub-functions f. However, it does enable using a systematic approach to structuring input data from a common substrate of variables recorded by the ITS, in accordance with (1).

$$G(X|A, X') \xrightarrow{F, Kb} < y, \gamma(y) >, \qquad (1)$$

where y is the decision of the system; γ is the explanatory arguments.

It is problematic to implement the F process in one step, since it requires a series of different types of operations. We will take as a basis the description of the general model of stage-by-stage generalization (concentration) of data in the tutoring system [17], where the following stages were identified: statistical concentration ($S1$), metric concentration ($S2$), semantic concentration ($S3$) and logical concentration ($S4$). We will consider these stages from the perspective of the need for updating the logic with the "pointwise" involvement of the programmer.

The preparatory stage involves introducing new variables (V), modifying the database (B) to accommodate them, and implementing an algorithm to collect data about A, X and X' from the DEF. Next comes the implementation of items $S1$-$S4$, which can be described by a template (see Fig. 2-a) of the data processing process. In general, it will include the following:

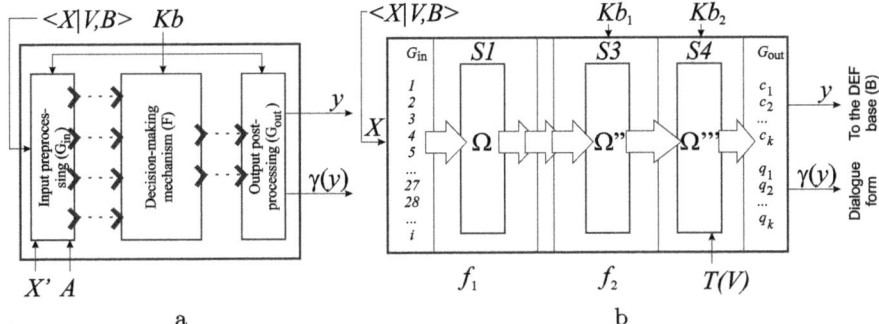

Fig. 2. An example of a scheme for integrating a new function into the ITS operation logic: in general form (a) and an example of detailing (b)

1. customization of the input data sampling (G_{in}) is done by means of the interactive form in Drag&Drop mode;
2. linking of the function to the event in the ITS (files f with the code are loaded into the repository of the ITS core through the form);
3. customization of output data representation after processing (G_{out}) is done by means of the interactive form in Drag&Drop mode;
4. customization of the explanation text template (T, master form).

Customization of the input data sampling involves specifying a variable from the V set, its loading mode (the last value, increment or the entire set from the DEF), delivery format, and the need for preprocessing (e.g., fuzzification). Then there is an indication of the file with the implementation of the function of algorithmic or logical processing (as a KB element), where the data from the previous stage are arranged in accordance with the sequence of arguments required for the calculation. The output data representation assumes defining the output format and the location in B where it should be saved (if necessary). Since the KB is formed in the knowledge representation language or in another form independent of the program code, its modification can be performed by third-party applications (e.g., loaded as an updated model file).

It should be noted that at any stage of S multiple operations can be performed, a separate stage can be skipped, and operations of the same level can be duplicated, forming a chain. Obviously, it is convenient to implement such a possibility of dispatching (forming a template) within the ITS in the form of a graphical designer storing the model of the decision-making act in the form of an independent model M. An example of such a sequence in the form of a scheme is shown in Fig. 2-b. In general, it can be derived from (1) by rewriting the original template in the form of (2)

$$G(M) : G_{in}(V, X|A, X') \xrightarrow[S1]{f_1, Kb_1} \Omega \xrightarrow[S2]{f_2, Kb_2} \Omega' \xrightarrow[S3]{f_3, Kb_3}$$
$$\Omega'' \xrightarrow[S4]{f_4, Kb_4} G_{out}(V, y) \xrightarrow{T} < y, \gamma >, \qquad (2)$$

where Ω is a set of values of variables generated by the next stage of generalization according to the model M during the transition from G_{in} to G_{out}.

The ITS reaction R following $S4$, which is implemented after the decision is made, implies elaboration of the form of recording the results of the made decision in the system log, DEF modification and changes in the interface part. Obviously, the stages of embedding V, B and R are implemented by the staff ITS developer together with the one who develops a set of algorithms f of the newly embedded or modified decision-making logic F. It is possible to achieve full independence in developing new functions with deep integration into the learning environment (without involving a staff programmer) only when the ITS project reaches the stage when its own language (e.g., like in MatLAB [5]) or pseudo-language (e.g., like in [9]) is embedded in it. In modern practice of developing online platforms, a promising solution is to use the Python language core on the server side: the programmer uploads the ready-made code to the server and can use it to implement the required functionality.

As can be seen from (2), the elements F and Kb can be substituted in accordance with the new or updated logic either by the developer of the functions of individual reactions to ITS events (if the code is modified) or by the knowledge engineer (if only the decision-making scheme M and knowledge fragments are modified). In the latter case, when modifying Kb, the standard KB editor for the rules of the system whose engine integrates the mechanism of the recommender system into the ITS is used. For example, it can be applied to get inference using precedent technology, production rules, or using black board technology [8].

Note that the sequence of generalization stages S itself can also be repeated several times between the single event call G_{in} and the presentation of the decision G_{out}, if this is required by the ITS operation logic. For example, to make decisions using mapping tools [14] it is necessary to obtain two particular (intermediate) decisions and only then synthesize the final one. This will complicate the detailed dispatching scheme (similar to Fig. 2-b), but the integration scheme from the ITS perspective will have the same template as in the scheme shown in Fig. 2-a.

4 Case Study

Let us consider the process of applying the proposed method using an example. For this purpose, we will use the experimental ITS AESU applied in the educational process of the Siberian Federal University. The development of this ITS in a number of areas, including research on reactions to events shown in Fig. 1 assumes that decision-making mechanisms are systematically updated. At the same time, each researcher works on its functionality independently, which gives rise to the problem of asynchronous modification of the system components without significant changes to the entire ITS by a staff programming administrator.

The logic of the intelligent scheduler of the experimental ITS is based on the use of the mechanism of recommender (expert) systems with a knowledge base in the form of production rules of E. Post [10] and a decision tree (model M) and the call of external handler functions. For this purpose, the flm format in the FLM_Builder program is used, which allows not only to form and test M elements, but also to unload decision-making models for further use in various languages (C++, Pascal, Python). For ITS AESU the web service of the FLM_Builder software package for Python programming language is used [15], which supports the processing of variables by the fuzzy logic mechanism (fuzzification according to [19]). A special module FLM_modul.py is used for integration. The general scheme of organization of the system elements responsible for decision-making is shown in Fig. 3). Thus, within the framework of the experimental ITS not only the mechanisms #1 and #4, but also option #6 from Table 1 is used.

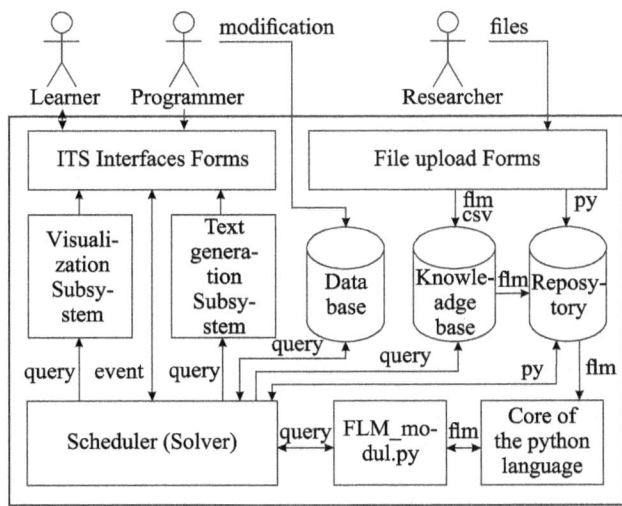

Fig. 3. Interaction of the decision-making components of ITS AESU

Let's consider a specific case. Let's assume that, upon the *onClick* event (the "Check" button), when assessing the results of passing a series of test tasks, the existing logic for assessment of the level of knowledge (a simple calculation of the percentage of correct answers by the function f_1 from the repository F) is replaced by f_1', which additionally assesses the level of development of the competencies C (the function f_1, which assumes the use of a set of expert opinions in the form of a fragment of the knowledge base according to the approach from [16]). The input will be the data on learner's answers X, and at the output y will be presented as a set of values (a number in the interval $[-1; 1]$), which will correspond to the expert system's coefficient of confidence in the development of each competency from A. Data on the dynamics of the assessments X' are not required in this function. Therefore, we will describe the transition $f_1 \to f_1'$ for the existing conditions as a set of the following stages:

1. introduction of variables v_k into the learner model, corresponding to the assessments of the competencies c_k, providing for the subsequent output of their values in the form of a dialogue with the names $\$k$ based on the results of processing (done by the programmer);
2. formation of a decision model M, consisting of stages of processing the answers (f_2) based on the fragment of the knowledge base Kb_1 ($S3$), fuzzification of the quantitative result Kb_2 ($S4$) and preparation of the dialogue template λ to explain the obtained decision (done by the researcher);
3. implementation of the function G_{in}, selecting variables from the DEF about all answers (stage $S1$) for the current date (vector of values X, done by the researcher);
4. filling the knowledge base Kb_1 with expert assessments according to [4], corresponding to the methodology [16] (the file in flm format, done by the researcher);
5. implementation of the function for calculating the assessments of the competencies f_2 for each of the generalized v_k (k quantitative assessments, done by the researcher);
6. formation of the fragment Kb_2 based on the results of the expert survey, allowing implementation of the fuzzification of the assessment from the qualitative scale Q (the file in flm format, done by the researcher);
7. filling in the field with the text template λ to explain an arbitrary v_k (e.g., "Assessment of the competency "c_k" development level" assessed as "q_k")
8. uploading all the algorithms to the repository by the researcher and adding data to the ITS KB, testing the result together with the staff programmer.

By replacing f_1 with the function f_1' the decision scheme M is accessed, the structure of which is shown in Fig. 2-b. The new function is a black box for the calling function and can be updated again (e.g., during debugging), but without involvement of the staff programmer, if the specification of inputs and outputs M as not changed). In this case, the variant $G_{in} \xrightarrow{S1} \Omega \xrightarrow{S3} \Omega'' \xrightarrow{S4} \Omega''' \xrightarrow{T} G_{out}$ is implemented, i.e. the generalization stage $S2$ is skipped (it is not needed here).

Let's consider another case. Let us assume that it is required to synthesize an individualized composition of didactic material (depth of study, degree of control) in an e-course (an individualized model W relative to k initial elements) for the individual needs of a learner (A). In response to the *onClick* event ("Go to course content" button), after the input questionnaire and testing, the course is assembled using the mechanism of expert systems and mapping. This will require implementing a comprehensive analysis by (2) according to the afferent synthesis approach. Let us put the arguments corresponding to the target indicators (A) of the current parameters of the learning situation, the cross-curricular links and the basic course configuration into the function f_1. The returned result should be expressed in the formation of a vector of didactic units included in the course with a certain depth of study and the required level of control y, as well as a decision-making protocol for explanations $\gamma(y)$. The decision is made in accordance with the following enlarged stages:

1. collecting all input data in the form of a single parametric map and delivering it to the input f_1 (done by the programmer);
2. forming a decision-making model M consisting of the stages of processing individual variables from the parametric map (f_2) based on the fragment of the knowledge base Kb_1 ($S3$), fuzzification of the quantitative result Kb_2 ($S4$) and preparing a dialogue template λ to explain the obtained decision in three steps (done by the researcher):
   (a) forming a combined cognitive map of knowledge diagnosis (built-in function);
   (b) forming a particular decision of the learner model (f_3, Kb_3);
   (c) forming a particular decision of the teacher model (f_4, Kb_4);
   (d) forming a compromise decision of the tutor model (f_5, Kb_5);
3. implementing the function G_{in} and filling W by G_{out} (done by the researcher);
4. filling the knowledge bases (flm format files, done by the researcher);
5. implementing the functions for calling expert systems and analyzing the combined map (done by the researcher);
6. filling the field with the text template λ to explain the answers to questions like "Why is \$$w_k$ included in my course?", "Why should I study \$$w_k$ as part of the course?", "Why is this form of control chosen for \$$w_k$?", which can be addressed to an arbitrarily selected didactic unit or topic of the individualized course (done by the researcher);
7. loading of all algorithms into the repository by the researcher and adding data to the ITS KB, testing the result together with the staff programmer.

This task was described in more detail in [15], where not only the structure of Kb_4 and characteristic functions for fuzzyfication are given (see Fig. 4), but also an example of the process of calculating a particular decision for the Simulation Modeling course for a specific student is shown.

It is obvious that all actions of the staff programmer in these cases are dictated not by personal initiative, but by the result of coordinated work with the knowledge engineer (researcher). The researcher is responsible both for implementing a new fragment of the KB or modifying an existing one, as well as compiling a decision-making scheme and developing (perhaps not independently)

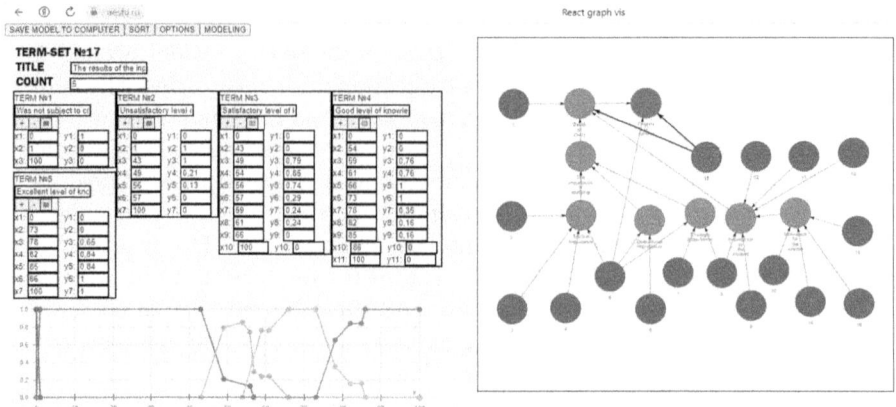

Fig. 4. Screenshot of FLM_Builder service interface for forming expert system models [15]

new functions for the repository F. Moreover, the logic of a particular scheme M can be completely revised (any functions, sub-stages, KB fragments can be added) without further involvement of the staff programmer, if the "interfaces" of the black box remain unchanged.

5 Results

Experimental testing of the proposed approach has allowed us to update many decision-making algorithms and update the knowledge base in ITS AESU without significant changes in the common code. Previously, work on integrating individual decision-making functions into the ITS took up a significant amount of time: more than 60% of the time was spent on programming when integrating updated decision-making methods. Now researchers perform the function of a knowledge engineer approximately 70% of the time and "get distracted" by adjusting interfaces and supplementing the code (mainly by calling procedures from the repository and forming algorithm modules) only when assembling their part of the project. The architecture of the system operation and the intelligent scheduler itself are not changed in the process of updates. This enables us to speed up the process of updating functionalities, reducing the risks of "spoiling" the logic of other decision-making procedures.

We have achieved the greatest practical results in the process of integrating cognitive visualization tools with decision-making logic and feedback synthesis. Thus, in 2024 alone, the tasks of individualization of the composition of didactic material and assessment of the learning situation were rethought and brought to a new level [15]; and new types of cognitive maps (combined and cross-cutting) were built into the general decision-making logic [14]). This enabled us to speed up the debugging and testing of the decision-making logic for synthesizing the recommendations by the intelligent scheduler without the programmer's repeated involvement: the interval between subsequent tests was approximately 2 weeks with different types of maps and their combinations. For more details on the latest experimental results concerning the process of individualizing the composition of the e-course, see [17]. This made it possible to increase the number of researchers actively working with the system from 3 to 8, and shift the emphasis in the work to the methodological and knowledge component.

Among the difficulties associated with this approach, the following should be noted. Firstly, the introduction of new functions involving complex program processing is still performed at the source code level and has not undergone significant changes, since it is not the logic of decision output that is updated, but the mechanisms themselves. This problem is partially removed due to the fact that the modification of the database and responsible sections of the code is done directly by the staff programmer, and not by the researchers. Secondly, researchers are required to have a high level of culture in performing knowledge engineering work. Thirdly, not all functions of this approach have yet been fully implemented on the basis of the experimental ITS, which complicates the full-fledged quantitative assessment of its implementation. In particular, the stage $S1$ and linking of G_{in} with M are still done in a semi-manual mode (at the code level), and the stage R is traditionally left entirely to the programmer. We understand the work on finalizing this functionality, and this work is in progress.

6 Conclusion

Addressing the need for simplified method for updating the ITS logic and flexible localization to the requirements of a particular educational institution or innovative teacher will accelerate the creation of more effective tutoring systems that meet the principles of Explanatory Artificial Intelligence (XAI). Shifting the focus from programming to working with knowledge is the direction in which tutoring systems will develop most intensively [7]. The approach we propose enables to take further steps in this direction and suggests further development.

Our current research areas in the field of implementing the ITS logic are the comprehensive development of all fragments of the knowledge base responsible for the implementation of all events from the scheme shown in Fig. 1. In parallel, we are improving the cognitive visualization module to fully implement the cross-cutting approach [17] to decision-making in the experimental ITS.

References

1. Anokhin, P.K.: The functional system as a unit of organism integrative activity. In: Systems Theory and Biology. pp. 376–403. Springer (1968). https://doi.org/10.1007/978-3-642-88343-9_15
2. Baker, R.S.: Stupid tutoring systems, intelligent humans. Int. J. Artif. Intell. Educ. **26**, 600–614 (2016)
3. Brusilovsky, P.: AI in education, learner control, and human-AI collaboration. Int. J. Artif. Intell. Educ. **33**(1560–4306), 15 (2023). https://doi.org/10.1007/s40593-023-00356-z

4. Buchanan, B., Shortliffe, E.: Rule-based Expert System: The MYCIN Experiments of the Stanford Heuristic Programming Project. Addison-Wesley, New York (1984)
5. Chaturvedi, D.K.: Modeling and simulation of systems using MATLAB and Simulink. CRC press (2017)
6. Despotović-Zrakić, M., Marković, A., Bogdanović, Z., Barać, D., Krčo, S.: Providing adaptivity in moodle lms courses. J. Educ. Technol. Soc. **15**(1), 326–338 (2012)
7. Du Boulay, B., Mitrovic, A., Yacef, K.: Handbook of artificial intelligence in education. Edward Elgar Publishing (2023). https://doi.org/10.4337/9781800375413
8. Jackson, P.: Introduction to Expert Systems. Addison-Wesley Pub. Co., Reading, MA (1999)
9. Mishina, S., Kornienko, D.: Setting up data exchange between information systems that automate accounting at the enterprise. J. Phys. Conf. Ser., 032018. IOP Publishing (2021). https://doi.org/10.1088/1742-6596/2094/3/032018
10. Post, E.L.: Introduction to a general theory of elementary propositions. Am. J. Math. **43**(3), 163–185 (1921). https://doi.org/10.2307/2370324
11. Rybina, G., Grigoriev, A.: Modern architectures of intelligent tutoring systems based on integrated expert systems: features of the approach to the automated formation of the ontological space of knowledge and skills of students. Pattern Recognit Image Anal. **33**(3), 491–497 (2023). https://doi.org/10.1134/S1054661823030409
12. Skinner, B.F.: Teaching machines: from the experimental study of learning come devices which arrange optimal conditions for self-instruction. Science **128**(3330), 969–977 (1958)
13. Troussas, C., Krouska, A., Sgouropoulou, C.: Enhancing human-computer interaction in digital repositories through a mcda-based recommender system. Adv. Hum.-Comput. Interact. **2021**(1), 7213246 (2021). https://doi.org/10.1155/2021/7213246
14. Uglev, V.: Cognitive maps of knowledge diagnosis (CMKD): the essence of the method, classification, characteristics and synthesis principles. In: Novel & Intelligent Digital Systems Conferences. pp. 594–605. Springer (2024). https://doi.org/10.1007/978-3-031-73344-4_51
15. Uglev, V.: Implementation of decision-making mechanism in the intelligent tutoring system based on the expert systems module. Pattern Recognit Image Anal. **34**(3), 744–750 (2024). https://doi.org/10.1134/S1054661824700615
16. Uglev, V., Shangina, E.: Assessment and visualization of course-level and curriculum-level competency profiles. In: International Conference on Computational Science and Its Applications. LNCS. pp. 478–493. Springer (2023). https://doi.org/10.1007/978-3-031-37105-9_32
17. Uglev, V., Smirnov, G.: A cross-cutting approach to analysis of the learning situation in its using a mapping mechanism. J. Integrated Design Process Sci. 1–16 (2024). https://doi.org/10.1177/10920617241289777
18. Wiener, N.: Cybernetics or Control and Communication in the Animal and the Machine. MIT press (2019)
19. Zadeh, L.A., Aliev, R.A.: Fuzzy Logic theory and applications: part I and part II. World Scientific Publishing, New Jersey, USA (2018)

Enhancing Pilot Training and Decision-Making Using Ontologies: A Cognitive Assistance Approach

Guy Carlos Tamkodjou Tchio[1(✉)], Roger Nkambou[1], Valéry Psyché[2], and Ange Adrienne Nyamen Tato[3]

[1] Université du Québec à Montréal, Montréal, Canada
carlos.tamkodjou@gmail.com
[2] Université TÉLUQ, Québec, Canada
[3] Université Laval, Québec, Canada

Abstract. This paper presents a cognitive assistance approach using ontologies to enhance pilot training and decision-making. A reference ontology, combining a domain ontology representing the aircraft's external environment and a task ontology describing flight procedures, is leveraged. Based on this, a synthetic pilot, developed using the ACT-R cognitive architecture, provides personalized cognitive assistance to pilots, helping them in their training and decision-making processes. The synthetic pilot adapts to individual learning preferences and progress, offering tailored feedback and guidance. The aim is to increase pilots' skills and enhance aviation safety through this personalized ontological cognitive assistance.

Keywords: Ontologies · Domain Ontology · Task Ontology · ACT-R · Synthetic Pilot · Cognitive Assistance · Modeling · SWRL Rules · Graph Theory

1 Introduction

Pilot training and decision-making are crucial for flight safety, despite technological advances and persistent challenges [1]. Ontologies, by enabling a formal and shared knowledge representation [2], help enhance training and decision-making in critical situations [3].

This paper proposes an innovative ontology-based cognitive assistance approach to improve pilot training and decision-making. This approach is based on the use of a reference ontology combining two aspects: a domain ontology describing the external environment of the aircraft as well as the execution environment of complex piloting tasks, and a task ontology modeling piloting procedures as well as expert knowledge in the aviation domain. On this ontological basis, a synthetic pilot based on the ACT-R cognitive architecture, recognized for its ability to faithfully model human behavior in complex environments [4], is developed using the PyACTR Python library.

In this context, our research addresses the following research questions: Can a synthetic pilot that simulates human cognition and relies on expert knowledge of aircraft piloting procedures effectively assist a human pilot in performing their tasks, thereby enhancing their training and decision-making capabilities ? How can such a synthetic pilot be built?

To answer these questions, we propose three hypotheses. First, a reference ontology can support the modeling of complex procedural knowledge related to aircraft piloting tasks, detailing the necessary information associated with the execution environment for each task. Second, the ACT-R cognitive architecture can effectively model human pilot behavior. Third, integrating a reference ontology of piloting procedures into an ACT-R-based cognitive agent can effectively assist human pilots, while enhancing their training and decision-making capabilities.

The synthetic pilot developed based on these hypotheses aims to provide cognitive assistance to human pilots, helping them in their learning and decision-making processes.

The reference ontology, based on NASA's Air Traffic Management ontologies [5, 32, 33] and those by Courtemanche et al. [6], has been adapted for our context and will serve as the synthetic pilot's declarative knowledge base, while procedural knowledge will be managed through production rules and Semantic Web Rule Language (SWRL) rules for automatic task execution.

2 Related Work

While it's impossible to cover every aspect, we've listed below a few of the works that have laid a solid foundation for our research.

Wu et al. [7] propose an ontology-based approach to model aircraft and improve maintenance management systems without addressing pilot training. Insaurralde and Blasch [8] suggest an ontology-based knowledge representation for decision-making in avionics, but it does not cover pilot training or use cognitive architecture. Yousefzadeh et al. [9] develop an ontology for air safety messages to enhance risk analysis and controller training, but it lacks a cognitive approach to decision-making. Stefanidis et al. [10] present the ICARUS ontology, which is used for general aviation but does not integrate cognitive assistance for pilot training or decision support. Insaurralde and Blasch [11–13] propose an ontology-based approach for advanced air traffic management decision-making, integrating cognitive architecture, but it does not focus on pilot training or simulating human cognitive processes like ACT-R. Salvucci [4] applies the ACT-R cognitive architecture to model driver behavior, potentially applicable to pilots, but does not use ontologies. Klaproth et al. [14] exploit ACT-R for pilot decision-making in emergencies but do not use ontologies. Oltramari and Lebiere [15] integrate ontologies with ACT-R for problem-solving without addressing training or decision-making.

The works presented above have contributed to the formalization of knowledge in various domains, but none have actively leveraged the aviation expertise formalized in an ontology to provide cognitive assistance to pilots during their training and decision-making. The research conducted by Tamkodjou et al. [16–18] addresses this challenge by integrating pilots' expert knowledge within an ontology to provide cognitive support to pilots during flight task execution. More precisely, Tamkodjou et al. [16] introduce a cognitive agent based on the ACT-R cognitive architecture, integrating an ontological reference model to simulate, in a manner like human pilots, a task involved in aircraft takeoff. In contrast, Tamkodjou et al. [17] present an ACT-R cognitive agent that integrates an ontological reference model to simulate the complete normal takeoff procedure prescribed by domain experts. Lastly, in [18], the authors focus on managing urgent and abnormal situations during takeoff, again combining ACT-R with an ontological reference model. The approach we propose in this paper aims to combine the three approaches presented by Tamkodjou et al. [16–18] while proposing a system that supports pilots in their training and decision-making.

3 Reference Ontology for the Synthetic Pilot

The reference ontology used by our synthetic pilot combines the Air Traffic Management (ATM) ontology developed by NASA [5] and the reference model proposed by Courtemanche et al. [6, 19], with some adaptations.

3.1 NASA Air Traffic Management Ontology (Atmonto)

The NASA ATM Ontology [5, 20, 32, 33] formally represents air traffic management knowledge, including classes, properties, and relationships related to air navigation, aircraft, airport infrastructures, airline management, and meteorological data.

In the synthetic pilot simulation, the atmonto variant (see Fig. 1) is used, built on the foundational ontology atmontoCore, which comprises five components: NAS (airspace structures), ATM (air traffic management), data (airport-related weather and operations), equipment (aircraft systems), and general (temporal and spatial concepts).

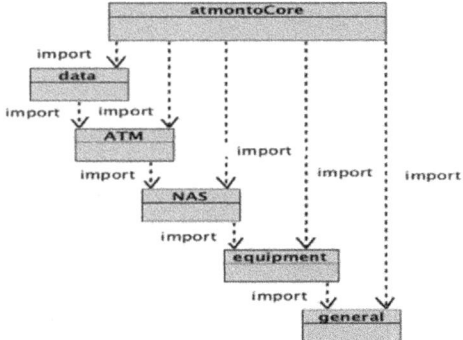

Fig. 1. Air Traffic Management Ontology Class Diagram.

3.2 Ontological Reference Model for Aircraft Piloting Procedures

The proposed reference model [6, 19] formalizes aircraft piloting knowledge through two closely linked components: the domain ontology and the task ontology.

The domain ontology is a terminological framework specific to aircraft piloting, serving as a semantically structured data dictionary to support complex piloting tasks. It exhaustively models elements of the cockpit's internal environment, the external environment, and the aircraft's systems. Its architecture revolves around a central class, "Environment," which includes both the aircraft's interior and exterior environments. This central class includes three specialized subclasses: "AircraftOutsideComponent," representing external components; "AircraftSystems," grouping aircraft systems; and "AircraftInsideEnvironment," modeling the internal environment.

The task ontology, on the other hand, forms the core of the reference model. It structures the execution parameters required for complex piloting tasks. It captures key elements to model human problem-solving processes specific to the aeronautical domain. The task ontology decomposes problem-solving by integrating contextual elements closely linked to the theory formalized in the domain ontology. It provides domain-specific terminology and a framework to represent cognitive processes involved in piloting problem-solving.

Its architecture is structured around a main class, "Task," which includes several classes dedicated to specific roles. These classes define various task aspects, including the person in charge of its execution ("Person"), roles of involved personnel ("Capability"), preconditions for completion ("Precondition"), associated constraints ("Constraint"), actions on the environment and parameter values ("Action"), task workload ("Attention"), and execution status ("ExecutionStatus").

Although distinct, the domain and task ontologies are strongly interconnected through semantic links. Each constraint in the task ontology references a specific environmental parameter and its acceptable value range, as defined in the domain ontology. The same mechanism links actions in the task ontology to corresponding parameters in the domain ontology, specifying actions to be performed on the environment.

The class diagrams presenting the main groups of the domain ontology, as well as the key classes of the task ontology and their relationships, are detailed in [16–18].

4 Cognitive Synthetic Pilot

Our proposal introduces a cognitive synthetic pilot, leveraging a reference ontology and the ACT-R cognitive architecture to enhance pilot training and decision-making.

The reference ontology combines NASA's ATM ontology with the ontological reference model described earlier. We have modified the rules of the ontological reference model governing access to the atmontoCore and atmonto external resources. Our reference ontology includes a domain ontology and a task ontology, enabling structured knowledge representation. The domain ontology provides vocabulary and concepts for the execution environment, while the task ontology defines problem-solving structures for tasks like piloting, supporting informed decision-making and efficient execution.

A cognitive architecture is a computational framework modeling human cognitive processes, including perception, attention, memory, reasoning, and decision-making. It offers a unified theory of cognition and can be implemented in artificial systems to replicate human-like intelligence [21–23]. We chose the ACT-R cognitive architecture for its proven ability to replicate human cognition. This decision aligns with the criteria outlined in Newell and Sun's desiderata [21].

ACT-R (Adaptive Control of Thought-Rational), developed by John R. Anderson and colleagues at Carnegie Mellon University in the 1970s [23], is a widely studied cognitive architecture. Grounded in information processing theory, it simulates and explains human cognitive processes. ACT-R comprises interconnected modules representing cognitive functions like perception, attention, memory, reasoning, and learning. These modules collaborate to generate complex behaviors. Key modules include the visual module (sensory input), the motor module (environmental actions), the declarative module (factual knowledge), the procedural module (production rules), and the Pattern Matching module (coordination). Chunks, or information packets, enable data transfer between modules. Their flow supports the perception-reasoning-action cycle, replicating human cognition.

ACT-R has been successfully applied to model many aspects of human cognition in complex tasks such as aircraft piloting [14, 24]. The modular architecture of the synthetic pilot based on ACT-R is shown in Fig. 2.

Our cognitive agent comprises interconnected modules working together, each with specific functionalities:

- Declarative module: Stores and manages knowledge from the reference ontology, including domain and task ontologies, as well as the current state of the piloting task.
- Episodic module: Enables the synthetic pilot to recall past experiences, aiding decision-making, reasoning, and adaptation to current situations.
- Goal module: Directs and focuses the synthetic pilot's attention, facilitating action planning and execution to achieve task objectives.
- Procedural module: Organizes and controls actions using production rules, supporting decision-making and goal achievement as defined by the goal module.
- Perceptual module: Captures and processes sensory inputs from aircraft sensors and instruments, enabling the synthetic pilot to perceive and interpret its environment.
- Motor module: Translates the synthetic pilot's decisions into concrete actions on the aircraft.
- Pattern Matching module: Analyzes the reference ontology to detect deviations from standard takeoff procedures and error management protocols. It selects production rules and activates relevant modules to address these deviations.

With its modular ACT-R-based architecture, the synthetic pilot leverages the reference ontology to assist pilots like a human instructor, enhancing training and decision-making during normal takeoffs or incidents that occur during takeoff. The synthetic pilot manages the following incidents:

- Engine failure after V1 [25–29];
- Rejected Takeoff after V1 [25, 27, 28];
- Reactive Windshear at Takeoff [25, 27, 28, 30];
- Traffic alert and Collision Avoidance System (TCAS) Event [27, 28];
- Dual engine failure with fuel remaining [27–29];
- Stall recovery [25, 27, 28, 31].

In aviation, "V1" refers to decision speed. It is a critical speed during an aircraft's takeoff phase. Specifically, V1 is the speed at which the aircraft reaches a point where the decision must be made between continuing takeoff or aborting and braking in case of emergency, such as an engine malfunction or other critical issue. Once the aircraft has reached the V1 speed, the decision to abort takeoff becomes riskier than continuing takeoff.

TCAS is an on-board collision-avoidance system used in aviation. Its main role is to monitor the airspace around an aircraft and alert pilots to other aircraft nearby that may pose a collision threat.

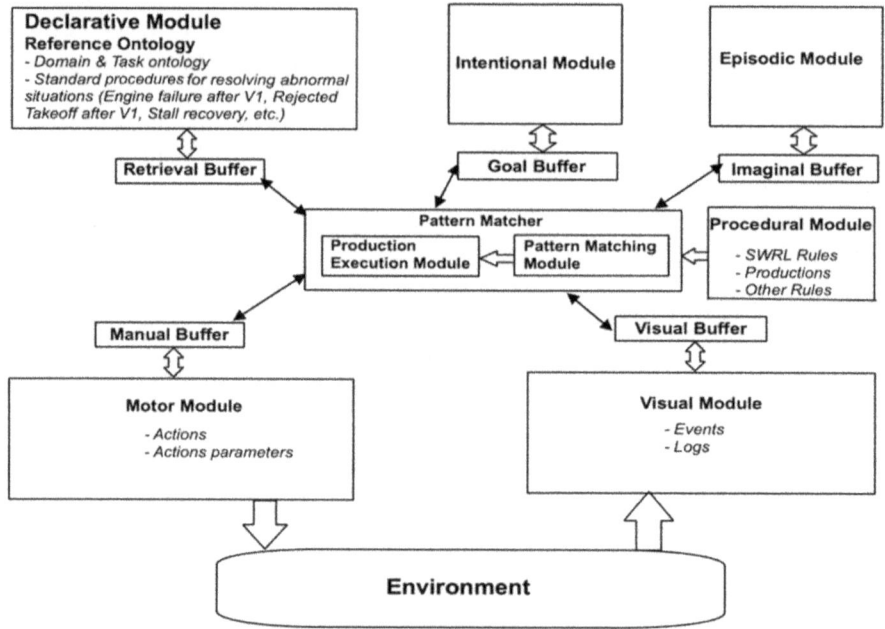

Fig. 2. Synthetic Pilot Operating Architecture.

5 Implementation Methodology and Results

5.1 Implementation Methodology

In order to implement the cognitive synthetic pilot based on the reference ontology, we wrote the algorithm shown in Algorithm 1.

The algorithm outlines how the synthetic pilot interacts with the environment and makes decisions based on available information.

Algorithm 1 : Cognitive Assistance Algorithm

Input : Reference Ontology R_O, Pilot Task to be Performed P_T
Parameter : Takeoff T_O, Engine failure after V1 EF_{V1}, Rejected Takeoff after V1 RT_{V1}, Reactive Windshear at Takeoff RW_{TO}, TCAS Event TC_{Ev}, Dual engine failure with fuel remaining DF_{FR}, Stall recovery S_R, Current Task C_T, Objective O_B
Output : Execution Time E_T, Directed Graph D_G, Task T

1: read(P_T), $O_B = goal(P_T)$ (Read and set Task to be Performed as the goal.)
2: The current task is set as the initial task (1000, 1400, 1076, 1251, 1201, 1176, or 1350).
   if $P_T == T_O$ **then** $C_T = 1000$
   else if $P_T == DF_{FR}$ **then** $C_T = 1400$
   else if $P_T == EF_{V1}$ **then** $C_T = 1076$
   else if $P_T == RW_{TO}$ **then** $C_T = 1251$
   else if $P_T == RT_{V1}$ **then** $C_T = 1201$
   else if $P_T == TC_{Ev}$ **then** $C_T = 1176$
   else if $P_T == S_R$ **then** $C_T = 1350$
   end if
3: status = Executed (The current task status is set to Executed.)
   Repeat the actions below until the current task is task P_T (task to be Performed).
4: **repeat**
5:    $D_G = generated\_path(D_G, O_B)$ (Generate the directed graph with the current task (C_T) as the starting node and task P_T as the ending node. To do this, we use the python package NetworkX.)
6:    print(D_G) (Display the directed graph in the visual interface. To do this, we use the python packages Pyvis and Matplotlib.)
7:    $T = next\_task(D_G)$ (Select the new current task in the directed graph D_G. As the graph is directed, the tasks are chronologically linked.)
8:    status = swrl(C_T) (The status will be set to Executed if C_T was executed successfully, NotExecuted otherwise. Our SWRL rules can be used to find out the status of a given task.)
9:    **if** status == Executed **then**
10:      $C_T = T$ (The current task C_T is set to the next task T.)
11:      $E_T = pattern\_matcher(C_T, R_O)$ (The cognitive agent uses its complex pattern matching mechanism to execute task C_T and cognitively assist the pilot. It proposes actions by selecting the production rules and modules to be activated to manage the current task.)
12:      print(E_T) (Display execution time E_T.)
13:   **end if**
14: **until** $T == P_T$
15: buffers = [P_T, O_B, E_T, C_T, D_G, T]
16: **return** Buffers

The process begins by defining the main objective and determining the initial task based on the goal, such as normal takeoff (1000), engine failure after V1 (1400), rejected takeoff after V1 (1076), reactive windshear at takeoff (1251), TCAS event (1201), dual engine failure with fuel remaining (1176), or stall recovery (1350). These initial task numbers are assigned according to domain expert guidelines. A directed graph is then generated, with the current task as the starting node and the goal as the final node. The cognitive agent then successively selects the new tasks to perform in the graph. For each task, the cognitive agent uses its complex pattern matching mechanism. Relying on the knowledge formalized in the reference ontology and the defined production rules, it executes the task and makes personalized recommendations to the human pilot, thus contributing to his training. The time required to complete the task is also displayed. This iterative process continues until the initial goal is reached. During this procedure, the synthetic pilot shares the various possible choices with the human pilot, thus improving his decision-making capabilities in both normal and critical contexts.

To make the reference ontology directly executable, SWRL rules have been defined. These rules enable the synthetic pilot, for a given task, to determine its execution status based on the conditions and constraints previously defined in the reference ontology, ensuring automated and consistent decision-making in the cognitive system. Figure 3 shows an example of a SWRL rule for evaluating a task such as 1205 involved in resolving the critical situation Rejected Takeoff after V1. The rule is designed to validate tasks which have two type 1 constraints and a precondition which is itself a task.

```
Task(?t), canBeExecutedBy(?t,?capability), canExecute(?capability,?t),
Person(?p), isResponsible(?p, ?spt), hasCapability(?p, ?capability),
hasSuperTask(?t, ?spt1), hasExecutionStatus(?spt1, LiveExecution),
hasPreCondition(?t, ?pc1),
hasExecutionStatus(?pc1, Executed),
    hasConstraint(?t, ?const1), hasConstraintType(?const1, ?ctype1),
    equal(?ctype1, 1), hasEvaluationCriteria(?const1, ?ev1),
    hasExactValue(?const1, ?ex_val1), hasActualValue(?ev1, ?ac_val1), equal(?ex_val1, ?ac_val1),
    hasConstraint(?t, ?const2), hasConstraintType(?const2, ?ctype2),
    equal(?ctype2, 1), hasEvaluationCriteria(?const2, ?ev2),
    hasExactValue(?const2, ?ex_val2), hasActualValue(?ev2, ?ac_val2), equal(?ex_val2, ?ac_val2)
-> hasExecutionStatus(?t, Executed)
```

Fig. 3. SWRL Rule for Evaluating a Task such as 1205.

The cognitive synthetic pilot was developed using specialized technologies to model, simulate, and visualize pilot decision-making processes. PyACTR, a Python library based on the ACT-R cognitive architecture, simulated pilots' cognitive processes. Owlready2 was used to create, manage, and query the reference ontology in OWL format, while Pellet, an inference engine, enabled logical deductions from axioms and relationships. SWRL (Semantic Web Rule Language) defined logical rules related to task execution. For task representation, NetworkX generated and manipulated directed graphs, with Pyvis providing web-based visualizations and Matplotlib supporting 3D rendering. Protégé, an ontology editor, facilitated the development and management of the reference ontology, and UML (Unified Modeling Language) enabled visual representation of concepts and relationships. Figure 4 provides a graphical representation of the reference ontology using the Protégé ontology editor, focusing on task 1076, which is a subtask of the Engine Failure after V1 super-task.

5.2 Results

To evaluate our model, we conducted several series of tests. We had the synthetic pilot perform several normal takeoffs as well as takeoffs involving various incidents described

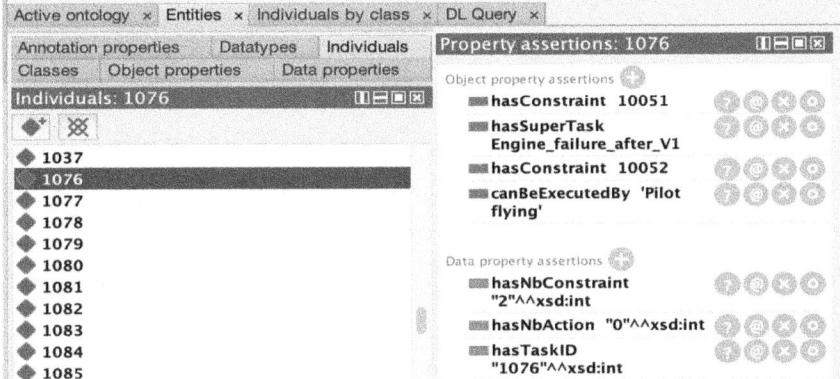

Fig. 4. Graphical Representation of Task 1076 from the Reference Ontology.

earlier, such as Engine Failure After V1, Rejected Takeoff after V1, Reactive Windshear at Takeoff, TCAS Event, Dual engine failure with fuel remaining, and Stall recovery. For each scenario, we executed the previously described Algorithm 1 with the synthetic pilot. In each case, we compared the results obtained by the virtual agent with the expected results, based on the procedures established by aviation experts. Figure 5 shows a portion of the state-transition diagram of the reference procedure for handling the abnormal situation Dual engine failure with fuel remaining. The complete procedure, comprising over 200 complex states, is too large to present in full, so we have only shown the initial and final parts of the diagram, as is the case for other procedures.

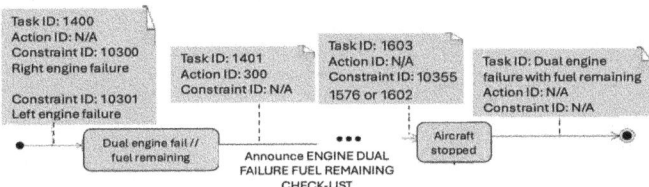

Fig. 5. An Extract from the Reference State-Transition Diagram of the Dual Engine Failure with Fuel Remaining Resolution Procedure.

We then compared the tasks dynamically generated by the directed graph produced by the synthetic pilot with those expected at each stage, taken from the reference ontology, which integrates expert knowledge of the domain. Figure 6 shows part of the directed graph generated by the synthetic pilot to solve the Dual engine failure with fuel remaining situation, while Fig. 7 shows the preconditions and constraints required to solve the first task (1400) and the last task (Dual_engine_failure_with_fuel_remaining) of the reference ontology associated with the same procedure.

To rigorously validate the results produced by the synthetic pilot, we assessed the compliance between the tasks dynamically generated in the directed graph (G_1) (Fig. 6)

68   G. C. Tamkodjou Tchio et al.

Fig. 6. An Extract from the Directed Graph of the Dual Engine Failure with Fuel Remaining Resolution Procedure.

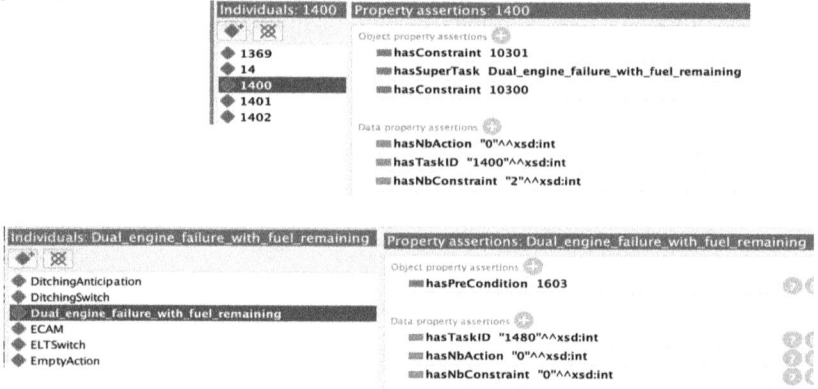

Fig. 7. Preconditions and Constraints for the First Task (1400) and the Last Task (Dual_engine_failure_with_fuel_remaining) of the Reference Ontology.

and the reference procedures established by experts, recorded in the reference state-transition diagram (G_2) (Fig. 5). For this purpose, we used the Graph Edit Distance (GED) as a comparison metric. GED measures the minimal cost of a sequence of operations (insertion, deletion, or substitution of nodes or edges) required to transform one graph into another. This approach enables precise quantification of structural differences between graphs [34]. This metric evaluates the following key aspects:

- Node Matching: Verifying that all tasks (nodes) from the reference state-transition diagram are present in the synthetic pilot's graph. For example, in the *Dual Engine Failure with Fuel Remaining* scenario (Fig. 5), we confirmed that critical tasks such as "1400" (initial task) and "Dual_engine_failure_with_fuel_remaining" (final task) were included in the generated graph (Figs. 5 and 6).
- Arc Consistency: Validating that the transitions between tasks in the generated graph conform to the procedural logic defined in the reference ontology. This includes verifying sequential and conditional dependencies between tasks, such as the preconditions and constraints illustrated in Fig. 7. A generated transition is therefore considered valid if and only if it complies with the logical constraints and preconditions defined in the reference ontology.

$$\text{GED}(G_1, G_2) = \min_{(e_1,\ldots,e_k) \in T(G_1,G_2)} \sum_{i=1}^{k} c(e_i) \quad (1)$$

where $T(G_1, G_2)$ denotes the set of edit paths transforming G_1 into G_2, and $c(e) \geq 0$ is the cost of each graph edit operation e (vertex insertion, vertex deletion, vertex substitution, edge insertion, edge deletion, edge substitution, etc.).

By achieving 100% node matching and arc consistency across all tested scenarios ($\text{GED}(G_1, G_2) = 0$, as no operation is required, and $c(e) = 0$), we confirmed that the graphs generated by the synthetic pilot faithfully reproduced the structure and logic of the reference state-transition diagrams defined by piloting standards.

The results obtained enabled us to validate the synthetic pilot's ability to handle take-offs in both normal and critical situations, in line with expert guidelines. Additionally, the directed task graph generated at each stage by the synthetic pilot reveals a remarkable capacity for adaptation. Indeed, for certain tasks where the reference model had not foreseen an exit situation (dead ends), our synthetic pilot was able to exploit the transitions between tasks in the graph to find solutions deemed appropriate.

Although the reference ontology has already been validated by aviation experts, a further study with experienced pilots is required. This will confirm the relevance and reliability of the results obtained by the cognitive agent, thereby strengthening the validity of our approach.

The synthetic pilot enhances personalized pilot training and decision-making through two distinct modes: autonomous and interactive modes.

In autonomous mode, the cognitive agent independently executes a selected procedure, displaying aircraft environmental data and relevant parameters such as constraint evaluation criteria, action parameters, and preconditions. This enables pilots to observe and understand complete takeoff procedures, including both normal and critical scenarios, reinforcing their learning and decision-making skills. Figure 8 illustrates an example.

In interactive mode, the synthetic pilot guides the human pilot step by step, requesting expected values, displaying reference ranges, and providing real-time recommendations. If deviations occur, the synthetic pilot assists in corrective actions, acting as an intelligent coaching system. This interactive support helps pilots refine their execution of procedures and improves their ability to respond effectively in complex situations. An example of execution is shown in Fig. 9.

```
(3.55, 'PROCEDURAL', 'RULE SELECTED: retrieve: ValeurParametreAction')
(3.6, 'PROCEDURAL', 'RULE FIRED: retrieve: ValeurParametreAction')
(3.6, 'g', 'MODIFIED')
(3.6, 'retrieval', 'START RETRIEVAL')
(3.6, 'PROCEDURAL', 'CONFLICT RESOLUTION')
(3.6, 'PROCEDURAL', 'NO RULE FOUND')
(3.65, 'retrieval', 'CLEARED')
(3.65, 'retrieval', 'RETRIEVED: word(cat= ValeurParametreAction, form= Aucune)')
(3.65, 'PROCEDURAL', 'CONFLICT RESOLUTION')
(3.65, 'PROCEDURAL', 'RULE SELECTED: scan: word')
(3.7, 'PROCEDURAL', 'RULE FIRED: scan: word')
(3.7, 'g', 'MODIFIED')
(3.7, 'imaginal', 'MODIFIED')
(3.7, 'retrieval', 'CLEARED')
(3.7, 'PROCEDURAL', 'CONFLICT RESOLUTION')
(3.7, 'PROCEDURAL', 'RULE SELECTED: done')
(3.75, 'PROCEDURAL', 'RULE FIRED: done')
parsed_word Aucune
(3.75, 'g', 'EXECUTED')
(3.75, 'g', 'MODIFIED')
(3.75, 'imaginal', 'CLEARED')
```

Fig. 8. Autonomous Mode.

The two modes of operation (stand-alone and interactive) enable pilots to receive personalized training tailored to their specific needs and skill levels. This dual approach to personalized training not only enhances learning efficiency, but also prepares pilots to face a variety of situations with confidence and competence, thus contributing to overall aviation safety.

```
(1.25, After Actions : True
(1.25, Current constraint : 10001
(1.25, Waiting Dataref Value : CrossWind = >? 5
(1.9,  Constraint : 10001  c_type == [2]
(1.95, value ==  5.0
(1.95, minValue ==  0.0
(1.95, maxValue ==  20.0
(1.95, Constraint 10001 => hasConstraintPermission : ConstraintOk
(1.95, Current constraint : 10021
(1.95, Waiting Dataref Value : TailWind = >? 100
(2.15, Constraint : 10021  c_type == [1]
(2.2,  value ==  100.0
(2.2,  exact_value ==  0.0
(2.2,  Waiting Input Dataref c_type 0 | 1 : TailWind = >? 0
(3.35, Constraint 10021 => hasConstraintPermission : ConstraintOk
(3.4,  After Constraint : True
(3.4,  After SuperTask : True
(3.4,  Task 1003 => hasExecutionStatus : Executed
(3.4,  After Precondition : True
(3.45, Current action : 4
(3.45, actionParameter : BrakeLeft   , actionValue: 0.0
```

Fig. 9. Interactive Mode.

6 Conclusion and Future Works

This study addresses the research questions mentioned in the introduction, and validates the hypotheses formulated by presenting a cognitive assistance approach using ontologies to improve pilot training and decision-making processes. By combining a domain ontology describing the aircraft's external environment and a task ontology describing flight procedures, we have developed a cognitive synthetic pilot based on the ACT-R cognitive architecture. The proposed approach demonstrates the potential of ontologies and cognitive computing to enhance pilots' capabilities and reinforce aviation safety. It helps reduce the risk of human error, while promoting continuous, personalized learning of optimal flight procedures. By providing a formal, shared representation of aeronautical domain knowledge, the reference ontology enables the synthetic pilot to reason and provide relevant support both during normal takeoffs and in abnormal situations occurring during takeoff. The two modes of operation of the synthetic pilot, autonomous and interactive, offer flexibility in personalized training and decision support.

Nevertheless, we must acknowledge certain limitations of our approach. The synthetic pilot relies exclusively on the expert knowledge formalized in the reference ontology, as well as on ACT-R's built-in learning mechanisms, such as reinforcement learning and statistical learning. This dependence could restrict the system's ability to adapt to situations not foreseen by the ontology, or to capture the full complexity of human behavior in dynamic and varied flight contexts.

Future work will aim to extend the tests to realistic flight simulators, such as X-Plane, and to specific aircraft models, like the Airbus A320, to evaluate the robustness and flexibility of the system. Furthermore, although the reference ontology has been validated by aviation experts, it will be essential to consolidate the findings of this study by evaluating the system with real users, particularly pilots and domain experts. An important area for improvement involves integrating machine learning techniques to enhance the synthetic pilot's knowledge and enable it to learn from real flight data, with the aim of accurately replicating human pilot behavior. Finally, it will be crucial to conduct an in-depth study in close collaboration with pilots and civil aviation authorities to address the ethical and regulatory considerations associated with the use of the training platform.

Acknowledgments. This work was supported by the NSERC Alliance program [grant number ALLRP 549083–19]. We are thankful to CRIAQ, Bombardier, CAE, and BMU for their financial support.

References

1. Dismukes, R.K., Berman, B.A., Loukopoulos, L.D.: The Limits of Expertise: Rethinking Pilot Error and the Causes of Airline Accidents. Aldershot, Hampshire, England, Ashgate (2007)
2. Gruber, T.R.: A translation approach to portable ontology specifications. Knowl. Acquis. **5**(2), 199–220 (1993)
3. Insaurralde, C. C., Blasch, E., Sabatini, R.: Ontology-Based situation awareness for air and space traffic management. In: 2022 IEEE/AIAA 41st Digital Avionics Systems Conference (DASC), pp. 1–8 (2022). https://doi.org/10.1109/DASC55683.2022.9925810
4. Salvucci, D.D.: Modeling driver behavior in a cognitive architecture. Hum. Factors **48**(2), 362–380 (2006). https://doi.org/10.1518/001872006777724417
5. Keller, R.M.: The NASA Air Traffic Management Ontology: Technical Documentation. National Aeronautics and Space Administration, Technical Memo NASA/TM-2017–219526 (2017a)

6. Courtemanche, M. A., Tato, A., Nkambou, R.: Ontological reference model for piloting procedures. In: Crossley, S., Popescu, E. (eds) Intelligent Tutoring Systems. ITS 2022. LNCS, vol. 13284. Springer, Cham (2022). https://doi.org/10.1007/978-3-031-09680-8_9
7. Wu, Y., Ebrahimipour, V., Yacout, S.: Ontology-based modeling of aircraft to support maintenance management system. In: Guan, Y., Liao, H. (eds.) Proceedings of the 2014 Industrial and Systems Engineering Research Conference (2014)
8. Insaurralde, C. C., Blasch, E.: Ontological knowledge representation for avionics decision-making support. In: 35th Digital Avionics Systems Conference (DASC), Sacramento, CA, USA (2016)
9. Yousefzadeh Aghdam, M., Kamel Tabbakh, S.R., Mahdavi Chabok, S.J., Kheyrabadi, M.: Ontology generation for flight safety messages in air traffic management. J. Big Data **8**(1), 1–21 (2021). https://doi.org/10.1186/s40537-021-00449-3
10. Stefanidis, D., Christodoulou, C., Symeonidis, M., et al.: The ICARUS ontology: a general aviation ontology developed using a multi-layer approach. In: Proceedings of the 10th International Conference on Web Intelligence, Mining and Semantics (WIMS 2020), pp. 21–23. Association for Computing Machinery (2020). https://doi.org/10.1145/3405962.3405983
11. Insaurralde, C.C., Blasch, E.: Uncertainty in avionics analytics ontology for decision-making support. J. Adv. Inform. Fusion (JAIF) **13**(2), 255–274 (2018)
12. Insaurralde, C. C., Blasch, E.: Ontologies in Aeronautics. In: Durak, U., Becker, J., Hartmann, S., Voros, N. (eds.) Advances in Aeronautical Informatics, pp. 67–85. Switzerland, Springer (2018b). https://doi.org/10.1007/978-3-319-75058-3_6
13. Insaurralde, C.C., Blasch, E.: Situation awareness decision support system for air traffic management using ontological reasoning. AIAA J. (2022). https://doi.org/10.2514/1.I010989
14. Klaproth, O. W., Halbrügge, M., Russwinkel, N.: ACT-R Model for Cognitive Assistance in Handling Flight Deck Alerts. (2019). from https://api.semanticscholar.org/CorpusID:243856698
15. Oltramari, A., Lebiere, C.: Mechanisms meet content: integrating cognitive architectures and ontologies. In: AAAI Fall Symposium: Advances in Cognitive Systems (2011). https://api.semanticscholar.org/CorpusID:12466118
16. Tamkodjou Tchio, G.C., Courtemanche, M.A., Tato Nyamen, A.A., Nkambou, R., Psyché, V.: Integrating an Ontological Reference Model of Piloting Procedures in ACT-R Cognitive Architecture to Simulate Piloting Tasks. In: Frasson, C., Mylonas, P., Troussas, C. (eds.) Augmented Intelligence and Intelligent Tutoring Systems. ITS 2023. LNCS, vol. 13891, pp. 199–213. Springer, Cham (2023). https://doi.org/10.1007/978-3-031-32883-1_16
17. Tamkodjou Tchio, G.C., Nkambou, R., Tato Nyamen, A.A., Psyché, V.: Towards cognitive coaching in aircraft piloting tasks: building an ACT-R synthetic pilot integrating an ontological reference model to assist the pilot and manage deviations. In: Sifaleras, A., Lin, F. (eds.) Generative Intelligence and Intelligent Tutoring Systems. ITS 2024. LNCS, vol. 14798, 183–194. Springer, Cham (2024). https://doi.org/10.1007/978-3-031-63028-6_16
18. Tamkodjou Tchio, G. C., Nkambou, R., Tato Nyamen, A. A., Psyché, V.: Handling of abnormal aircraft takeoff procedures: cognitive modeling of an act-r synthetic pilot integrating an ontological reference model. In: Mylonas, P., Kardaras, D., Caro, J. (eds.) Novel and Intelligent Digital Systems: Proceedings of the 4th International Conference (NiDS 2024). LNNS, vol. 1170. Springer, Cham (2024). https://doi.org/10.1007/978-3-031-73344-4_38
19. Courtemanche, M. A., Tato, A., Nkambou, R.: Automatic execution of the ontological piloting procedures. In: Frasson, C., Mylonas, P., Troussas, C. (eds.) Augmented Intelligence and Intelligent Tutoring Systems. ITS 2023. LNCS, vol. 13891, 29–41. Springer, Cham (2023). https://doi.org/10.1007/978-3-031-32883-1_3
20. Keller, R. M.: The NASA Air traffic management ontology (atmonto) (Version 1.0). National Aeronautics and Space Administration (2018). https://data.nasa.gov/ontologies/atmonto

21. Kotseruba, I., Tsotsos, J.: 40 Years of cognitive architectures: core cognitive abilities and practical applications. Artifi. Intell. Rev., 17–94 (2020). https://doi.org/10.1007/s10462-018-9646-y
22. Newell, A.: Unified Theories of Cognition. Harvard University Press (1990)
23. Anderson, J.R.: How Can the Human Mind Occur in the Physical Universe? Oxford University Press (2007)
24. Salvucci, D.D.: An Integrated model of eye movements and visual encoding. Cogn. Syst. Res. **1**(4), 201–220 (2001)
25. Airbus.: Flight Crew Operating Manual: Part 3 Flight Operations. A319 / A320 / A321 (2006a)
26. Airbus.: Flight Crew Operating Manual: Part 4 FMGS Pilot's Guide. A319 / A320 / A321 (2006b)
27. Airbus.: Quick Reference Handbook: A318 / A319 / A320 / A321 (2012)
28. Haroon, K.: A320 Abnormal Procedures. The airline pilots forum & resource (2020). https://www.theairlinepilots.com/forumarchive/a320/a320-abnormalprocedures.pdf
29. V-Prep.: V-Prep: A320 Engine Failure After Takeoff Training [vidéo]. YouTube (2017). https://www.youtube.com/watch?v=KyWBCiQYRVM
30. V-Prep.: V-Prep: A320 Predictive and Reactive Windshear [vidéo] (2018a). https://www.youtube.com/watch?v=Z-ptBJD326M&t=65s
31. V-Prep.: V-Prep: A320 Stall Recovery Procedure [vidéo] (2018b). https://www.youtube.com/watch?v=8YFNmXmYijI
32. Keller, R.M.: The NASA Air Traffic Management Ontology: Technical Documentation (Technical Memo NASA/TM-2017-219526). National Aeronautics and Space Administration (2017b)
33. Keller, R.M.: Air Traffic Management (ATM) Ontology: Includes Core Classes and Properties. National Aeronautics and Space Administration (2017c). https://data.nasa.gov/ontologies/atmontoCore/doc/
34. Serratosa, F.: Redefining the graph edit distance. SN COMPUT. SCI. **2**, 438 (2021). https://doi.org/10.1007/s42979-021-00792-5

Enhancing Intelligent Tutor for Program Element Scope Training: Lessons Learned

Nikita Moskalenko, Andrey Sidor, and Oleg Sychev(✉)

Volgograd State Technical University, Volgograd, Russia
o_sychev@vstu.ru
https://vstu.ru

Abstract. In this paper, we describe the enhancement of an intelligent tutoring system for teaching details of program-element scope in the C++ programming language. We expanded the range of learned content, introduced hints with informative descriptions, and provided detailed feedback on errors during premature completion of a learning problem. In addition to scope and visibility, the new tutor can also teach the concept of object lifetime and data flow direction. We conducted an experiment to evaluate the effects of the tutor improvements on the learning process. The results showed that while the overall level of learning gains increased, the gains in some of the topics remained the same and for the most complex topic, they decreased because the students were distracted by the new material. It shows that when expanding intelligent tutors, the teachers should also consider expanding the time spent with the tutor. It was also shown that the students who actively used hints learned significantly more than the students who ignored that feature.

Keywords: Intelligent tutors · Introductory programming · Constraint-based tutors

1 Introduction

Intelligent Tutoring Systems (ITS) have emerged as a promising solution for delivering personalized, adaptive, and scalable instruction in different areas of education, including computer science. They are designed to replicate the skills, behaviors, and methodologies of human instructors by leveraging advanced artificial intelligence technologies to create a more "intelligent" learning experience [19]. By mimicking human teaching approaches, ITS provide an interactive, data-driven learning environment capable of addressing the diverse needs of learners.

One of the key advantages of ITS is the delivery of tailored feedback and guiding learners through complex concepts [3,8]. This personalized support fosters deeper engagement and ensures that learners can progress at their own pace, tackling challenges that might otherwise hinder their understanding [18]. Furthermore, ITS offer scalability, which makes them highly effective in reaching a broad audience without compromising the quality of instruction.

ITS excel in their ability to adapt instructional content to the level of knowledge and skill of the learner. Using diagnostic data, ITS determine the content, timing, and method of presentation of the course content. They offer step-by-step demonstrations for beginners, while more advanced learners encounter increasingly complex scenarios that foster independent problem solving [22]. Furthermore, certain ITS incorporate automated learning problem generation to create personalized exercises aligned with the learner's needs [12]. Dynamic adaptation ensures that learners engage with content that matches their needs, making the learning process more efficient and effective.

This ability of ITS to tailor instruction is particularly valuable in domains such as introductory programming, where abstract and foundational concepts often pose significant challenges to learners. Concepts like scope, which define the accessibility of variables, functions, and objects within a program, require precise understanding to avoid common misconceptions. However, many learners find it difficult to grasp [25]. Adapting to the needs of each learner, ITS can play a crucial role in addressing these difficulties and improving comprehension.

Understanding the rules governing scope remains one of the most challenging aspects of learning programming. Previous studies [10,13] have highlighted common misconceptions about variables and parameter passing. They show that learners frequently develop incorrect and contradictory mental models of scope early during their learning.

The intelligent tutoring system, described in [27], demonstrated effectiveness in teaching the object scope to novice programmers. After studying with ITS, the participants significantly improved their performance in mastering the concept of element visibility in the C++ programming language. However, the described ITS was limited to one kind of learning problems and to providing feedback on errors. Also, some of the feedback messages were not informative. For example, when a learning problem was completed prematurely, the message "Error: not all the correct answers were selected" was displayed. That generic message did not provide learners with clear information about specific answers that were missing and did not explain the reasons why those lines had to be in the correct answer.

In this study, we aim to see if adding other kinds of learning problems on the topic and providing hints will help the students learn the topic or they would not have any effect or hinder the learners. We propose enhancements to the described ITS that should address the described limitations: expanding the range of learning-problem kinds, enhancing some of the feedback messages, and introducing the hint feature that can describe a correct action in the given circumstances with the reason for its correctness and demonstrate worked examples if used continuously. We then evaluate the new ITS and compare the results with the previous evaluation. Our first question was would introducing the features described above cause increase in learning gains of the students; we study that by comparing the results of the students using the two versions of tutor. Our second question concerned the effects of the hint feature on the students who used it voluntarily: to study that, we compared the results of the students who used hints and for those who had access to them but didn't use them.

2 Related Works

The development of ITS has been a prominent focus in educational technology, with various approaches designed to enhance learning experiences across different domains. These systems aim to provide personalized support and feedback to learners, simulating the guidance of a human tutor. In this section, we review notable examples of ITS implementations.

The study [2] presents the deployment architecture of an ITS based on the Moodle learning platform. The proposed system integrates artificial intelligence algorithms, including an optimized ant colony algorithm, to support online education and implement advanced instructional strategies in computer science courses. The ITS provides user authentication, feedback, hints, solutions, and a history of user actions. Furthermore, it monitors student progress to dynamically adjust their learning path according to individual needs. The system is also accessible via smartphones, which makes it particularly valuable for users with limited access to personal computers.

The study by O'Rourke et al. [21] explores the concept of automatic generation of interactive scaffolding tools in ITS. One of the primary advantages of this approach is its ability to dynamically adapt the level of support based on the learner's progress, enabling personalized learning experiences. The system can offer hints and step-by-step guidance tailored to the learner's current state, thereby improving engagement with the material and boosting motivation. However, this approach also has limitations. The generation of high-quality scaffolding tools requires complex analytical algorithms and can be resource-intensive, particularly for non-standard learning problems. Nonetheless, that work makes a significant contribution to the field of educational technology automation, demonstrating how interactive scaffolding tools can enhance learning outcomes.

The study of Cavalcanti et al. [5] shows that automatic feedback in online learning environments helps learners identify and correct their mistakes and fosters confidence and autonomy. That underscores the importance of developing effective feedback mechanisms for complex fields like programming education, where the adaptability and timeliness of feedback are critical for success.

An ITS on the scope of program elements was presented by Fernandes and Kumar [7]. They proposed a tutoring platform aimed at teaching program-element scope concepts during an introductory programming course. They developed an interactive tutor that supports learners in grasping the principles of variable and function scope through targeted examples and exercises. The system assigns learning problems to users and provides feedback, clarifying errors, and offering detailed explanations to facilitate a clearer and more engaging learning experience. To assess the system's efficacy, the authors conducted an experimental study with student participants. The findings revealed that the tutor significantly improved learners' comprehension of scope-related concepts. The system's limitation is that it predominantly focuses on fundamental scope concepts, which might restrict its usefulness for advanced learners.

Another approach to developing ITS is described in [16]. That work presents a constraint-based approach to building ITS, inspired by Stellan Ohlsson's theory of learning from errors [20]. Ohlsson proposed representing knowledge as constraints that define what must be true, rather than generating explicit solution paths. A notable effect of this approach is that constraint-based systems do not provide feedback in scenarios where they do not have knowledge, unlike model-tracing approaches. In model-tracing systems, if a learner performs an action that does not match the known solution path, the system often deems the action incorrect.

When errors occur because of the learner's actions, constraint-based systems provide feedback based on the violated constraints. This feedback aligns with the theory of learning; it informs the learner about the violated principle, explains how it was breached, and reiterates the correct principle. The constraints can also be used to correct the learner's response, offering hints or suggestions on what to do or fix next. The disadvantage of Mitrovic's approach is that the constraints are defined using the correct answer, not the problem formulation, so the messages cannot inform the learner why their answer is wrong for the given problem, only about the difference between the learner's answer and correct answer.

Several successfully implemented tutors use the constraint-based approach, including SQL-Tutor (for teaching SQL queries in relational databases) [17], EER-Tutor (for conceptual database design) [6], CAPIT (for teaching English punctuation rules) [14], LBITS (for vocabulary expansion), and NORMIT (for data normalization) [15]. These tutors have been tested and have demonstrated their effectiveness in improving learning outcomes.

The studies by Sykes and Franek [28,29] present a prototype of an ITS for learning Java programming that demonstrates several good features. The authors introduce an innovative learning approach based on cognitive science and Artificial Intelligence, enabling a personalized educational experience. The system incorporates interactive components, such as automated code verification and a feedback mechanism, which facilitate a deeper understanding of the material. But the authors do not provide empirical data on system testing in real-world conditions, making it difficult to objectively assess its effectiveness. Also, the system is limited compared to instructor-led learning and may face challenges in handling complex logical errors. Overall, this development appears promising but requires further research and refinement to validate its practical applicability.

Butz et al. described a web-based ITS designed to teach programming [4]. The system uses Bayesian networks for implementing adaptive learning by tailoring feedback and assignments to the learner's needs. The web-based platform ensures accessibility to a wide range of users, lowering entry barriers. However, Bayesian networks are complex and require significant computational resources to accurately construct knowledge models. The system primarily targets introductory-level programming, which may limit its effectiveness for advanced learners.

Another notable ITS example is presented by Sychev et al. [27]. It employs both human- and machine-readable domain models, such as cognitive process graphs [26], to teach learners how to manage variable scopes and uses multi-level text modeling to generate natural-language feedback [1]. The system integrates human expertise in constructing domain models; it underwent preliminary evaluation, demonstrating statistically significant improvements in participants' performance after just 12 min of interaction. Usability testing confirmed the system's practicality and user-friendliness, although learners who repeatedly made the same errors showed smaller learning gains.

This research highlights the potential of cognitive modeling using cognitive process graphs to develop highly effective tutoring systems. Beyond improving learning efficiency, this approach allows for addressing complex challenges, such as dynamic learning problem generation and maintaining pedagogical dialogue. These capabilities significantly enhance the adaptability of ITS, bringing them closer to the responsiveness of human tutors.

3 Tutor Improvements

One of the important limitations of the ITS we enhanced [27] was that it supported only one kind of learning problem: selecting program objects (variables, fields, types, etc.) that are visible on a certain line with a certain prefix. That left out the concept of element lifetime and limited the ways the users could assess object scopes. We added three new kinds of learning problems to the tutor, using the framework developed by Krygin et al. [11].

The learning problems of the first new type require learners to identify the lines of code where a given variable is visible (see Fig. 1). That is the inverse problem to the learning problem of original tutor. The input to this problem consists of C++ source code, a variable or class property along with the line where it is declared, and an optional prefix. Learners must analyze the provided code and select the lines where the specified variable or property is visible.

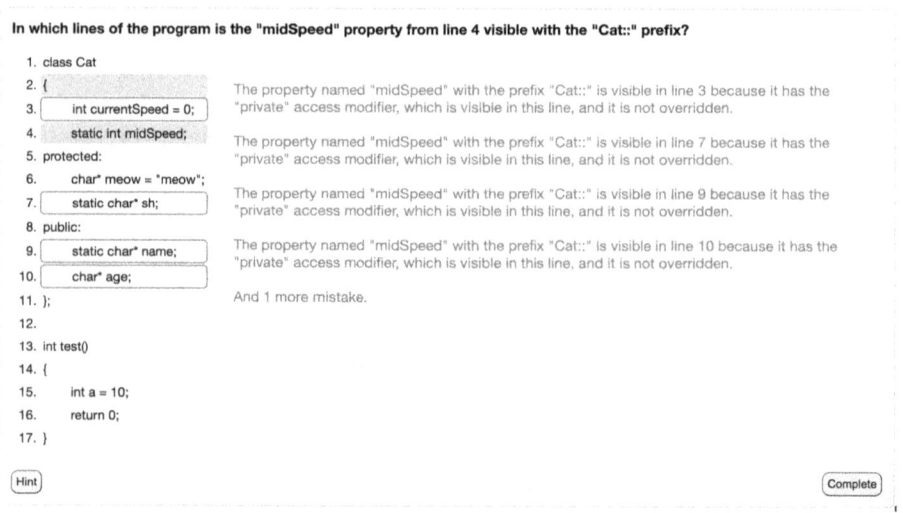

Fig. 1. An example of the learning problem of the first type

The learning problems of the second type are devoted to the variable lifetime (see Fig. 2), which cannot be defined on static code. The learners are presented with C++ source code, its execution trace, and a variable or class property declared in that code. The problem requires learners to find the lines of execution trace where the variable exists, thus connecting static program analysis with dynamic execution behavior. This type of learning problem helps address misconceptions related to memory usage and the inability of learners to trace code execution linearly, as discussed in [10].

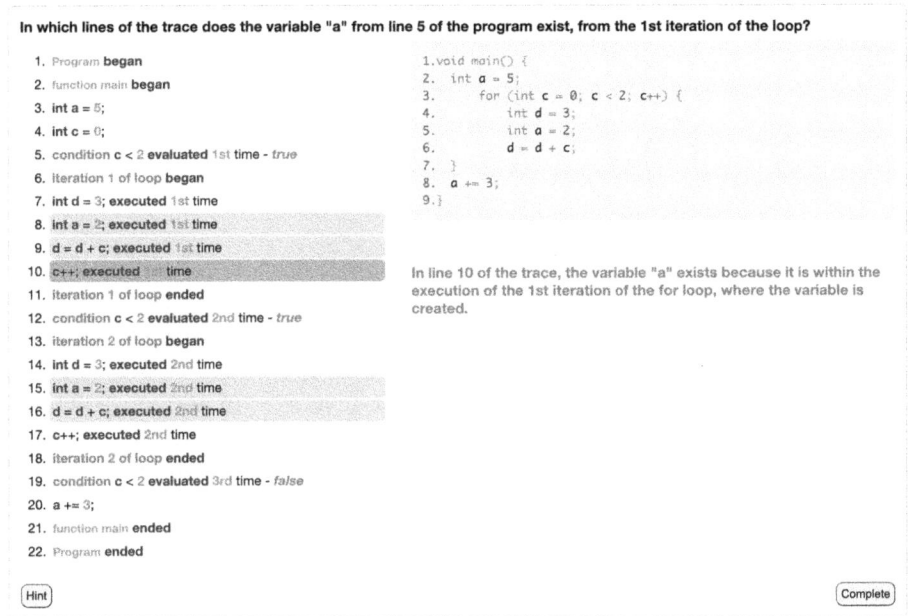

Fig. 2. An example of the learning problem of the second type

The problems of the third kind focus on data flow during expression evaluation (see Fig. 3). The problem formulation includes an expression and the list of used variables for which the learner should determine the data flow direction (input, output, or both input and output). The expressions can contain standard C++ operators and function calls. The function prototypes including parameter directions are provided so that the learner knows what the used functions do to their parameters. This type of learning problem addresses misconceptions related to the roles of variables in the program, as highlighted in [23].

The integration of these new learning problems into the ITS has resulted in a more comprehensive coverage of topics related to the scope, lifespan, and usage of variables and other program elements. Consequently, the system now facilitates the identification and explanation of a wider range of learner errors.

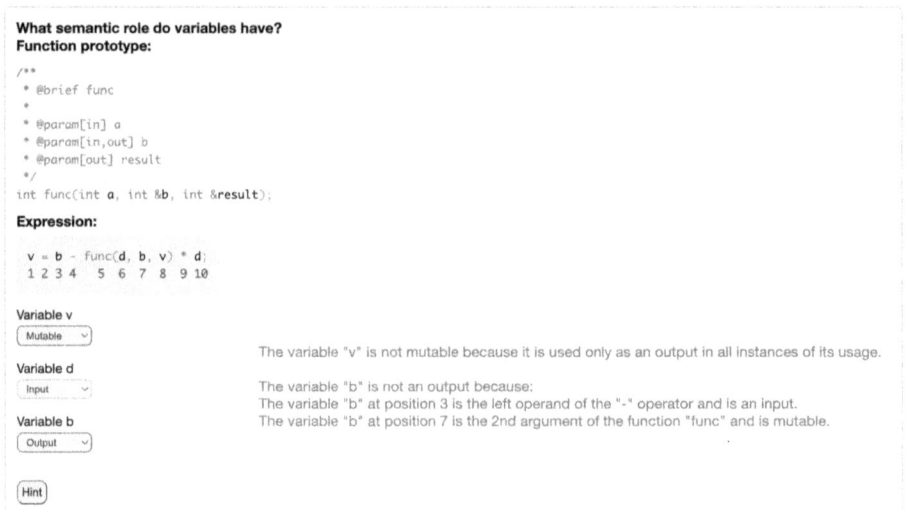

Fig. 3. An example of the learning problem of the third type

This enhancement not only supports more nuanced feedback but also promotes a more robust understanding of these foundational programming concepts.

Another important modification of the first version of the tutor was the introduction of informative hints. Hints are used by learners when they do not know which step to do next and include not only highlighting the correct step in the learner's controls but also providing a textual explanation of why that step is correct in the given circumstances. The hints aim to guide learners toward the correct solution and avoid a trial-and-error process. If used systematically, they can provide fully worked examples of solving the relevant problem. The generation of these hints relies on the Thought Process Graph, which is also used to identify correct and incorrect answers [26]. An example hint is shown in Fig. 2: it is highlighted in green and positioned below the program code.

To adapt to the current situation, the hint templates incorporate parameters derived from the variables determined during the execution of the Thought Process Graph. The templates of these hints are associated with the green nodes of the Thought Process Graph, which represent the correct answers and allow customizing messages according to the reasons for the correctness of the relevant problem-solving steps.

We also improved feedback on errors by providing informative feedback messages upon premature learning problem completion. Some learning problems do not require the learner to select all the objects in the problem formulation. An example of the error message on premature problem completion is shown in Fig. 1. The message is highlighted in red and is positioned to the right of the learning problem. To achieve this, we developed supplementary Thought Process Graphs for every learning problem; those graphs are used when the learner pushes the button "Complete". These graphs assess whether all the correct answer options have been selected and, if some of them haven't, generate an error message. Those graphs resemble the main graphs used to verify the learner's answer, but they use loops to analyze all the options, and they are inverted (the error is not pressing the correct options). That aligns with the logical validation of learning problem completion and can be expressed as follows:

$$ProblemCompleted \iff \forall x \in Options, (x \notin Selected \Rightarrow x \notin Correct), \quad (1)$$

where:

- *"Options"* refers to the set of all available answer options;
- *"Selected"* denotes the options chosen by the learner;
- *"Correct"* represents the set of correct answers.

Under the hood, we changed the logic of solution verification, optimizing the Thought Process Graph (described in [27]) for the initial learning problem supported by the old tutor. The old version used nested loops to identify overlapping variables as shown in Fig. 4(a), which sometimes iterated over the same objects twice or more. We replaced it with a single loop with a better object selection criterion as shown in Fig. 4. That allowed us to increase the tuytor's performance and avoid weeding out duplicated error messages.

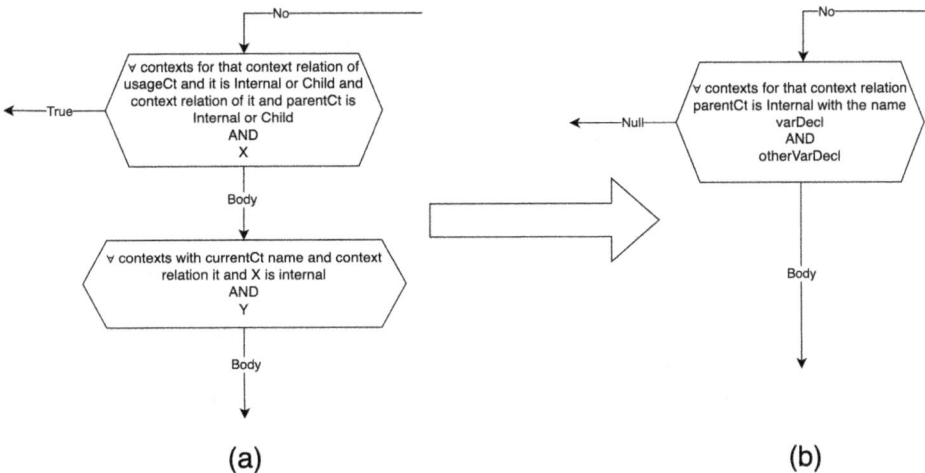

Fig. 4. An example of improving the Thought Process Graph for solution verification: (a) previous version; (b) improved version

4   Evaluation

To evaluate the proposed system modifications, we conducted testing with a number of volunteer students of Volgograd State Technical University majoring in software engineering (most of them were second and third-year undergraduate students). We divided the participants randomly into two groups: the first group (17 students) used the old intelligent tutor described in [27]; the second group (18 students) used the improved version of the tutor. Both groups did the following:

1. pass a pre-test assessing baseline knowledge of the topic;
2. use the tutor assigned to your group to complete a set of exercises;
3. pass a post-test measuring knowledge levels after using the system;
4. participate in a survey evaluating user experience.

Pre-tests and post-tests for both groups contained learning problems with identical topics and were based on a shared pool of learning problems (ranging from 6 to 10 unique learning problems). This approach minimized systematic bias associated with recalling correct answers after testing but kept the learning problems basically the same. The pre-test and post-test for the two study groups contained five learning problems about variable lifetime, visibility, and dataflow direction. The maximum possible test score was 5 points.

We measured several parameters of student learning, including Absolute Learning Gain (ALG) and Relative Learning Gain (RLG) to study the efficiency of the tutors. ALG represents the difference between post-test and pre-test scores, while RLG is the absolute learning gain divided by the maximum possible learning gain; it is calculated as: $RLG = \frac{pre-post}{5-pre}$, where "pre" and "post" represent test scores before and after using the tutor, respectively, and 5 is the maximum possible test score. The RLG metric provides a more objective measure of progress because the participants with a higher initial level of knowledge have limited absolute learning gains but have to master more complex elements of the educational material to advance their knowledge. In order to evaluate the effect of hints, we measured Average Error Rate (AER), which is the mean percentage of incorrect answer choices made by the student among all the incorrect choices available in a given learning problem.

Table 1 presents the mean values and standard deviations of these parameters for both versions of the tutor.

The learning gains were higher for the improved version of the tutor for learning problems 1, 2, and 5; the older tutor turned out better for learning problem 4. The problem of learning problem 4 can be explained by the fact that in the new tutor, the participants had more material to learn in one experimental session, so some of the more complex details might be missed. That means that the new tutor should be used in several learning sessions instead of one because it covers more material.

We used the t-test to identify statistically significant differences between the measured parameters, with the significance threshold of $p < 0.05$. It assumes normally distributed data, so we tested the datasets for normality using the ShapiroWilk test. The RLG scores from the students using the two versions of the tutor were normally distributed according to the ShapiroWilk test with $p = 0.21$ (the group of students who used the improved tutor version $N = 18$) and $p = 0.42$ (the group of students who used the original tutor $N = 17$). A two-sample t-test with equal variances indicated that the difference in the total RLG

Table 1. Learning gains achieved by the students using the two versions of tutor.

Parameter	Previous tutor				Improved Tutor			
	PRE	POST	ALG	RLG	PRE	POST	ALG	RLG
1. Determine the lines of trace where the variable exists								
Mean	0.57	0.43	−0.13	−1.21	0.53	0.77	0.24	0.39
Std. dev.	0.24	0.25	0.29	2.66	0.31	0.24	0.38	0.85
2. Determine the lines of code where the local or global variable is visible								
Mean	0.64	0.65	0.01	−0.13	0.74	0.8	0.06	0.28
Std. dev.	0.24	0.26	0.31	1.18	0.2	0.21	0.3	0.5
3. Determine the lines of code where the class property is visible with a prefix								
Mean	0.65	0.9	0.25	0.44	0.55	0.82	0.27	0.5
Std. dev.	0.26	0.11	0.3	0.57	0.28	0.21	0.28	0.46
4. Determine the lines of code where the class property is visible								
Mean	0.56	0.81	0.25	0.45	0.58	0.74	0.16	0.22
Std. dev.	0.21	0.25	0.35	0.66	0.22	0.26	0.31	0.99
5. Determine the data flow directions of variables in an expression								
Mean	0.51	0.62	0.11	0.23	0.63	0.84	0.2	0.34
Std. dev.	0.15	0.22	0.17	0.47	0.34	0.24	0.44	0.7
Total								
Mean	2.93	3.41	0.48	0.23	3.05	3.91	0.86	0.43
Std. dev.	0.46	0.57	0.51	0.25	0.71	0.7	0.77	0.41

between the two tutoring systems was statistically significant ($p = 0.042$), which supports the improvement in learning outcomes for the group trained with the improved tutor ($0.43 > 0.23$). Pre- and post-test results for the improved tutor were also normally distributed: the ShapiroWilk test for the group of students who used the improved tutor version: $p = 0.97$ (pre-test), $p = 0.21$ (post-test). The difference between them is also statistically significant (3.91 (post) > 3.05 (pre), with t-test $p = 0.00018$), which proves that the students learned new content.

On the level of individual learning problems, the distribution of RLG scores for learning problem 1 does not follow the normal distribution according to the ShapiroWilk test ($p = 0.00007$ for the students using the improved tutor, $p = 0.00003$ for the students using the original version). Therefore, instead of the t-test, the MannWhitney U test was used, which revealed a statistically significant difference between the samples ($p < 0.05$). This shows that the improved tutor covers that topic better. That learning problem addresses the topic of object lifetime, which was not covered in the old version of the tutor. This indicates that introducing new kinds of learning problems helps students better understand the concept of "object visibility and lifetime." For the other learning problems, the RLG values are not normally distributed according to the ShapiroWilk test and are not statistically significant based on the MannWhitney U test. However, it is worth noting that the RLG for learning problem 5, which also represents a new kind of learning problem, is higher in the improved tutor version. This further supports the conclusion that new kinds of learning problem enhance learning of the topic.

To find out whether the hint feature helped the students learn, we analyzed AER values for students who used hints and those who did not. On average, students who used hints had a lower average AER ($AER = 0.37$) compared to those who did not use them ($AER = 0.52$). The behavior of students who solved learning problems without hints can be described as a trial-and-error approach: when solving difficult learning problems, they either guessed randomly or selected all the available options in turn to identify the correct one. According to the ShapiroWilk test, the data follows a normal distribution: for the group of students that used hints ($N = 9$) $p = 0.16$ and the group of students that did not ($N = 9$) $p = 0.95$. The difference in AER between the groups is statistically significant based on the Student's t-test ($p = 0.019$).

We also studied the effect of using hints on learning gains. The students who used hints voluntarily had a mean RLG of 0.63; those who did not had a mean RLG of 0.23. The learning gains followed a normal distribution according to the ShapiroWilk test for both the student group that used hints ($p = 0.13$) and the group that did not ($p = 0.34$). The difference between their learning gains was statistically significant according to the t-test ($p = 0.016$), which supports the hypothesis that hints contribute to more effective learning.

User experience was assessed using the User Experience Questionnaire (UEQ) [24]. The survey consisted of 26 items, each rated on a scale from -3 to 3 (ranging from negative to positive evaluation). The questions were presented to assess various criteria: perspicuity (4 items), efficiency (4 items), dependability (4 items), stimulation (4 items), novelty (4 items), and attractiveness (6 items), covering different aspects of user perception. The survey results for both the old and the new tutors are presented in Table 2. It can be seen that the students saw the improved tutor as a slighter better tool, but the difference wasn't statistically significant. The responses on the attractiveness scale show good internal consistency for both the previous and the improved tutors, with Cronbach's alpha between 0.8 and 0.9. For the remaining scales, the internal consistency is acceptable ($0.7 < a < 0.8$).

Table 2. User Experience Questionnaire results

Scale	Attractiveness	Perspicuity	Efficiency	Dependability	Stimulation	Novelty
Previous tutor						
Mean	1.56	1.50	1.72	1.17	1.33	1.06
Variance	1.10	1.15	1.23	0.79	1.24	1.11
Improved Tutor						
Mean	1.61	1.89	1.78	1.22	1.39	1.17
Variance	1.09	1.13	1.06	1.31	1.33	1.20

5 Conclusion

In this paper, we described an improvement of an intelligent tutor for program element scope, that enhanced error messages on premature learning-problem completion, expanded the range of the supported learning problems, and introduced the hint feature describing the next correct step in the given situation.

The conducted study revealed that expanding the range of learning problems and introducing hints into the ITS significantly enhanced students' learning outcomes. These improvements are especially evident in learning problems covering previously unexplored topics, where statistically significant performance gains were observed. But the results in the previously covered topics could decrease slightly. As was noted in the study by Jordan et al. [9], attempting to cover an extensive amount of material within a limited timeframe may overwhelm students and hinder effective learning because of high cognitive learning. To enhance educational outcomes, instructional content should be segmented into key concepts that can be meaningfully absorbed within each session. In our experiment, we tested all the kinds of learning problems simultaneously, which can result in cognitive overload. So when using the advanced tutor, we recommend spreading training using different kinds of learning problems over several sessions to lower the cognitive load.

Students who used hints demonstrated a more thoughtful approach to learning and made fewer mistakes, which resulted in significantly lower percentage of incorrect responses. They also had higher learning gains. As highlighted in the study by Zhao [30], providing feedback in the form of explanations for both correct and incorrect answers helps deepen understanding, enhances memory retention and promotes engagement in the learning process. The tutor's feedback improvements (adding hints and enhancing existing messages for some kinds of errors) allowed for increased learning gains students get from interacting with the tutor as the evaluation showed.

Our further work will focus on increasing the adaptive capabilities of the tutor and implementing automatic learning-problem generation to ensure that the tutor will never run out of learning problems to give to students. We are also planning to evaluate the tutor with a bigger cohort of students, which may require several years to achieve.

References

1. Anikin, A., Sychev, O., Gurtovoy, V.: Multi-level modeling of structural elements of natural language texts and its applications. In: Samsonovich, A.V. (ed.) BICA 2018. AISC, vol. 848, pp. 1–8. Springer, Cham (2019). https://doi.org/10.1007/978-3-319-99316-4_1
2. Binh, H.T., Trung, N.Q., Duy, B.T.: Responsive student model in an intelligent tutoring system and its evaluation. Educ. Inf. Technol. **26**(4), 4969–4991 (2021). https://doi.org/10.1007/s10639-021-10485-4
3. Burns, H.L., Capps, C.G.: Foundations of intelligent tutoring systems: an introduction. In: Foundations of Intelligent Tutoring Systems, pp. 1–19. Routledge (1988)

4. Butz, C.J., Hua, S., Maguire, R.B.: A web-based intelligent tutoring system for computer programming. In: Proceedings of the 2004 IEEE/WIC/ACM International Conference on Web Intelligence, WI 2004, pp. 159–165. IEEE Computer Society, USA (2004)
5. Cavalcanti, A.P., et al.: Automatic feedback in online learning environments: a systematic literature review. Comput. Educ. Artif. Intell. **2**, 100027 (2021). https://doi.org/10.1016/j.caeai.2021.100027
6. Elmadani, M., Mitrovic, A., Weerasinghe, A., Neshatian, K.: Investigating student interactions with tutorial dialogues in EER-Tutor. Res. Pract. Technol. Enhanc. Learn. **10**(1), 1–21 (2015). https://doi.org/10.1186/s41039-015-0013-1
7. Fernandes, E., Kumar, A.N.: A tutor on scope for the programming languages course. ACM SIGCSE Bull. **36**(1), 90–93 (2004). https://doi.org/10.1145/1028174.971332
8. Gutierrez, F., Atkinson, J.: Adaptive feedback selection for intelligent tutoring systems. Expert Syst. Appl. **38**(5), 6146–6152 (2011). https://doi.org/10.1016/j.eswa.2010.11.058
9. Jordan, J., Wagner, J., Manthey, D.E., Wolff, M., Santen, S., Cico, S.J.: Optimizing lectures from a cognitive load perspective. AEM Educ. Train. **4**(3), 306–312 (2019). https://doi.org/10.1002/aet2.10389
10. Kaczmarczyk, L.C., Petrick, E.R., East, J.P., Herman, G.L.: Identifying student misconceptions of programming. In: Proceedings of the 41st ACM Technical Symposium on Computer Science Education, SIGCSE 2010, pp. 107–111. Association for Computing Machinery, New York (2010). https://doi.org/10.1145/1734263.1734299
11. Krygin, A.I., Gumerov, M.R., Moskalenko, N.A., Sychev, O.A.: A framework for developing intelligent tutoring systems based on domain models in the form of decision trees. Pattern Recognit Image Anal. **34**(3), 710–716 (2024). https://doi.org/10.1134/s1054661824700561
12. Kumar, A.N.: Generation of problems, answers, grade, and feedback–case study of a fully automated tutor. J. Educ. Resour. Comput. **5**(3), 3 (2005). https://doi.org/10.1145/1163405.1163408
13. Ma, L., Ferguson, J., Roper, M., Wood, M.: Investigating and improving the models of programming concepts held by novice programmers. Comput. Sci. Educ. **21**(1), 57–80 (2011)
14. Mayo, M., Mitrovic, A., McKenzie, J.: Capit: an intelligent tutoring system for capitalisation and punctuation. In: Proceedings International Workshop on Advanced Learning Technologies. IWALT 2000. Advanced Learning Technology: Design and Development Issues, pp. 151–154 (2000). https://doi.org/10.1109/IWALT.2000.890594
15. Mitrovic, A.: Normit: a web-enabled tutor for database normalization. In: International Conference on Computers in Education, Proceedings, vol. 2, pp. 1276–1280 (2002). https://doi.org/10.1109/CIE.2002.1186210
16. Mitrovic, A., Martin, B., Suraweera, P.: Intelligent tutors for all: the constraint-based approach. IEEE Intell. Syst. **22**(4), 38–45 (2007). https://doi.org/10.1109/mis.2007.74
17. Mitrovic, A., Ohlsson, S.: Evaluation of a constraint-based tutor for a database language. Int. J. Artif. Intell. Educ. (1999)
18. Mitrovic, A., Ohlsson, S., Barrow, D.K.: The effect of positive feedback in a constraint-based intelligent tutoring system. Comput. Educ. **60**(1), 264–272 (2013). https://doi.org/10.1016/j.compedu.2012.07.002

19. Nwana, H.: Intelligent tutoring systems: an overview. Artif. Intell. Rev. **4**(4) (1990). https://doi.org/10.1007/bf00168958
20. Ohlsson, S.: Constraint-based student modelling. J. Interact. Learn. Res. **3**(4), 429 (1992)
21. O'Rourke, E., Andersen, E., Gulwani, S., Popović, Z.: A framework for automatically generating interactive instructional scaffolding. In: Proceedings of the 33rd Annual ACM Conference on Human Factors in Computing Systems, CHI 2015, pp. 1545–1554. Association for Computing Machinery, New York (2015). https://doi.org/10.1145/2702123.2702580
22. Phobun, P., Vicheanpanya, J.: Adaptive intelligent tutoring systems for e-learning systems. Procedia. Soc. Behav. Sci. **2**(2), 4064–4069 (2010). https://doi.org/10.1016/j.sbspro.2010.03.641
23. Qian, Y., Lehman, J.: Students' misconceptions and other difficulties in introductory programming: a literature review. ACM Trans. Comput. Educ. **18**(1), 1–24 (2017). https://doi.org/10.1145/3077618
24. Schrepp, M., Hinderks, A., Thomaschewski, J.: Construction of a benchmark for the user experience questionnaire (UEQ). Int. J. Interact. Multimedia Artif. Intell. **4**, 40–44 (2017). https://doi.org/10.9781/ijimai.2017.445
25. Strömbäck, F., Haglund, P., Berglund, A., Berglund, E.: The progression of students' ability to work with scope, parameter passing and aliasing. In: Proceedings of the 25th Australasian Computing Education Conference, ACE 2023, pp. 39–48. Association for Computing Machinery, New York (2023). https://doi.org/10.1145/3576123.3576128
26. Sychev, O.: Educational models for cognition: methodology of modeling intellectual skills for intelligent tutoring systems. Cogn. Syst. Res. **87**, 101261 (2024). https://doi.org/10.1016/J.COGSYS.2024.101261
27. Sychev, O., Sidor, A., Karpenko, P.: Embedding process knowledge in cyber-social systems on the example of cognitive tutor to teach scope. J. Integr. Des. Process Sci. **27**(3–4), 248–262 (2024). https://doi.org/10.1177/10920617241289701
28. Sykes, E.R., Franek, F.: An intelligent tutoring system prototype for learning to program javatm. In: Proceedings of 3rd IEEE International Conference on Advanced Technologies (2003)
29. Sykes, E.R., Franek, F.: A prototype for an intelligent tutoring system for students learning to program in java (TM). In: Proceedings of the IASTED International Conference on Computers and Advanced Technology in Education, pp. 78–83 (2003)
30. Zhao, Y.: The impact of cognitive load theory on online learning outcomes for adolescent students. J. Educ. Humanit. Soc. Sci. **18**, 50–55 (2023). https://doi.org/10.54097/ehss.v18i.10946

Mapping AI Tools in Education: A Topic Modeling Analysis of Cognitive, Metacognitive, and Affective Insights

Michael Pin-Chuan Lin[1](✉) , Arita Li Liu[2], Saeed Saffari[3], Daniel Chang[2] , and Jeeho Ryoo[4]

[1] Mount Saint Vincent University, Halifax, NS, Canada
`michael.lin@msvu.ca`
[2] Simon Fraser University, Burnaby, BC, Canada
`{arita_liu,dth7}@sfu.ca`
[3] Dalhousie University, Halifax, NS, Canada
`Saeed.Saffari@dal.ca`
[4] Fairleigh Dickinson University, Vancouver, BC, Canada
`j.ryoo@fdu.edu`

Abstract. The rapid rise of Artificial Intelligence (AI) tools prompts educators to revisit how learning theories inform instruction and assessment. While AI supports personalization, adaptive feedback, and automation, its alignment with established learning theories remains unclear. This study examines how AI tools engage cognitive, metacognitive, and affective dimensions using an open dataset of AI-powered educational tools. Using topic modeling techniques and cluster analysis, we identify thematic categories and their alignment with Bloom's Taxonomy, the Two-Level Model of Metacognition, and Control-Value Theory. Findings show a strong emphasis on lower-order processes (e.g., Remembering and Understanding), with fewer designed for higher-order thinking. Some tools enable self-monitoring and reflection, but few support strategic learning. In the affective domain, AI enhance motivation via personalization but lacks emotional adaptation. These results highlight the need for theory-informed AI design to promote deeper, self-regulated, and emotionally responsive learning.

Keywords: AI in Education · Cognitive Learning · Metacognitive Learning · Affective Learning · Topic Modeling · Educational Technology · AI and Pedagogy

1 Introduction

The emergence of AI reshapes teaching, learning, assessment, and administration (Chiu et al., 2023). Research (e.g., Chang et al., 2023; Lin et al., 2024a, 2024b) on AI in education (AIEd) highlights that AI-driven tools enhance engagement, personalize instruction, and improve grading efficiency, offering tailored support to learners and instructors. Particularly, AIEd is conceptualized as a dynamic actor: a subject that interacts with learners, a mediator assisting instructors, and a supplementary aid providing data-driven insights (Xu and Ouyang, 2022). The evolving AI-learner interaction is categorized into three paradigms: AI-directed (learners as recipients), AI-supported (learners collaborating with AI), and AI-empowered (learners taking leadership roles) (Ouyang and Jiao, 2021). While these frameworks highlight AI's role in education, its alignment with established learning theories, such as cognitive load theory (Sweller, 1988), self-regulated learning (SRL) (Zimmerman, 2000), and self-determination theory (SDT) (Ryan and Deci, 2000), remains underexplored.

Effective learning integrates cognitive, metacognitive and affective processes. Instructional frameworks, such as Bloom's Taxonomy (Bloom et al., 1956) guide structured knowledge acquisition, while cognitive theories, such as schema theory (Anderson and Pearson, 1984) explain how knowledge is organized and retrieved. AI tools may support these aspects through adaptive feedback and personalizing instruction. Metacognitive theories, particularly Zimmerman's (2000) SRL framework, highlight learners' regulation and monitoring of their learning. Affective learning, which is integral to motivation theories like SDT (Ryan and Deci, 2000) and Control-Value Theory (CVT) highlight motivation and engagement—areas where AI seeks to contribute through gamification and personalized pathways (Lin et al., 2024a). Despite these theoretical links, it remains unclear whether AI tools effectively support these dimensions. This study addresses this gap by mapping AI tool functionalities onto cognitive, metacognitive, and affective lens.

2 Literature Review and Theoretical Framework

2.1 AIEd: Cognitive, Metacognitive, and Affective Dimensions

Recently, AI has increasingly been integrated into education, supporting cognitive skill development, metacognition, and affective engagement. AI tools facilitate knowledge structuring, reasoning, and problem-solving, contributing to the development of higher-order skills (Liu et al., 2024; Valdivia et al., 2024). Additionally, AI tutoring and writing assistants aid metacognitive development by fostering planning and self-monitoring strategies (Shen and Tao, 2025). Personalized AI-based interventions enhance intrinsic motivation and engagement, fostering SRL by encouraging learners to take greater control over their learning processes (Lai et al., 2023). To better understand AI's role in education, we examine its impact on learning through three theoretical lenses: Bloom's Taxonomy for cognitive processes, the Two-Level Model of Metacognition for self-regulation, and CVT for affective engagement.

2.2 AI and Cognitive Development: Bloom's Taxonomy

Anderson and Krathwohl's (2001) revised Bloom's Taxonomy offers a structured lens to examine AI's role in cognitive development, organizing cognitive processes from lower-order skills like Remembering to higher-order skills like Creating. Research shows AI tools often support foundational tasks such as knowledge acquisition and knowledge retention (Bai et al., 2023; Liu et al., 2024; Pergantis et al., 2025; Shanmugasundaram and Tamilarasu, 2023). Some studies suggest AI can assist with higher-order processes, such as problem-based learning and application (Valdivia et al., 2024), though challenges remain in helping students transfer AI-generated insights to real-world contexts (Elim, 2024). While tools like ChatGPT have shown to support complex tasks (Essel et al., 2024), it is still unclear how AI can be systematically designed to scaffold the full range of cognitive demands in Bloom's framework, particularly beyond foundational knowledge.

2.3 AI and Metacognitive Dimension – Two-Level Model of Metacognition

The Two-Level Model of Metacognition (Nelson and Narens, 1994) distinguishes between object-level cognition (tasks engagement) and meta-level cognition (monitoring and regulation). Within this framework, AI can function as a meta-level support system by offering structured prompts, reverse prompting, reflection opportunities, and adaptive feedback to enhance SRL (Chang et al., 2023; Lin and Chang, 2023). For instance, recent evidence has pointed out that AI-powered writing tools can offer feedback (Shen and Tao, 2025), develop planning and self-monitoring strategies (Chang et al., 2023), and provide just-in-time feedback (Liu et al., 2023). However, these metacognitive functions rely on the AI's underlying cognitive processing capabilities, making their effectiveness dependent on how learners engage with and prompt the tools. This cognitive-metacognitive interdependence also raises concerns about "Metacognitive laziness", where students offload critical thinking to AI (Ahmad et al., 2023; Zhai et al., 2024). Thus, drawing on Nelson & Narens' model, effective AI integration must recognize this dependency and focus on how students actively leverage AI's cognitive affordances to support metacognitive regulation.

2.4 AI and Affective Dimension: CVT

AI-driven learning environments enhance student motivation by offering personalized, interactive, and adaptive experiences. Instead of a one-size-fits-all approach, AI tools adjust content to individual needs, fostering autonomy and engagement (Valdivia et al., 2024). When students perceive AI as supporting intrinsic motivation, they engage more deeply with learning materials and exhibit higher acceptance of the technology (Lai et al., 2023). Features like adaptive feedback, gamification, and tailored recommendations further sustain interest and promote self-directed learning (Huang et al., 2023).

The CVT of achievement emotions (Pekrun, 2006; Pekrun et al., 2002) explains how students' perceptions of control over their learning and the value they assign to tasks shape their emotional and motivational states. Based on CVT, AI can enhance student motivation by (a) increasing perceived control through adaptive feedback and tailored learning pathways and (b) enhancing subjective value by aligning AI-generated content with students' interests and academic goals.

However, AI-driven instructions may not always promote long-term engagement. If AI's recommendations are too prescriptive or inflexible, students may feel disconnected from their learning process, leading to lower intrinsic motivation (Chiu et al., 2023). To sustain meaningful engagement, AI tools should support learner autonomy, choice, and meaningful interactions, ensuring students remain actively involved in shaping their learning experiences (Lin et al., 2024a, 2024b; Seo et al., 2021).

2.5 Current Study: Addressing Gaps

Despite the growing integration of AI in education, gaps remain in understanding how AI tools systematically support learning processes. Therefore, borrowing from Bloom's framework, we examine the functionalities of AI-powered tools through the lens of three theoretical frameworks to evaluate their potential impacts and provide insights into how they align with educational goals and instructional strategies. We address the following research questions:

1. In what ways do current AI-powered tools serve educational purposes?
2. What cognitive, metacognitive, and affective aspects of learning do current AI-powered tools aim to enhance?

3 Methods

This study employs topic modeling to analyze AI-powered tools and their alignment with cognitive, metacognitive, and affective learning dimensions. Topic modeling is a widely used unsupervised machine learning technique for identifying latent themes in large textual datasets (Blei et al., 2003), making it particularly suitable for examining the large text of AI tool descriptions in the data. By applying Latent Dirichlet Allocation (LDA), this study uncovers underlying patterns in how AI tools are designed, categorized, and utilized in educational contexts.

3.1 Data Collection and Analysis

The dataset for this study was sourced from an open dataset (Bureau, 2023) containing 4000 AI tools across 50 categories, including content generation, productivity, business, marketing, programming, and education. Tools were filtered based on alignment with predefined educational topics such as AI writing, interactive learning, language learning, research assistance, and personalized education. To ensure relevance and feasibility, the top 20% of tools were selected based on (1) completeness of descriptions, (2) website functionality, and (3) educational applicability. This percentile-based sampling methods, commonly used in research (Bornmann and Williams, 2013), enhances interpretability and ensures a structured analysis of AI's role in cognitive, metacognitive, and affective learning.

Preprocessing. Preprocessing is a crucial phase in topic modeling as it improves data consistency and interpretability (Roberts et al., 2013; Blei et al., 2003). This study used R and Python for thorough data cleaning. First, all text was converted to lowercase to standardize the input format. Punctuation, numeric values, and stopwords were removed to reduce noise and ensure that irrelevant elements did not influence the modeling process. The stopword removal process used a standard stopword list augmented with additional domain-specific terms, following best practices for educational and technical datasets

(Feinerer et al., 2008; Rinker, 2018). Lemmatization was applied to group related words (e.g., "analyze" and "analyzed") under a single term, improving semantic coherence as noted by Skorkovská (2012).

Determining the Number of Topics. To identify the optimal number of topics (K), this study applied Structural Topic Modeling (STM) using the tm (Feinerer et al., 2008) and stm (Roberts et al., 2019) packages in R. Multiple evaluation metrics (e.g., Methlagl et al., 2024) were employed to assess the model's performance:

- **Held-Out Likelihood:** Evaluates the model's predictive performance and its ability to generalize its learned knowledge to unseen data.
- **Residuals:** Identifies discrepancies between observed and predicted values.
- **Semantic Coherence:** Ensures meaningful topic formation.
- **Lower Bound:** Assesses model stability and convergence.
- After testing multiple iterations, the K value with the highest semantic coherence and stability was selected (Roberts et al., 2019).

Topic Modeling Process. Once the optimal number of topics was determined, LDA was run in Python using the *nltk* and *Gensim* libraries. The model was executed multiple times to ensure stable topic distributions. The output included a ranked list of keywords for each topic, with weights showing their contribution.

Topic Interpretation and Labeling. Topic interpretation was conducted manually by reviewing the top-weighted words within each topic to balance relevance and clarity when assigning topic names (Sievert and Kenneth, 2014). Each topic was assigned a descriptive label that corresponded to AI functionalities, such as AI tools for education, research, writing, summarization, coding, and presentations.

Mapping Topics to Learning Dimensions. After assigning descriptive labels, the identified topics were systematically mapped to specific AI tool categories to evaluate their thematic relevance. Some tools aligned closely to a single topic, while others spanned multiple categories due to their multifunctional nature. For instance, tools categorized under educational support often incorporated summarization features, illustrating the overlapping and integrated nature of modern AI tools. This overlap highlighted the versatility of many AI tools, which simultaneously support tasks such as instructional content creation, research assistance, and presentation enhancements. Thus, this mapping process provides a structured analysis of how AI tools contribute to different learning contexts.

Cluster Analysis. To analyze how AI tools align with cognitive, metacognitive, and affective learning dimensions, this study employed text preprocessing, keyword matching, and clustering techniques (Jain, 2010). AI tool descriptions were normalized through lowercasing, stopword removal, lemmatization, and tokenization to ensure data consistency. Using a curated list of keywords derived from established theoretical frameworks, exact and fuzzy matching (via Levenshtein distance) identified relevant terms for each learning dimension. Each AI tool receives a relevance score based on keyword occurrences and contextual alignment with each dimension. Multiple model runs and parameter adjustments were conducted to ensure the stability of these classifications. The AI tools were then grouped into three categories: Cognitive, Metacognitive, and Affective. This clustering process was based on their strongest alignment scores. A manual review by two researchers further validated the results, refining topic assignments for accuracy. To refine classification, a k-means cluster analysis was conducted using Cognitive, Metacognitive, and Affective scores. Standardization was performed via z-score normalization, and 47 outliers exceeding z-score threshold ($|z| > 3$) were removed before finalizing cluster analysis, which included a total of 798 tools.

4 Results

4.1 RQ1. In What Ways Do the AI-Powered Tools Serve Educational Purposes?

This section presents the findings from the topic modeling process, which analyzed the descriptions of AI tools to identify key thematic categories. The primary goal was to classify AI tools based on their applications in writing, education, and research. To determine the optimal number of topics (K), diagnostic metrics such as held-out likelihood, residuals, semantic coherence, and lower bound values were evaluated.

As shown in Fig. 1, diagnostic plots generated in R guided the selection of K = 8 as the optimal number of topics. The Semantic Coherence plot was especially informative, indicating that K = 8 produced well-defined and interpretable topics with minimal overlap or fragmentation. At this value, the model captured distinct thematic groupings that balanced clarity and specificity.

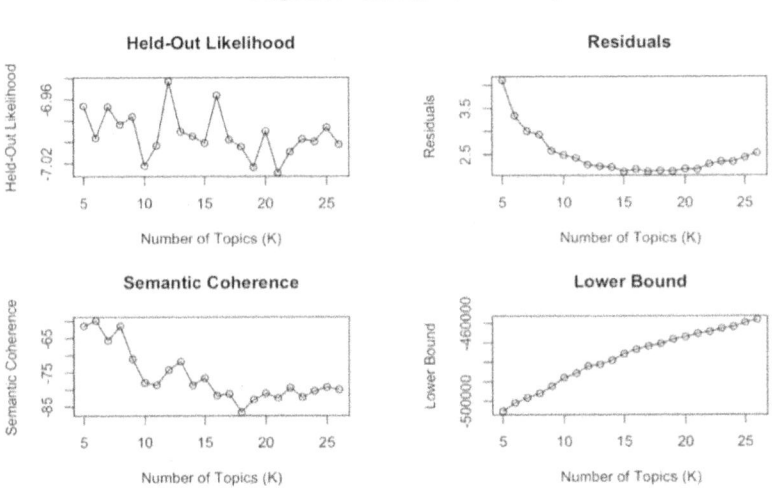

Fig. 1. Diagnostic Values by Number of Topics

Identified Topics and Their Descriptions. After finalizing K = 8, the LDA model was run to extract top-ranked words for each topic, and descriptive labels were assigned based on word distributions. The resulting eight topics reflect the primary functions of AI-powered tools across educational and professional contexts.

The frequency distribution of AI tool categories is presented in Table 1. Results indicate that tools supporting textual generation and research tasks are dominant. Content Creation and Generation (28.9%) and Summarization and Research Assistance (25.8%) together comprise over half the dataset, suggesting a productivity-oriented focus in current AI tool development. In contrast, Interactive Learning and Educational (2.3%) and Language Learning and Communication (3.4%) tools are underrepresented, highlighting a potential gap in AI support for personalized, student-centered learning.

Table 1. Frequency of Topics

Topic	Description	Frequency	Proportion (%)
Content Creation and Generation	Tools for content creation, essay writing, and article generation	258	28.9%
Summarization and Research Assistance	Systems for summarizing, retrieving, and analyzing documents	231	25.8%
Writing Enhancement and Grammar Support	Tools focused on essay writing, grammar checking, and structure support	116	13.0%
General Writing and Text Processing	Platforms for text formatting, paraphrasing, and stylistic refinement	108	12.1%
Coding Skill Development	Tools for code suggestions, debugging, and software development	71	7.9%
Data Analysis and Business Insights	Applications for customer insights, research data, and team collaboration	59	6.6%
Language Learning and Communication	Tools for vocabulary, feedback, and interactive language use	30	3.4%
Interactive Learning Support	Platforms that support student-centered, dynamic, and animated learning	21	2.3%

4.2 RQ2. What Cognitive, Metacognitive, and Affective Aspects of Learning Do the AI-Powered Tools Aim to Enhance?

The optimal number of clusters was determined using the elbow method, with four clusters selected for the final analysis (Fig. 2). Table 2 presents descriptive statistics for each cluster, while Table 3 reports ANOVA results, confirming detectable differences across clusters ($p < .001$ for all dimensions). The eight topical categories of AI tools are not mutually exclusive within the cognitive, metacognitive, and affective dimensions; although each category has distinct goals, many tools span multiple aspects of learning. To illustrate their distribution across both the four clusters and the eight topical categories, we present representative examples: *QuizWhiz* and *AIQuizMe* (Content Creation and Generation), *ExplainPaper* and *DocuAsk* (Summarization and Research Assistance), *Wordtune* and *AI Buddy* (Writing Enhancement and Grammar Support), *AI Code Mentor* and *Dev Codes* (Coding Skill Development), *TreeMind*, *CoolMindMaps* and *Mathly* (Interactive Learning Support), and *Langotalk* and *LearnLingo* (Language Learning and Communication).

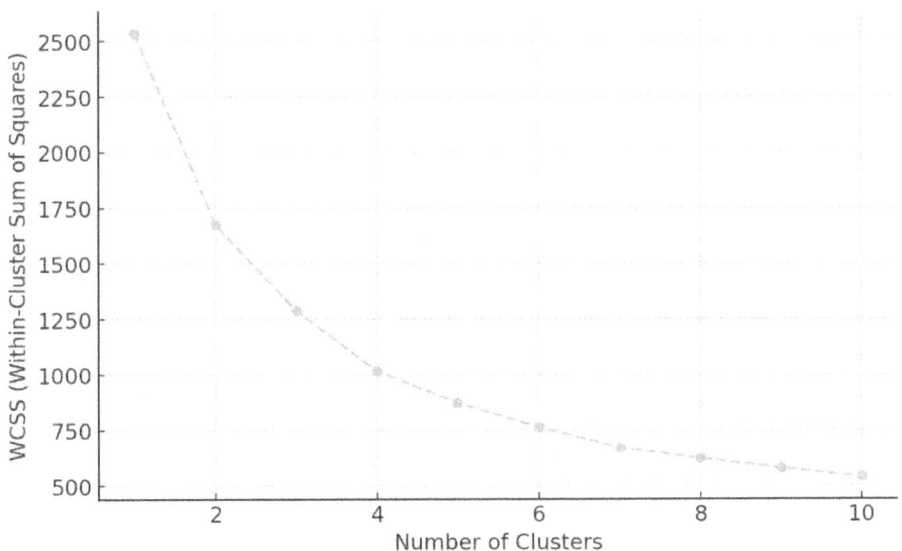

Fig. 2. WCSS VS. Number of Clusters

Table 2. Descriptive Statistics

Cluster	Cognitive		Metacognitive		Affective	
	M	SD	M	SD	M	SD
1 (n = 425)	1.06	1.00	0.53	0.49	1.40	1.01
2 (n = 105)	5.67	1.43	1.17	1.00	4.09	1.99
3 (n = 158)	1.66	1.10	0.82	0.62	5.25	1.63
4 (n = 110)	1.63	1.26	2.80	0.72	2.84	1.59

Cluster One: Consists of tools with low scores across all dimensions ($M = 1.06$, 0.53, 1.40, respectively), indicating minimal engagement in cognitive, metacognitive, or affective support. Cluster Two is characterized by high cognitive scores ($M = 5.67$) and moderate affective support ($M = 4.09$), suggesting these tools focus on cognitive development while incorporating some motivational elements. Cluster Three emphasizes affective support ($M = 5.25$) while offering moderate cognitive and metacognitive features, likely designed to enhance learner engagement. Finally, Cluster Four stands out for high metacognitive scores ($M = 2.80$), indicating tools that prioritize self-monitoring and regulation in learning.

Cognitive Support (Cluster Two): AI-powered tools in this group primarily support Remembering, Understanding, Analyzing, and Creating, based on Bloom's taxonomy. Content generation tools such as *QuizWhiz* and *AIQuizMe* reinforce information retrieval and self-assessment through quiz-based learning. Research assistance tools, including *ExplainPaper* and *DocuAsk*, help to simplify and enhance the processing of complex information to promote Understanding through interactive text highlighting, question-based exploration, and AI-generated explanations. Summarization tools like *Eightify Explore* and *Summary Box* aid efficient information extraction by summarizing video content linked to specific timestamps, supporting knowledge organization. Through interactive learning, AI-powered mind-mapping tools like *TreeMind* and *CoolMindMaps* enhance the structuring and retention of complex knowledge.

AI-driven data analysis tools support Analytical thinking, with *Deepnote* enabling learners to visualize data through customize charts and graphs, while *Elicit* facilitates evidence synthesis and cross-study comparisons in research. Coding skill development such as *AI Code Mentor* and *AI Dev Codes* support learning programming through reviewing, optimizing, and debugging learner codes, and facilitating understanding code by providing detailed explanations for code sections. However, few AI tools in the data explicitly support cognitive processes of Applying and Evaluating, revealing a gap in current AI tools development focusing on higher-order cognitive processes.

Table 3. Analysis of Variance

	F-statistic	p-value
Cognitive	482.23	<.001
Metacognitive	376.02	<.001
Affective	335.54	<.001

Affective Support (Cluster Three): From the perspective of CVT (Pekrun, 2006), AI-powered tools in this cluster enhance learners' perceived control and task value by providing personalized assistance, adaptive guidance, and cognitive load reduction. Writing assistants like *AI Buddy* and *Wordtune* offer tailored feedback and scaffolding, improving learners' confidence and engagement. Research tools such as *Research PAL* and *ExplainPaper* simplify complex information, easing cognitive load and promoting learner autonomy. By fostering a sense of control and task relevance, these tools contribute to positive emotions and sustained motivation. Nevertheless, while AI tools excel in personalization through adaptive feedback and tailored support, their ability to dynamically respond to learners' emotional states remains limited. Most AI tools prioritize task personalization rather than real-time emotional adaptation, reducing their capacity to respond to fluctuating engagement and motivation.

Metacognitive Support (Cluster Four): AI tools in this cluster focus on planning, self-monitoring, and strategic regulation. For example, writing assistance tools such as *ReviewGPT* enhances metacognitive awareness by providing real-time feedback on grammar, clarity, tone, and coherence, allowing learners continuously monitor and refine writing. Similarly, interactive learning support tools such as *Mathly* supports self-reflection on problem-solving strategies by enabling students to compare their reasoning with the AI's explanations and promoting error analysis and strategic adjustments.

However, while some AI tools facilitate self-reflection and progress tracking, few provide comprehensive guidance on strategic planning, adaptive metacognition, or SRL strategies. This limitation may imply that while AI can assist in monitoring and evaluating learning, its ability to guide students in setting goals, adjusting study tactics, and regulating their learning remains largely undeveloped.

5 Discussion and Implication

Findings from this study provide a structured analysis of how AI-powered tools engage users with cognitive, metacognitive, and affective learning dimensions, highlighting both their potential and limitations. We found that the AI tools from the dataset mainly claim to support lower-order cognitive processes, such as Remembering and Understanding, through quizzing, summarization, and explanations. Yet, their functionalities for facilitating higher-order thinking remain limited. While some AI tools assist with knowledge retrieval and comprehension, fewer support Applying and Evaluating, which are essential for problem-solving and critical thinking. For instance, in computing education, AI simulators can challenge students to design and test coding skills, but AI tools must go beyond simple feedback to engage learners in deeper reasoning and iterative problem-solving. However, moving beyond cognitive processes, AI tools can build on these cognitive functionalities and enhance motivation and engagement by providing personalized feedback and reducing cognitive load, aligning with CVT (Pekrun, 2006). Nevertheless, most AI tools lack robust emotional adaptation, meaning they do not dynamically adjust responses based on learners' affective states, such as frustration and disengagement (Vistorte et al., 2024). To address this, future research should explore affect-based AI-powered systems that integrate emotion recognition to provide adaptive support in real-time (Fernández-Herrero, 2024; Jia and Tu, 2024). These advancements could mitigate disengagement and improve long-term learning retention.

Metacognitive support is another critical area where AI tools show promise but require further refinement. As theorized by Nelson and Narens (1994), there is an interdependent relationship between cognition and metacognition. While some tools claim to assist with self-monitoring and reflection, they often assume learners to have sufficient cognitive strategic resources for self-regulation. Furthermore, AI tools like *ReviewGPT* and *Mathly* claim to help students track progress and identify errors, but very few provide metacognitive prompts or visualizations (i.e., learning analytics) that facilitate goal-setting, strategic planning, or long-term learning adjustments (Fernandes et al., 2024). To date, to achieve these metacognitive purposes for learning, learners are required to actively prompt cognitive AI tools. This phenomenon explains when these AI tools claim to support metacognitive learning functions, students often do not have enough cognitive resources to function metacognitively. Instead, they heavily rely on AI-generated responses without critically analyzing or reflecting on their own learning process. In this way, students may miss opportunities to develop independent SRL strategies. To address this, future AI-driven learning tools should consider incorporating adaptive learning pathways, goal-setting recommendations, and iterative self-assessment mechanisms SRL (Chang et al., 2023; Lin et al., 2024a; Ng et al., 2024).

Another key finding of this study is that many AI-powered tools prioritize productivity over deeper learning experiences. The largest cluster of tools analyzed did not explicitly focus on cognitive, metacognitive, or affective learning support, reinforcing concerns that AI integration in education is often driven by convenience rather than pedagogical alignment. Previous research emphasizing the importance of aligning AI development with educational theories (Ouyang and Jiao, 2021; Xu and Ouyang, 2022). Without careful pedagogical integration, AI risks promoting passive learning behaviours and metacognitive laziness (Ahmad et al., 2023; Zhai et al., 2024). To maximize AI's educational impact, we recommend designing AI as a scaffolding tool rather than a substitute for cognitive engagement, ensuring that it supports active, self-regulated, and meaningful learning.

For AI-powered tools to be effective in education, several key areas require further development. Current AI tools primarily support lower-order cognitive processes but need to expand to facilitate higher-order thinking, including Applying and Evaluating knowledge based on Bloom's taxonomy. Additionally, AI-driven tutors should incorporate real-time affective recognition to respond dynamically to students' emotions, enhancing motivation and engagement. In the metacognitive domain, we recommend AI tools to provide beyond corrective feedback to guide learners in goal-setting, self-monitoring, and adaptive learning strategies. Addressing these gaps can transition AI-powered tools from productivity aids to intelligent learning partners that foster deeper, and more independent SRL.

Despite these potential advancements, this study has limitations. First, the dataset may not fully represent the diversity of AI tools in education, particularly those developed after 2023. Furthermore, the focus on the top 20 percent of tools, selected for their completeness, functionality, and educational relevance, may introduce selection bias. While this approach enhances interpretability and analytical clarity (Bornmann and Williams, 2013), it may overlook insights from less prominent or emerging tools that could offer innovative pedagogical value. Additionally, the reliance on textual descriptions in topic modeling may not capture the full range of tool functionalities or contextual applications. Finally, the study emphasizes functional and theoretical alignments, without accounting for broader social, philosophical, and ethical considerations surrounding AI adoption in education (Ouyang and Jiao, 2021). Future research should address these dimensions to ensure responsible, inclusive, and contextually aware implementation of AI in learning environments.

Acknowledgments. This research was supported by the Social Sciences and Humanities Research Council of Canada (SSHRC), 430-2024-00269 (Michael Lin).

Disclosure of Interests. The authors have no competing interests to declare that are relevant to the content of this article.

References

Ahmad, S.F., et al.: Impact of artificial intelligence on human loss in decision making, laziness and safety in education. Human. Soc. Sci. Commun. **10**(1), 1–14 (2023). https://doi.org/10.1057/s41599-023-01787-8

Anderson, R.C., Pearson, P.D.: A schema-theoretic view of basic processes in reading comprehension. In: Pearson, P.D., Barr, R., Kamil, M.L., Mosenthal, P. (eds.) Handbook of Reading Research, pp. 255–291. Longman Inc., New York (1984)

Anderson, L., Krathwohl, D.A.: Taxonomy for Learning, Teaching and Assessing: A Revision of Bloom's Taxonomy of Educational Objectives. Longman, New York (2001)

Bai, L., Liu, X., Su, J.: ChatGPT: the cognitive effects on learning and memory. Brain-X **1**(3), e30 (2023). https://doi.org/10.1002/brx2.30

Blei, D.M., Ng, A.Y., Jordan, M.I.: Latent Dirichlet allocation. J. Mach. Learn. Res. **3**(Jan), 993–1022 (2003)

Bloom, B.S., Engelhart, M.D., Furst, E.J., Hill, W.H., Krathwohl, D.R.: Taxonomy of Educational Objectives: The Classification of Educational Goals. Handbook I: Cognitive Domain. David McKay Company, New York (1956)

Bornmann, L., Williams, R.: How to calculate the practical significance of citation impact differences? An empirical example from evaluative institutional bibliometrics using adjusted predictions and marginal effects. J. Informet. **7**(2), 562–574 (2013). https://doi.org/10.1016/j.joi.2013.02.005

Bureau, O.: AI Tools - Open Dataset - 4000 tools / 50 categories. Harvard Dataverse, V1, UNF:6:0OQxqyCsirkXlwENiEcEcQ (2023). https://doi.org/10.7910/DVN/QLSXZG

Chang, D.H., Lin, M.P.C., Hajian, S., Wang, Q.Q.: Educational design principles of using AI Chatbot that supports self-regulated learning in education: goal setting, feedback, and personalization. Sustainability **15**(17) (2023). https://doi.org/10.3390/su151712921

Chiu, T.K.F., Moorhouse, B.L., Chai, C.S., Ismailov, M.: Teacher support and student motivation to learn with Artificial Intelligence (AI) based chatbot. Interact. Learn. Environ. **32**(7), 3240–3256 (2023). https://doi.org/10.1080/10494820.2023.2172044, https://www.frontiersin.org/journals/education/articles/10.3389/feduc.2024.1418006/full

Chiu, T.K., Xia, Q., Zhou, X., Chai, C.S., Cheng, M.: Systematic literature review on opportunities, challenges, and future research recommendations of artificial intelligence in education. Comput. Educ. Artif. Intell. **4**, 100118 (2023). https://doi.org/10.1016/j.caeai.2022.100118

Elim, E.H.S.Y.: Promoting cognitive skills in AI-supported learning environments: the integration of bloom's taxonomy. Education **3–13**, 1–11 (2024). https://doi.org/10.1080/03004279.2024.2332469

Essel, H.B., Vlachopoulos, D., Essuman, A.B., Amankwa, J.O.: ChatGPT effects on cognitive skills of undergraduate students: receiving instant responses from AI-based conversational large language models (LLMs). Comput. Educ.: Artif. Intell. **6**, 100198 (2024). https://doi.org/10.1016/j.caeai.2023.100198

Feinerer, I., Hornik, K., Meyer, D.: Text mining infrastructure in R. J. Stat. Softw. **25**(5), 1–54 (2008). https://doi.org/10.18637/jss.v025.i05

Fernández-Herrero, J.: Evaluating recent advances in affective intelligent tutoring systems: a scoping review of educational impacts and future prospects. Educ. Sci. **14**, 839 (2024). https://doi.org/10.3390/educsci14080839

Fernandes, D., et al.: AI makes you smarter, but none the wiser: the disconnect between performance and metacognition. arXiv preprint arXiv:2409.16708 (2024). https://doi.org/10.48550/arXiv.2409.16708

Huang, A.Y., Lu, O.H., Yang, S.J.: Effects of artificial Intelligence-Enabled personalized recommendations on learners' learning engagement, motivation, and outcomes in a flipped classroom. Comput. Educ. **194**, 104684 (2023). https://doi.org/10.1016/j.compedu.2022.104684

Jain, A.K.: Data clustering: 50 years beyond K-means. Pattern Recogn. Lett. **31**(8), 651–666 (2010). https://doi.org/10.1016/j.patrec.2009.09.011

Jia, X.H., Tu, J.C.: Towards a new conceptual model of AI-enhanced learning for college students: the roles of artificial intelligence capabilities, general self-efficacy, learning motivation, and critical thinking awareness. Systems **12**(3), 74 (2024). https://doi.org/10.3390/systems12030074

Kilinç, H.K., Keçecioğlu, Ö.F.: Generative artificial intelligence: a historical and future perspective. J. Eng. Smart Syst. **12**(2), 47–58 (2024). https://doi.org/10.21541/apjess.1398155

Lai, C.Y., Cheung, K.Y., Chan, C.S.: Exploring the role of intrinsic motivation in ChatGPT adoption to support active learning: an extension of the technology acceptance model. Comput. Educ. Artif. Intell. **5**, 100178 (2023). https://doi.org/10.1016/j.caeai.2023.100178

Lin, M.P.-C., Chang, D.: CHAT-ACTS: a pedagogical framework for personalized chatbot to enhance active learning and self-regulated learning. Comput. Educ. Artif. Intell. **5**, 100167 (2023). https://doi.org/10.1016/j.caeai.2023.100167

Lin, M.P.-C., Chang, D.H., Winne, P.H.: A proposed methodology for investigating student-chatbot interaction patterns in giving peer feedback. Educ. Tech. Res. Dev. (2024a). https://doi.org/10.1007/s11423-024-10408-3

Lin, M.P.-C., Liu, A.L., Poitras, E., Chang, M., Chang, D.H.: An exploratory study on the efficacy and inclusivity of AI technologies in diverse learning environments. Sustainability **16**(20), 8992 (2024b). https://doi.org/10.3390/su16208992

Liu, C., Hou, J., Tu, Y.F., Wang, Y., Hwang, G.J.: Incorporating a reflective thinking promoting mechanism into artificial intelligence-supported English writing environments. Interact. Learn. Environ. **31**(9), 5614–5632 (2023). https://doi.org/10.1080/10494820.2021.2012812

Liu, M., Zhang, L.J., Biebricher, C.: Investigating students' cognitive processes in generative AI-assisted digital multimodal composing and traditional writing. Comput. Educ. **211**, 104977 (2024). https://doi.org/10.1016/j.compedu.2023.104977

Methlagl, M., Taslimi, N.J., Rudloff, C., Majcen, J.: Exploring research topics and trends in early childhood education using structural topic modeling. SN Soc. Sci. **4**(10), 183 (2024). https://doi.org/10.1007/s43545-024-00982-x

Nelson, T.O., Narens, L.: Why investigate metacognition? In: Metcalfe, J., Shimamura, A.P. (eds.) Metacognition: Knowing About Knowing. MIT Press (1994). https://doi.org/10.7551/mitpress/4561.001.0001

Ng, D.T.K., Tan, C.W., Leung, J.K.L.: Empowering student self-regulated learning and science education through ChatGPT: a pioneering pilot study. Br. J. Edu. Technol. **55**, 1328–1353 (2024). https://doi.org/10.1111/bjet.13454

Ouyang, F., Jiao, P.: Artificial intelligence in education: the three paradigms. Comput. Educ. Artif. Intell. **2**, 100020 (2021). https://doi.org/10.1016/j.caeai.2021.100020

Pekrun, R.: The control-value theory of achievement emotions: assumptions, corollaries, and implications for educational research and practice. Educ. Psychol. Rev. **18**(4), 315–341 (2006). https://doi.org/10.1007/s10648-006-9029-9

Pekrun, R., Goetz, T., Titz, W., Perry, R.P.: Academic emotions in students' self-regulated learning and achievement: a program of qualitative and quantitative research. Educ. Psychol. **37**(2), 91–105 (2002). https://doi.org/10.1207/S15326985EP3702_4

Pergantis, P., Bamicha, V., Skianis, C., Drigas, A.: AI Chatbots and cognitive control: enhancing executive functions through Chatbot interactions: a systematic review. Brain Sci. **15**(1), 47 (2025). https://doi.org/10.3390/brainsci15010047

Rinker, T.W.: qdap-tm Package Compatibility (2018). http://cran.nexr.com/web/packages/qdap/vignettes/tm_package_compatibility.pdf

Roberts, M.E., Stewart, B.M., Tingley, D., Airoldi, E.M.: The structural topic model and applied social science. In: Advances in Neural Information Processing Systems Workshop on Topic Models: Computation, Application, and Evaluation, vol. 4, no. 1, pp. 1–20 (2013)

Roberts, M.E., Stewart, B.M., Tingley, D.: STM: an R package for structural topic models. J. Stat. Softw. **91**(2), 1–40 (2019). https://doi.org/10.18637/jss.v091.i02

Ryan, R.M., Deci, E.L.: Self-determination theory and the facilitation of intrinsic motivation, social development, and well-being. Am. Psychol. **55**(1), 68–78 (2000). https://doi.org/10.1037/0003-066X.55.1.68

Seo, K., Tang, J., Roll, I., Fels, S., Yoon, D.: The impact of artificial intelligence on learner–instructor interaction in online learning. Int. J. Educ. Technol. High. Educ. **18**(1), 54 (2021). https://doi.org/10.1186/s41239-021-00292-9

Sievert, C., Shirley, K.: LDAvis: a method for visualizing and interpreting topics. In: Chuang, J., Green, S., Hearst, M., Heer, J., Koehn, P. (eds.) Proceedings of the Workshop on Interactive Language Learning, Visualization, and Interfaces, pp. 63–70. Association for Computational Linguistics (2014). https://doi.org/10.3115/v1/W14-3110

Shanmugasundaram, M., Tamilarasu, A.: The impact of digital technology, social media, and artificial intelligence on cognitive functions: a review. Front. Cogn. **2**, 1203077 (2023). https://doi.org/10.3389/fcogn.2023.1203077

Shen, X., Tao, Y.: Metacognitive strategies, AI-based writing self-efficacy and writing anxiety in AI-assisted writing contexts: a structural equation modeling analysis. Int. J. TESOL Stud. **7**(1), 70–87 (2025). https://doi.org/10.58304/ijts.20250105

Skorkovská, L.: Application of lemmatization and summarization methods in topic identification module for large scale language modeling data filtering. In: Sojka, P., Horák, A., Kopeček, I., Pala, K. (eds.) Text, Speech and Dialogue, pp. 191–198. Springer, Heidelberg (2012)

Sweller, J.: Cognitive load during problem solving: effects on learning. Cogn. Sci. **12**(2), 257–285 (1988). https://doi.org/10.1207/s15516709cog1202_4

Valdivia, A.E.O., Osorio, C.M., Velasco-Bejarano, B., Vargas-Rodríguez, Y.M.: Evaluating cognitive and affective development in chemistry students using AI-supported problem-based learning. Am. J. Educ. Res. **12**(11), 447–454 (2024). https://doi.org/10.12691/education-12-11-5

Vistorte, A.O.R., Deroncele-Acosta, A., Ayala, J.L.M., Barrasa, A., López-Granero, C., Martí-González, M.: Integrating artificial intelligence to assess emotions in learning environments: a systematic literature review. Front. Psychol. **15**, 1387089 (2024). https://doi.org/10.3389/fpsyg.2024.1387089

Xu, W., Ouyang, F.: A systematic review of AI role in the educational system based on a proposed conceptual framework. Educ. Inf. Technol. **27**(3), 4195–4223 (2022). https://doi.org/10.1007/s10639-021-10774-y

Zhai, C., Wibowo, S., Li, L.D.: The effects of over-reliance on AI dialogue systems on students' cognitive abilities: a systematic review. Smart Learn. Environ. **11**(1), 28 (2024). https://doi.org/10.1186/s40561-024-00316-7

Zimmerman, B.J.: Chapter 2—Attaining self-regulation: a social cognitive perspective. In: Boekaerts, M., Pintrich, P.R., Zeidner, M.: (eds.) Handbook of Self-regulation, pp. 13–39. Academic Press (2000). https://doi.org/10.1016/B978-012109890-2/50031-7

Unravelling Emotional Nuances: A Cross-Linguistic Analysis of Sentiment Differences in Multilingual Movie Versions

Adam Wynn[1]($^{\boxtimes}$), Jingyun Wang[1], and Xiaoyan Li[2]

[1] Durham University, Durham, UK
{adam.t.wynn,jingyun.wang}@durham.ac.uk
[2] Kyushu University, Fukuoka, Japan

Abstract. To facilitate automatic knowledge creation for the learners of intercultural communication, we propose a pipeline that combines AI analytics with human-in-the-loop evaluation. A case study was conducted on the English and Japanese versions of the film 'Spirited Away'. Speech segments from both versions were extracted and processed using Valence-Arousal-Dominance (VAD) scores and discrete emotion classification, generated by pre-trained Wav2Vec 2.0 models. The segments with the highest discrepancies in emotions were identified for further analysis by a group of human raters. This approach not only improves the understanding of emotional differences in dubbed media but also benefits researchers studying cross-cultural communications by assisting knowledge discovery and the creation of knowledge pools. These insights may also contribute to the design of intelligent tutoring systems (ITS) for cross-cultural communication education, enhancing the overall learning experience for learners.

Keywords: Cross-linguistic analysis · Speech Emotion Recognition · Cultural Learning · Emotion Perception · Wav2Vec 2.0

1 Introduction

Cross-cultural communication education focuses on developing the students' knowledge of how to operate in a culture other than in their own [3]. However, it is time-consuming for instructors to prepare suitable materials manually. This challenge is particularly significant when it comes to addressing emotional differences across cultures, as emotion is deeply tied to an individual's cultural background. Whilst some researchers consider emotion to be a universal construct and that a large part of emotional experience is biologically based, emotion is also heavily influenced by the environment an individual grew up in [4]. Therefore, the way humans express emotions can vary across different languages due to different cultural backgrounds [7].

However, in the field of cross-linguistic sentiment analysis, existing tools tend to focus on text rather than speech, leaving gaps in the comparison of emotional nuances across languages [18]. Developing tools that account for these cultural differences, especially in speech, could significantly enhance educational resources in cross-cultural communication, enabling students to better understand how emotion varies across cultural contexts.

On the other hand, the emotional discrepancies between the same word or phrase under different cultural settings could, when translated directly, often cause confusion, and even lead to conflicts [9]. Analysing emotional content across languages manually is a complex and time-consuming process, especially when dealing with spoken audio. Human annotators often face challenges in consistently identifying and categorizing emotions because emotional perception is subjective where different raters might interpret the same audio in different ways based on their cultural background. Identifying subtle emotional cues requires in-depth knowledge of both languages and culture [17]. Moreover, emotional experiences are often dulled when listening in a second language compared to a listener's native language [2]. Intelligent tutoring systems (ITS) could address these challenges by integrating AI-driven emotion analysis into language learning environments, providing students with real-time feedback on how emotional expression varies across languages.

Therefore, this paper aims to design a AI-based pipeline to support the exploration of the subtle emotional differences between multilingual versions of movies and facilitate the automatic creation of knowledge pools for learners of intercultural communications. To achieve this, a series of deep learning models automatically identify and extract segments of audio, eliminating the need for manual inspection of each sentence. Subsequently, for effectiveness evaluation we conducted a case study on the movie 'Spirited Away' by examining the sentiment conveyed in the audio of the English and Japanese versions to discover the segments that are significantly different in emotion.

In particular, this paper compares how native English and Japanese speakers, as well as non-native bilingual speakers, perceive emotional content in these identified segments. The focus group discussions highlight the importance of a "human-in-the-loop" approach and the importance of human input in understanding emotions that may be missed by AI models alone, and the data analysis is intended to explore how these differences can inform the design of intelligent tutoring systems (ITS) for intercultural communication education, enabling more accurate and culturally aware learning experiences for students.

By automating the process of detecting emotional disparities in subtitles, we aim to facilitate cross-cultural communication analysis and foster a deeper understanding of how cultural contexts shape linguistic expression. This project has the potential to streamline research efforts and contribute to the broader field of intercultural studies. Through the development process of the pipeline, we aim to answer the following research questions:

- **RQ1:** Are the Valence-Arousal-Dominance (VAD) model and discrete emotion classification models appropriate for analysing cross-linguistic emotional content in audio data?
- **RQ2:** How do individuals from different cultural and linguistic backgrounds perceive emotional content in the audio of English and Japanese versions of the same movie, and what implications does this have for education?

In this pipeline, we have, for the first time, devised a subtitle matching algorithm with high accuracy, trained an emotion classification model using high-dimensional audio representations, and performed quantitative analysis to extract discrepancies using the projected VAD states. Through this project, we contribute to the field of cross-linguistic sentiment analysis and provide valuable insights into how cultural differences shape emotional perception for researchers and learners of cross-cultural communication. The findings could inform ITS design, allowing for adaptive learning experiences that help students develop a deeper understanding of how cultural contexts influence emotional expression. By combining the power of AI-based analytics with human expertise, this paper proposes a robust pipeline that extracts the emotional nuances of language and contributes to the advancement of cross-linguistic sentiment analysis.

2 Related Work

2.1 Emotional Theory

In the study of emotions, there are two primary approaches to representing emotion: using Discrete Emotions and the VAD model. Central to the discrete approach is Ekman's identification of six basic emotions: anger, joy, surprise, disgust, fear, and sadness [4]. These emotions, which are fundamental to human experience, form the basis for many psychological and computational models in understanding emotional responses across different cultures and contexts, making them critical to sentiment analysis and cross-cultural emotional studies.

Another approach which quantifies emotions and provides a more detailed view of emotional expression, is the Valence-Arousal-Dominance (VAD) model [12] that represents emotions as a 3-dimensional vector with each dimension ranging from -1 to 1. Valence ranges from negative to positive and expresses the pleasant or unpleasant feeling about something, arousal measures the intensity of the emotion ranging from calm to excitement, and dominance reflects the level of control, from submissive to dominant. This model has been widely adopted in psychological studies and more recently in machine learning for sentiment analysis [16]. By capturing emotions in this multidimensional space, the VAD model offers a more nuanced understanding of emotional expression, particularly in cross-cultural contexts, providing the foundation for further computational approaches, such as audio processing and speech recognition.

2.2 Audio Processing

To prepare continuous speech signals for machine learning models, several preprocessing steps are necessary, including noise reduction and feature extraction.

Noise reduction algorithms reduce unwanted background noise in audio recordings. Traditionally, noise reduction algorithms such as the noisereduce algorithm [13] consist of spatial filtering but if the entire recording has inconsistent noise levels, the de-noised audio outputs will be unsuitable for audio processing. To address this, deep learning approaches, such as Nvidia's CleanUNet model [6], propose to leverage encoder-decoder architectures and self-attention mechanisms to achieve more effective denoising.

Traditional methods for feature extraction involve breaking down raw waveforms into frames, and performing windowing techniques and Fourier transforms to convert signals from the time domain to the frequency domain. Features such as Mel Frequency Cepstral Coefficients [15] have been widely used to capture essential acoustic features, particularly for speech and music processing [14].

2.3 Speech Emotion Recognition

Deep learning enables the use of the rich high-dimensional representations of audio segments, and subsequently allows us to translate this encoding into emotion scores using a decoder model. A prominent example is Wav2vec 2.0 [1] which employs a transformer network to build a contextualised representation, trained similarly on a contrastive task that requires 100 times fewer data. Wav2vec 2.0 proposed several variants, including XLSR-Wav2vec 2.0 (XLSR), which learns cross-lingual speech representations by performing the contrastive training task in more than 56,000 h in 53 languages and outperforms the best-known results over several benchmarks. However, Wav2vec models are not robust to noisy speeches so speech segments should be de-noised before processing them. Alternatively, HuBERT [5] uses hidden units that are analogous to word tokens in BERT to transform speech data into a more language-like structure.

Pepino et al. (2021) investigated the use of Wav2Vec 2.0 embeddings for speech emotion recognition (SER) by leveraging multiple layers of the pre-trained model with adaptive weighting. Their approach applied transfer learning, utilizing a version of Wav2Vec 2.0 fine-tuned for automatic speech recognition (ASR) to enhance SER performance. However, they discovered that ASR fine-tuning can discard features crucial for emotion recognition, such as pitch, which is unnecessary for ASR but plays a key role in SER.

3 Methodology

In this paper, a novel machine learning pipeline is devised to extract instances of emotional misalignment in the movie, as shown in Fig. 1. In this section, each step of the pipeline will be illustrated in detail. To preliminarily evaluate our pipeline, we apply it to the analysis of the movie *Spirited Away*, by Hayao Miyazaki. The source audio in both Japanese original and English-dubbed audio is in raw waveform (.wav) format, sampled at 16 kHz.

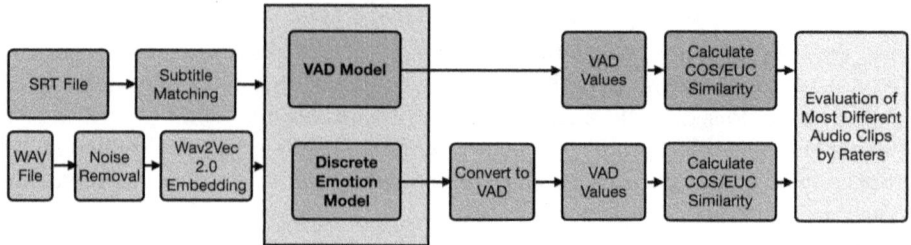

Fig. 1. Overall Pipeline involving AI Emotion Detection and Human Evaluation

3.1 Timestamp Matching and De-noising Operation

The corresponding subtitles in Japanese and English were obtained from Netflix in SubRip Subtitle (.srt) format. The Japanese subtitle file consists of 1,466 lines, whereas the English subtitle file consists of only 1,119 lines. However, the number of lines in the two subtitle files is different due to the differences in length and grammatical nature of the two languages. This along with accessibility captions gives rise to mismatching timestamps. In order to process texts and audio segments, the subtitle files are pre-processed to find the matching timestamps.

An algorithm to match and merge the subtitles in two languages is designed. We take each pair of timestamps in the Japanese subtitles, and attempt to match a pair of timestamps in the English subtitles where the start and end timestamps are both within a short threshold of the corresponding Japanese start and end timestamps. For unmatched subtitles, the start times were matched using the same threshold, while the end times were matched with an increased threshold in subsequent subtitle entries across both languages. If a match is found, the timestamps and subtitles for all entries between the start and end are merged, resulting in a pair of subtitles with the same duration. Any remaining unmatched entries are discarded. This algorithm maximizes the number of subtitle matches while ensuring that no two matched pairs have overlapping timestamps. As a result, we obtained 1,080 matched pairs of subtitles in both languages.

Given that noisy backgrounds significantly impair model performance [11], a denoising preprocessing step was incorporated into the pipeline to reduce the impact of noise in the subsequent models. The denoising process was applied to the audio segments using the CleanUNet model [6] to remove white noise, and also efficiently remove background music. This denoising operation also reduces the audio to a single channel for subsequent processing.

3.2 Audio Sentiment Analysis

After obtaining the denoised audio, we now predict the sentiment conveyed by the audio by leveraging the XLSR53-Wav2Vec 2.0 model [16] for its robustness to audio perturbations and fair gender accuracy. The extracted speech embeddings are then processed by the VAD model and the Discrete Emotion Model independently, as described below.

VAD Model. VAD analysis is performed using the pre-trained speech emotion recognition model as described Wagner et al. [16]. In the implementation, the denoised audio segments were first transformed into the log Mel frequency spectrum using the audeer package. The default parameters were used including a sampling rate 16 kHz, 1,024 hidden layer units and default dropout of 0.2. The final linear layer outputs three logit values corresponding to the Valence, Arousal and Domiance scores of the speech segment.

During pre-training, Concordance Correlation Coefficient (CCC) loss was employed alongside the Adam optimiser. During run-time, the logits are passed through a Tanh layer to yield normalised VAD values between 0 and 1. We then linearly interpolated to correspond to the original VAD psychological model.

Discrete Emotion Model. Leveraging the representational power of the Wav2Vec 2.0 model, two standalone 6-class emotion recognition models were trained for English and Japanese. The training process is set to run for 10 epochs, using a batch size of 4 with a learning rate of 1e−4 to optimize performance.

The two emotion classification models were trained on noise-free versions of the JVNV dataset [19] for Japanese and the RAVDESS dataset [8] for English. For both datasets, we maintained an equal gender ratio in the speech samples, as well as ensured similar dataset sizes and audio recording lengths. A batch size of 100 was used, with a learning rate starting at $1e^{-4}$. The discrete model achieved an accuracy of 90.5% for the RAVDESS dataset and 98.6% for the JVNV dataset using 5-fold validation. The datasets were balanced for emotion and gender to ensure fairness and reduce potential biases, and across languages, we ensured similar dataset sizes and recording lengths.

Table 1. Emotion Dimension Values for Ekman's six basic emotions [4]

	Valence	Arousal	Dominance
Anger	−0.43	0.67	0.34
Joy	0.76	0.48	0.35
Surprise	0.4	0.67	−0.13
Disgust	−0.6	0.35	0.11
Fear	−0.64	0.6	−0.43
Sadness	−0.63	0.27	−0.33

For each speech segment in both languages, a predicted probability for each of the six emotions is obtained. To compare the emotions quantitatively, we compute a *weighted average VAD score* by applying the VAD coordinates of each of the six basic emotions (see Table 1) weighted by the predicted probability. This method allows for a nuanced analysis of complex emotional states, enabling distance measures between predictions in both languages. For example, a prediction of 50% happiness and 50% surprise can be evaluated continuously between their VAD scores rather than discretely.

3.3 Evaluation Metrics

For the predicted VAD values generated by the VAD and Discrete Emotion models, the audio segments with the highest discrepancies were identified using two measures: cosine similarity and Euclidean distance across each dimension. Cosine similarity provides a similarity score ranging from -1 to 1 and is insensitive to relative magnitude. This is particularly useful for assessing the similarity in the type of emotion conveyed rather than its intensity. However, it is less effective when the same emotion is expressed in both languages but with varying intensities.

Conversely, Euclidean distance is heavily influenced by magnitude, ranging from 0 (indicating identical VAD scores) to infinity. This measure is beneficial for comparing the intensity of emotions; for instance, it can effectively capture the difference in intensity of surprise conveyed between two speech segments. However, Euclidean distance can be affected by the scale of dimensions, as differences in the arousal dimension might disproportionately outweigh differences in the dominance dimension. To evaluate our pipeline, the top 10 audio segments with the highest distances are further analysed.

4 Results

Having identified the sentences with the largest emotional disparities using the machine learning pipeline, we intend to showcase the instances where the emotional interpretations diverged the most. In this study, the audio of the top 10 sentences for each metric (available at https://github.com/adamtwynn/Unravelling-Emotional-Nuances) were manually analysed by four raters: Rater A (native British English speaker, male, aged 20–25), Rater B (native Japanese speaker, female, aged 20–25), and Raters C and D (both proficient in both languages but not native, both female aged 40–50, D is a researcher in Cross-cultural Communications). Many of the sentences were the same across both metrics so any duplicates were removed from the analysis resulting in 15 audio samples for the VAD Model and 11 for the Discrete Model.

4.1 VAD Model Analysis

Each rater was first individually asked to answer the following questions which correspond to valence, arousal and dominance: "Does the English audio sound more positive than the Japanese audio?", "Does the English audio have more energy than the Japanese audio?", and "Does the English audio sound more in control than the Japanese audio?" and could answer on a scale from -2 (significantly less positive/energy/in control) to 2 (significantly more positive/energy/in control) with the option of adding an open comment for each audio clip.

To assess interrater reliability across raters, intraclass correlation coefficients (ICC) were calculated for each VAD dimension. Results indicated poor agreement for valence (ICC = −0.163, 95% CI [−0.25, 0.04], p = 0.951) and slight agreement for dominance (ICC = .103, 95% CI [−0.09, 0.42], p = 0.170), whilst fair agreement was observed for arousal (ICC = 0.287, 95% CI [0.05, 0.60], p = 0.008). Raters were more consistent when evaluating differences in energy levels (arousal) and the lower agreement for valence and dominance likely reflects the greater subjectivity and complexity involved in interpreting emotion across languages.

After each rater rated the top 10 audio clips for each metric, a focus group discussion was held to identify sentences where the raters had disagreements in their evaluations and to further discuss their ratings. Overall, out of the 15 sentences Rater A and B identified three sentences, and Rater D identified four sentences as having the same valence, arousal and dominance in both English and Japanese whereas rater C found no sentences with matching emotional expressions. This suggests that at least 11 out of the 15 sentences identified by the VAD Model contain differences in sentiment and are meaningful for cross-linguistic sentiment analysis.

Individual Rating Result Analysis. Rater A, the native English speaker, found that the valence and dominance of English and Japanese were similar on average (Valence: M=0.07, SD=0.8; Dominance: M=−0.13, SD=0.83). The mean value for arousal (M = −0.53, SD = 1.06) suggest a slight tendency to perceive the Japanese audio as more arousing and having more energy for the selected sentences compared to the English audio. Rater A also commented that the English audio often conveys more exaggerated or heightened emotions and hears sarcasm when the Japanese version sounds more angry. The Japanese audio is commented as sounding more in control and more accepting of situations particularly when the English version sounds worried. Rater B, the native Japanese speaker showed that Japanese valence (M=−0.4, SD=1.12) and arousal (M=−0.4, SD=1.24) were stronger than English indicating that the Japanese audio is slightly more negative with less energy. Similar to Rater A, the dominance mean (M=0.00, SD=0.84) suggests the rater on average thought dominance was similar in both language versions.

Raters C and D are proficient in both English and Japanese. Rater C rated the English audio, with a higher mean valence score (M=0.86, SD=0.86), while the arousal mean (M=−0.21, SD=1.31) indicates a slightly calmer interpretation of the Japanese audio. The dominance mean (M=0.00, SD=1.15) suggests that this rater thought dominance was similar in both language versions. Rater C identified the Japanese audio as more worried and intense, often conveying feelings of anger or frustration, whereas the English audio was perceived as more relaxed and more straightforward in delivery, and lacked energy compared to the Japanese version. In contrast, Rater D's scores for valence (M=−0.13, SD=1.18), arousal (M=−0.40, SD=1.18), and dominance (M=−0.33, SD=1.29) indicate a slight tendency to perceive the Japanese audio as more negative, arousing, and dominant. According to Rater D's comments, the Japanese version was often described as more direct and commanding while the English version appeared softer and more friendly, sometimes altering the meaning of the sentence, as seen in examples like 「イヤっ行かないでここにいてお願い」 (Please don't go)" in Japanese versus "No, don't leave me, I don't want to be alone" in English.

In summary, across the four raters, the Japanese audio is often described as more direct and intense, with stronger expressions of anger and worry, and the English audio, is typically seen as more calm and less emotional. The overall mean values across all raters: valence (0.13), arousal (−0.39), and dominance (−0.10), suggest that while English was generally perceived as slightly more positive in valence, Japanese tended to be more arousing and controlling. However, both Rater B and Rater C reported a mean dominance score of 0 which could suggest that the concept of dominance was hard to hear in the audio especially as differences in valence and arousal were found and emotional differences were mentioned in the open comments.

Focus Group Discussion for VAD Model. In the focus group, sentences with rater disagreement were discussed. The first pair of sentence where raters disagreed (A: 0, 1, 0; B: 0, 2, 1; C: 0, −1, 0; D: 1, 0 −1) was "Welcome. Always nice to see you." and 「いらっしゃいませお早いお着きで」. Rater A commented that the English sounded exaggerated, possibly because British English speakers don't use the phrase "Welcome" as frequently as in Japanese. Rater B, the native Japanese speaker felt that the Japanese version lacked the depth of feeling conveyed and the emotion wasn't as strong. Rater C (proficient in both languages) noted that the English version sounded less passionate, and rater D (also proficient in both) commented that the English version felt friendlier, while the Japanese sounded more in control. Moreover, the Japanese audio translated directly to "Welcome, please quickly get dressed," which may have affected the perception of dominance.

The sentence pair "Shoot, this is clearly harassment" (ちぇっ！見えすいたイビリしやがって) also had varying emotional interpretations among the raters (A: 0, −1, 1; B: −1, −1, 0; C: 0, 1, 0; D: 1, −1, 1). Rater A explained that the English audio sounded more sarcastic than angry, a nuance that the other raters did not pick up on. Rater B commented that English sounded more like complaining and the Japanese version was less strong and professional. Rater C noted that the Japanese version felt more emotional, slightly angry and "kuyashii", which translates to a feeling of frustration or regret over something unfair, and the English audio was more straightforwardly angry. Finally, Rater D commented that the Japanese version expressed stronger personal feelings, and similar to Rater B, the English version felt more professional and in control.

Another pair of sentence where raters disagreed (A: 1, −2, −1; B: −2, −1, 0; C: 1, −2, Not Clear; D: −1, −1, 2) was "He's destroying everything. It's costing us a fortune." (何をグズグズしてたんだいこのままじゃ大損だ). Rater A commented that Japanese sounded angrier and Rater C noted that the English version conveyed more disgust, whereas the Japanese version felt angrier, hence more negative. On the other hand, Rater B noted that the Japanese version sounded more acted and the anger didn't sound genuine. Rater D observed that the Japanese version criticized someone's behaviour personally, with a sense of threat for future consequences, while the English version emphasised that the damage had already been done, focusing on the fact that everything was already ruined.

Overall, the focus group discussion revealed how factors such as cultural nuances, as well as the raters' language background could cause differences in how the raters interpreted the emotion of English and Japanese audio clips. The discussion also highlighted the complexity of emotions, with raters often struggling to classify a single emotion in a single utterance and it was also noted that raters' opinions could change after listening again to the same audio.

4.2 Discrete Emotion Model Analysis

To evaluate the discrete model, at first each rater was individually asked to assign one of six possible emotions (angry, disgust, fear, happy, sad and surprised) to both the English and Japanese audio and also provided open-ended comments; then a focus group discussion was conducted. Interrater reliability was assessed using Fleiss' Kappa ($\kappa = 0.34$), indicating fair agreement among raters. Overall, Rater B found that all 11 sentences conveyed the same emotion in both languages, whilst Rater A identified 2 sentences with different emotions, Rater C identified 3, and Rater D identified 8. It is worth mentioning that rater D (a researcher in Cross-cultural Communications) highlighted that 6 out of 8 sentences are related to fear and the fear emotion in Japanese was weakened or absent in the English version.

Individual Rating Result Analysis. Rater A frequently identified fear as the dominant emotion. In the English audio, fear was selected five times, along with disgust and surprise twice, and sadness appeared once. For the Japanese audio, fear was also the most common emotion, identified five times, with angry, disgust, surprise, and sad each selected once. In rater A's open-ended responses they often felt that fear was more intense in the Japanese version, while anger, although present in both versions, was portrayed with a more restrained tone in the English audio.

In Rater B's evaluation of the audio, the same emotion was portrayed for both English and Japanese. Fear was identified in 6 out of 10 clips, anger appeared twice, and happy and disgust were each identified once for both the English and Japanese audio. Despite the ratings being the same, Rater C frequently described emotions in the Japanese audio as more powerful or expressive.

Rater C also identified fear as the dominant emotion in the English audio (5 times), and sadness and surprise appeared twice. For the Japanese audio, fear was again the dominant emotion, appearing six times, with sadness twice, and angry and surprise chosen once. In their open-ended responses, Rater C often commented on the increased emotional intensity in the Japanese audio. They remarked that the Japanese characters expressed stronger feelings, noting the louder, more direct expressions of emotions such as anger and sadness. For example, the Japanese version of a scene conveyed a greater sense of frustration, whereas the English counterpart seemed subtler or less emotionally charged.

Rater D's evaluation presented more variation in the emotions selected. For the English audio, they identified fear four times, anger three times, and surprise twice, disgust and sadness once each. In the Japanese audio, fear appeared three times, angry three times, sadness twice, and surprise twice. Rater D discussed that fear and anger, were more subdued in the English audio and was more urging than angry.

In summary, across the four raters, fear was the most consistently identified emotion in both the English and Japanese versions but its intensity differed across languages, with the Japanese audio frequently perceived as more emotionally charged. Anger and sadness were also commonly noted, particularly in the Japanese version, where several raters highlighted how emotions like anger and sadness were conveyed with greater emotion intensity.

Focus Group Discussion for Discrete Model. As with the VAD model, sentences were identified where the raters disagreed on their evaluations. One sentence was 「血！わかる？血！」 ("That's blood! Get it! It's blood"). In English this sentence was localised as "I got germs, see". As the sentences were not literally translated, this may have influenced the raters' scores. Rater A (native English) heard disgust in the English audio and fear in the Japanese. Rater B (native Japanese) perceived anger in both versions, explaining that it sounded like the speaker was angrily showing something. Raters C and D (proficient in both languages) felt surprise in the English audio and fear in the Japanese. Only Rater A detected disgust in English, but everyone agreed it was not heard in the Japanese version whilst C and B noted that the Japanese speaker's voice conveyed surprise, which was less apparent in English.

The next pair of sentences was "It's water" (水だ). Rater A heard surprise in the English audio and fear in Japanese, commenting that the English sounded more shocked, whereas Rater B perceived fear in both versions. Rater C detected a mix of surprise and happiness in both, noting that emotions are often more complex than a single label which highlights a limitation of our AI model, which can only classify one emotion per utterance. Rater D heard surprise in the English version and happiness in the Japanese, suggesting they interpreted the discovery of water positively, possibly influenced by the content of the sentence. All raters agreed that the English audio sounded more surprised overall.

Another pair of sentences identified was "Sen, I am sorry I called you a dope before!" (せーん！お前のことどんくさいって言ったけど). Rater A heard disgust in both versions, noting that the Japanese audio sounded more like shouting, edging toward anger but still expressing disgust. They commented that the speaker didn't seem to want to apologize, especially in the English version. Rater B perceived happiness in both. It was discussed that in general, the raters selected the "happy" emotion when they perceived the audio as generally positive, even when "happy" may not have been the most accurate emotion as it was the closest emotion out of happiness, sadness, fear, anger, surprise and disgust. Rater C detected sadness, interpreting both speakers as feeling sorry, though the Japanese version was louder. Rater D heard sadness in the English audio but anger in the Japanese, attributing this to the use of the 'kedo' particle, which made the Japanese version sound more confrontational.

Moreover, in the focus group it was discussed that the native English rater (Rater A) deliberately avoided focusing on the content of the dialogue and relied only on audio cues, unlike the other raters who, being bilingual, considered both the content and the emotional tone of the audio. Whilst the raters tried to not listen to the content, there was still a slight bias as it was difficult to completely disregard the content. This suggests a natural bias when humans label audio compared to the AI models which only have audio as input, as humans can't fully separate cultural knowledge from their evaluations. Whilst AI analyses audio without this bias, the group recognised that the raters' cultural knowledge was valuable, enhancing their interpretations and providing insights that AI alone might miss.

5 Conclusion, Limitations and Future Work

To facilitate automatic knowledge pool creation for the learners of intercultural communication, we developed a novel pipeline combining AI analytics and human-in-the-loop methods for the automated extraction of emotional discrepancies in film dubbing and conducted a case study on the English and Japanese versions of Spirited Away. To answer the first research question, our analysis suggest that whilst both the VAD and discrete models have their strengths, the discrete classification approach proved more intuitive for both human raters and AI when distinguishing between singular emotions. The VAD model was more effective for capturing the emotional depth of more complex audio segments, offering a more nuanced understanding of subtle differences in valence and arousal. However, the human annotators found the VAD approach hard to interpret when comparing it to their own emotional perceptions.

The focus group discussions highlighted the impact of cultural and linguistic backgrounds on emotional perception. To answer the second research question, the raters from different backgrounds often had different interpretations of the same audio clips, revealing how cultural context shapes emotional understanding. The AI models identified the utterances with the highest emotional discrepancies, but human raters offered insights into the emotional complexity that AI struggled to capture, such as detecting multiple emotions in a single utterance. This finding emphasises the importance of integrating human expertise into the analysis process to account for subjective emotional interpretations. Understanding these nuances can support the development of more effective teaching strategies for cross-cultural learners, particularly within ITS, by providing examples of emotional variation in speech and enhancing learners' ability to navigate cross-cultural communication challenges.

In summary, the analysis results indicate that our pipeline effectively identifies audio segments with emotional divergences, which are crucial for understanding how cultural backgrounds influence emotional nuances. In addition, the comparison of discrepancies under various metrics has provided insights into the subtleties of cross-linguistic emotional expression. However, the pipeline lacks the ability to capture contextual factors from audio utterances alone critical for accurate emotional interpretation. Furthermore, the English version of Spirited Away is dubbed, meaning the voice actors are not the same as in the original Japanese version which can create differences in how well emotions are expressed compared to the original actors [10], potentially affecting both AI and human emotional assessments. Additionally, the small sample size of movies and focus groups limits the generalisability of the findings. Future work will involve expanding the dataset to include a broader range of movies with multimedia data. We will also conduct evaluations with larger and more diverse focus groups to further explore how cultural differences influence emotional perception.

Acknowledgments. We would like to thank Peihang Li for their support with coding the pipeline during their undergraduate project at Durham University. We would also like to thank all of the raters for their participation in the focus group discussions.

Disclosure of Interests. The authors have no competing interests to declare that are relevant to the content of this article.

References

1. Baevski, A., Zhou, Y., Mohamed, A., Auli, M.: wav2vec 2.0: A framework for self-supervised learning of speech representations. In: Advances in Neural Information Processing Systems, vol. 33, pp. 12449–12460 (2020)
2. Bellini, C., Del Maschio, N., Gentile, M., Del Mauro, G., Franceschini, R., Abutalebi, J.: Original language versus dubbed movies: effects on our brain and emotions. Brain Lang. **253**, 105424 (2024) https://doi.org/10.1016/j.bandl.2024.105424, https://www.sciencedirect.com/science/article/pii/S0093934X24000476
3. Chiper, S.: Teaching intercultural communication: ICT resources and best practices. Procedia - Soc. Behav. Sci. **93**, 1641–1645 (2013). https://doi.org/10.1016/j.sbspro.2013.10.094, 3rd World Conference on Learning, Teaching and Educational Leadership
4. Ekman, P., et al.: Basic emotions. In: Handbook of Cognition and Emotion, vol. 98, no. 45–60, p. 16 (1999)
5. Hsu, W.N., Bolte, B., Tsai, Y., Lakhotia, K., Salakhutdinov, R., Mohamed, A.: Hubert: self-supervised speech representation learning by masked prediction of hidden units. IEEE/ACM Trans. Audio Speech Lang. Process. **29**, 3451–3460 (2021)
6. Kong, Z., Ping, W., Dantrey, A., Catanzaro, B.: Speech denoising in the waveform domain with self-attention. In: ICASSP 2022-2022 IEEE International Conference on Acoustics, Speech and Signal Processing (ICASSP), pp. 7867–7871. IEEE (2022)
7. Lim, N.: Cultural differences in emotion: differences in emotional arousal level between the east and the west. Integr. Med. Res. **5**(2), 105–109 (2016). https://doi.org/10.1016/j.imr.2016.03.004

8. Livingstone, S.R., Russo, F.A.: The ryerson audio-visual database of emotional speech and song (ravdess): a dynamic, multimodal set of facial and vocal expressions in North American English. PLoS ONE **13**(5), e0196391 (2018)
9. Monaghan, L.: Perspectives on intercultural discourse and communication (2012). https://doi.org/10.1002/9781118247273.ch2
10. Naranjo, B.: The role of emotions in the perception of natural vs. play-acted dubbing: an approach to angry and sad vocal performances. Meta **66**(3), 580–600 (2021). https://doi.org/10.7202/1088351ar
11. Radford, A., Kim, J.W., Xu, T., Brockman, G., McLeavey, C., Sutskever, I.: Robust speech recognition via large-scale weak supervision. In: International Conference on Machine Learning, pp. 28492–28518. PMLR (2023)
12. Russell, J.A., Mehrabian, A.: Evidence for a three-factor theory of emotions. J. Res. Pers. **11**(3), 273–294 (1977)
13. Sainburg, T., Gentner, T.Q.: Toward a computational neuroethology of vocal communication: from bioacoustics to neurophysiology, emerging tools and future directions. Front. Behav. Neurosci. **15**, 811737 (2021)
14. Spanias, A., Painter, T., Atti, V.: Audio Signal Processing and Coding. Wiley (2006)
15. Tiwari, V.: MFCC and its applications in speaker recognition. Int. J. Emerg. Technol. **1**(1), 19–22 (2010)
16. Wagner, J., et al.: Dawn of the transformer era in speech emotion recognition: closing the valence gap (2022). https://doi.org/10.48550/ARXIV.2203.07378
17. Wierzbicka, A.: Emotions across languages and cultures: Diversity and Universals (1999). https://doi.org/10.1017/CBO9780511521256
18. Xia, Y., Shin, S.Y., Kim, J.C.: Cross-cultural intelligent language learning system (CILS): leveraging AI to facilitate language learning strategies in cross-cultural communication. Appl. Sci. **14**(13), 5651 (2024). https://doi.org/10.3390/app14135651
19. Xin, D., Jiang, J., Takamichi, S., Saito, Y., Aizawa, A., Saruwatari, H.: JVNV: a corpus of Japanese emotional speech with verbal content and nonverbal expressions. IEEE Access (2024)

A Method and Semi-automated AI Tool Supporting Tutors in Preparing Audio-Tactile Exercises for Blind Students

Mateusz Kawulok, Michał Maćkowski(✉), and Maria Rosiak

Department of Distributed Systems and Informatic Devices, Silesian University of Technology, Gliwice, Poland
`michal.mackowski@polsl.pl`

Abstract. The article presents a method and tool that use deep learning to enable the preparation of educational graphic materials adapted to the needs of visually impaired people, focusing on supporting the teacher's work in adapting exercises to an alternative audio-tactile form. The challenges educators face, the proposed alternative in the form of an artificial intelligence tool, and the research carried out are presented. The research group comprised 9 teachers with extensive experience working with visually impaired students, and the study spanned one semester in a high school setting. The proposed evaluation method encompassed several factors, including a comparison of the effectiveness of the obtained artificial intelligence models for image analysis, a comparison of the time required for exercise preparation in contrast to previously used solutions, the usability scale of the proposed system measured by subjective indicators, and the reduction of the workload of the tutor by using a standard task-load index. The findings suggest that the proposed method and the teacher support tool attain high-efficiency scores in the quality of the classifier and markedly reduce the workload necessary to adapt educational material to the needs of blind individuals. Further development of the tool toward generative models can contribute to the creation of a comprehensive and automated adaptation tool, thereby reducing exercise preparation time to the requisite minimum.

Keywords: Alternative Method of Audio-Tactile Presentation · Blind Students Education · Automated Tool for Exercises Preparation

1 Introduction

In the modern era, education is increasingly dependent on the integration of digital and interactive materials. These materials have been shown to facilitate greater student engagement with the subject matter, thereby enhancing the efficacy of the learning process [1]. Frequently, these materials are presented in graphic formats, engaging the visual sense and concurrently encouraging creative thinking. However, it is important to note that using materials is not universally accessible, particularly for students who are blind, whose cognitive processes are often affected by their visual impairment [2]. In such cases, the employment of specific adaptive tools becomes imperative to surmount the aforementioned barriers [3].

In recent years, we have observed an emergence of solutions that facilitate accessibility for blind individuals with regard to educational materials [4]. These solutions can be categorized into two primary groups: audio [5, 6] and audio-touch [7]. The former encompasses screen readers, which have attained ubiquity in contemporary electronic devices [5]. The latter encompasses more comprehensive approaches, exemplified by dynamic information adaptation systems such as dot-matrix displays [8]. However, most of these solutions are designed solely for students with sight impairments. Presently, tutors lack the tools to adapt materials into alternative formats for subsequent use on educational platforms, reducing the time required to prepare such content [9]. It is a critical issue, as the process can be time-consuming and labor-intensive for the individual adopting the materials or sources in question [10]. Additionally, while digital materials are relatively straightforward to adapt, the images found in educational textbooks are typically presented in paper form, making them difficult to adapt to the needs of individuals with visual impairment [11, 12].

In the context of the broader endeavor to support the education of students with blindness, it is crucial to consider the needs of teachers, as they can significantly impact the proliferation of didactic materials and, consequently, enhance learning outcomes among students [11]. Moreover, using correctly adapted images employing the audio-tactile method has been shown to positively influence students' engagement in educational activities, thereby serving as an additional motivator for addressing challenging issues [12].

Our prior research [13–15] has enabled the development of an educational platform designed to support the teaching of students who are blind through the use of tactile printouts in conjunction with a web and mobile application (Fig. 1). A recurring concern identified in our previous studies was the absence of an automated preparation process for educational materials [13, 16]. This observation motivated us to devise a method and a tool to automate the adaptation of educational materials, encompassing both traditional and digital formats, to align with the requirements of visually impaired individuals. When employed in conjunction with the existing platform, our approach will yield a comprehensive and user-friendly solution.

In light of the prevailing trend of employing artificial intelligence (AI) to automate rudimentary processes, it was determined that deep learning would be utilized to address the aforementioned limitations. An initial review of the extant literature [17–19] revealed that this approach has been met with considerable success in numerous applications involving object detection in visual media.

This study presents our semi-automatic adaptation tool, which was designed to assist teachers in the process of preparing exercises. The tool allows for the scanning of a traditional mathematical graph, followed by analysis using an object detection model to identify all elements that are important from the perspective of a blind person. The model's results automatically generate an adapted image in a web editor, which can be further corrected or modified.

The primary objective of the research study is to evaluate the efficacy of a proposed object detection model training in conjunction with a developed web-based editor. This evaluation will encompass both quantitative and qualitative analyses, with the aim of assessing the tool's usability in the creation of exercises for students with visual impairments. The central research questions address the reduction of tutors' workload and the acceleration of the process, thereby aiming to enhance efficiency and reduce time-consuming educational material adaptation.

A tactile image aligned with the visual content displayed on the tablet screen with additional 3D printed frame.

When a student who is blind touches an element on the tactile image, the alternative description is read aloud in a authors' mobile application.

Fig. 1. The proposed audio-tactile approach.

2 Related Works

Recent years have witnessed a rapid development of tools such as educational and e-learning platforms, as well as assistive technologies, including screen readers and screen magnifiers, served to facilitate the use of digital materials by individuals with disabilities. In the field of human sciences education, text is the fundamental source of information, which can be efficiently scanned, recognized and read using speech synthesizers, for example.

Research indicates that people who are blind process cognitive information similarly to that of sighted students. However, they must rely on alternative means of information acquisition, such as haptic or audial senses, which, as noted by the authors of papers [20, 21], impose certain disadvantages. It is essential to acknowledge the necessity of preparing educational materials, media, or techniques that facilitate the learning requirements of all students. Teachers should be given a range of materials on effective methods of teaching students with blindness and a variety of supplementary handouts to ensure equitable access to the learning process for all students [22, 23].

Despite the rapid advancements in information technology, disparities in access to information persist among sighted students and their blind peers. It is particularly evident in the context of multimedia platforms and technical data comprising specific symbols or diverse formats, which are inaccessible to blind individuals. Consequently, existing technologies are inadequate in transforming such data to make it accessible to blind individuals [24]. A similar challenge is evident in mathematics and STEM disciplines, where the presentation of information to students and their subsequent comprehension appears to be particularly arduous for those with visual impairments.

In the field of materials adaptation for the visually impaired, several notable concepts have emerged. One such idea, outlined in a research paper [25], involves using segmentation and contour detection methods to render images in a format suitable for subsequent tactile printing. The approach's strength lies in its capacity to accentuate thickened regions while streamlining the overall drawing to its fundamental contours, thereby enhancing its accessibility and navigability for users with diverse visual abilities. A similar approach with a suitable tool was also presented by the authors in the paper [26].

Another concept related to adapting graphics for the visually impaired was the analysis of images found in school textbooks [11]. It involved scanning and analyzing the image and subsequently filtering it into a segment pertaining to the image and its corresponding text. The two components were processed independently: the first into an image in SVG format and the second into text in Braille. The integration of these components resulted in a composite graph with the adapted descriptions applied. This approach offers the benefit of preparing the image in a print-ready format; however, it operates only on a single sense—touch—thus, a person who is blind must physically remove their finger from the currently touched element in order to read the description.

In AI, a particularly interesting concept for addressing the challenge of adaptation involves the integration of 3D printing [27]. The implementation of braille text combined with these printouts serves to foster the development of spatial imagination. In this context, the pivotal role of artificial intelligence lies in the classification and selection of pertinent image components to be prioritized during the printing process. The implementation of this solution results in the generation of a 3D object, accompanied by the classification description in Braille from the trained model.

Another approach related to AI and adaptation involves the use of the text-to-image method [28]. The authors employed language models, transformers, and encoders to create a simple printable graphic from text input. A key drawback of the solution was that the range of elements it could generate was limited to only a few basic categories, such as animals and flowers. Consequently, generating intricate images, such as scientific graphics, may encounter challenges.

This paper proposes a methodology to automate the preparation of educational materials made by teachers, focusing on preparing educational materials for blind students. The methodology employs AI methods to boost the detection of elements in images. The paper also discusses the potential for creating a complete and semi-automatic solution to reduce teachers' workload while working with blind students. The proposed approach and tool will benefit from the achievements of existing research in terms of processing the graphics themselves. Concurrently, our research will also propose new, faster, and more accurate models. These models will allow for the simultaneous removal of unnecessary elements of the graph and the conversion of the graph into an SVG format suitable for tactile printing.

3 Materials and Methods

3.1 Deep Learning Methods Used

The research used the YOLO (You Only Look Once) neural networks [29], which represent deep learning models derived from the convolutional neural network (CNN) approach. These networks are regarded as one of the most rapid modern solutions for object detection. A notable advantage of utilizing YOLO is its reduced resource consumption [30] in comparison to other contemporary solutions, such as R-CNN (Region CNN) [31] and Faster R-CNN [32]. A notable advantage of YOLO over Vision Transformers (ViT) [33] is its ability to preserve the input image with all objects marked, a feature that Transformers, being treated with a vector input, often lose [34]. The development of this neural network commenced in 2015 and has been continuously refined to the present, with the most recent iteration, YOLOv11 [35], released in 2024. To prepare this solution for teachers as a rapid, accurate and efficient tool that requires few resources, we used the YOLO networks as the primary deep learning algorithm. The primary evaluation methodologies employed in the designated network category entail comparing Precision, Recall and Average Precision values. Furthermore, the output confusion matrix analysis is a valuable information source.

3.2 Proposed Solution

The developed tool employs a web application integrated with a YOLO model. The network output has been modified to generate a text file containing all the recognized classes and their relative position on the graph, in addition to the graphical result depicting detected objects. This file then serves as the input for a designed web SVG editor, which draws an image based on the given information. The teacher can then modify the image using standard means, such as dragging and dropping elements and changing graph parameters (e.g. line thickness, function parameters). Furthermore, the tutor can delete unwanted elements and add new ones to the graph. The result can be saved as an SVG file.

The SVG editor, as depicted in Fig. 2, has been developed using standard web technologies, namely JavaScript, HTML5 and CSS. It functions as both an AI-integrated solution and a standalone application, capable of producing in vector-format images. The primary features encompass user interaction through drag-and-drop functionality, modification of function formulas, and adjustment of graphical parameters such as line thickness. The user can create an image based on an existing one using the proposed deep learning models, or alternatively, can create a new SVG file from scratch using the proposed controls to draw basic objects. The result can be saved as a vector graphic file for later use.

The purpose of the process described above was to reduce the time required for image preparation in a form that can be used by the educational system to add descriptions to elements and then be printed out on a braille printer and used with the mobile learning application.

3.3 Dataset and Model Training

The primary phase of the research concentrated on developing deep learning models. Until then, the dataset comprised images of graphs from mathematical textbooks and images generated using Python scripts. The current research used additional data generation deemed essential due to the comparatively limited number of examples from the abovementioned category. The proposed scripts were created to emulate real-world examples as closely as possible, including the generation of additional descriptions and

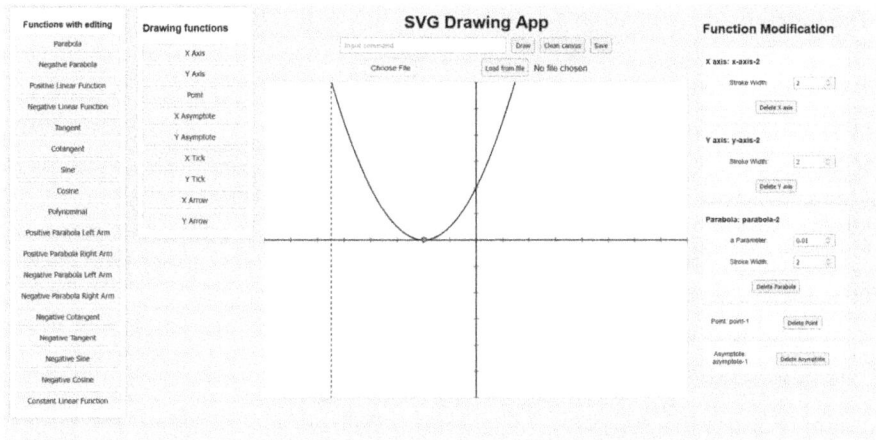

Fig. 2. The proposed SVG web editor.

non-essential elements of graphs, which are not needed from the point of view of the process of exploration by the visually impaired. Concurrently, identifying elements on graphs that are crucial for the learning process of blind individuals was undertaken. It facilitated the graph decomposition that would serve to represent the object classes in subsequent stages. The proposed division is illustrated in Fig. 3.

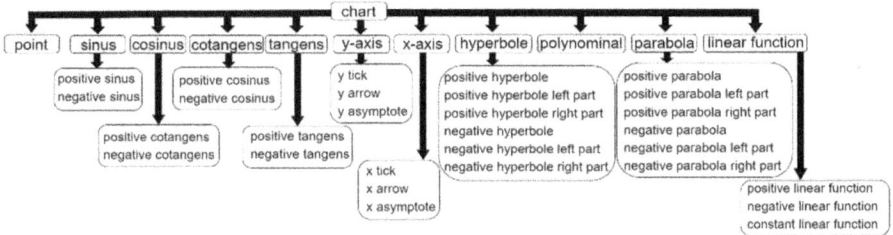

Fig. 3. The proposed mathematical graph decomposition.

It is important to observe the classes that are directly dictated by the adaptation for the blind; for example, in the parabola branch, a division is observed between the negative and positive representation, as well as between the right and left arm of the function. It is a direct consequence of the audio-tactile approach, where, in many cases, each element has a different sound description.

The second phase of the research centered on training the models on the selected YOLO versions, with the final dataset comprising almost 40,000 examples that had been labelled. The training was conducted using YOLOv5 and YOLOv8, which were selected based on prior research [36] that indicated these two versions achieved the best results in earlier evaluation iterations. The dataset was then divided into two splits to verify the influence of the data separation percentage on the final results. The proposed divisions were as follows:

- The training set contains 90% of the images, while the validation set contains 10%.
- The training images are 80%, the validation images are 10%, and the test images are 10%.

The training process involved 100 epochs for each submodel identified within the selected YOLO versions. YOLOv5 presents 10 submodels, with five operating on an input image of 640 × 640 pixels and the remaining five on a 1280 × 1280 input image. Similarly, YOLOv8 provides five submodels, each operating on an input image of 640 × 640 pixels. After each training process, the results obtained were stored for subsequent comparison.

3.4 Research Group

The author evaluated the proposed tool during one semester at the high school level. The research group comprised educators from an educational facility for the blind in Poland. The participants had to meet the following inclusion criteria:

- Candidates must have at least three years of experience teaching blind and visually impaired students.
- Ideally, the candidate should have experience teaching mathematics or other sciences that utilize graphs of functions to illustrate information.

Among the tutors employed at the facility, nine were found to meet the specified inclusion criteria and thus participated in the study. Before working with the tool, teachers received instructions on utilizing the proposed solution, encompassing the processes of scanning images and utilizing the SVG editor.

The study conducted two phases of evaluation of the proposed tool. The initial phase included comparing the obtained results of the model training, analyzing the confusion matrix of the best model, and performing a real-world scenario test for the models with the highest parameter values. The subsequent phase entailed comparing the average time required for a teacher to prepare 10 images for the exercises, both with and without the proposed tool. Moreover, the research employed a subjective System Usability Scale (SUS) [37] to assess the perceived usefulness of the proposed tool. The statements from the survey are presented in Table 1. Finally, a comparison of the workload of teachers was conducted using a NASA-TLX test [38, 39].

In addition, the teachers were invited to share their perspectives on the proposed tool in the following domains: (1) Its potential application in the creation of exercises, (2) Its ease of use and integration into existing practices, and (3) The method's strengths and limitations.

4 Results

4.1 Model Results

The training results for the 90% training data and the 10% validation data are shown in Table 2.

Table 1. List of SUS Test Statements.

No.	SUS Test Statement
1.	I found the SVG image preparation tool easy to use
2.	I found the tool unnecessarily complex
3.	I felt that the tool's functions were well-integrated and logically organized
4.	I think most teachers would struggle to learn how to use this tool without special training
5.	I felt confident using the tool to adapt materials
6.	I found the tool frustrating to use
7.	The tool's features worked well for preparing and editing SVG images
8.	Using this tool requires too much effort
9.	Most of the tool's features were easily accessible when I needed them
10.	Overall, I am not satisfied with this tool

Table 2. Results for the training set of 90%, with the validation set of 10%.

	YOLOv5				YOLOv8			
Submodel	Precision	Recall	AP_{50}	$AP_{50:95}$	Precision	Recall	AP_{50}	$AP_{50:95}$
n	0.718	0.944	0.759	0.567	0.710	0.948	0.751	0.575
s	0.753	0.939	0.858	0.665	**0.873**	**0.948**	**0.930**	**0.739**
m	**0.825**	**0.929**	**0.904**	**0.712**	0.833	0.946	0.911	0.725
l	0.816	0.919	0.901	0.709	0.857	0.949	0.925	0.739
x	0.794	0.925	0.896	0.704	0.858	0.953	0.921	0.734
n v6	0.662	0.910	0.718	0.526	-	-	-	-
s v6	0.671	0.901	0.730	0.539	-	-	-	-
m v6	0.729	0.951	0.787	0.607	-	-	-	-
l v6	0.729	0.953	0.771	0.595	-	-	-	-
x v6	0.738	0.932	0.795	0.617	-	-	-	-

The findings suggested that the proposed deep learning method is a suitable candidate for final implementation. In the case of YOLOv5, the optimal model was the medium one, while in the case of YOLOv8, the optimal model was the small one. Both models attained an AP_{50} and a Recall value above 90%. Additionally, the precision rate was found to be consistently high, with values exceeding 80%. A notable observation was that the models exhibited superior performance when the input size was set to 640 × 640, compared to the larger size of 1280 × 1280.

Table 3 shows the results obtained for the 80% training, 10% validation, and 10% test data.

Table 3. Results for the training set of 80%, validation set of 10% and test set of 10%.

	YOLOv5				YOLOv8			
Submodel	Precision	Recall	AP_{50}	$AP_{50:95}$	Precision	Recall	AP_{50}	$AP_{50:95}$
n	0.721	0.933	0.746	0.557	0.727	0.945	0.806	0.625
s	0.735	0.939	0.806	0.617	0.846	0.947	0.912	0.722
m	**0.795**	**0.936**	**0.901**	**0.709**	**0.852**	**0.945**	**0.921**	**0.733**
l	0.799	0.930	0.890	0.697	0.746	0.929	0.843	0.667
x	0.762	0.947	0.880	0.690	0.845	0.947	0.911	0.725
n v6	0.655	0.911	0.719	0.527	-	-	-	-
s v6	0.670	0.906	0.731	0.539	-	-	-	-
m v6	0.719	0.956	0.759	0.581	-	-	-	-
l v6	0.739	0.952	0.802	0.623	-	-	-	-
x v6	0.736	0.946	0.780	0.602	-	-	-	-

The second experimental dataset provided further confirmation of the observations from the previous training evaluation, with comparable results obtained. The confusion matrix for the best performing model is shown in Fig. 4.

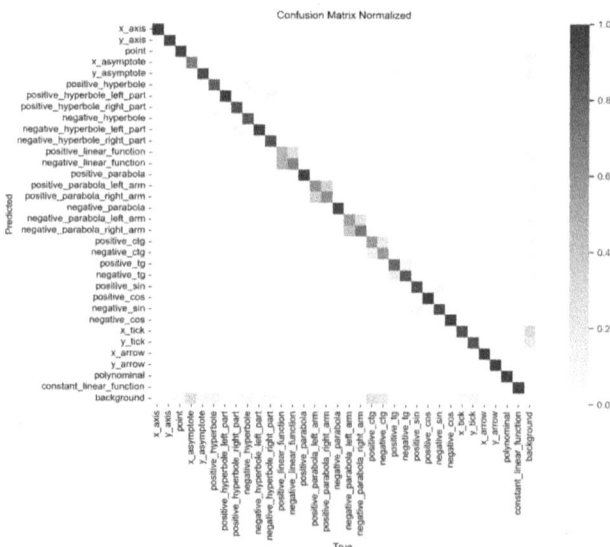

Fig. 4. Confusion matrix for the best model – YOLOv8s 90% and 10% data split.

The confusion matrix obtained for the YOLOv8s (Fig. 4) indicates that every object class was detected with good or almost perfect accuracy. The most common mistakes made by the network were related to linear functions and parabolas. In the case of linear functions, the network frequently misidentified positive graphs as negative. In the case of parabolas, the network frequently confused the arms of the function. It is noteworthy that the network demonstrated a high degree of accuracy in identifying trigonometric functions, a category that had previously posed challenges.

In addition, a real-world scenario experiment was proposed in which the best models from the selected versions were tested on a new set of 100 generated and scanned images. The results obtained are shown in Table 4.

Table 4. Results of the conducted real-world scenario test on 100 images.

Model	Correctly classified objects (%)
YOLOv5m 90/10 data split	94.95
YOLOv8s 90/10 data split	95.51

The results obtained for the proposed real-world scenario test further confirmed the observations made from the training parameters. The YOLOv8s achieved slightly better results in detecting all objects on the generated images, but only by about 0.5%.

4.2 Tool Experiences Results

The results of the time comparison for preparing an exercise, representing the average time required to prepare 10 exercises, are shown in Table 5.

Table 5. The average time needed to prepare an exercise without and with the proposed tool.

Teacher No.	1.	2.	3.	4.	5.	6.	7.	8.	9.	**Avg.**
Previous methods (mm:ss)	28:21	20:38	32:12	24:38	29:53	18:42	41:27	23:33	15:49	**26:08**
Proposed Tool (mm:ss)	15:43	14:52	20:14	18:43	17:03	14:21	21:36	17:48	12:23	**16:58**

Teachers who employed the conventional methods needed more time to prepare an exercise than those who used the proposed tool, with the discrepancy in time sometimes reaching 20 min. The variation in the time required by each teacher can be attributed to their experience in creating adapted exercises and their computer skills. In instances where the duration of preparing the exercise was minimal, as in the case of teacher number 9, the proposed tool exhibited the least impact, reducing the average preparation time by a mere 3 min. Conversely, in the case of teacher number 7, a substantial average time reduction of 10 min was observed. On average, the utilization of the tool resulted in a 10-min reduction in the preparation time for adapted exercises.

Table 6 shows the results obtained for the proposed System Usability Scale (SUS) test, according to the statements from Table 1.

Table 6. The results of the conducted SUS test.

Question No.	1.	2.	3.	4.	5.	6.	7.	8	9.	10.
Average Response	4.6	2.1	4.5	2.3	4.8	1.7	4.3	2.2	4.7	1.9
Average Score	3.6	2.9	3.5	2.7	3.8	3.3	3.3	2.8	3.7	3.1

The final SUS score based on Table 6 is 81.75, which demonstrates that the tool under consideration is highly usable. Furthermore, the results indicated that the tool can be further developed and integrated into the process of preparing materials for blind and visually impaired individuals. As indicated by the available data, values exceeding 80 are generally regarded as acceptable outcomes [40].

Table 7 shows the results of the NASA TLX test. The time parameter was not taken into account, as it was evaluated in a separate experiment described above. Moreover, since the task did not involve strict time constraints, the perceived urgency to complete it quickly wasn't a relevant factor in assessing the overall workload.

Table 7. The results of the conducted NASA-TLX test.

	Previous method	Proposed tool
Mental demand	78.4	45.7
Physical demand	74.1	28.2
Temporal demand	X	X
Performance	76.8	39.5
Frustration	55.0	33.7
Effort	72.5	26.8
Total score	71.4	34.8

The final evaluation centered on the teacher's workload in preparing the exercises. The findings indicated that the implementation of the proposed tool resulted in a comprehensive enhancement of key parameters, as evidenced by a decline in values. The most pronounced changes were observed in the Effort category, while the least significant improvements were noted in the Frustration category. According to the literature, the total scores indicate that the system helps reduce the required workload [41].

4.3 Teacher Opinions

In addition to the results obtained in the proposed, an open questionary on 3 mentioned topics was conducted. In response to the first question (1), one teacher said: *"The proposed tool was very useful for me during the process of preparing exercises. Previously I had to use special SVG editors, which sometimes were a bit too complicated for the purpose I wanted them for."* When asked about the second issue (2), another tutor said the following: *"I'm using the educational platform for my classes, and the created tool really helps me to work with it. It was easy to use with no setup required which is an additional benefit for me"*. Responding to the third (3), another tutor said: *"The strengths are visible for me at first sight – the possibility of faster exercise preparation means a lot to me. A big downside is however the lack of creating the descriptions. Now having the graphical file, I still have to do the last step manually".*

The collected opinions serve to further substantiate the tool's practicality and offer valuable insights into the steps that should be taken in the future.

5 Discussion and Conclusions

The integration of semi-automated image preparation functionality enables educators to optimize their time management, particularly in the context of exercise preparation for students engaged in learning through the educational platform. The incorporation of AI algorithms serves to underscore the novel and contemporary character of the solution, while the utilization of a dedicated web editor obviates the necessity for additional tool installation, further streamlining the overall process.

The findings of the present study suggest that the proposed tool has yielded notable advancements in the realm of education for the visually impaired. The efficacy of the proposed models has been substantiated by the positive outcomes observed in the teacher surveys and usability tests. These outcomes further underscore the positive impact of the research, as evidenced by the results of the workload tests. While the tool has been found to facilitate the process of exercise preparation to a considerable extent, it is important to note that certain limitations remain. These shortcomings will be addressed in forthcoming studies.

The primary constraint concerns the audio-tactile approach and the utilization of the tool. The proposed solution currently serves to prepare the image in a format compatible with authors' platform; however, it does not facilitate the generation of alternative descriptions that can be read aloud by the tool employed by students. This step remains to be performed manually by teachers. The integration of generative language models to generate these alternative descriptions or backbones would significantly enhance the process of exercise adaptation, thereby empowering educators to create a more extensive array of materials for students.

Another limitation is intimately associated with the proposed models. Their fundamental operational principle is predicated on mathematical representations found in textbooks. One potential avenue for further development is to employ them in other graphic-related subjects, such as physics, geography, and chemistry. Another promising avenue for development is to train the models to adapt hand-drawn images, which would assist teachers in creating exercises from the ground up. Both approaches appear to have potential applications in future research.

Acknowledgments. This publication was supported by the Excellence Initiative - Research University Program in Silesian University of Technology, grant number: 02/110/RGJ24/1027.

References

1. Tuma, F.: The use of educational technology for interactive teaching in lectures. Ann. Med. Surg. **62**, 231–235 (2021). https://doi.org/10.1016/J.AMSU.2021.01.051
2. van Garderen, D., Scheuermann, A., Jackson, C.: Developing representational ability in mathematics for students with learning disabilities: a content analysis of grades 6 and 7 textbooks. Learn. Disabil. Q. **35**, 24–38 (2012). https://doi.org/10.1177/0731948711429726
3. DePountis, V.M., Pogrund, R.L., Griffin-Shirley, N., Lan, W.Y.: Technologies used in the study of advanced mathematics by students who are visually impaired in class-rooms: teachers' perspectives. J. Vis. Impair. Blind. **109**, 265–278 (2015). https://doi.org/10.1177/0145482X1510900403
4. Soares, M.d.S., Furukawa, C.A., Cagnin, M.I., Paiva, D.M.B.: Accessible learning objects: a systematic literature review. Univers. Access. Inf. Soc. **23**, 1931–1945 (2024). https://doi.org/10.1007/s10209-023-01025-7
5. Khan, A., Khusro, S.: An insight into smartphone-based assistive solutions for visually impaired and blind people: issues, challenges and opportunities. Univers. Access. Inf. Soc. **20**, 265–298 (2021). https://doi.org/10.1007/s10209-020-00733-8
6. Sabourin, C.J., Merrikhi, Y., Lomber, S.G.: Do blind people hear better? Trends Cogn. Sci. **26**, 999–1012 (2022). https://doi.org/10.1016/j.tics.2022.08.016
7. Zeinullin, M., Hersh, M.: Tactile audio responsive intelligent system. IEEE Access **10**, 122074–122091 (2022). https://doi.org/10.1109/ACCESS.2022.3223099
8. dot Pad 320 Graphic Tablet User Guide. https://manuals.plus/dot/pad-320-graphic-tablet-manual. Accessed 15 Jan 2025
9. Race, L., et al.: Designing while blind: nonvisual tools and inclusive workflows for tactile graphic creation. In: ASSETS 2023 - Proceedings of the 25th International ACM SIGACCESS Conference on Computers and Accessibility (2023). https://doi.org/10.1145/3597638.3614546
10. Plazar, J., Meulenberg, C.J.W., Kermauner, A.: Science education for blind and visually impaired children. Metodički ogledi: časopis za filozofiju odgoja. **28**, 167–190 (2021). https://doi.org/10.21464/MO.28.1.10
11. Jayant, C., Renzelmann, M., Wen, D., Krisnandi, S., Ladner, R., Comden, D.: Automated tactile graphics translation: in the field. In: ASSETS'07: Proceedings of the Ninth International ACM SIGACCESS Conference on Computers and Accessibility, pp. 75–82 (2007). https://doi.org/10.1145/1296843.1296858
12. Namdev, R.K., Maes, P.: An interactive and intuitive STEM accessibility system for the blind and visually impaired. In: 8th ACM International Conference on PErvasive Technologies Related to Assistive Environments, PETRA 2015 – Proceedings (2015). https://doi.org/10.1145/2769493.2769502
13. Maćkowski, M., Kawulok, M., Brzoza, P., Spinczyk, D.: Methods and tools supporting the learning and teaching of mathematics dedicated to students with blindness. Appl. Sci. **13** (2023). https://doi.org/10.3390/app13127240
14. Maćkowski, M., Brzoza, P., Kawulok, M., Knura, T.: Mobile e-learning platform for audio-tactile graphics presentation. In: Miesenberger, K., Kouroupetroglou, G., Mavrou, K., Manduchi, R., Covarrubias Rodriguez, M., Penáz, P. (eds.) Computers Helping People with Special Needs, pp. 82–91. Springer, Cham (2022)
15. Mackowski, M., Brzoza, P., Kawulok, M., Meisel, R., Spinczyk, D.: Multi-modal presentation of interactive audio-tactile graphics supporting the perception of visual information by blind people. ACM Trans. Multimedia Comput. Commun. Appl. **19** (2023). https://doi.org/10.1145/3586076

16. Maćkowski, M., Brzoza, P.: Accessible tutoring platform using audio-tactile graphics adapted for visually impaired people. Sensors **22** (2022). https://doi.org/10.3390/s22228753
17. Sarshartehrani, F., Mohammadrezaei, E., Behravan, M., Gracanin, D.: Enhancing e-learning experience through embodied AI tutors in immersive virtual environments: a multifaceted approach for personalized educational adaptation. In: Sottilare, R.A., Schwarz, J. (eds.) Adaptive Instructional Systems, pp. 272–287. Springer, Cham (2024)
18. Koraishi, O.: Teaching English in the age of AI: embracing ChatGPT to optimize EFL materials and assessment. Lang. Educ. Technol. **3** (2023)
19. Davis, C., Bush, T., Wood, S.: Artificial intelligence in education: enhancing learning experiences through personalized adaptation. Int. J. Cyber IT Serv. Manag. **4**, 26–32 (2024). https://doi.org/10.34306/ijcitsm.v4i1.146
20. Bishop, V.E.: Teaching Visually Impaired Children. 3rd edn. Charles C Thomas Publisher Ltd., Springfield, IL (2004)
21. Lahav, O., Hagab, N., El Kader, S.A., Levy, S.T., Talis, V.: Listen to the models: sonified learning models for people who are blind. Comput. Educ. **127**, 141–153 (2018). https://doi.org/10.1016/j.compedu.2018.08.020
22. Klingenberg, O.G., Holkesvik, A.H., Augestad, L.B.: Research evidence for mathematics education for students with visual impairment: a systematic review. Cogent Educ. **6**, 1626322 (2019). https://doi.org/10.1080/2331186X.2019.1626322
23. Opertti, R., Brady, J.: Developing inclusive teachers from an inclusive curricular perspective. Prospects (Paris). **41**, 459–472 (2011). https://doi.org/10.1007/s11125-011-9205-7
24. Regec, V.: Mathematics in inclusive education of blind students in secondary schools in the Czech Republic. Procedia Soc. Behav. Sci. **174**, 3933–3939 (2015). https://doi.org/10.1016/j.sbspro.2015.01.1136
25. Ferro, T.J., Pawluk, D.T.V.: Automatic image conversion to tactile graphic. In: Proceedings of the 15th International ACM SIGACCESS Conference on Computers and Accessibility, ASSETS 2013 (2013). https://doi.org/10.1145/2513383.2513406
26. Crombie, D., Lenoir, R., McKenzie, N., Ioannidis, G.: The bigger picture: automated production tools for tactile graphics. In: Miesenberger, K., Klaus, J., Zagler, W.L., Burger, D. (eds.) Computers Helping People with Special Needs, pp. 713–720. Springer, Heidelberg (2004)
27. See, A.R., Advincula, W.D.: Creating tactile educational materials for the visually impaired and blind students using AI cloud computing. Appl. Sci. **11**, 7552 (2021). https://doi.org/10.3390/APP11167552
28. Dzhurynskyi, Y., Mayik, V., Mayik, L.: Enhancing accessibility: automated tactile graphics generation for individuals with visual impairments. Computation 2024, vol. 12, p. 251 (2024). https://doi.org/10.3390/COMPUTATION12120251
29. Gallagher, J.E., Oughton, E.J.: Surveying You Only Look Once (YOLO) multispectral object detection advancements, applications, and challenges. IEEE Access **13**, 7366–7395 (2025). https://doi.org/10.1109/ACCESS.2025.3526458
30. Aboyomi, D., Daniel, C.: A comparative analysis of modern object detection algorithms: YOLO vs. SSD vs. faster R-CNN. ITEJ (Inf. Technol. Eng. J.) **8** (2023). https://doi.org/10.24235/itej.v8i2.123
31. Girshick, R., Donahue, J., Darrell, T., Malik, J.: Rich feature hierarchies for accurate object detection and semantic segmentation. In: 2014 IEEE Conference on Computer Vision and Pattern Recognition, pp. 580–587 (2014). https://doi.org/10.1109/CVPR.2014.81
32. Ren, S., He, K., Girshick, R., Sun, J.: Faster R-CNN: towards real-time object detection with region proposal networks. In: Cortes, C., Lawrence, N., Lee, D., Sugiyama, M., Garnett, R. (eds.) Advances in Neural Information Processing Systems. Curran Associates, Inc. (2015)
33. Dosovitskiy, A., et al.: An image is worth 16x16 words: transformers for image recognition at scale. arXiv abs/2010.11929 (2020)

34. Arkin, E., Yadikar, N., Xu, X., Aysa, A., Ubul, K.: A survey: object detection methods from CNN to transformer. Multimed. Tools Appl. **82**, 21353–21383 (2023). https://doi.org/10.1007/s11042-022-13801-3
35. Khanam, R., Hussain, M.: YOLOv11: an overview of the key architectural enhancements. arXiv abs/2410.17725 (2024)
36. Kawulok, M., Maćkowski, M.: YOLO-type neural networks in the process of adapting mathematical graphs to the needs of the blind. Appl. Sci. **14**, 11829 (2024). https://doi.org/10.3390/APP142411829
37. Hyzy, M., et al.: System usability scale benchmarking for digital health apps: meta-analysis. JMIR Mhealth Uhealth **10**, e37290 (2022). https://doi.org/10.2196/37290
38. Hart, S.G., Staveland, L.E.: Development of NASA-TLX (Task Load Index): results of empirical and theoretical research. In: Hancock, P.A., Meshkati, N. (eds.) Advances in Psychology, pp. 139–183. North-Holland (1988). https://doi.org/10.1016/S0166-4115(08)62386-9
39. Cao, A., Chintamani, K.K., Pandya, A.K., Ellis, R.D.: NASA TLX: software for assessing subjective mental workload. Behav. Res. Methods **41**, 113–117 (2009). https://doi.org/10.3758/BRM.41.1.113
40. Bangor, A., Kortum, P.T., Miller, J.T.: Determining what individual SUS scores mean: adding an adjective rating scale. J. Usabil. Stud. Arch. **4**, 114–123 (2009)
41. Prabaswari, A.D., Basumerda, C., Utomo, B.W.: The mental workload analysis of staff in study program of private educational organization. IOP Conf. Ser. Mater. Sci. Eng. **528**, 012018 (2019). https://doi.org/10.1088/1757-899X/528/1/012018

AI-Powered Tutoring for Novice Programmers: Supporting Students Throughout Project Development

Juan Diego Lugo Sánchez[1(✉)], Brena Marques Ribeiro[2], Rubén Manrique[1], and Kelly Garcés[1]

[1] Universidad de los Andes, Bogotá, Colombia
{jd.lugo,rf.manrique,kj.garces971}@uniandes.edu.co
[2] University of São Paulo, São Paulo, Brazil
brena.marques@usp.br

Abstract. The context of this study is an introductory programming course where high school students often struggle with a proprietary graphics library used for animation/video game development projects, exacerbated by the limited availability of teaching assistants. This results in delayed and inefficient resolution of students' queries, impacting their learning experience and self-perception towards programming. We developed an AI-powered tutor designed to offer constructive tips and guide students through their coding errors without providing direct solutions. Surveys results indicate that the AI tutor effectively addresses common student queries, and improves the correctness and completeness of student code.

1 Introduction

Large Language Models (LLMs) represent the latest advancement in chatbot technology. These models are designed to understand and generate human-like text by training on vast datasets using deep learning techniques. LLMs like OpenAI's GPT (Generative Pre-trained Transformer) have fundamentally changed how chatbots operate.

In recent years, the use of Large Language Models (LLMs) as tools to assist in everyday tasks has expanded significantly, highlighting their potential as educational assistants.

The articles [3,7,8] collectively examine student satisfaction with ChatGPT feedback during programming tasks and the overall efficiency of language models (LLMs). Among the findings, GPT-4 was rated the highest in terms of effectiveness. The studies also noted that while students developed faster reasoning skills for task solving when guided by GPT suggestions, they struggled more with complex tasks in the absence of these suggestions. Similarly, multiple studies have analyzed the role of LLMs in computational problem-solving. GitHub Copilot research on an introductory programming course [1] showed that prompt engineering techniques improved its problem solving rate from 47.6% to 60.9%, highlighting the pedagogical value of refining prompts. Another study explored the use of GPT-3.5 as a virtual teaching assistant in McGill University's COMP202 course [5], showing that while it outperformed human TAs in clarity and participation in general inquiries, human oversight remained essential. Furthermore, integrating AI tutors [10] into the Artemis platform demonstrated benefits such as continuous guidance and real-time feedback, although students sometimes found the feedback too generic. A study by Jošt et al. (2024) [2] examined LLM reliance in a React programming course, revealing that although LLM improved efficiency and comprehension, overreliance on them for code generation correlated with lower grades. Collectively, these studies emphasize the potential and limitations of LLMs in programming education, addressing issues of effectiveness, ethical concerns, and student dependency.

Like aforementioned related work this study investigates the application of LLMs as learning tools aimed at clarifying doubts and identifying errors in the codes of students working on a programming course offered by Universidad de los Andes in partnership with the CSBridge iniciative.[1]

The participating students are part of an initiative aimed at reducing the opportunity gap in programming education for high school students in their final three years. At the end of the course, each student presents a final project that assesses their learning. However, recurring issues have been noted with a proprietary graphics library designed specifically for teaching animation and video game development. The high demand and limited supply of teaching assistants (referred to as Section Leaders) frequently impede the timely and efficient resolution of students' queries.

To address these challenges, we developed an AI-powered tutor leveraging a commercial LLM API. This tutor is designed to provide clear and objective answers, guiding students through their errors and suggesting potential approaches for their coding projects. The focus is on offering constructive tips rather than direct solutions, thereby promoting independent learning while ensuring adequate support. By providing efficient and tailored assistance, the AI tutor enhances knowledge access and complements the efforts of human tutors, thereby enriching the overall educational experience and enabling students to overcome programming challenges more independently.

The paper is structured as follows. Section 2 discusses the context of this research. Section 3 describes the proposal, followed by preliminary results in Sect. 4. Finally, conclusions and future work are presented in Sect. 5.

2 Context

In 2019, for the first time, the Department of Systems and Computing Engineering at Universidad de los Andes collaborated with CSBridge, under the guidance of professors from Stanford University in the United States to offer a introduction to programming course. This initiative aims to enhance the programming learning experience for both women and men, fostering greater motivation for continued engagement in programming.

---

[1] https://csbridge.stanford.edu/.

The department has conducted the course four times -in 2019, 2022, 2023, and 2024–with each session hosting 100 high school students in their last three years of study. While the initial edition saw the participation of 20 girls, subsequent editions included at least 50 girls. The course, structured as an intensive two-week program, features daily sessions, each four hours long. These sessions begin with a 45-minute lecture on Python programming concepts for the entire cohort, followed by practical work in smaller groups, addressing tasks such as problem-solving, function completion, and final project development, led by advanced computer science students (section leaders).

Perception surveys are administered at the beginning and end of each cohort to evaluate: i) students' self-perception towards programming, and ii) their course experience. Recent results indicate:

- Initially, most students disagreed or strongly disagreed with the notion that "innate natural intelligence is needed to code," which was the desired response. However, post-course perceptions were more divided, with some students agreeing or strongly agreeing with this statement.
- The majority of students reported a good or very good course experience. Practical and dynamic exercises positively impacted their learning, whereas the final project caused significant stress and demotivated some students.

We hypothesize that these outcomes are interconnected. The final project, scheduled for the course's last two days, likely increased stress levels, adversely affecting students' self-perception towards programming. To address this, in 2023, we revised the project's structure, dividing it into several parts–an inspiration part, an ideation part, a planning part, a development part, and a closure–to be completed progressively throughout the course. Section leaders observed that this new approach fostered a sense of accomplishment as students completed each milestone, thus preventing disappointment or frustration. Nonetheless, certain challenges remain:

- Students often struggle with the graphics library needed for animation and video game projects. The short training period is insufficient for some students to master the library, and discrepancies between web development environments and desktop IDEs (e.g., PyCharm, Visual Studio Code) exacerbate these difficulties.
- Many students find it challenging to perform basic animation tasks, such as positioning or moving graphical elements correctly within valid screen areas. Recognizing common patterns in these projects and aiding students in applying appropriate solutions is essential.
- Each section leader is responsible for 10 students, but due to the diverse backgrounds of the students, leaders frequently lack the time to address all concerns effectively.

These challenges prompted us to explore the potential of AI-based tutors to assist students during project development. The goal is not to replace section leaders, whose guidance is invaluable, but to provide a supplementary tool available during and beyond camp hours, enabling students to make swift progress in coding their projects.

3 Solution

The proposed solution was built through multiple iterations in which two specific tools (i.e., OpenAI Assistant Client and Diffy) were used to obtain different prototypes of tutor.

3.1 OpenAI Assistant Client-Based Approach

Initially, a prototype was built on top of the OpenAI Python library and the GPT-4o model API, and through the 'Assistant client', an initial prompt was structured based on the literature review, which highlighted the importance of including: i) a description of the role the LLM would take; ii) the context in which the assistant should work. Apart from that, we added three parts to the prompt, namely: iii) the student's question; iv) the student's wrong code; and v) graphics library code (along with documentation for each function). Therefore, the resulting prompt is as follows below, notice that the elements between ≪ ≫ were replaced by concrete inputs sent to the LLM.

> *Role: You are going to act as a tutor for high school students who are learning to program and building a project in Python.*
>
> *Context: Below is the problem faced by a student while programming her project, the library she is using in her project, you will also be given incorrect code written by the student, your task is to give suggestions on how the student can fix her code based on the Python library and syntax. You should only improve the correctness of the code, without worrying about the style.*
>
> *<< Student'squestion >>*
> *<< Incorrectcode >>*
> *<< Graphicslibrarycode >>*

At first, the results obtained by the assistant achieved a good general performance with multiple questions; however, it is notorious for the "loss of attention" by the language model. This is partially solved by prompt engineering, where a general context and a role were expressed together with specific steps to be performed and the delimitation of elements for the identification of each section, i.e. the third step uses [] to delimit the student code in the prompt.

> *Below is the problem a student faces when programming her project, the library she is using in her project, you will also be given incorrect code written by the student, your task is to give hints on how the student can fix her code based on the Python library and syntax. You should only help improve*

the correctness of the code, without worrying about style. Recall not to include a complete code that provides an answer. They are high school students who are learning to program and building a project in Python, you must detect if the code is well or poorly solved and from the student's question respond by the following steps:

-First, Empathize with the student, use crutches like Mmmm or Ash, and let them know that you are going to solve the problem together.
-Second, read the method of the canvas object associated with this problem, you will find it in triple quotes "'.
-Third, make the code yourself and compare it with the one the student has, which you will find in square brackets [].
-Fourth, understand where the student's doubt lies and explain where the fault lies in the code.
-Fifth, generate an answer in the format.
-Finally, check that under no circumstances does the answer given contain code
"' The methods of the graphics library are:

The primary challenge encountered was the prompt's length, which led to performance issues and exceeded cost constraints–specifically, the token expenditure increased significantly due to the extensive context stored in just a few uses. To address this, we considered switching LLM tools, moving from an'assistant' model to direct API calls, complemented by a client that enables faster iterations and modifications. Ultimately, we selected Diffy for its versatility and ease of implementation, particularly due to its no-code environment.

3.2 Diffy-Based Approach

In Diffy, we designed three distinct tutors, referred to as Assistant 1, Assistant 2, and Assistant 3. These assistants follow two different workflows: Assistant 1 operates within an independent flow, while Assistants 2 and 3 share another flow, though each uses a different language model. To improve control over response generation, we divided the original prompt into multiple sub-prompts, allowing for more precise adjustments to specific elements of the output.

Chatflow of Assistant 1. This flow relies on OpenAI ChatGPT-4o and includes the steps illustrated in Fig. 1 which are described below.

(1) Knowledge retrieval: our approach focuses on extracting the most relevant knowledge based on the student's query. We follow a Retrieval-Augmented Generation (RAG) framework [4], where our Knowledge Base consists of a Python library, including its docstrings and code. The text is divided into chunks, each corresponding to a specific function and its documentation. These chunks are then converted into vectors and stored in a vector database. When a student's submits a query, we retrieve the four most similar vectors to generate a relevant response.

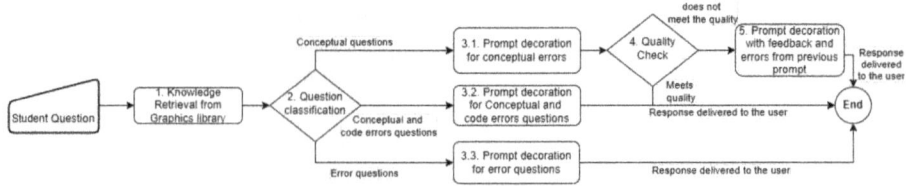

Fig. 1. Chatflow structured for assistant 1

(2) Question classification: this node classifies the user's question into one of three categories based on the input: 'conceptual question,' 'code errors,' or 'conceptual and code errors.' We found that tailoring the prompt to the question type significantly improves the quality of the answers.

(3) Initial prompt decoration: based on the classification, the chatflow adjusts the prompt by adding instructions and contextual information to enhance the relevance of the response. At this stage, depending on the question type, the answer is either delivered directly to the user or reviewed to ensure it adequately addresses the student's query.

(4) Quality check: An evaluation is conducted using another prompt. In this step, instructions and guidelines for a correct answer are provided, as it is not desirable to deliver the answer directly. If the evaluation determines that the initial response is correct, it is delivered to the student. Otherwise, the answer is regenerated with feedback from the evaluation and then provided to the user. This additional verification step is necessary due to a loss of quality in responses when attempting to explain programming concepts from a course for which the LLM lacks conceptual context beyond the library used.

(5) Final prompt decoration: This step ensures that the correct answer aligns with the course content. This is particularly important because the library contains functions with names that may lead to errors.

It is worth noting that we initially planned to include the quality check step in a loop, allowing for multiple iterations as needed, following the approach of Liu et al. However, Diffy does not support cycles, permitting only a single verification. Given this limitation and our focus on quality, we decided to design the chatflow of assistants 2 and 3, where validations are performed earlier in the process to provide the LLM with better context.

3.3 Chatflow of Assistants 2 and 3

The second and third chat flows are illustrated in Fig. 2. While they follow the same structure, their key difference lies in the LLM used: Assistant 2 relies on OpenAI ChatGPT-4o, while Assistant 3 uses Gemini 1.5 Pro. The goal of this new flow was to generate more focused responses–providing greater specificity and richer information.

(1) Knowledge Retrieval operates in the same way that assistant 1.

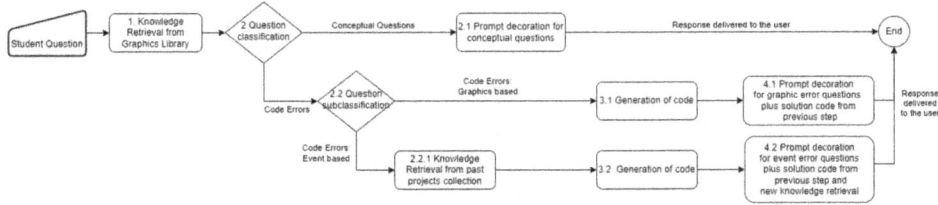

Fig. 2. Chatflow structured for assistant 2 and 3

(2) Question classification is now divided into two main categories and two subcategories: code questions and conceptual questions. Among these, event and graphics questions are subcategories of code questions.

(2.1) Prompt decoration for conceptual questions: For conceptual questions, a different approach is taken compared to that of Assistant 1. Instead of providing guidelines at the moment of answer generation, the conceptual scope of the response is predefined by setting specific guidelines based on the concepts covered in the course, particularly those related to the graphics library. Subsequently, the final response is delivered to the user.

(2.2) Question subclassification: Because of a problem identified when answering questions about event handling in Python–specifically (the use of the mouse or keyboard), we decide to classify code error questions into two subcategories (i.e., events and graphics). The problem was that responses often included functions and libraries that, while correct, relied on complex programming concepts that were not suitable for an introductory programming course. After subclassification, if question are marked as graphics-based the flow continues with steps 3 and 4. Otherwise, in case of event-based question, the flow pursuits with a retrieval step (2.2.1). Once the knowledge retrieval is integrated it, the flow follows steps 3 and 4.

(2.2.1) Past projects retrieval: For events questions, we introduce a second round of knowledge retrieval. However, this time, the retrieval is performed on previous student projects from past camps, which have been pre-filtered to remove anti-patterns and bad practices. This allows for the extraction of relevant examples of event usage within the context and guidelines of the camp.

(3) Generation of code: A block was introduced to generate a code solution prior to response generation. This code helps us to constraint the prompt. When providing a solution, the responses tended to focus more on explanation rather than directly delivering the solution. This approach makes it appear that the response is not directly generated by the assistant but rather derived from a predefined solution, enabling more effective control and constraint mechanisms.

(4) Prompt decoration for graphic or event questions: This step makes a fine tuning of the prompt incorporating information from the knowledge retrieval step and the generated code solution.

4 Validation

4.1 Methodology

The camp hosts a large group of students each year; however, evaluating this type of tool after the event poses significant challenges. These challenges stem from both logistical constraints and the need for parental permissions, as most participants are minors. To address this, a survey is conducted with ten (10) section leaders from the previous camp, who can offer valuable insights into the learning process of multiple students. The survey follows a standardized structure, asking each section leader to review the answers generated by the three chat flows (1, 2, and 3) in response to three common questions a camp student might ask.

1. Scenario 1: *"I have an error creating the oval and I don't know how to center it either"*.
2. Scenario 2: *"How can I set an image, how do I set a timer without crashing the program?"*
3. Scenario 3: Free question.

These scenarios were chosen to cover the most common questions students ask during the camp, particularly regarding canvas placement, graphical object creation, and event handling. Additionally, section leaders were allowed to ask their own questions, allowing for feedback beyond the predefined scenarios and uncovering potential gaps.

Afterward, each section leader evaluates the chat flow on a scale from 0 to 10, where 0 represents 'deficient' and 10 signifies 'excellent,' based on the following four criteria:

Correctness: Evaluates whether the answers generated by the assistant are correct in terms of Python code, which implies checking if the code provided works without errors, meets the requirements set in the prompt and follows the standard conventions of Python and the Graphics library.

Completeness: Analyzes whether the answers are complete; meaning that the answers must comprehensively address all parts of the problem or question posed, without leaving out relevant information or steps necessary for the student to understand and execute the code successfully.

Truthfulness: Examines the accuracy of the information provided; it is about making sure that everything the assistant presents as part of the answer is true and corresponds to the knowledge and good practices taught during the camp, both in terms of theory and implementation in Python.

Understandability: Assesses how easy it is for a high school student to understand the answers. Explanations should be clear, appropriate for their level of knowledge, and presented pedagogically, with examples that facilitate understanding and avoid overly technical or advanced language. Interested readers can have access to the survey through this link: Survey

4.2 Results and Analysis

Quantitative Analysis. Table 1 shows the average score per criterion obtained for each designed flow. Note that the table does not show the full names of the criteria, but rather an abbreviation: *Cor* refers to correctness and *Com* to completeness, *Tru* to truthfulness, and *Und* to understandability. At first glance, these results show that the three assistants have very even grades to the criteria evaluated, ranging from 6,27 to 8,13 out of 10.

Table 1. Average score per criterion for each assistant

Assistants	Assistant 1				Assistant 2				Assistant 3			
Criteria	Cor	Com	Tru	Und	Cor	Com	Tru	Und	Cor	Com	Tru	Und
Average	7,87	7,77	7,33	6,27	7,87	7,57	7,20	6,67	7,63	6,90	8,13	7,00

The previous results suggest a uniform average behavior among the different assistants. This may be partly because chatflow 1 served as the foundation upon which Chatflows 2 and 3 were built. However, we wondered whether each assistant might have a particular strength, to identify the best aspects of each and integrate them into a new version of the chat soon. For this reason, we continued analyzing the data from a quantitative and qualitative point of view. Figure 3 presents scores box plots obtained by the chatflows in each of the scenarios presented in the survey. When reading Fig. 3 by *columns* to visualize the performance of each assistant across the scenarios we can observe:

- For Assistant 1 (which uses OpenAI ChatGPT) we can highlight its high and stable correctness which indicates that the quality check step, which verifies answers before delivering the final response, is working well. Additionally, it demonstrates solid completeness in the first and third scenarios, meaning that the answers generally address the problems in their entirety. Some variability is observed in the second scenario, the one related to events. However, the main issues lie in understandability, as it shows the greatest dispersion, with lower average values. This suggests that the verification and feedback steps may be introducing more technical or overly detailed responses, making comprehension more difficult for students.
- For the Assistant 2 (which uses OpenAI ChatGPT) we can observe a balance between correctness and understandability; as both metrics show a more even distribution. This suggests that the assistant is able to deliver correct answers without sacrificing clarity.
- Assistant 3 (which uses Gemini) demonstrates higher average understandability compared to the other two assistants. In terms of correctness, its performance is acceptable, although it exhibits greater dispersion. While it is not as accurate as Assistant 1, it still achieves a reasonable level of correctness. Assistant 3 also exhibits greater dispersion in truthfulness. This suggests that the model may be "hallucinating" or generating responses that are not always

aligned with the best practices of the course. In some scenarios, this assistant displays greater variability in completeness, indicating that certain responses may not fully address all aspects needed by the student.
- When comparing the performance of assistants 2 and 3 that share the same workflow but differs in the underlying LLM model we observe the following: The variation in the used LLM model appears to result in differences in terms of code accuracy; Gemini-based assistant being the more accurate overall. This behavior may be partly due to the fact that Gemini had a better interpretation of the code content that resulted from the step of past projects knowledge retrieval.

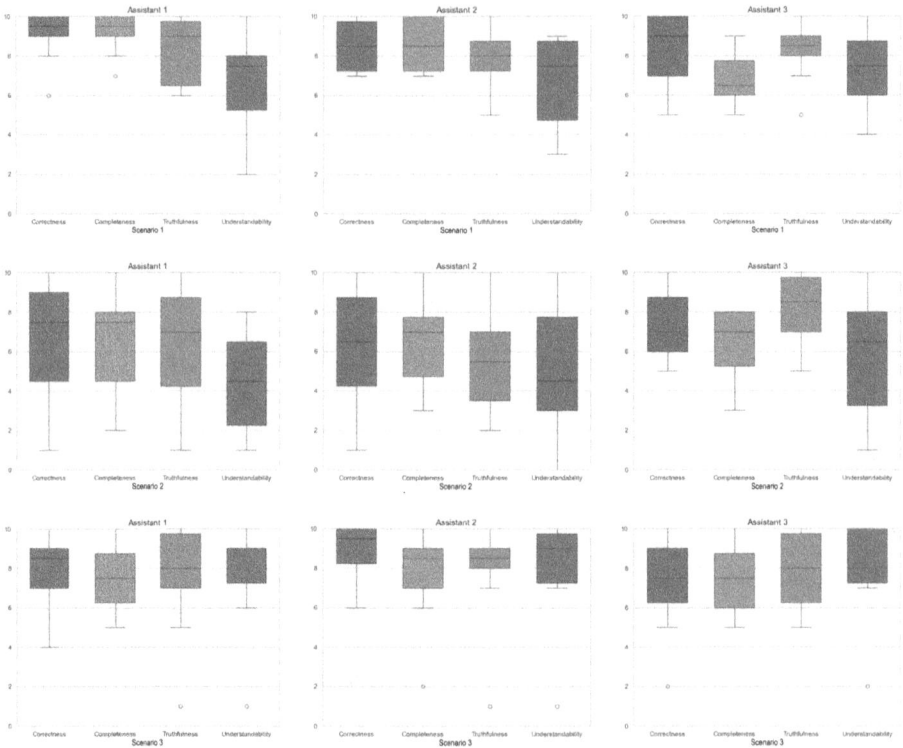

Fig. 3. Scenarios results

Qualitative Analysis. Given that the results are not quantitatively conclusive, we decided to peruse each survey submission (both multiple-choice and open-ended questions) to identify expectation bias in the ratings. Table 2 summarizes the rating and comments that a particular subject assigned to Assistant 3 for each scenario.

Table 2. Comments from a section leader over Assistant 3 performance

Scenario 1				
Ratings:	Cor	Com	Tru	Und
	9	3	9	1
Comment:	No comments			
Scenario 2				
Ratings:	Cor	Com	Tru	Und
	1	2	1	5
Comment:	Lack of code explanations (snippets are very helpful) and limited coverage of the overall project structure			
Scenario 3				
Ratings:	Cor	Com	Tru	Und
	10	10	10	10
Comment:	Very clear and the information is correct			

The ratings given by the respondent to Assistant 3 show a marked inconsistency between scenarios, suggesting the presence of bias in their evaluation. In the first and second scenarios, the assistant received low ratings for completeness and understandability, which could be attributed to the absence of code snippets in the chatflow response–an aspect the respondent highlighted as important in their comments. However, in the third scenario, where the question was open-ended (how to generate multiple colored squares?) and possibly aligned with subject's interest, she gave perfect ratings. This behavior could be explained by expectation bias, where the respondent penalizes answers that do not meet a specific criterion (in this case, the presence of code examples). Additionally, anchoring bias (first impression bias) may have played a role, where a negative experience in the second scenario influenced their overall perception of the assistant, leading to lower ratings in other aspects.

Overall, this pattern suggests that the chatflow evaluation is influenced not only by objective performance criteria but also by the respondent's individual expectations, prior experiences in former scenarios, and the nature of the question itself.

Lessons Learned. Based on these results, we plan to develop a new chatflow that incorporates the steps and features that contribute the most to the aforementioned quality criteria:

- *Question classification:* this step helps tailoring the prompt to the student's question type.
- *Knowledge retrieval:* On one hand, retrieving information from the graphics library provides the LLM with more context about the functions available for

developing animation and video game projects. On the other hand, retrieving past code projects enriches the LLM context with code examples related to the use of graphics or events. However, this context may sometimes be insufficient compared to the extensive prior knowledge the LLM has about Python. As a result, this prior knowledge may occasionally take precedence in the responses.
- *Generation of code*: This step allows us to refine the prompt; when generating a response, the answers tended to emphasize explanation rather than simply providing the solution.
- *Code-based LLM:* models such as Gemini or other specialized coding models may help to fine-tune the expected behavior in detail.

4.3 Threads to Validity

Below, we outline the threats to the validity of this study according to the dimensions identified by [11]. Regarding construct validity, the survey was designed based on previously validated surveys from the literature on related topics [6,9]. As for internal validity, fully controlling this threat when designing a survey is challenging, as any error in a question may influence respondents' answers. To mitigate this, the survey was reviewed by two senior researchers before being disseminated among section leaders. In terms of external validity, we acknowledge the limitation of having only 10 respondents, which restricts the generalizability of the findings. Conducting similar surveys with a larger number of respondents, ideally high school students, would be beneficial. We plan to implement this in the next iteration of the course. A potential threat to validity in this study arises from suggestions to perform comparisons that are not appropriate for the experimental context, such as comparing the agents performance with human section leaders. Given the structure of the course, the section leaders provide guidance and are largely responsible for providing personalized assistance in small groups. In this context, the AI tutor is introduced: to address simple coding queries and free up leaders time so they could focus on supporting students with more complex or conceptual issues. Therefore, a direct comparison of performance would not have been meaningful, nor would it have aligned with the current context.

5 Conclusion and Future Work

The introduction of AI-based tutors to support students in learning programming has proven to be a promising strategy. However, challenges such as generating coherent responses, contextual limitations, and the need to adapt to students' knowledge levels required refinements in the adopted approach. In our case the transition from an OpenAI Assistant Client-based model to the Diffy platform allowed greater control over the generated responses, enabling the segmentation of interactions and more targeted knowledge retrieval. Structuring the assistants into different workflows and separating the responsibilities for code generation and explanations contributed to more effective responses aligned with the educational goals of the course. Our results indicate that LLM can be a valuable tool to complement the work of section leaders, providing continuous support and reducing the difficulties faced by students. However, it is essential to ensure that its use does not lead to excessive dependency and that learning occurs autonomously and meaningfully. Future improvements may include improving response evaluation mechanisms, expanding the knowledge base used by tutors, and conducting a long-term analysis of the impact of the tool on student motivation and performance.

References

1. Denny, P., Kumar, V., Giacaman, N.: Conversing with copilot: exploring prompt engineering for solving cs1 problems using natural language. In: Proceedings of the 54th ACM Technical Symposium on Computer Science Education (SIGCSE 2023) (2023). https://doi.org/10.1145/3545945.3569823,
2. Jost, G., Taneski, V., Karakatic, S.: The impact of large language models on programming education and student learning outcomes. Appl. Sci. **14**(4115) (2024). https://doi.org/10.3390/app14104115
3. Koutcheme, C., Dainese, N., Sarsa, S., Hellas, A., Leinonen, J., Denny, P.: Open source language models can provide feedback: evaluating LLMs' ability to help students using GPT-4-as-a-judge. In: Proceedings of the 2024 on Innovation and Technology in Computer Science Education, vol. 1, pp. 52–58 (2024)
4. Lewis, P., et al.: Retrieval-augmented generation for knowledge-intensive NLP tasks (2021). arxiv:2005.11401
5. Liu, M., M'hiri, F.: Beyond traditional teaching: Large language models as simulated teaching assistants in computer science. Proceedings of the 55th ACM Technical Symposium on Computer Science Education (SIGCSE 2024) (2024). https://doi.org/10.1145/3626252.3630789
6. Mychalski, A.: Exploration of domain-specific conversational systems as a means to enhance obstetric emergency care. Master's thesis, Universidad de los Andes (2024). https://hdl.handle.net/1992/75222
7. Nie, A., et al.: The GPT surprise: offering large language model chat in a massive coding class reduced engagement but increased adopters' exam performances. Technical report, Center for Open Science (2024)
8. Pankiewicz, M., Baker, R.S.: Navigating compiler errors with AI assistance-a study of GPT hints in an introductory programming course. In: Proceedings of the 2024 on Innovation and Technology in Computer Science Education, vol. 1, pp. 94–100 (2024)
9. Salazar-Lara, C., Arias Russi, A.F., Manrique, R.: Bridging the gap in health literacy: harnessing the power of large language models to generate plain language summaries from biomedical texts. medRxiv (2024). https://doi.org/10.1101/2024.07.02.24309847, https://www.medrxiv.org/content/early/2024/07/03/2024.07.02.24309847
10. Vadaparty, A., et al.: Cs1-LLM: Integrating LLMs into cs1 instruction. In: Proceedings of the 2024 Innovation and Technology in Computer Science Education (ITiCSE 2024) (2024). https://doi.org/10.1145/3649217.3653584
11. Wohlin, C., Runeson, P., Höst, M., Ohlsson, M.C., Regnell, B.: Experimentation in Software Engineering. Springer, Cham (2012)

Language Models for Educational Question Generation: Practical Challenges, Personalization Opportunities, and Parameter Optimization

Jason Bernard(✉) and Sabine Graf

Athabasca University, Athabasca, AB T9S 3A3, Canada
{cbernard,sabineg}@athabascau.ca

Abstract. Language models (LMs) are a new technology attracting research interest in many fields, including educational technology, for their ability to generate media, including text, from a prompt. For teachers creating new questions is a time-consuming process yet essential for developing and confirming a learner's understanding of the material. This research extends existing research on LM-based question generation by investigating what challenges exist when developing a question generator to support both teachers and learners. In addition, to support personalization, the generation of questions at three difficulty levels is investigated. Finally, different settings are systematically evaluated for creating the best possible questions. Using training data from a course, two small LMs, Gemma 7B and Gemma-7B-it (instruction pre-tuned), were trained under 84 experimental settings. 7 prompts styles (10 prompts each), plus 9 human-generated prompts, for each course unit were used for each experimental setting. It was found that considerable manual effort to prepare the training data and extract the generated questions from the LM's response was required. Depending on the settings, a question with the proper difficulty was generated between 61.5% and 67.4% of the time. Gemma-7B-it improved overall quality but struggled to generate beginner-level questions. Sentences granularity with unit-only training was found to be best. Roleplaying-style prompts created the best questions, and prompt engineering was critical for LM control. Furthermore, LM-generated prompts were found to be better than human-created prompts.

Keywords: Small Language Models · Question Generation · Teacher Support · Learner Support · Generative AI

1 Introduction

Question generation has been a research subject for decades [e.g., 1–4]. Recent advances with language models (LMs), which can create high-quality text, or other media, from a prompt [5, 6], has spurred a renewed interest particularly within the context of educational technology [7–12]. Within the educational context, question generation can be used to support both teachers and learners.

Dating back to Bloom's Taxonomy [13, 14], it has been well known that different questions can encourage learning in varying ways, with each question style having a purpose. Convergent (closed) questions might be useful for beginners, while divergent (open) questions promote more critical thinking [13–16]. Questions promote engagement from students, and help confirm the learner's knowledge [15, 16]. However, creating variant questions just to cover each layer of Bloom's Taxonomy [13, 14] is a considerable effort, let alone considering the pedagogical ideas discovered since then.

Hence, for teachers, automatic question generation offers the opportunity to create questions for varying pedagogical purposes without the substantial increase in workload that would be required to do so manually. Even in non-adaptive settings, question generation is useful when creating a new course, or when course content has changed.

The generated questions support learners by promoting learning and engagement [15–17]. Providing many questions in a course can support the learning process and help students prepare for exams. Automatic question generation creates also the opportunity to provide questions personalized to the student based on a student model (a set of characteristics about the student that can be queried) [18], which potentially creates a pathway from beginner to critical thinker by asking increasingly more open questions as the student progresses.

Prior related works [e.g., 7–12] have focused on evaluating generated questions using well-known natural language processing metrics, such as Perplexity [7, 10], BLEU [7, 8, 10], METEOR [8, 9], and ROUGE [8, 9]. Such preliminary work is vital for determining if LMs can produce coherent questions, and the results have been promising. However, missing from such work is an investigation into the relevance and quality of such questions from an educational perspective as well as the challenges that can occur when developing a question generator in practice for an educational setting.

In addition, research into the generation of personalized questions where, for example, the difficulty of a question is matched with a learner's knowledge level is in a very early stage. A preliminary study [12] examined the difficulty of generated questions when no personalization prompting is provided. They found they were often too easy and unengaging, and stated difficulty and engagement as an area for improvement.

Furthermore, other studies [19, 20] have found that the optimal settings for creating LMs that produce meaningful results vary from problem to problem and need to be examined systematically by experimentation. To date, no such analysis exists for educational question generation.

With the gaps mentioned in the previous three paragraphs in mind, the aim of this paper is to fill in these knowledge gaps by developing an LM-based educational question generator for a course, systematically using different LM settings. The challenges in development are reported on via observations during the development process. To investigate the LM's capability for creating personalized questions, half the prompts include a specified difficulty level. The resulting questions are then evaluated for how well they match the specified difficulty level. The optimal settings are found by evaluating the questions and comparing the average results. The following research questions represent these goals:

- RQ1: How can a practical LM-based educational question generator be developed and what challenges emerge from such development?

- RQ2: How effective is such an LM in creating personalized questions?
- RQ3: What are the optimal settings for such LM to generate the best questions for educational use?
  - RQ3a: Are instruction pre-tuned models optimal for educational question generation?
  - RQ3b: With respect to training data, how does granularity and scope affect educational question generation?
  - RQ3c: How does any interaction between granularity and scope affect educational question generation?
  - RQ3d: What is the optimal prompt style for educational question generation?
  - RQ3e: How effective are LM-generated prompts in comparison to human-created prompts for educational question generation?

2 Related Works

While LMs dominate the current landscape for question generation, the earliest comparable works focused on question answering about images [1, 2], followed by works exclusively on question generation [3, 4]. These works focused on different neural networks algorithms and could even be considered pre-cursor research to LMs. Following the release of the earliest viable LMs, question generation research increased dramatically in number [e.g., 21, 22] although still in the context of imagery [23] or conversational AI [21, 22]. Only very recently has research begun for question generation using LMs for educational purposes; however, already there have been several attempts [7–12]. Taken in all, there is a clear multi-decade consensus of the value for automatic question generation.

The predominant methodology used for LM-based question generation in education [7–12] is to take the newest released version of an LM and fine tune it with one or more known large, curated data sets such as SQuAD [24], S2ORC [25], or learningQ [26]. The trained LM is evaluated using one or more NLP metrics such as perplexity [27], BLEU [28], ROUGE [29], and METEOR [30]. Such research is valuable as they confirm that questions can be generated that are of high quality from an NLP perspective, i.e., they are readable, similar in structure to human-generated questions, and are not just copies of the training data. Collectively, the studies report successful results vis a vis the NLP metrics [7–11], but the questions are not evaluated pedagogically, with Bulathwela and colleagues [7] stating this would be the necessary next step.

One issue arises from the training data used. The datasets used in other works, while large and provide the ground truth required for the NLP metrics, are quite shallow when considering a particular educational subject [10, 11]. For example, SQuAD [24] has over 100,000 questions and answers, and 50,000 unanswerable questions. However, this is spread over all human knowledge ranging from pop stars to scientific topics. For example, considering the educational topic of software engineering (the course subject selected for this research), there are only three entries: 1. The contribution of Estonian scientists on software engineering, 2. A description of software quality assurance, and 3. Changes in contemporary computer science. This would not be enough information for the model to create meaningful questions for a course in software engineering. For clarity, other studies acknowledge these datasets are intended for reading comprehension and not to provide specialized knowledge to the LM [7, 9–12].

The work most related to this one is a multiple-choice question generator for two courses where teachers were used to evaluate the generated questions [12]. They found that the questions (with answers) were correct, but found the level of difficulty too low, and hence the questions unengaging. While our work focuses on short answer questions instead of multiple-choice questions, we also investigate the pedagogical quality as well as how well an LM can create questions at different difficulty levels (RQ2).

In addition, the prior works [7–12] use a limited number of setting variables, often only varying the model, and compare results to each other. Other studies [19, 20] have examined the individual parameters that control LMs for the general text generation task and found that the parameters should be evaluated on a problem-by-problem basis. Hence leading to RQ3, which is to find the optimal settings for educational question generation as this has not been done previously.

3 Methodology

This section describes and justifies the approaches used for this research. It begins by describing the pre-evaluation processes for model selection, prompt generation, as well as data selection and processing. It then describes the metrics used: difficulty matching, relevance, and quality.

3.1 Model Selection

This research focused on choosing freely available LMs towards making free and open tools; however, there are many to choose from of differing sizes. The decision was made to focus on small language models (SLMs) as there is evidence they can perform better on specialized tasks [31]. In addition, SLMs are more portable, and have less computational training costs, which promotes accessibility to more users as described by Fawzi and colleagues [11], who also found that SLMs were just as effective as LLMs for question generation. The best definitions that could be found in the literature suggested LMs with less than 10B parameters might be considered small as of late 2024 [5, 6].

According to a past study [19], there is a lack of certainty concerning the effectiveness of instruction pre-tuning and that it should be evaluated on a per problem basis, which led to forming RQ3a to fill in this knowledge gap for educational question generation. Therefore, the selected model should have an instruction pre-tuned variant.

The last criterion was to find models that have been used extensively in research suggesting robustness. Gemma-7B [32] and Gemma-instruct-7B [32] were selected as they met all requirements. The models were further fine-tuned using training data.

3.2 Data Selection and Processing

The training data consists of the learning materials of a course to capture specialized knowledge. The primary restriction is the learning materials had to digitally exist, i.e.

no paper textbook. It was also decided to avoid courses that focused on programming or mathematics, as these require specialized model training [33–35]. An online software engineering course met these criteria and so was selected. The training data consisted of the SWEBOK textbook [36], scholarly papers, and web pages.

Fine tuning current LM models, commercial or public, for text generating tasks requires text data. Such text data was extracted from the PDFs (i.e., SWEBOK and the scholarly papers) manually. While it can be automated using Python libraries, this was found to be inefficient as undesirable text (titles, page numbers, journal name, etc.) was interwoven into the data in a way that was difficult to remove either automatically or manually. Additionally, PDFs with multiple columns were often converted with the columns interwoven which is also difficult to correct. For some PDFs, this was an issue even with manual extraction, but easier to control. ChatGPT was used for converting PDFs to text when manual extraction caused an excessive number of errors. While ChatGPT is effective, it is much slower than manual extraction and has a cost which is contrary to the goal of creating free, open tools. As such, an automatic error correction tool was created, which can fix many common errors (e.g., ligatures, words split by "-", etc.), and organize the content into paragraphs. The data was manually checked for accuracy, while resolving any errors not fixed automatically.

All the web pages for the course were scrapped manually for two reasons. Automatic web scraping may sometimes be detected and blocked. Even more so than the PDFs, web pages include non-learning material, such as ads, which are not easily skipped automatically.

3.3 Training Data

Following pre-processing, the data was converted into training data to then fine-tune the LMs. In their review, Zhang and colleagues [37] state that LM training data may be subdivided into the document, paragraph (one or many paragraphs), sentence, and keyword. To be comprehensive, the data has been subdivided into all the fully completed paragraphs on a page (multiple paragraphs), henceforth called "page", paragraph (one only), and sentence granularities. The documents used by Zhang and colleagues [37] are not as large as scholarly papers or textbooks, which could not be used due to real-world memory limitations. Keyword training data is used for tasks where specific text outputs are desired based on a knowledge graph produced from the keywords, which is not the case for this research.

The three granularities are the second experimental parameter and are used to answer RQ3b. Table 1 shows the amount of data by granularity and course unit following data extraction.

The third experimental parameter, which relates to RQ3c, is an attempt to either confuse the LM or provide additional context for the LM by using training data from the whole course rather than just the unit's learning material. As the long-term goal is to obtain domain-independence, this is an especially critical question to answer. If the LM is confused by even course-level data, then it might be incredibly confused by larger domain scopes. In contrast, additional material that is closely related to the unit may provide additional context and could also improve question generation.

Table 1. The size of the training data by unit and granularity.

Unit	Pages	Paragraphs	Sentences	Total Words
Scope of Software Engineering	32	298	795	21080
Software Requirements	26	334	882	31240
Software Design	44	566	1348	40396
Software Construction Approaches	27	220	658	27371
Software Maintenance	67	898	2070	45950
Software Engineering Process	86	886	2441	46591

3.4 Prompt Style and Engineering

To answer RQ3d, the last experimental parameter is prompt style and engineering. Due to performance differences, experimenting with many styles is recommended [19]. There are many styles of prompts. For this research the following were selected: Zero Shot [7, 9, 11], Few Shot [38], Chain-of-Thought [8], Direct Instruction [39], Roleplaying [39], Contextual [39], and Decomposition [39].

Prompts were created from templates that could be used across all units. For each style, ten prompt templates were generated by ChatGPT, as LLMs have been found to be effective prompt engineers [40]. In addition, nine human-generated prompt templates (which is the focus of existing works [7–9, 11]) were created, one in each style plus two additional ones for the roleplaying and contextual styles to account for student vs. teacher roles or context. All human-generated prompts were rolled into one category for a total of eight experimental prompt categories which are used to answer RQ3d and RQ3e. In total, 79 templates were created for a total of 474 prompts across the 6 units.

Finally, to answer RQ2, half of the prompts specify a desired difficulty level (beginner, intermediate, or advanced). The prompts either request a single question at one difficulty level, with each difficulty guaranteed to exist, or to generate a set of three related questions at each difficulty level. The other half of prompts do not explicitly ask for a specific difficulty.

Questions were automatically extracted from the LM response to each prompt looking for sentences ending with "?", a "Question" marker, or phrases like "The question might be: ...". However, there were many issues, so some manual work was done to further process the extracted data (as further discussed in Sect. 5.2).

3.5 Experimental Settings

In summary, the experimental settings for this research consist of a model selection (Gemma 7B and Gemma 7B-it), with the training data used to fine-tune the LMs under different granularity values (Page, Paragraph, and Sentence), training data scopes (Unit-level, Course-level), and then a base case with no fine tuning for each model for a total of

14 settings. While prompts are considered a parameter when computing the evaluation metric, all prompts were sent to the LM following training. Every setting is executed for all 6 units giving a total of 84 experiments.

All experiments were trained using 4 x v100 cards, each with 32 GB of VRAM. Memory requirement reduction was achieved using low-rank adaptation (LoRA) rank 4. A batch size of 10 was used over 20 epochs.

3.6 Evaluation Process and Metrics

The metrics for evaluating the questions generated are somewhat different than related works [7–12], which used NLP metrics. In this research, the focus is on pedagogical usefulness and the metrics are designed for this purpose. The questions generated were assessed by one of the researchers, a software engineering expert with 20 years of industry experience, and university-level teaching experience.

As the questions were evaluated blindly, all generated questions were categorized as beginner, intermediate, or advanced. For questions generated using a prompt with a specified difficulty, the assessed difficulty is compared to the prompted difficulty, resulting in a Difficulty Match metric. If the prompted difficulty and assessed difficulty are the same, then this is scored as 1; if they are off by one category (e.g., a beginner and intermediate or advanced and intermediate pairing), it is scored as 0.5; otherwise, 0. Questions generated without a specified difficulty were ignored for this calculation.

Each question is also evaluated from 1 to 5 for Relevance and Quality, with a higher score being better. Relevance measures how well the question matches the course unit. Quality measures the overall sense of whether the question is useful, understandable/readable, and pedagogically sound. Initially, a Readability metric was considered; however, there were so few issues (less than 1% had even minor issues) that this was wrapped into Quality.

For calibration purposes, a basic but sound question such as "What are the principles of software engineering?" was scored as 3 for quality. Higher quality scores were given to questions that would have superior phrasing, promote more engagement from the learner, or focused on vital aspects of software engineering as judged by the expert. Lower quality was given to questions that were either phrased confusingly, yes/no questions, or wildly off-topic (e.g., "What does software design mean for your afterlife?"). Given the relationship between quality and difficulty level (e.g., advanced level questions are mostly of higher quality than beginner level questions), the quality was computed using only those questions generated from a prompt without a specific difficulty.

All the metrics above were averaged across models, and prompt styles. For the granularities, averages were taken for each granularity at the unit and course level, given that both parameters are related to the training data. The averages were compared to find the best settings, or prompt style to answer all research questions except RQ3e. For that question, the comparison is made between the average over all LM-generated categories to the average of the human-created category.

4 Results and Evaluation

To begin, the quantitative results are provided as averages across different experimental settings to show which parameter settings provide the best questions. Table 2 provides the results when averaging for the two LM models. Tables 3 and 4 provide the results when averaging across granularities, with Table 3 being for unit-level training data, and Table 4 when using the entire course's data. Finally, Tables 5 and 6 (split only due to the size) provide the results when averaged across prompt styles.

In terms of model selection, the average for difficulty matches are close to each other with 64.1% for 7B, and 65.0% for 7B-it (as shown in Table 2). However, the mismatches are caused for different reasons in each. The distribution of difficulties indicates that 7B tended to produce more beginner-level questions (41.7%) than 7B-it (18.2%), which mainly produced intermediate-level questions (61.6%), and these tendencies account for much of the mismatches. Both also had the interesting quirk of asking complex essay-style or programming questions as beginner-level questions, although this was more common with 7B-it.

For average relevance and quality, 7B-it was better for every unit except the first, indicating that it is the better choice for generating education questions. For Unit 1, an examination of the questions showed that both models seemed confused by the word "Scope" in the unit title. Many of the questions were related to system design or requirements and generated questions concerning "scoping a system", and not as the unit is intended, an introduction to software engineering. 7B-it perhaps owing to better reasoning, was more confused than 7B about the meaning of "scope" causing a larger decrease in relevance scores. Due to the confusion caused by "scope", while all results are provided, the discussion in the following paragraphs focuses on the other five units and another average row has been added to the tables "Avg w/o U1".

Table 2. The effects of instruction tuned model on the evaluation metrics: difficulty match % (DM), average relevance ($\overline{\text{Rel}}$), and average quality ($\overline{\text{Q}}$). The best results are bolded.

Unit	Gemma 7B			Gemma 7B Instruct		
	DM	$\overline{\text{Rel}}$	$\overline{\text{Q}}$	DM	$\overline{\text{Rel}}$	$\overline{\text{Q}}$
SoSE	**69.7%**	**3.32**	2.71	67.4%	2.98	**2.92**
SReq	62.1%	4.66	2.88	**62.5%**	**4.84**	**3.66**
SDes	**63.8%**	4.52	2.82	62.1%	**4.84**	**3.25**
SConst	57.8%	4.43	2.83	**61.6%**	**4.82**	**3.52**
SMaint	66.0%	4.73	2.89	**71.6%**	**4.89**	**3.47**
SEProc	**65.2%**	4.67	2.86	64.5%	**4.87**	**3.48**
Average	64.1%	4.39	2.83	**65.0%**	**4.54**	**3.38**

When looking at granularity and scope, from the unit-only results (Table 3), "Sentences" performed best overall with difficulty match %, relevance and quality scores of

65.6%, 4.70 and 3.08. For the course-level data results (Table 4), there is no conclusive best as the top for each metric is the base model for DM, "Pages" for quality, and "Sentences" for relevance. The unit-only results are consistently better than when using the entire course data for training (except relevance with paragraphs). The decreases are small, but indicate a possible confusion effect, which should be examined further.

Prior to examining the different prompt styles, an issue with automatic question extraction needs to be discussed. As mentioned, automatic extraction looked for questions based on a "?", a "Question" marker, or a phrase like "The question might be…". Two prompt styles exhibited issues with this approach. Often questions generated from Few Shot prompts were obfuscated by intermediary questions that required additional manual parsing. The chain-of-thought prompt response would often contain a method for finding questions and then provide several questions and answers, making the intended question unclear.

Table 3. The effects of granularity using unit-only data: difficulty match % (DM), average relevance ($\overline{Rel}$), and average quality ($\overline{Q}$). Also, includes the base case where no training data is used. The best results are bolded.

Unit	Base			Pages			Paragraphs			Sentences		
	DM	$\overline{Rel}$	$\overline{Q}$	DM	$\overline{Rel}$	$\overline{Q}$	DM	$\overline{Rel}$	$\overline{Q}$	DM	$\overline{Rel}$	$\overline{Q}$
SoSE	70.4%	3.00	2.88	**72.1%**	2.82	2.63	65.5%	2.95	2.83	65.1%	**3.60**	**2.97**
SReq	**70.1%**	4.63	3.06	62.7%	**4.77**	3.11	57.0%	4.42	2.86	60.3%	**4.77**	**3.15**
SDes	**69.2%**	4.53	2.84	64.1%	4.53	2.82	57.3%	**4.73**	**2.94**	68.1%	4.71	3.01
SConst	57.1%	4.45	2.91	**64.6%**	**4.59**	3.11	60.8%	4.46	**3.15**	58.9%	4.46	**3.15**
SMaint	67.3%	4.68	2.96	70.4%	**4.80**	3.03	**75.3%**	**4.80**	3.12	72.0%	4.76	2.97
SEProc	61.6%	4.69	3.02	62.6%	4.76	3.00	67.6%	4.79	2.98	**68.5%**	**4.81**	**3.10**
Average	65.8%	4.33	2.95	**66.1%**	4.38	2.95	63.9%	4.36	2.98	65.5%	**4.52**	**3.06**
Avg w/o U1	65.1%	4.60	2.96	64.9%	4.69	3.01	63.6%	4.64	3.01	**65.6%**	**4.70**	**3.08**

In looking at the results for the prompts (Tables 5 and 6), three prompt styles emerge as excellent picks: Few Shot, Direct Instruction, and Roleplaying. Roleplaying has the highest quality (3.18). Few Shot on the other hand has the highest average difficulty matching and relevance scores with 67.4% and 4.94 respectively. However, taking into account the manual work required for Few Shot, then Roleplaying seems the better option as little manual work was required for it. If the Few Shot results are ignored, Direct Instruction would have the highest difficulty match (64.3%), second-best quality (3.12), and second-best relevance (4.76), making it a potential selection for personalizing questions. Overall, it depends on whether the issues surrounding the Few Shot responses can be resolved, but this requires further investigation.

In terms of LLM vs Human generation of prompts, the "Human" category includes human-generated prompts across all styles. To compare it with LLM generated prompts,

Table 4. The effects of granularity using all six units training data: difficulty match % (DM), average relevance ($\overline{\text{Rel}}$), and average quality ($\overline{Q}$). Also, includes the base case where no training data is used. The best results are bolded.

Unit	Base			Pages			Paragraphs			Sentences		
	DM	$\overline{\text{Rel}}$	$\overline{Q}$	DM	$\overline{\text{Rel}}$	$\overline{Q}$	DM	$\overline{\text{Rel}}$	$\overline{Q}$	DM	$\overline{\text{Rel}}$	$\overline{Q}$
SoSE	70.4%	3.00	2.88	**75.6%**	2.31	**2.95**	71.7%	3.14	2.82	60.8%	**3.39**	2.71
SReq	**70.1%**	4.63	3.06	64.0%	4.72	3.08	62.1%	4.75	3.03	61.2%	**4.81**	**3.11**
SDes	**69.2%**	4.53	2.84	64.3%	4.69	2.91	63.8%	4.63	**2.96**	66.0%	**4.79**	2.92
SConst	57.1%	4.45	2.91	61.5%	4.49	**2.93**	**62.1%**	4.45	2.84	59.2%	**4.55**	2.88
SMaint	67.3%	4.68	2.96	**69.2%**	4.76	2.99	66.0%	**4.82**	3.08	68.9%	4.81	3.03
SEProc	61.6%	4.69	3.02	63.6%	**4.68**	**3.03**	62.5%	4.61	2.82	**68.5%**	4.49	2.92
Average	65.8%	4.33	2.95	**66.4%**	4.28	**2.99**	64.7%	4.40	2.93	64.1%	**4.47**	2.93
Avg w/o U1	**65.1%**	4.60	2.96	64.5%	4.67	**2.99**	63.3%	4.65	2.95	64.8%	**4.69**	2.97

Table 5. The effects of different prompt styles: difficulty match % (DM), average relevance ($\overline{\text{Rel}}$), and average quality ($\overline{Q}$). Also, includes the base case where no training data is used. The best results across Tables 5 and 6 are bolded.

Unit	Zero Shot			Few Shot			Chain-of-Thought			Direct Instruction		
	DM	$\overline{\text{Rel}}$	$\overline{Q}$	DM	$\overline{\text{Rel}}$	$\overline{Q}$	DM	$\overline{\text{Rel}}$	$\overline{Q}$	DM	$\overline{\text{Rel}}$	$\overline{Q}$
SoSE	65.6%	2.84	2.76	**71.5%**	**3.68**	**3.07**	67.9%	2.31	2.52	61.4%	3.02	2.62
SReq	57.8%	4.76	3.20	62.0%	**4.96**	3.15	55.8%	3.91	2.53	64.3%	4.84	**3.29**
SDes	59.3%	4.39	2.81	**66.7%**	**4.95**	3.05	64.1%	4.26	2.67	65.8%	4.84	3.10
SConst	60.0%	4.83	3.02	**63.7%**	**4.87**	3.17	61.1%	3.76	2.80	56.4%	4.80	**3.22**
SMaint	64.1%	4.96	3.14	76.2%	**4.97**	3.00	**78.1%**	4.26	2.42	65.0%	4.92	3.16
SEProc	66.3%	4.75	2.98	68.4%	**4.95**	3.05	55.6%	4.43	2.65	**70.0%**	4.39	2.73
Average	62.2%	4.42	2.99	**68.1%**	**4.73**	3.08	63.8%	3.82	2.60	63.8%	4.47	3.04
Avg w/o U1	61.5%	4.74	3.03	**67.4%**	**4.94**	3.08	62.9%	4.12	2.61	64.3%	4.76	3.12

the average of the results across all prompt styles (except "Human") were calculated and are DM = 63.6%, $\overline{\text{Rel}}$=4.66, and $\overline{Q}$=3.00, which beats all three of the human-generated scores. This is a useful finding as it means that prompts generation can be automated and such automation would even lead to better results.

Table 6. The effects of different prompt styles: difficulty match % (DM), average relevance ($\overline{\text{Rel}}$), and average quality ($\overline{Q}$). Also, includes the base case where no training data is used. The best results across Tables 5 and 6 are bolded

Unit	Roleplaying			Contextual			Decomposition			Human		
	DM	$\overline{\text{Rel}}$	$\overline{Q}$	DM	$\overline{\text{Rel}}$	$\overline{Q}$	DM	$\overline{\text{Rel}}$	$\overline{Q}$	DM	$\overline{\text{Rel}}$	$\overline{Q}$
SoSE	67.3%	3.06	3.01	71.2%	2.78	2.84	68.4%	2.31	2.85	69.3%	2.91	2.56
SReq	58.7%	4.88	3.24	**68.4%**	4.62	3.14	66.7%	4.67	2.99	63.1%	4.64	2.96
SDes	61.2%	4.89	**3.14**	60.2%	4.45	2.88	64.4%	4.54	2.78	62.8%	4.50	2.81
SConst	57.0%	4.82	3.21	57.0%	4.47	2.97	54.7%	4.51	3.04	61.1%	4.38	2.88
SMaint	70.0%	4.91	**3.18**	69.6%	4.74	3.03	65.2%	4.68	2.93	65.2%	4.68	3.00
SEProc	66.4%	4.84	**3.15**	60.8%	4.62	3.07	64.5%	4.73	2.96	63.9%	4.70	2.98
Average	63.4%	4.57	**3.15**	64.5%	4.28	2.98	64.0%	4.24	2.93	64.2%	4.30	2.87
Avg w/o U1	62.7%	4.87	**3.18**	63.2%	4.58	3.02	63.1%	4.62	2.94	63.2%	4.58	2.93

5 Lessons Learned

This section discusses additional observations made while conducting this research.

5.1 The Prompt is (Almost) Everything

In general, LMs like to be verbose, for example, providing explanations for their response, or thinking in steps such as: "Step 1 - What is software maintenance?", "Step 2 - What are the types of software maintenance?", etc. This makes question extraction complicated because there is considerable unneeded surrounding text, and the LMs do not respond in predictable ways, making templating challenging.

If something is not specified, and sometimes even when it is, the LMs will fill in the blanks. For example, in some roleplaying prompts saying "I am a teacher preparing a quiz, I need a question ..." would have the LM return a multitude of questions even though only a singular question was asked for. Changing this to "I am a teacher. I need only one more question to finish writing my quiz,..." resolved the issue. This highlights that – with the current state of LMs – to focus the LM properly towards reliably producing a good response, for example, a single educational question on a specific topic, it is preferable to have the prompts automatically generated in lieu of being created by the end user. Automatic prompt engineering research has already discovered successful approaches [40–42], so this should not be a difficult challenge.

It was further observed that when 7B-it (and 7B to a lesser degree) would generate a non-question response, it would be instructions on how a teacher might create a question. This crossed all prompt styles, which suggests an internal predisposition towards supporting teachers for question generation.

5.2 Using Language Models is Labor Intensive

There has been a multi-decade research effort to create question generators, with recent efforts focusing on LMs to reduce the manual workload required. Surprisingly, using the LMs in this research required much more manual labor than might be expected.

At the front end, preparing the training data was a time-consuming task. This is not the fault of the LMs per se, only that current public and commercial LMs need training data in text form, and there are difficulties when extracting text from PDFs.

Then on the back end, it is not a case of just executing the prompts and getting a question as the response is cluttered with unneeded text. This might be ignorable in a commercial context where the end user can focus on the part of the response in which they are interested, but for the educational context, this is not reasonable. For example, if a student asks for a question, then they need to be given a question and not an explanation for how the question was created, why it is appropriate, and certainly not the answer, all of which are common with the LMs response seen in this study.

While a reasonable effort was made to extract the question automatically (and for some prompt-styles this was sufficiently successful for experimental purposes), it was decidedly non-trivial and certainly not conclusively solved. While the 7B-it model performed best, it also was the most problematic for issues that required manual intervention owing to displaying its thinking more.

6 Conclusions

This research investigated using Gemma 7B and Gemma7B-it to generate educational questions. The goal was to discover what challenges might occur when building such a generator for a real-world scenario. This means using training data from a real course to capture specialized knowledge and to extract questions from the response so they can be used. As personalization is a key advantage using automated tools, prompting for questions to be generated at three difficulty levels was investigated. Additionally, several settings, prompt styles, and human versus LM-generated prompting were all evaluated to see which provides the best questions from a pedagogical point of view.

Considering one of the main goals is to reduce workload, the main issue is the amount of manual labor required to use an LM for educational question generation. Extracting training data from PDF files was a time consuming largely manual process as the data was interwoven with non-learning material text (page number, author names, etc.) and with multi-column documents sometimes between columns horizontally instead of vertically. Similarly, the LMs provide a lot of extra text in their response that had to be filtered out even after automatic extraction.

In addition to the observed challenges when using an LM to generate questions for a real course, this research has identified that a model pre-tuned for instructions is better for generating questions, although, they struggle somewhat at generating beginner questions. Both models exhibited a quirk of asking long essay-style and programming questions as beginner-level questions. While the prompt is the main lever towards generating better questions, dividing the data into sentences allows the LM to generate better questions; however, only when training using unit-only data. This has potential practical implications as this would require training a LM per unit. The results also suggest that roleplaying style prompts are best for question generation in practice, with direct instruction being another possibility especially for personalization.

The main limitation of this work is that it cannot be certain that the findings on parameter optimization translate to other courses or broader domains, as prior studies suggest that optimal settings can vary even for closely related tasks [19, 20].

The future for this research is promising and varied. Clearly, one direction will be to work on resolving the challenges discovered in this study. The LM will also be extended to generate an answer along with the question, grade an answer, and provide feedback on the answer provided to it, which will be evaluated in a user study. Finally, the domain scope will be broadened to include additional computer science topics to ensure these findings hold.

Acknowledgements. The authors acknowledge the support of the National Science and Engineering Research Council of Canada (NSERC) [RGPIN-2020-05837].

Disclosure of Interests. The authors have no competing interests to declare that are relevant to the content of this article.

References

1. Ren, M., Kiros, R., Zemel, R.: Exploring models and data for image question answering. In: Advances in Neural Information Processing Systems, vol. 28 (2015)
2. Malinowski, M., Rohrbach, M., Fritz, M.: Ask your neurons: a neural-based approach to answering questions about images. In: 2015 IEEE International Conference on Computer Vision, pp. 1–9. IEEE, Santiago, Chile (2015). https://doi.org/10.1109/ICCV.2015.9
3. Du, X., Shao, J., Cardie, C.: Learning to ask: neural question generation for reading comprehension. In: Proceedings of the 55th Annual Meeting of the Association for Computational Linguistics (Volume 1: Long Papers), pp. 1342–1352. Association for Computational Linguistics, Vancouver, Canada (2017). https://doi.org/10.18653/v1/P17-1123
4. Zhou, Q., Yang, N., Wei, F., Tan, C., Bao, H., Zhou, M.: Neural question generation from text: a preliminary study. In: 6th Natural Language Processing and Chinese Computing, Dalian, China, 8–12 November 2017, Proceedings 6, pp. 662–671. Springer, Cham (2018)
5. Lu, Z., et al.: Small Language Models: Survey, Measurements, and Insights (2024). https://doi.org/10.48550/ARXIV.2409.15790
6. Zhao, W.X., et al.: A Survey of Large Language Models (2023). https://doi.org/10.48550/ARXIV.2303.18223
7. Bulathwela, S., Muse, H., Yilmaz, E.: Scalable educational question generation with pretrained language models. In: Artificial Intelligence in Education, pp. 327–339. Springer, Cham (2023). https://doi.org/10.1007/978-3-031-36272-9_27
8. Zhang, Z., Chen, J., Shi, W., Yi, L., Wang, C., Yu, Q.: Contrastive learning for knowledge-based question generation in large language models (2024). https://doi.org/10.48550/ARXIV.2409.13994
9. Maity, S., Deroy, A., Sarkar, S.: Investigating large language models for prompt-based open-ended question generation in the technical domain. SN Comput. Sci. **5**, 1128 (2024). https://doi.org/10.1007/s42979-024-03464-2
10. Vachev, K., Hardalov, M., Karadzhov, G., Georgiev, G., Koychev, I., Nakov, P.: Leaf: multiple-choice question generation. In: Advances in Information Retrieval, pp. 321–328. Springer, Cham (2022). https://doi.org/10.1007/978-3-030-99739-7_41

11. Fawzi, F., Amini, S., Bulathwela, S.: Small generative language models for educational question generation. In: Proceedings of the NeurIPS Workshop on Generative Artificial Intelligence for Education. New Orleans, LA, USA (2023)
12. Ling, J., Afzaal, M.: Automatic question-answer pairs generation using pre-trained large language models in higher education. Comput. Educ. Artif. Intell. **6**, 100252 (2024)
13. Bloom, B.S., Engelhart, M.D., Furst, E., Hill, W.H., Krathwohl, D.R.: Handbook I: Cognitive Domain, pp. 483–498. N. Y. David McKay (1956)
14. Anderson, L.W., Krathwohl, D.R.: A Taxonomy for Learning, Teaching, And Assessing: A Revision of Bloom's Taxonomy of Educational Objectives, Complete Addison Wesley Longman Inc., Upper Saddle River (2001)
15. Tofade, T., Elsner, J., Haines, S.T.: Best practice strategies for effective use of questions as a teaching tool. Am. J. Pharm. Educ. **77**, 155 (2013)
16. Neal, M.-A.: Engaging students through effective questions. Educ. Can. **51**, n1 (2011)
17. Ertmer, P.A., Sadaf, A., Ertmer, D.J.: Student-content interactions in online courses: the role of question prompts in facilitating higher-level engagement with course content. J. Comput. High. Educ. **23**, 157–186 (2011). https://doi.org/10.1007/s12528-011-9047-6
18. VanLehn, K.: Student modeling. Found. Intell. Tutor. Syst. 55–78 (2013)
19. Leidinger, A., Van Rooij, R., Shutova, E.: The language of prompting: what linguistic properties make a prompt successful? In: Findings of the Association for Computational Linguistics, pp. 9210–9232. Association for Computational Linguistics, Singapore (2023)
20. Sclar, M., Choi, Y., Tsvetkov, Y., Suhr, A.: Quantifying language models' sensitivity to spurious features in prompt design or: how i learned to start worrying about prompt formatting (2023). https://doi.org/10.48550/ARXIV.2310.11324
21. Singh, D., Reddy, S., Hamilton, W., Dyer, C., Yogatama, D.: End-to-end training of multi-document reader and retriever for open-domain question answering. In: Advances in Neural Information Processing Systems, pp. 25968–25981. Curran Associates, Inc. (2021)
22. Zaib, M., Zhang, W.E., Sheng, Q.Z., Mahmood, A., Zhang, Y.: Conversational question answering: a survey. Knowl. Inf. Syst. **64**, 3151–3195 (2022)
23. Ben Abacha, A., Sarrouti, M., Demner-Fushman, D., Hasan, S.A., Müller, H.: Overview of the VQA-med task at imageclef 2021: visual question answering and generation in the medical domain. In: Proceedings of the CLEF 2021 Conference and Labs of the Evaluation Forum-Working Notes, 21–24 September 2021 (2021)
24. Rajpurkar, P., Zhang, J., Lopyrev, K., Liang, P.: SQuAD: 100,000+ Questions for Machine Comprehension of Text (2016). http://arxiv.org/abs/1606.05250
25. Lo, K., Wang, L.L., Neumann, M., Kinney, R., Weld, D.S.: S2ORC: The Semantic Scholar Open Research Corpus (2019). https://doi.org/10.48550/ARXIV.1911.02782
26. Chen, G., Yang, J., Hauff, C., Houben, G.-J.: LearningQ: a large-scale dataset for educational question generation. In: Proceedings of Interenational AAAI Conference on Web Social Media, vol. 12 (2018)
27. Jelinek, F., Mercer, R.L., Bahl, L.R., Baker, J.K.: Perplexity—a measure of the difficulty of speech recognition tasks. J. Acoust. Soc. Am. **62**, S63–S63 (1977)
28. Papineni, K., Roukos, S., Ward, T., Zhu, W.-J.: BLEU: a method for automatic evaluation of machine translation. In: Proceedings of the 40th Annual Meeting on Association for Computational Linguistics, p. 311. Association for Computational Linguistics, Philadelphia, Pennsylvania (2001). https://doi.org/10.3115/1073083.1073135
29. Barbella, M., Tortora, G.: Rouge metric evaluation for text summarization techniques. SSRN Electron. J. (2022). https://doi.org/10.2139/ssrn.4120317
30. Banerjee, S., Lavie, A.: METEOR: an automatic metric for MT evaluation with improved correlation with human judgments. In: Proceedings of the ACL Workshop on Intrinsic and Extrinsic Evaluation Measures for Machine Translation and/or Summarization, pp. 65–72 (2005)

31. Sinha, N., Jain, V., Chadha, A.: Are Small Language Models Ready to Compete with Large Language Models for Practical Applications? (2024). https://doi.org/10.48550/ARXIV.2406.11402
32. Gemma (2024). https://ai.google.dev/gemma
33. Lopez, C., Morrison, M., Deacon, M.: Language models for generating programming questions with varying difficulty levels. Eur. Publ. Soc. Innov. Rev. **9**, 1–19 (2024)
34. Fan, A.X., Zhang, R.H., Paquette, L., Zhang, R.: Exploring the Potential of Large Language Models in Generating Code-Tracing Questions for Introductory Programming Courses (2023). https://doi.org/10.48550/ARXIV.2310.15317
35. Shen, J.T., et al.: MathBERT: A Pre-trained Language Model for General NLP Tasks in Mathematics Education (2021). https://doi.org/10.48550/ARXIV.2106.07340
36. Washizaki, H.: Guide to the Software Engineering Body of Knowledge (SWEBOK Guide), Version 4.0. IEEE Computer Society (2024)
37. Zhang, R., Guo, J., Chen, L., Fan, Y., Cheng, X.: A Review on question generation from natural language text. ACM Trans. Inf. Syst. **40**, 1–43 (2022)
38. Schick, T., Schütze, H.: True few-shot learning with prompts—a real-world perspective. Trans. Assoc. Comput. Linguist. **10**, 716–731 (2022)
39. White, J., et al.: A Prompt Pattern Catalog to Enhance Prompt Engineering with ChatGPT (2023). https://doi.org/10.48550/ARXIV.2302.11382
40. Zhou, Y., et al.: Large Language Models are Human-Level Prompt Engineers (2022). https://doi.org/10.48550/ARXIV.2211.01910
41. Ye, Q., Axmed, M., Pryzant, R., Khani, F.: Prompt Engineering a Prompt Engineer (2023). https://doi.org/10.48550/ARXIV.2311.05661
42. Jin, C., et al.: APEER: Automatic Prompt Engineering Enhances Large Language Model Reranking (2024). https://doi.org/10.48550/ARXIV.2406.14449

A Negotiation and Explainable Approach to Automatically Reduce Cognitive Conflicts and Enhance Learner Model Accuracy in an Intelligent Tutoring System for Propositional Logic

Evandro Costa[1]([✉]), Emanuele Silva[2], Priscylla Silva[2,3], Marlos Silva[4], Leandro da Silva[1], and Dante Costa[1]

[1] Federal University of Alagoas, Maceió, Brazil
{evandro,leandrodias}@ic.ufal.br
[2] Federal Institute of Alagoas, Maceió, Brazil
emanuele.tuane@ifal.edu.br, priscylla.silva@usp.br
[3] University of São Paulo, São Paulo, Brazil
[4] Federal Institute of Sergipe, Aracaju, Brazil
marlos.silva@ifs.edu.br

Abstract. This paper introduces an open learner model approach that enhances transparency by allowing students to engage in a negotiation process with the system, collaboratively improving the model's accuracy, especially working within an ITS for propositional logic, particularly supporting students in theorem-proof using inference rules, deriving proofs. By enabling students to review and discuss discrepancies in their learner model, the system reduces cognitive conflicts that arise from misalignment between the student's self-perception and the system's assessment. We analyze student-system interactions in this logic tutoring environment and demonstrate that negotiation-driven learner modeling enhances the accuracy of the system's understanding of student knowledge, potentially allowing metacognitive engagement and self-regulation. Our findings highlight the potential of explainable and interactive learner models to improve the effectiveness of ITSs, particularly in domains requiring logical reasoning and structured problem-solving.

Keywords: Open learner model · Negotiated learner model · Personalization · Explainability · Intelligent Tutoring Systems

1 Introduction

The field of Intelligent Tutoring Systems (ITSs) is characterized by its adaptive and personalized approach, providing instruction and interaction tailored to the need of the individual learners through the creation and maintenance of learner models [6]. Early approaches adopted for learner models often kept them hidden from the learners and were only accessible to the system, but recent research has advocated for open learner models, allowing learners to inspect their contents. This openness offers opportunities for developing skills in reflection, metacognition and other areas [1,3,5]. Furthermore, this shift has also introduced numerous challenges, particularly in enhancing model accuracy and reducing uncertainty.

This paper addresses the issue of enhancing the accuracy of the learner model in open learner modeling by proposing an automated approach for negotiated open learner modeling with explainability support. This approach allows students to collaborate with the system in refining their learner models. Specifically, we develop a problem-based tutoring system that engages learners in solving logic proof problems withing propositional logic. Our approach adopts a Bayesian network structured as a curriculum topic graph, allowing to represent student model, which is dynamically updated based on their performance. A negotiation mechanism detects and resolves cognitive conflicts when students examine information inferred by the system about their models, that is, when discrepancies arise between the system's evaluation and the learner's perspective. We conducted experiments in Logic courses with computer science and computer engineering students. Our findings indicate that the incorporation of negotiated learner models reduces conflicts between students and tutors compared to scenarios without negotiation. Furthermore, the results show that the learner model was enhanced through this process, suggesting that the negotiation mechanism positively influenced the resolution of cognitive conflicts. This approach to negotiated open learner modeling aligns with some recent trends in ITS research.

We found only a few studies that explored methods to negotiate open learner modeling. The work in [1] brings different approaches for OLM. The work in [2] describes a framework to provide services on open learner modeling. Our approach aligns with little studies, such as the works in [7,8], which prioritize improving learner model accuracy through negotiation mechanisms within open learner modeling frameworks. The work in [3] follows a relevant approach oriented to VR games. These systems, similar to ours in some aspects, enable students to contest the ITS's assessment and propose revisions to their learner model. The main contribution of this research is a new OLM negotiation approach and the results of a study comparing student- and system-initiated negotiation events, as well as the proposed negotiation protocol.

2 Our Approach on Open Learner Modeling

Our work divides the learner model into two parts: the tutor model (M_t) and the self-assessment model (M_s). The tutor model (M_t) is built using the solutions that the student submits to the ITS; this part of the model reflects the student's actual performance in the problem-solving activity. The M_t can be understood as the tutor's assessment of the student's knowledge. The self-assessment model (M_s) is built using the students' degree of confidence in the solutions they submit to the system, and this part of the model reflects the students' assessment of their knowledge. Whenever students solve problems in the system, they must report on a scale of 0 to 10 how confident they are in the answer.

Although the system builds and updates both M_t and M_s, control over them is differentiated. The ITS controls M_t, and the student controls M_s. Thus, the system has complete autonomy over M_t, being responsible for this part of the model so that only the system can make and authorize any changes to it. The student has control over Ms, making the final decision regarding any changes to this part of the model.

To create the student model, we start by constructing a curriculum using a tree structure. Each node in this tree represents a specific topic in the propositional logic domain that the students are required to master, and it is referred to as a *pedagogical unit*. In our study, each pedagogical unit corresponds to a *rule of inference* for the students to understand. The entire curriculum structure includes 6 inference rules: Modus Ponens, Modus Tollens, Hypothetical syllogism, Disjunctive syllogism, conjunction, addition.

The M_t and M_s models are represented by Bayesian Networks (BNs), following the approach proposed by [4]. These models share the same structure but differ in how evidence is incorporated. The building of these BNs is based on the curriculum structure. We utilize a Dynamic Belief Network (DBN) to represent the models, consisting of two parts: (i) *Domain-general Knowledge*, representing the learner's overall knowledge of the domain, and (ii) *Task-specific Knowledge*, representing the learner's knowledge related to specific problems.

Domain-general knowledge is derived from the curriculum structure defined for the Propositional Logic domain. Figure 1 presents the Bayesian network for Domain-general Knowledge, containing two types of nodes: (i) Pedagogical Unit (PU), representing a student skill, which may be a parent to other PU nodes or a set of problem nodes, and (ii) Problem Set (PS), representing the student's knowledge of a specific set of problems, where each set contains problems of the same difficulty level.

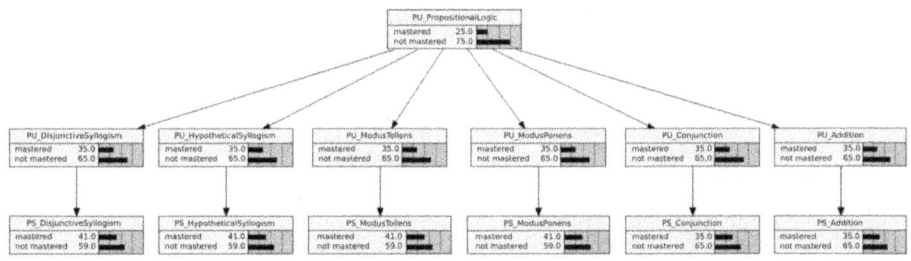

Fig. 1. The BN Structure of the Domain-general knowledge part of DBN Model

Task-specific knowledge is generated at runtime and built from the students' solutions. When a student completes a problem, the probabilities of all relevant nodes are updated. This part includes a problem node (P), which represents the student's probability of solving the problem, and one or more solution nodes (S), representing all submitted solutions to a problem.

3 Negotiation Mechanism

The negotiation mechanism, a key component within the ITS framework, serves as a dynamic interface where students interact collaboratively with the system. This mechanism is a win-win solution, benefiting both the system and the student. For the system, it enables more accurate modeling of student knowledge, leading to more trustworthy decisions. For the student, it promotes metacognitive development and self-regulated learning, embodying the concept of personalized and learner-centered education.

Before explaining how the negotiation mechanism works, we must define *cognitive conflict* between the student and the system. Visualizing both parts of the open learner model allows students to identify differences between the self-assessment and tutor models. These differences in values in the models demonstrate that there is a conflict of opinions between the system and the student. To reduce the conflicts of opinion, a negotiation mechanism was created. In this mechanism, the student has autonomy over their opinion (self-assessment model), being able to change it whenever necessary, and the system has autonomy over its opinion (tutor model). The students can begin a negotiation process when they disagree with the tutor's belief about their knowledge in a pedagogical unit. The system will start a negotiation process when it detects a cognitive conflict between its and student beliefs. This conflict can be detected when the difference between the tutor's belief and the student's belief is outside the range specified as acceptable by the system.

In the negotiation process with the student, the system must choose from predefined negotiation strategies. Each strategy defines the nature of the interaction and the objectives to be achieved during the negotiation. The first strategy, ***Support***, aims to boost students' confidence in their performance and enhance their perceived knowledge. This strategy is used when the value of a pedagogical unit in the student's self-assessment model is lower than the tutor model. The second strategy, ***Persuasion***, aims to help the student understand and accept the system's evaluation. This is used when the student tries to change a value in the tutor model or when the value in a pedagogical unit in the student's self-assessment model is higher than the tutor's model. For every dialogue move initiated by the student, the system will respond with a corresponding dialogue move determined by the selected negotiation strategy. This structured interaction aims to resolve discrepancies between the student's self-assessment and tutor models, fostering a more accurate and reflective learning process.

The interaction between the student and the system is based on predefined standard moves for both parties. The valid dialogue moves include: a) **Show unit value**: Displays the current value of a pedagogical unit; b) **Justify**: Provides an explanation for the current belief or a request to modify a belief; c) **Modify**: Changes the value of a pedagogical unit; d) **Request**: Asks for a justification regarding a pedagogical unit's value; e) **Suggest**: Proposes a new value for a pedagogical unit; f) **Accept**: Agrees with a justification or a suggested value for a pedagogical unit; g) **Reject**: Disagrees with a justification or a suggested value for a pedagogical unit; h) **Reject**: Disagrees with a justification or a suggested value for a pedagogical unit; i) **Close**: Ends the negotiation; and j) **Requires proof**: Allows the student to answer questions to demonstrate their knowledge.

These moves facilitate structured interactions, ensuring clarity and consistency in the student and system negotiation process. Both the student and the system can initiate a negotiation. This allows for two distinct scenarios in the negotiation process between the student and the tutor:

1. The tutor disagrees with the student's self-assessment model (M_s) and attempts to persuade the student to modify it;
2. The student disagrees with the tutor's model (M_t) and attempts to persuade the tutor to modify it.

3.1 System-Initiated Negotiation

For the system to initiate a negotiation in a unit of the self-assessment model, two conditions must be satisfied:

1. The student must have solved at least two questions in the pedagogical unit since the last negotiation;
2. The difference between the unit value in the self-assessment and the tutor model must be at least 25 points, indicating a significant conflict. This threshold was chosen because the difference between knowledge levels is approximately 25 (on a scale of 0 to 100). This condition is the identification of a cognitive conflict

If both conditions are met, the system will start a negotiation, the goal of which is to persuade the student to accept an adjustment in the self-assessment model. The dialogue flow for system-initiated negotiations is illustrated in Fig. 2. During the negotiation, the system will suggest a new value for the pedagogical unit, and the student can accept the new value, reject the new value, propose a new one, or reject and stop the negotiation. If the student proposes a new value for the unit, the system will accept it if it is within 10 points above or below the current value in the tutor model.

When the system initiates a discussion about a particular pedagogical unit, it presents information about the student's performance in that unit to justify negotiation and the new value proposed by the system. The information shown to the student will depend on the negotiation strategy chosen by the system, which is determined by the following conditions:

1. If the unit value in the self-assessment model is lower than in the tutor model, the system will adopt the ***Support*** strategy. This strategy aims to demonstrate to the students that their knowledge of a pedagogical unit is greater than they believe, encouraging them to adjust their confidence level to match the tutor model;

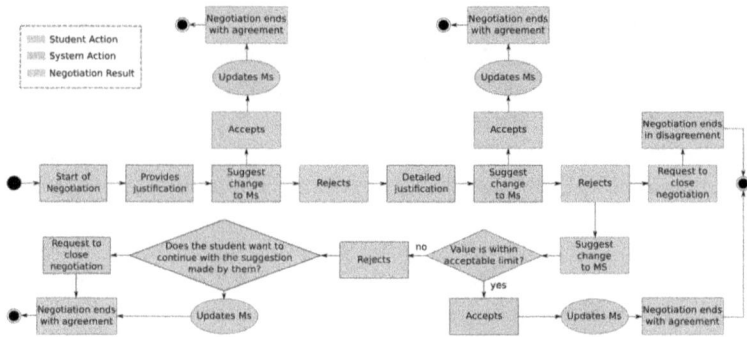

Fig. 2. Dialogue Flow for System-Initiated Negotiations

2. If the unit value in the self-assessment model is higher than in the tutor model, the system will adopt the ***Persuasion*** strategy. This strategy aims to show the student that they are overestimating their knowledge and to persuade them to lower their confidence level to align with the tutor model.

3.2 Student-Initiated Negotiation

Upon reviewing their student model, students may disagree with the tutor model regarding their knowledge in a specific pedagogical unit. If the student has answered at least two questions since their last negotiation, they can initiate a negotiation process to persuade the system to modify the pedagogical unit's value. The dialogue flow for student-initiated negotiations is illustrated in Fig. 3.

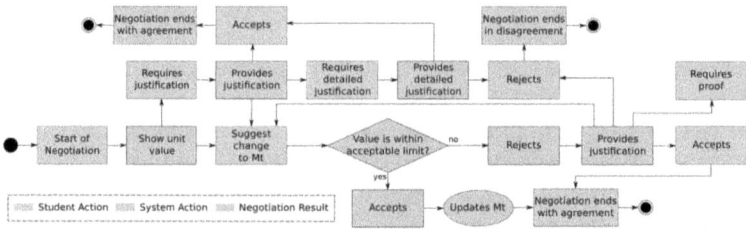

Fig. 3. Dialogue Flow for Student-Initiated Negotiations

When student proposes a new value for a pedagogical unit, the system will accept it if the proposed value is within 10 points above or below the current value in the tutor model. If the system disagrees with the student's proposed value, the student can request the system to initiate a proof process. During this process, the system will present two problems to the student: i) **Analysis Problem**: The system provides a problem with a solution and asks the student to evaluate the correctness of the solution. This step aims to verify the student's ability to understand and apply their knowledge about the pedagogical unit involved in the negotiation; and ii) **Synthesis Problem**: The student must solve a problem using their knowledge of the pedagogical unit involved in the negotiation.

If the student provides the correct answers for both the analysis and synthesis problems, the system will calculate a new value for the pedagogical unit that has been negotiated and show this new value to the student. The tutor model will be updated if the student agrees with the new value. If not, the negotiation process will end.

4 Experiment

The main objective in this study is to investigate the effect of a negotiation mechanism on cognitive conflicts in a student model within an intelligent tutoring system for propositional logic. Specifically, we seek to answer the question: Can the negotiation mechanism reduce conflicts of opinion between the student and the system? To address this question, we conducted an experiment with 25 computer science students from the Federal University of Alagoas. The students began with a class on propositional logic, covering six inference rules: modus ponens, modus tollens, hypothetical syllogism, disjunctive syllogism, conjunction, and addition. They were provided with an overview of the ITS and its features, along with an introduction to the interfaces and possible interactions, including negotiations.

We initialized all models with the same probabilities for each student, setting a basic knowledge level of 0.25 in the logic unit. The system included 25 assignments, all available for students to complete. We instructed the students to solve the assignments step by step, using only the inference rules studied. We divided the information about the students into two groups: a control group, which built the models without the negotiation mechanism, and an experimental group, which interacted with the model that included the negotiation mechanism. The students used the system for two hours and were advised to review the self-assessment and tutor models after completing the assignments. As part of the experiment, four types of models were created for each student, categorized as follows: i) **Self-assessment model without negotiation**: this model is based on the student's confidence levels and cannot be visualized or negotiated; ii) **Tutor model without negotiation**: this model is based on the student's solutions and cannot be visualized or negotiated; iii) **Self-assessment model with negotiation**: this model is based on the student's confidence levels and cand be visualized and negotiated; and iv) **Tutor model with negotiation**: this model is based on the student's solutions and can be visualized and negotiated.

To analyze the results, we conducted a comparison between the self - assessment model and the tutor model. Our aim with this comparison was to identify the degree of agreement between the student's self - assessment model, based on the student's confidence levels, and the tutor model, which evaluates responses according to the inference rules of the intelligent tutoring system. This analysis allowed us to observe whether the student's and system's opinions were aligned and how the negotiation mechanism impacted this relationship.

We used the Pearson correlation coefficient and the Weighted Kappa coefficient to quantify the degree of agreement between the student and the system. These metrics allow us to measure, respectively, the linear relationship between variables and the categorical agreement adjusted for the possibility of chance agreement. Furthermore, we used the Bland-Altman plot, also known as the Tukey mean-difference plot. This plot provides a visualization of the agreement between the models by comparing the differences and averages of the scores obtained by students in both groups. It allows us to visualize the bias, error, and outliers. Through this analysis, we were able to identify the impact of the negotiation mechanism on the student model and gain insights into the alignment of responses between the student and the system.

5 Results and Discussion

Throughout the experiment, there were a total of 168 negotiations (160 agreements and 8 disagreements). The students initiated 148 negotiations during the experiment, while the system initiated 20 negotiations. Approximately 89% of the negotiations were resolved through the value suggestion mechanism, in 9% of the negotiations the student had to confirm their knowledge by answering two questions, and in 2% of the negotiations the student accepted the tutor system's justification. The chart in Fig. 4 provides an overview of negotiations categorized by pedagogical unit. The Modus Ponens and Hypothetical Syllogism have the highest number of negotiations, 37 and 36, respectively. Moreover, the ITS initiated negotiations more often (7 times) in Modus Ponens, while students proposed the negotiations more frequently (32 times) in Hypothetical Syllogism. The ITS did not start negotiations for the Conjunction and Addition units. Meanwhile, all negotiations in the Modus Tollens, Disjunctive Syllogism, and Conjunction units concluded with an agreement.

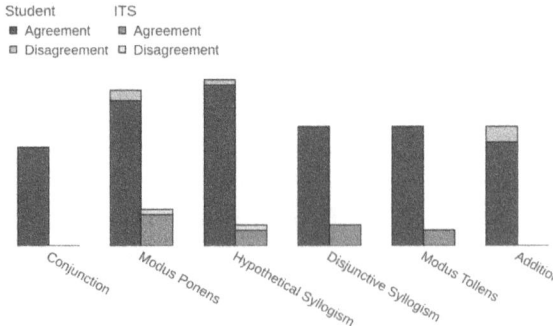

Fig. 4. Overview of Negotiations Categorized by Pedagogical Unit.

The chart in Fig. 5 presents the distribution of adjustments made to the models during negotiations. Most adjustments were within the expected range and the outliers can be explained by the following cases: i) Students could modify the values of the Ms even if the system did not agree, allowing them to set values significantly higher or lower than the current ones; ii) When values in Ms were significantly higher than those in Mt, the system could suggest a significant decrease in the student's belief, hence some outliers with low values in Modus Ponens and Hypothetical Syllogism units; iii) and When values in Ms were significantly lower than those in Mt, the system could suggest a significant increase in the student's belief, hence some outliers with high values.

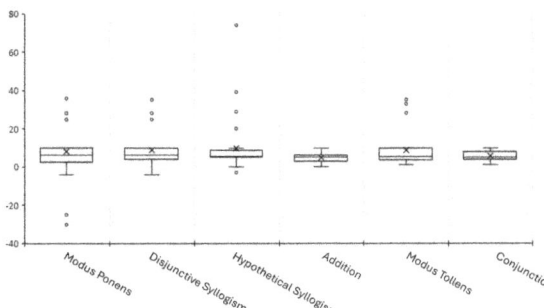

Fig. 5. The figure depicts the distribution of model adjustments across different pedagogical units. The y-axis represents the size of the adjustment made in each negotiation

The Pearson correlation coefficient (denoted as ρ) quantifies the strength and direction of a linear relationship between two continuous variables. A value closer to 1 indicates a stronger positive correlation between the variables. To conduct Pearson Correlation Analyses, we collected data on the values of all pedagogical units from both the self-assessment and tutor models. We then applied the Pearson correlation to examine whether a correlation exists between the levels of knowledge measured by the self-assessment and the tutor models. Initially, we computed the Pearson correlation between the self-assessment and tutor models without negotiation (as illustrated in Fig. 6a). Subsequently, we repeated this analysis for the self-assessment and tutor models with negotiation (as depicted in Fig. 6b).

In Fig. 6a, the scatter plot shows the relationship between the self-assessment and tutor models without negotiation. The plot shows a positive linear trend with a Pearson correlation coefficient of $\rho = 0.65$. In Fig. 6b, the scatter plot presents the relationship between the self-assessment and tutor models with negotiation. Figure 6b shows a higher positive linear relationship, as evidenced by a correlation coefficient of $\rho = 0.89$. This result suggests a closer alignment between the values of negotiated models. These findings indicate that negotiated models exhibit stronger correlations compared to non-negotiated models.

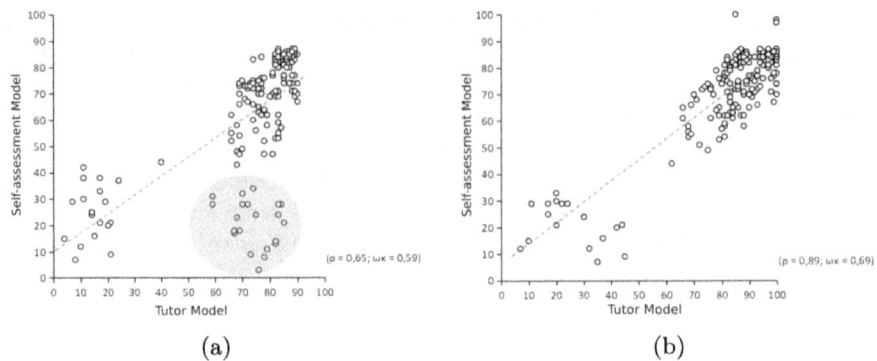

Fig. 6. (a) Pearson Correlation Analysis between Self-assessment and Tutor Models **without** Negotiation, (b) Pearson Correlation Analysis between Self-assessment and Tutor Models **with** Negotiation

In the scatter plot of the models without negotiation (Fig. 6a), we noticed samples where the tutor's belief exceeded the student's belief. This occurred when students lacked confidence in their answers, even when they were correct. These samples are highlighted in the blue area of Fig. 6a. In these cases, the tutor models believed that the student's knowledge was greater than 50, while the students themselves assessed their knowledge as less than 40. This demonstrates the students' lack of confidence in their own knowledge, which is a crucial aspect of metacognition - the ability to monitor and regulate one's own thinking and learning processes.

Looking at Fig. 6b, the scatter plot of the models with negotiation, we can observe that these samples disappear, indicating that during the negotiation process, students become aware of the disparity between their beliefs and the system's beliefs, leading them to adjust their self-assessment models to higher values. This adjustment reflects a significant development in metacognitive awareness, as students actively reflect on their own understanding and recognize the need for adjustment based on feedback from the system. By participating in this negotiation process, students not only improve the accuracy of their self-assessment but also enhance their metacognitive skills, which are essential for effective learning and problem-solving in various contexts.

The Kappa agreement test was used to measure the level of agreement between the models. Kappa is a widely used measure of agreement that not only assesses whether agreement exceeds chance expectations but also quantifies the degree of agreement. This coefficient is calculated based on the number of matching responses, specifically, the instances where the value assigned by the tutor model matches that assigned by the self-assessment model. Therefore, higher Kappa values indicate greater agreement between the models. Given that values within each unit range from 0 to 100, even a one-point difference between unit values in each model can be considered a significant difference. Therefore, we chose to use weighted Kappa (wk), which assigns different weights to disagreements/agreements (e.g., mild, moderate, severe) to understand their impact better. As a result, closer unit values in compared models correspond to higher agreement.

The weighted Kappa value between the models without negotiation was 0.59, with a 95% confidence interval of (0.139, 1.0), indicating moderate agreement. On the other hand, the weighted Kappa between the models with negotiation was 0.69, with a 95% confidence interval of (0.4578, 0.928), indicating substantial agreement. Therefore, the models showed higher agreement when negotiation was employed than when it was not.

We used the Bland-Altman plot to evaluate the level of disagreement between the self-assessment and tutor models, both with and without negotiation. A Bland-Altman plot is a statistical tool used to assess the agreement between two different methods of measuring the same quantity. It's a visual representation that helps determine if there is a systematic difference between the two methods (bias) and how much the measurements vary. With this method is possible to define if the two methods produce similar results, if one method consistently overestimates or underestimates compared to the other and identify any data points that deviate significantly from the general pattern. Our goal was to verify whether introducing negotiation mechanisms reduced the level of disagreement between the models compared to their non-negotiated counterparts. The outcomes of these analyses are presented in Fig. 7a and 7b, with Fig. 7a showing the Bland-Altman plot for models without negotiation and Fig. 7b displaying the same for models with negotiation.

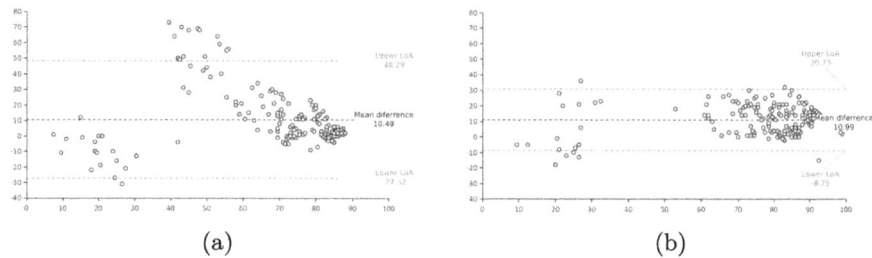

Fig. 7. (a) Bland-Altman Plot for Models **without** Negotiation, (b) Bland-Altman Plot for Models **with** Negotiation

In Fig. 7a, the mean difference between non-negotiated models is calculated as 10.49. The central line is close to zero, indicating there is just a little bias between the methods. However, the wide range of Limits of Agreement (±37.8), the dispersion of the data and the great number of points outside the limits, suggest poor agreement between the student model and the tutor model. Conversely, Fig. 7b shows a mean difference of 10.99 between negotiated models. The central line is also close to zero, indicating there is just a little bias between the methods. Moreover, the narrower range of Limits of Agreement (±19.7), the clustering of the data and the small number of points outside the limits, suggest closer agreement between the student model and the tutor model. These observations lead to the conclusion that the introduction of negotiation mechanisms results in improved agreement between the self-assessment and tutor models.

6 Conclusion

In this paper we presented an approach for an open learner modeling, exploring the potential of incorporating negotiation facilities over the learner model within an ITS for propositional logic. Thus, in this approach, the negotiated learner model within this ITS is collaboratively updated and maintained by both the system and the learner. The novelty of this proposed approach is twofold: the representation of the learner's knowledge through Bayesian networks associated with the curriculum structure, and the provision of an updating learner model method that includes an automated negotiation mechanism to solve cognitive conflicts arising from problem-solving evaluation processes. Thus, we contribute to the field of negotiated learner modeling by employing explicit negotiation and explanation support in dialogue, facilitating the acquisition of cognitive and metacognitive skills within a propositional logic domain characterized by justified belief, thereby advancing existing approaches in the literature.

References

1. Bull, S.: There are open learner models about! IEEE Trans. Learn. Technol. **13**(2), 425–448 (2020). https://doi.org/10.1109/TLT.2020.2978473
2. Bull, S., Kay, J.: SMILI: a framework for interfaces to learning data in open learner models, learning analytics and related fields. Int. J. Artif. Intell. Educ. **26**(1), 293–331 (2016). https://doi.org/10.1007/s40593-015-0090-8
3. Chen, Y., Kay, J., Yoo, S.: Feedback and open learner models in popular commercial VR games: a systematic review. In: Wang, N., Rebolledo-Mendez, G., Matsuda, N., Santos, O.C., Dimitrova, V. (eds.) Artif. Intell. Educ., pp. 541–552. Springer Nature Switzerland, Cham (2023). https://doi.org/10.1007/978-3-031-36272-9_44
4. Conati, C., Gertner, A., Vanlehn, K.: Using Bayesian networks to manage uncertainty in student modeling. User Model. User-Adap. Inter. **12**(4), 371–417 (2002)
5. Costa, E., Silva, P., Magalhaes, J., Silva, M.: An open and inspectable learner modeling with a negotiation mechanism to solve cognitive conflicts in an intelligent tutoring system. In: Workshop and Poster Proceedings of the 20th Conference on User Modeling, Adaptation, and Personalization, pp. 47–52 (2012)
6. Hooshyar, D., Pedaste, M., Saks, K., Leijen, A., Bardone, E., Wang, M.: Open learner models in supporting self-regulated learning in higher education: a systematic literature review. Comput. Educ. **154**, 103878 (2020). https://doi.org/10.1016/j.compedu.2020.103878, https://www.sciencedirect.com/science/article/pii/S0360131520300774
7. Mabbott, A., Bull, S.: Student preferences for editing, persuading, and negotiating the open learner model. In: Ikeda, M., Ashley, K.D., Chan, T.W. (eds.) Intelligent Tutoring Systems, pp. 481–490. Springer, Berlin, Heidelberg (2006)
8. Thomson, D., Mitrovic, A.: Preliminary evaluation of a negotiable student model in a constraint-based its. Res. Pract. Technol. Enhanc. Learn. **05**(01), 19–33 (2010). https://doi.org/10.1142/S1793206810000797

Scaling Effective Characteristics of ITSs: A Preliminary Analysis of LLM-Based Personalized Feedback

Rachel Van Campenhout, Jeffrey S. Dittel, and Benny G. Johnson

VitalSource Technologies, Raleigh, NC 27601, USA
benny.johnson@vitalsource.com

Abstract. Intelligent tutoring systems (ITSs) have long held the gold standard for learning in digital learning environments. However, ITSs have historically required substantial authoring effort, limiting scaling. Computer assisted instruction has continued to be more widely available to students, and generative AI now enables richer student-computer interactions. One key feature of ITSs is the delivery of personalized feedback on student responses. In this paper, we discuss the nature of successful personalized feedback, the development of personalized feedback using generative AI as part of an automatic question generation system, and initial analysis of this feedback performance using data from students in a traditional university course.

Keywords: intelligent tutoring systems · computer assisted instruction · formative practice · feedback · learning by doing · artificial intelligence · large language models · personalization

1 Introduction

1.1 Intelligent Tutoring Systems

Intelligent tutoring systems (ITSs) are highly specialized learning environments with decades of research on their features and effects. ITSs refer to a specific type of environment that should be distinguished from computer assisted instruction (CAI). ITSs are typically highly adaptive, interactive, and learner-paced environments—created using computational models developed in the learning sciences, cognitive sciences, mathematics, computational linguistics, artificial intelligence, and other relevant fields [1]—that are intended to mirror the practices of expert human tutors [2]. VanLehn [3] describes ITSs as having an inner and outer loop, where the outer loop selects the learning task (possibly with adaptation and learner modeling) and the inner loop provides steps to solve problems with feedback, hints, or error codes provided as guidance. VanLehn [3] notes that CAIs typically have the outer loop but not the inner. From their meta-analysis, Steenbergen-Hu and Cooper [4] note that ITSs working processes "usually consist of delivering learning content to students, tracking and adapting to students' learning pace, assessing learning progress, and providing feedback" (p. 333). They also note that ITSs are stand-alone environments with unique instructional content and domain-specific knowledge—a contrast to many domain-independent technologies.

Intelligent tutoring systems have a long history of being some of the most effective learning environments of the digital learning era, though the true effect size of these systems has been the focus for several researchers. Early studies suggested effect sizes of ~ 2.0 standard deviations for human tutoring [5], ~ 1.0 for ITSs [6], and ~ 0.3 for CAI [7]. However, VanLehn's [8] meta-analysis found an ITS increase on test scores of 0.58 standard deviations, with tutors using step-based feedback increasing 0.76 standard deviations and the newer substep-based tutors only increasing 0.40 standard deviations. In their meta-analysis, Steenbergen-Hu and Cooper [4] found ITSs had a non-significant negative impact compared to human tutoring ($g = -0.25$), but a positive significant impact compared to traditional and computer instruction ($g = 0.37$) and an even larger impact over self-reliant learning or no-treatment controls ($g = 0.86$). This review remains consistent with prior expectations that ITSs were not as effective as human tutoring but more effective than all other learning treatments. However, Kulik and Fletcher's [9] review provides a critical lens on these results, citing inclusion of studies with environments not considered to be ITSs and non-conventional control groups. In their findings from 50 studies, the effect size of ITSs was 0.66 (a moderate to large effect). Compared to their estimation of human tutoring increasing gains by 0.40, the selection criteria in this review find that ITSs outperform human tutoring [9].

1.2 Features that Scale

Formative practice and immediate feedback are a critical component of ITSs. VanLehn [3] notes one hypothesis for why human tutoring could be so effective: "the frequent feedback of human tutoring makes it much easier for students to find flaws in their reasoning and fix their knowledge" (p. 200). In ITSs, feedback is designed to be similarly frequent, at the substep level to help correct mistakes in procedural knowledge. In CAIs, feedback is typically only given at the step level, on an answer [8]. The LISP ITS developed at Carnegie Mellon University showed that feedback minimized the time it took students to learn content and increased comprehension of the correct answer [10]. VanLehn [8] also notes that feedback is a key component of learning as it guides students to correct misconceptions and persist; should students not persist, they lose opportunities for learning.

Despite their effectiveness for learning, ITSs have historically required substantial authoring effort, limiting broad deployment. In their stead, CAIs have become prolific because they can take advantage of some learning features of ITSs. Formative practice with immediate, targeted feedback became a central learning tool for courseware learning environments, for example. Carnegie Mellon University's Open Learning Initiative studied formative practice placed alongside core text content at frequent intervals and found this method generates the doer effect, the learning science principle that proves doing practice is on average six times more effective for learning than reading alone [11, 12]. The doer effect research has been replicated in other learning contexts, showcasing the generalizability of this learning science principle [13]. When an ITS is not possible, learning by doing in CAI environments provides an effective alternative.

1.3 Feedback

An essential element of formative practice is the feedback provided to students after they respond. Extensive research shows both timing and type of feedback matter. Dunlosky et al. [14] showed that practice testing is most effective when paired with feedback. An analysis of Statistics courseware developed at Carnegie Mellon found that immediate, targeted feedback significantly reduced the time needed to achieve learning goals [15]. Immediate feedback is also associated with higher student satisfaction [16].

The specific type of feedback used in formative assessments has been shown to influence learning outcomes. Feedback is generally classified into three main categories: knowledge of results (KR), which indicates whether an answer is correct or incorrect; knowledge of correct response (KCR); and elaborative feedback (EF) [14, 16, 17]. Research suggests that KR alone is the least effective, as it provides no guidance for improvement, while KCR offers only marginally better outcomes [16]. EF, which typically combines KR or KCR with additional explanations, hints, or strategies, is more effective because it serves as a supplementary instructional tool [16]. For example, Anderson et al. [10] reported that repeat errors were significantly reduced when students received explanatory feedback (37%) compared to no feedback (60%). The approach of integrating formative practice with immediate, elaborative feedback formed the basis of the courseware created by Carnegie Mellon's Open Learning Initiative. This approach demonstrated both greater learning gains and reduced time to mastery compared to traditional instructional materials [15]. These same learning by doing environments were also used to prove the doer effect [11, 12].

1.4 Automatic Question and Feedback Generation

The scalability of ITSs—and most CAI environments—has typically been limited by the human effort required to author content. To scale the learning by doing method known to be highly effective for student learning [11–13], an automatic question generation (AQG) system was built to create questions and feedback from textbook content [18]. While there are many methods for developing AQG systems [19], this system was developed as a rule-based, expert-designed system without using large language models. Prior research has found automatically generated (AG) questions perform as well as human-authored questions on key performance metrics such as engagement, difficulty, persistence, and discrimination [20, 21]. This AQG system creates several types of AG questions, including fill-in-the-blank (FITB), matching, multiple choice, and free response. The questions open in a panel next to the textbook content, allowing students to refer back to the content if needed while they answer.

Feedback is given immediately, with every attempt receiving outcome (KR) feedback. For FITB questions, incorrect answers have two additional feedback options. *Context feedback* is an extended selection of the textbook passage where the question stem came from to provide students with more context to support their next attempt. *Common answer feedback* is a sentence selected from nearby in the textbook with the same answer word missing, to give students another example and help scaffold their next attempt. A randomized experiment found common answer feedback the most effective at increasing correct responses and persistence to the correct answer [22].

These feedback types, provided at the answer level, are both typical for CAIs [8] while also being appropriate for the type of learning in this environment. However, they lack a hallmark of ITS feedback: personalization—diagnosing specific errors and addressing them directly. It is here that large language models (LLMs) can enhance the existing AQG pipeline by providing personalized feedback for open-ended questions. While LLM technology has well-known limitations that must be guarded against, its strength in comparative language makes it a prime solution for evaluating free-response work. Research has already shown the viability of this approach, finding that LLMs generated more readable feedback with greater detail and consistency than human instructors, outperformed human instructors in providing information on effective feedback practices, and could provide feedback on the process of students completing the task [23, 24]. LLM feedback was found to generally adhere to fundamental principles of effective feedback [24]. Despite successes, a lightweight review process remains advisable because some errors persist [25].

In fall 2024, two new question types intended to foster deeper cognitive engagement were launched, with a generative AI-based feature for personalized feedback on open-ended responses. (1) **Exam-question writing**: students draft a test item for a textbook section, promoting synthesis. (2) **Compare-and-contrast (C&C)**: students explain the difference between two related glossary terms.

Although both new types employ generative AI for detailed feedback, the present analysis focuses on the C&C items. Studies on compare-and-contrast tasks show they enhance conceptual clarity and retention [26]. Moreover, the effect has been demonstrated in intelligent tutoring systems, where explanation-based practice led to superior transfer and reduced guesswork relative to mere answer submission [27].

The goals of this paper are to detail LLM technology as a method for generating personalized feedback for formative practice at scale and conduct an initial analysis of how students respond to this feedback in real-world course usage. By probing the following research questions, we investigate whether LLM-generated feedback can deliver individualized, elaborative guidance characteristic of ITSs without the historic authoring cost that limited scalability. The findings offer preliminary guidance on improving the generative feedback system.

- RQ1: What proportion of student second attempts show high textual overlap with the LLM-based feedback, and how is that proportion distributed across response-latency bands?
- RQ2: Do overlap and latency, individually or together, predict the likelihood that a second attempt is correct?

2 Methods

2.1 Question Generation and Answer Evaluation

The system identifies terms from the textbook's glossary that appear together or in close proximity within a single textbook section and share the same final word (e.g., "lactate threshold" and "ventilatory threshold"). The system generates the question using the template "Explain the difference between the terms '[Term 1]' and '[Term 2]'" which is added at a location ensuring the student has just read about both terms.

GPT-4o [28] was used for student response evaluation. When a student submits an answer, a short textbook excerpt containing each term's definition is provided alongside the student's text, ensuring course-specific grounding. A system message instructs the generative evaluator to maintain a professional, courteous tone, avoid profanity, and refuse unethical or offensive content. The LLM then succinctly determines whether the explanation accurately distinguishes the two terms. Because answers are open-ended, they are not strictly labeled as "right" or "wrong." Instead, key strengths in the student's response are identified, along with areas needing further elaboration or correction. If an answer is nonresponsive, a brief corrective explanation is offered. Setting temperature to 0 encourages concise, factual feedback aligned with textbook definitions, minimizing potential "hallucinations." Collectively, these design choices help ensure responsible use of generative AI, focusing on clarifying student misunderstandings without introducing extraneous or inappropriate content. Students are given the feedback immediately and may revise and resubmit their answer if desired. Personalization is currently answer-level; future iterations can include consideration of the learner's historical data.

2.2 Data Collection and Analysis

The data set for this study consists of student–question interaction events from a 100-level Introduction to Communication Studies course at a large public university in the United States. Practice counted for 10% of the course grade with a minimum of 80% completion required. Data were gathered between August 15 and December 26, 2024, during which the course assigned the AG questions in the VitalSource Bookshelf ereader platform. The ereader logs all student interactions under an anonymous identifier, and user consent for research and analytics is obtained via the platform's terms of use and privacy policy. No student demographic information was collected.

Data were grouped into student-question sessions, which are all actions by a student on a given question in chronological order. This yielded 5,022 sessions from 29 distinct questions and 198 students. While not a large-scale deployment, it reflects authentic usage of LLM-based questions under normal class conditions, providing a valuable real-world perspective. The data set is available in our open-source repository [29].

2.3 Classifying Correctness and Authenticity

Although the feedback system does not explicitly label the open-ended answers as right or wrong, C&C responses can be classified objectively. GPT-4o mini [30] was used to review each answer plus its feedback and judge whether a typical professor would deem the explanation "complete and correct." If the answer addressed the terms but was wrong or incomplete, it was marked incorrect; if it ignored one or both terms (e.g., "idk," random text) it was non-genuine. Thus, we obtained three answer categories: correct, incorrect, and non-genuine.

2.4 Student Answer Length

All recorded attempts, including initial answers and subsequent tries, were analyzed to gauge student answer length. Each response was split on whitespace to determine the number of tokens, which serves as a simple but sufficient proxy for response depth in this context. Since the platform does not permit completely blank submissions, zero-length entries do not occur. To illustrate how response length corresponds to the three attempt categories, the first (Q_1), second (Q_2, median) and third (Q_3) quartiles of answer length are reported for each category. Very short responses, for instance, frequently are non-genuine attempts, whereas longer answers can indicate more substantive effort or understanding. Because answer lengths were highly skewed, quartiles were chosen to better represent the distribution than, e.g., a single mean.

2.5 Time Interval from Feedback to Second Attempt

A time interval was measured for each scenario in which a student's initial attempt was incorrect or non-genuine and a subsequent attempt was submitted on the same question. This metric is defined as the elapsed time in seconds between the submission of the student's first attempt and the submission of the second attempt, serving as an approximation of how long the student potentially spent reading feedback and revising their explanation. This approach aligns with prior research in intelligent tutoring systems (ITS), where response latency or time on hints has often served as a proxy for reflection or cognitive engagement [8, 31]. Here, a short interval might indicate minimal attention to the LLM feedback, whereas a longer interval could suggest deeper consideration and revision of the student's initial answer.

To accommodate the typically skewed distribution of response times, Q_1–Q_3 are reported. Additionally, time intervals are subdivided by both the initial attempt's category (incorrect vs. non-genuine) and the outcome of the next attempt (correct, incorrect, or non-genuine). This structure highlights whether transitions—such as non-genuine → correct—generally involve additional time to incorporate feedback, whereas minimal intervals could indicate an immediate resubmission of LLM-generated text. We also discuss how these intervals may correlate with overlap detection to further elucidate the relationship between rapid resubmission and potential copying of the LLM's feedback.

2.6 Overlap of Second Attempt with LLM Feedback

When a second attempt was submitted following an incorrect or non-genuine first attempt, the text of that attempt was compared to the LLM-generated feedback from the preceding attempt to address RQ1. This aimed to detect potential copying of feedback into the student's new response and gauge how frequently a correct second attempt might reflect literal reuse of the feedback text rather than independent construction. Because the LLM feedback can sometimes amount to a fully formed model answer, identifying overlap in these cases is relevant for understanding whether students are actively composing their responses or simply replicating the provided solution.

Unlike for student answer length, the overlap analysis employed a minimal text preprocessing step: both the LLM feedback and the student's second-attempt text were lowercased and stripped of punctuation before splitting on whitespace. This preprocessing reduces noise from minor variations in case or punctuation. Boilerplate phrases occasionally produced by the LLM (e.g., "Ok, no problem") were not removed, as they were not prevalent enough to significantly distort the overlap measurements.

A token-level gestalt pattern matching procedure [32] was performed using Python's difflib.SequenceMatcher. Each pair of second-attempt answer and first-attempt feedback yielded a similarity ratio in the interval [0, 1], where 1 indicates an exact token-by-token match in the same order. Reordering of text reduces the ratio, penalizing partial rearrangements. This approach identifies all contiguous subsequences across entire responses, making it better suited for detecting literal copying than alternatives such as token-level Levenshtein distance. No threshold was established for labeling attempts as "copied" or "not copied," given that partial or revised reuse of the LLM feedback could reflect a continuum from mere copy-paste to legitimate paraphrasing and integration.

Only the immediate second attempt was analyzed, without examining subsequent attempts (third or fourth), as few sessions progressed beyond a second submission. For reporting, quartiles of overlap scores are grouped by (1) the initial attempt category (incorrect or non-genuine) and (2) the second attempt category (correct, incorrect, or non-genuine). These results are later related to the time-interval data to test RQ2, exploring whether quick resubmissions correspond to higher literal overlap. This approach acknowledges that literal copying does not necessarily preclude learning—some students may incorporate and rephrase feedback productively—yet highlights instances where minimal revision may reduce the potential for deeper understanding.

3 Results and Discussion

Table 1 summarizes the distribution of answer lengths (in words) by attempt category. Correct attempts had a median of 29 words (interquartile range 22–41), while incorrect attempts were shorter, with a median of 19 words (IQR 12–27). Non-genuine submissions stood out as extremely brief, with a median of only one word (IQR 1–4).

These differences suggest that correct explanations tend to include more elaboration or detail than incorrect ones. The extremely short nature of non-genuine responses (75% at four words or fewer) implies that they seldom engage meaningfully with the terms in the question.

Table 1. Descriptive statistics for student answer length (words) by attempt category.

Attempt	N	Q_1	Q_2 (Median)	Q_3
Correct	3,641	22	29	41
Incorrect	1,136	12	19	27
Non-Genuine	756	1	1	4

Having established that answer length often correlates with correctness, we next explore how rapidly students revised their answers and how heavily they relied on the LLM's feedback. To gain insight into whether LLM feedback contributed to learning, this analysis focuses on cases where the first attempt is incorrect (21.9%) or non-genuine (14.5%). We are interested in whether these students make a second attempt, and if so, how quickly and to what extent they reuse the LLM's feedback. Despite the option for resubmission, only 22.6% of non-correct first attempts had a second attempt, likely due to time, participation fulfillment, or perceived sufficiency of the LLM feedback.

Tables 2 and 3 report the time between the first and second attempts and the overlap ratio between the LLM's feedback and the student's subsequent response, categorized by transition type (e.g., incorrect to correct).

Table 2. Elapsed time (s) between first and second attempts by transition type.

First Attempt	Second Attempt	N	Q_1	Q_2 (Median)	Q_3
Incorrect	Correct	126	14	21.5	35.75
	Incorrect	16	43.5	61.5	103.5
	Non-Genuine	5	11	17	33
Non-Genuine	Correct	235	11	14	19.5
	Incorrect	13	23	57	94
	Non-Genuine	19	6.5	8	20.5

Table 3. Overlap ratio between LLM feedback and second attempt by transition type.

First Attempt	Second Attempt	N	Q_1	Q_2 (Median)	Q_3
Incorrect	Correct	126	.492	.745	.867
	Incorrect	16	.144	.204	.225
	Non-Genuine	5	.000	.000	.105
Non-Genuine	Correct	235	.714	.819	.946
	Incorrect	13	.224	.277	.378
	Non-Genuine	19	.000	.026	.076

Several notable patterns emerge, but our main interest is in cases where the second answer is correct, which can signify meaningful learning—or, alternately, superficial copying. Specifically, 85.7% of second attempts following an incorrect first answer ended up correct, whereas 88.0% of second attempts following a non-genuine first answer were correct. By examining the time intervals and feedback-overlap scores, we can gauge whether rapid turnaround and high verbatim similarity imply minimal processing (e.g., simple copy-paste), whereas longer intervals and lower overlap may suggest deeper engagement, such as reflecting and potentially revising the LLM's explanation into their own words. Some overlap may reflect appropriate uptake of scaffolding rather than mere copying, however, and so high-overlap/long-latency cases should be interpreted cautiously.

Overall, the clearest synergy between the two metrics is in non-genuine to correct answer transitions: a rapid turnaround ($Q_3 < 20$ s) and very high textual overlap (median $> .8$). This strongly suggests that many correct second attempts stem from direct insertion of the LLM's feedback with minimal modifications after receiving a "model solution." Future work might explore strategies to encourage more constructive engagement, e.g., by providing partial hints rather than fully elaborated model solutions, or by detecting copy-paste patterns in real time and prompting students to paraphrase. We also note that since the interface re-displays the question while feedback is still visible, this may cue textual reuse; an A/B test could help determine the size of that effect.

In cases where the first attempt was incorrect and the second was correct, overlap scores range from moderate to high (IQR .492–.867), and the median time interval (21.5 s) is notably longer than for non-genuine first attempts. Although the upper end of the overlap range still suggests significant reliance on the LLM's explanation, the lower overlap scores and longer time intervals may imply more genuine reflection and partial rewriting or paraphrasing rather than copying verbatim. Thus, while certain second attempts appear to incorporate the feedback heavily, the broader distribution points to a degree of genuine reflection or partial reworking of the provided content.

4 Conclusion

This preliminary exploration of LLM–driven feedback for compare-and-contrast glossary questions reveals promising signs that large language models can help scale aspects of intelligent tutoring systems. Though the feedback mechanism was evaluated only on C&C questions in one social science course, correctness rates climbed substantially after students received personalized feedback, suggesting its potential to guide them toward deeper understanding. Yet the data also reveal a tension between meaningful engagement and superficial copying: short intervals with high textual overlap frequently signal verbatim reuse of model solutions, whereas more moderate overlap and longer reflection times align with more substantive engagement.

By highlighting these varying patterns of student behavior, our results underscore the critical need to design mechanisms—such as partial hints, real-time copy-paste detection, and prompting for elaboration—that encourage constructive engagement rather than mere compliance. Although drawn from a single course's usage data, these insights illustrate both the value and challenges of adapting generative AI feedback for open-ended tasks at scale. Going forward, broader deployments and studies with pre- and post-assessments will help clarify how LLM-based feedback can emulate the most impactful features of ITSs to advance student learning.

References

1. Graesser, A.C., Conley, M., Olney, A.: Intelligent tutoring systems. In: Harris, K.R., Graham, S., Urdan, T. (eds.) APA Educational Psychology Handbook. Applications to Learning and Teaching, vol. 3, pp. 451–473. American Psychological Association, Washington, DC (2011)
2. Woolf, B.P.: Building Intelligent Interactive Tutors: Student-Centered Strategies for Revolutionizing E-Learning. Morgan Kaufman Publishers, Burlington MA (2009)
3. VanLehn, K.: The behavior of tutoring systems. Int. J. Artif. Intell. Educ. **16**(3), 227–265 (2006). https://dl.acm.org/doi/10.5555/1435351.1435353

4. Steenbergen-Hu, S., Cooper, H.: A meta-analysis of the effectiveness of intelligent tutoring systems on college students' academic learning. J. Educ. Psychol. **106**(2), 331–347 (2014). https://doi.org/10.1037/a0034752
5. Bloom, B.S.: The 2 sigma problem: the search for methods of group instruction as effective as one-to-one tutoring. Educ. Res. **13**, 4–16 (1984)
6. Anderson, J.R., Corbett, A.T., Koedinger, K.R., Pelletier, R.: Cognitive tutors: lessons learned. J. Learn. Sci. **4**, 167–207 (1995). https://doi.org/10.1207/s15327809jls0402_2
7. Kulik, C., Kulik, J.: Effectiveness of computer-based instruction: an updated analysis. Comput. Hum. Behav. **7**, 75–91 (1991). https://doi.org/10.1016/0747-5632(91)90030-5
8. VanLehn, K.: The relative effectiveness of human tutoring, intelligent tutoring systems, and other tutoring systems. Educ. Psychol. **46**(4), 197–221 (2011). https://doi.org/10.1080/00461520.2011.611369
9. Kulik, J.A., Fletcher, J.D.: Effectiveness of intelligent tutoring systems: a meta-analytic review. Rev. Educ. Res. **86**(1), 42–78 (2016). https://doi.org/10.3102/0034654315581420
10. Anderson, J.R., Conrad, F., Corbett, A.: Skill Acquisition and the LISP Tutor. Cogn. Sci. (13) (1989). https://doi.org/10.1207/s15516709cog1304_1
11. Koedinger, K. R., Kim, J., Jia, J., McLaughlin, E., Bier, N.: Learning is not a spectator sport: doing is better than watching for learning from a MOOC. In: Proceedings of the Second ACM Conference on Learning@Scale, pp. 111–120 (2015). https://doi.org/10.1145/2724660.2724681
12. Koedinger, K.R., McLaughlin, E.A., Jia, J.Z., Bier, N.L.: Is the doer effect a causal relationship? How can we tell and why it's important. In: Proceedings of the Sixth International Conference on Learning Analytics & Knowledge, pp. 388–397 (2016). https://doi.org/10.1145/2883851.2883957
13. Van Campenhout, R., Jerome, B., Johnson, B.G.: The doer effect at scale: investigating correlation and causation across seven courses. In: LAK'23: 13th International Learning Analytics and Knowledge Conference (LAK 2023) (2023). https://doi.org/10.1145/3576050.3576103
14. Dunlosky, J., Rawson, K., Marsh, E., Nathan, M., Willingham, D.: Improving students' learning with effective learning techniques: promising directions from cognitive and educational psychology. Psychol. Sci. Public Interest **14**(1), 4–58 (2013). https://doi.org/10.1177/1529100612453266
15. Lovett, M., Meyer, O., Thille, C.: The Open Learning Initiative: measuring the effectiveness of the OLI statistics course in accelerating student learning. J. Interact. Media Educ., 1–16 (2008). https://doi.org/10.5334/2008-14
16. Schaeffer, L.M., Margulieux, L.E., Chen, D., Catrambone, R.: Feedback via educational technology. Educ. Technol., 59–72 (2016)
17. Shute, V.J.: Focus on formative feedback. Rev. Educ. Res. **78**, 153–189 (2008). https://doi.org/10.3102/0034654307313795
18. Van Campenhout, R., Clark, M., Jerome, B., Dittel, J.S., Johnson, B.G.: Advancing intelligent textbooks with automatically generated practice: a large-scale analysis of student data. In: 5th Workshop on Intelligent Textbooks. The 24th International Conference on Artificial Intelligence in Education (2023). https://intextbooks.science.uu.nl/workshop2023/files/itb23_s1p2.pdf
19. Kurdi, G., Leo, J., Parsia, B., Sattler, U., Al-Emari, S.: A systematic review of automatic question generation for educational purposes. Int. J. Artif. Intell. Educ. **30**(1), 121–204 (2020). https://doi.org/10.1007/s40593-019-00186-y
20. Van Campenhout, R., Dittel, J.S., Jerome, B., Johnson, B.G.: Transforming textbooks into learning by doing environments: an evaluation of textbook-based automatic question generation. In: Third Workshop on Intelligent Textbooks at the 22nd International Conference on Artificial Intelligence in Education. CEUR Workshop Proceedings, pp. 60–73 (2021). http://ceur-ws.org/Vol-2895/paper06.pdf

21. Johnson, B.G., Dittel, J.S., Van Campenhout, R., Jerome, B.: Discrimination of automatically generated questions used as formative practice. In: Proceedings of the Ninth ACM Conference on Learning@Scale, pp. 325–329 (2022). https://doi.org/10.1145/3491140.3528323
22. Van Campenhout, R., Kimball, M., Clark, M., Dittel, J.S., Jerome, B., Johnson, B.G.: An investigation of automatically generated feedback on student behavior and learning. In: LAK '24: Proceedings of the 14th Learning Analytics and Knowledge Conference, pp. 850–856 (2024). https://doi.org/10.1145/3636555.3636901
23. Dai, W., et al.: Can Large Language Models Provide Feedback to Students? A Case Study on ChatGPT (2023). https://doi.org/10.35542/osf.io/hcgzj
24. Dai, W., et al.: Assessing the proficiency of large language models in automatic feedback generation: an evaluation study. Comput. Educ. Artif. Intell. **7** (2024). https://doi.org/10.1016/j.caeai.2024.100299
25. Jacobsen, L.J., Weber, K.E.: The promises and pitfalls of LLMs as feedback providers: a study of prompt engineering and the quality of AI-driven feedback (2023). https://doi.org/10.31219/osf.io/cr257
26. Alfieri, L., Nokes-Malach, T.J., Schunn, C.D.: Learning through case comparisons: a meta-analytic review. Educ. Psychol. **48**(2), 87–113 (2013). https://doi.org/10.1080/00461520.2013.775712
27. Aleven, V., Koedinger, K.R., Cross, K.M.: Tutoring answer explanation fosters learning with understanding. Artif. Intell. Educ. **10**(1), 151–158 (1999)
28. OpenAI. GPT-4o [Large language model] (2024a)
29. VitalSource Supplemental Data Repository (2025). https://github.com/vitalsource/data
30. OpenAI. GPT-4o mini [Large language model] (2024b)
31. Aleven, V., Koedinger, K.: Limitations of student control: do students know when they need help? In: Proceedings of the 5th International Conference on Intelligent Tutoring Systems, pp. 292–303 (2000)
32. Ratcliff, J.W., Metzener, D.E.: Pattern matching: the gestalt approach. Dr. Dobb's J. **13**(7), 46–51 (1988)

Leveraging LLMs for Bayesian and Deep Knowledge Tracing in the Logic-Muse Intelligent Tutoring System

Ange Tato[1]([✉]) and Roger Nkambou[2]

[1] Université Laval, Quebec, Canada
Ange-Adrienne.Nyamen-Tato@fse.ulaval.ca
[2] University of Quebec in Montreal, Montreal, Canada
nkambou.roger@uqam.ca

Abstract. Tracing learners' knowledge in a new domain or system is particularly challenging when no prior data is available. While expert input or prior knowledge can help design an initial model to estimate learners' knowledge, extracting expert knowledge often tacit and difficult to articulate can be cumbersome. This paper explores the use of large language models (LLMs), specifically ChatGPT, to construct a Bayesian network (BN) for knowledge tracing without relying on expert intervention or existing data. By identifying key domain knowledge elements, we demonstrate that a BN constructed using an LLM is as effective as one designed by domain experts. Furthermore, when integrated into a Deep Neural Network via Deep Knowledge Tracing (DKT), the LLM-based BN (as well as the Expert-based BN) significantly improves the performance of the traditional DKT model. Our findings suggest that LLMs offer a promising approach for developing adaptive learning models in domains with limited data.

Keywords: LLM · Knowledge tracing · Bayesian network · logical reasoning tutor

1 Introduction

A core challenge in developing adaptive interactive systems, such as intelligent tutoring systems (ITS), lies in designing the foundational knowledge structures that enable adaptive interactions. These structures encompass domain knowledge models (e.g., ontologies), production rules for problem-solving procedures, and probabilistic or neural models (e.g., Bayesian networks, neural networks) used to diagnose, classify, or predict learner behavior.

A key component of these systems is Knowledge Tracing (KT), which aims to estimate a learner's evolving knowledge state to predict future performance and inform personalized instruction [1]. Here, knowledge is treated as a latent variable, updated as learners engage with tasks. The key challenge is prediction: given a learner's interactions $(x_1, ..., x_t)$ up to time t, how will they perform at time $t+1$? This reduces to estimating the probability $P(x_{t+1}|x_1, ..., x_t)$. Common approaches like Bayesian Knowledge Tracing (BKT) and Deep Knowledge Tracing (DKT) [13] rely on historical data. However, a major obstacle in deploying such systems is the *cold start problem* [18], where insufficient historical data prevents accurate prediction during early learner interactions.

To address this, domain knowledge is often manually encoded into models such as Bayesian networks (BNs), which can bootstrap the system by representing expert assumptions about skill relationships and learning dependencies. However, this manual process introduces several bottlenecks: (a) expert availability is limited, (b) formalizing knowledge into BN structures is cognitively demanding, and (c) the process is labor-intensive and difficult to scale in educational contexts. This raises a critical research question: *Can a Bayesian network be constructed for a given domain without relying on expert input or pre-existing learner data?* Although data-driven methods provide partial solutions, they remain dependent on the availability of large, curated datasets, which may not exist in many domains, especially during initial system deployment. That is the case with Logic-Muse, an Intelligent Tutoring System for logical reasoning learning.

This paper presents a preliminary investigation into the use of LLMs as a scalable alternative for BN construction in Logic-Muse. The rest of the paper is organized as follows: Sect. 2 provides a quick review of BN construction and knowledge tracing in various perspectives. Section 3 describes the Logic-Muse Expert-based and LLM-based BNs. Section 3.1 presents a qualitative and structural comparison those BNs and their impact of KT. Section 4 concludes with a discussion of findings and future directions.

2 Building BN for Knowledge Tracing in Intelligent Tutoring Systems

2.1 When Experts Are Available

BN can be manually designed by domain experts [3,11]. In fact, a BN designed solely by experts refers to a probabilistic model in which the structure, causal relationships, and conditional probabilities are entirely defined manually by domain experts, without relying on data-driven learning or machine learning techniques. Experts determine which variables (skills, concepts, or factors) should be included in the network and establish causal dependencies between them. The probability tables are estimated subjectively, based on expert knowledge rather than empirical data.

2.2 When Prior Data Is Available

When relevant prior interaction data for problem solving are available, learning a Bayesian network means learning 1) conditional probability distributions (parameter learning) and 2) the graphical model of dependencies (structure learning) using machine learning techniques [17]. Several methods have also been proposed to simplify the task of experts by constructing the network using data [7]. For instance, Ramirez-Noriega et al. [9] introduce a technique for building BNs based on ontologies and information from Wikipedia. This approach constructs the qualitative component of the BN using classes and relationships from ontologies, while the quantitative component is derived from frequencies, hops, and a similarity measure between the ontology concepts represented by Wikipedia articles. The results showed a positive correlation of 0.647 between the method and the opinions of experts in the domain, as measured by the Spearman test. As a result, the method enables the construction of a BN that reflects knowledge in intelligent tutoring systems, similarly to how experts would build it, thus supporting the automatic creation of these systems.

2.3 Mixed Initiative Approaches

The approach can also follow a mixed initiative strategy, in which part of the Bayesian network is designed by experts and then enhanced through data-driven learning. A notable example of this is the Logic-Muse ITS, where the initial Bayesian network was constructed by experts [16] before being refined and extended using data-driven learning based on the Cognitive Diagnosis Model (CDM) [8]. In the case of Logic-Muse, the necessary data was collected from an experiment involving 294 learners.

3 Logic-Muse BNs Built from Experts and a LLM

3.1 The Logic-Muse Expert-Based BN

In Logic-Muse ITS, our focus is on learning propositional logical reasoning, specifically conditional reasoning, for which the initial Bayesian network was completely designed by experts, encompassing everything from the architecture to the definition of prior probabilities, as we will outline in the next section.

The Bayesian network designed by experts contains 29 reasoning skills (latent variables), 16 of which are directly connected to exercises (or items)(see Fig. 1). The prior probabilities and causal relationships between the different units of knowledge were also established beforehand by experts. It is worth noting that causality in this case materializes the influence of one unit of knowledge on the learning of the other. The leaf nodes are directly connected to the exercises, which are the evidence nodes. The skills involved in the Bayesian network include the inhibition of exceptions to the premises, the generation of counterexamples to the conclusion, and the ability to manage all the relevant models for familiar, counterfactual, and abstract situations.

For the evaluation, we used a sample of 294 participants, who completed 48 exercises covering 16 competencies (three items per skill). The items assessing conditional reasoning in Logic-Muse were based on the four logical forms of conditional reasoning: Modus Ponendo Ponens (MPP), Modus Tollendo Tollens (MTT), Affirmation of the Consequent (AC), and Denial of the Antecedent (DA). The MPP inference ("If P then Q, P is true, therefore Q is true") and

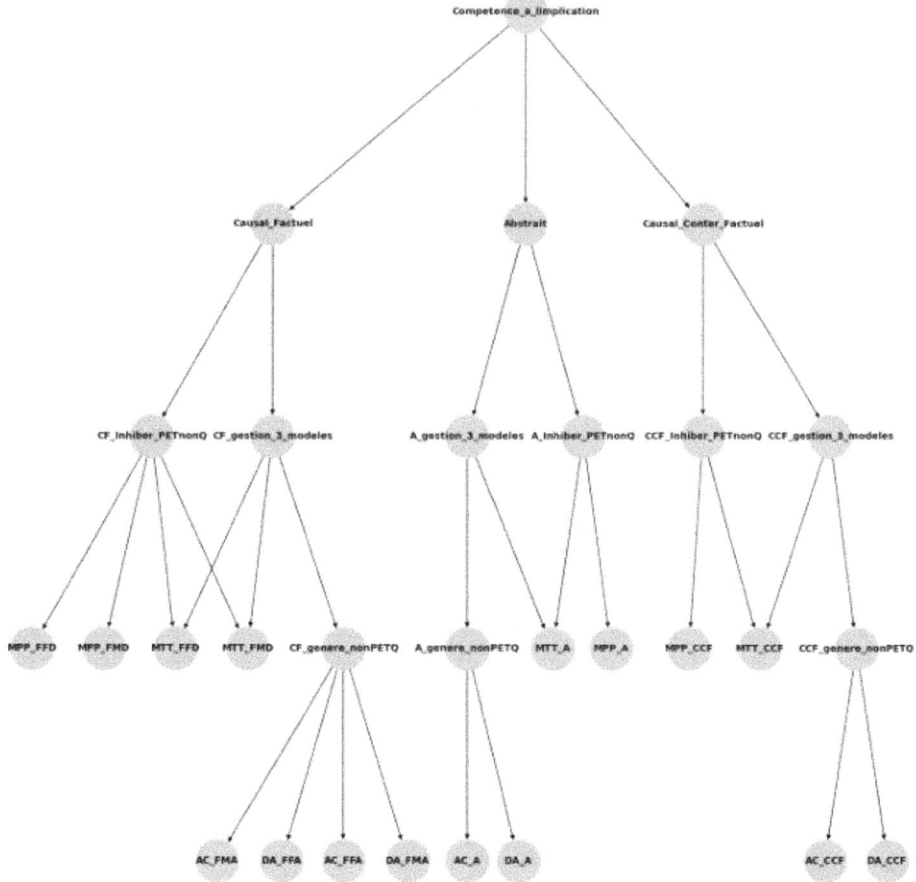

Fig. 1. Logic-Muse Expert-based BN

the MTT inference ("If P then Q, Q is false, therefore P is false") are both valid and lead to necessary conclusions. By contrast, the AC inference ("If P then Q, Q is true, therefore P is true") and the DA inference ("If P then Q, P is false, therefore Q is false") referred to as DA) are both invalid since their conclusions do not necessarily follow from the premises. These four logical forms are declined in 3 levels of content (factual, abstract and counterfactual) based on a developmental model of conditional reasoning [2,6].

Predicting the Learner's Behavior with the Expert-Based BN: The bayesian knowledge tracing (BKT) algorithm we implemented for this BN aims at predicting a learner's behavior (response) at time $t+1$, based on the answers provided between $t=1$ and t. At $t=0$, the prediction relies solely on the prior probabilities. We evaluated this expert-based model on 294 learners who answered 48 questions (16 skills × 3 exercises per skill). The confusion matrix is presented in Table 1 and the model performances are shown in Table 2.

Table 1. Confusion matrix for the expert-based model.

	Expert-based BN		
	Predicted Correct	Predicted Incorrect	Total
Actual Correct	7827	550	8377
Actual Incorrect	2818	2623	5441
Total	10645	3173	13818

Table 2. Expert-Based BKT Performance

Metric	Expert-based BN
Accuracy	0.76
Precision	0.74
Recall	0.93
F1-Score	0.82
AUC	0.708

3.2 The Logic-Muse LLM-Based BN

LLMs have demonstrated exceptional abilities in understanding, generating, and processing natural language. These models are pre-trained on vast text corpora and are often fine-tuned for specific downstream tasks. They have shown an advanced capacity to learn complex language patterns and structures, along with strong reasoning capabilities, enabling superior performance across a wide range of natural language processing tasks [4]. We hypothesized that if a LLM has been trained on relevant knowledge, it is highly likely that it can generate causal links between knowledge elements and assign conditional probabilities to them. The LLM tool used for the automatic generation of the BN was ChatGPT-4. We provided it with a comprehensive list of domain-specific skills and instructed it to generate a corresponding Bayesian network. The request was formulated as follows: *"Here is a list of skills related to first-order logical reasoning, specifically propositional logic. Generate a Bayesian network incorporating all these skill nodes. You must include prior probability tables and leverage your domain knowledge to establish links and logical probabilities."* Once generated, the Bayesian network was implemented using the PyBBN library[1] and further

---
[1] https://py-bbn.readthedocs.io/index.html.

refined by integrating exercise nodes (items) linked to their corresponding skills, similar to the Expert-based BN. The final Bayesian network includes all 29 reasoning skills (see Fig. 2), with 16 skills directly connected to exercises.

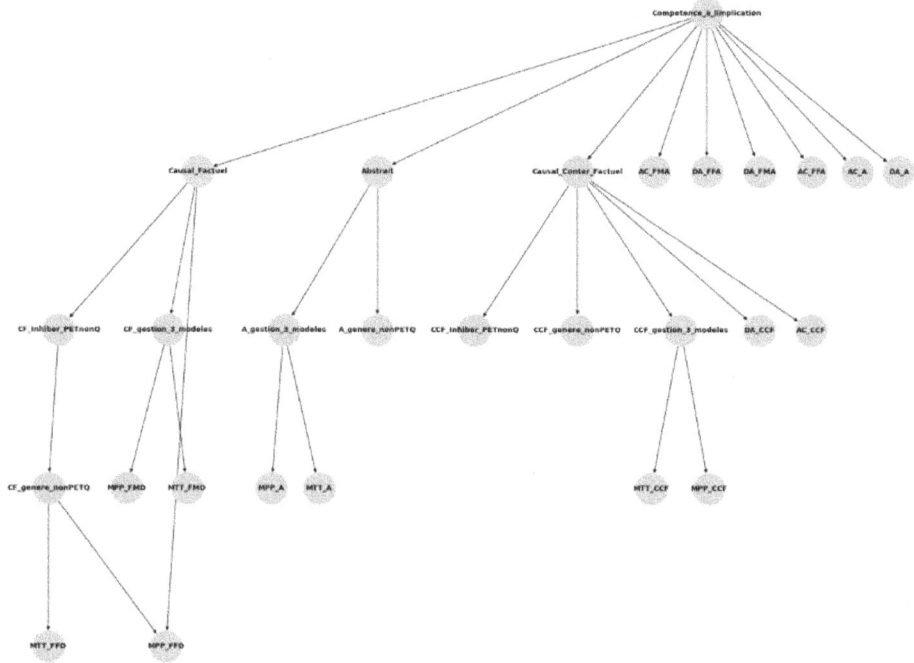

Fig. 2. Logic-Muse LLM-Based BN

As shown in Fig. 2, the LLM-based BN successfully established logical connections between the provided skills. Moreover, with a few exceptions, these connections closely resemble those in the expert-designed network. Similarly, the Conditional Probability Tables (CPTs) generated by the LLM (see Table 4) are also comparable to those proposed by experts (see Table 3). Additionally, although the exercise nodes were added at the final stage, the CPTs were still generated by the LLM. An important observation is that the 29 skills provided to the LLM were given without definitions—only their acronyms were supplied. This suggests that, in this specific case, the LLM tool was able to produce a BN nearly as effective as the expert-designed one in just one minute with few shot prompting. However, it is crucial to emphasize that human oversight remains necessary before deployment, as LLMs do not truly understand the semantics of the concepts and can easily produce incorrect or misleading information without proper human or external supervision [5]. LLMs generate responses based on patterns in data rather than genuine comprehension [10]. This implies that LLMs can confidently produce misinformation, hallucinate sources, or misinterpret context.

Table 3. Conditional Probability Tables (CPTs) for three skills provided by experts.

Skill	Parents	CPT (Experts)
`Competence_a_limplication`	None	True: 0.5, False: 0.5
`Causal_Factuel`	`Competence_a_limplication`	True → True: 0.9, False: 0.1 False → True: 0.3, False: 0.7
`Causal_Conter_Factuel`	`Competence_a_limplication`	True → True: 0.9, False: 0.1 False → True: 0.3, False: 0.7

Table 4. Conditional Probability Tables (CPTs) for three skills generated by the LLM.

Skill	Parents	CPT (LLM)
`Competence_a_limplication`	None	True: 0.7, False: 0.3
`Causal_Factuel`	`Competence_a_limplication`	True → True: 0.9, False: 0.1 False → True: 0.5, False: 0.5
`Causal_Conter_Factuel`	`Competence_a_limplication`	True → True: 0.8, False: 0.2 False → True: 0.4, False: 0.6

Predicting the Learner's Behavior with the LLM-Based BN: Using the same methodology as the expert-based BN, the LLM-based model was implemented in the BKT algorithm to predict learner responses at time $t+1$ based on their answer history from $t=1$ to t. Initial predictions at $t=0$ relied solely on prior probabilities. The resulting confusion matrix is shown in Table 5, and comparative performance metrics with the expert-based model are illustrated in Fig. 3. As shown, the LLM-based model's confusion matrix is well-aligned with that of the expert-based model, enabling a direct and fair comparison between the two.

Table 5. Confusion matrix for the LLM-based model.

	LLM-based BN		
	Predicted Correct	**Predicted Incorrect**	**Total**
Actual Correct	7871	506	8377
Actual Incorrect	2814	2627	5441
Total	10685	3133	13818

4 Discussion and Conclusion

We applied both models without modification for the knowledge tracing algorithm in Logic-Muse, comparing the two Bayesian networks in terms of predictive accuracy and structural consistency. As shown in Fig. 3, the AI-generated

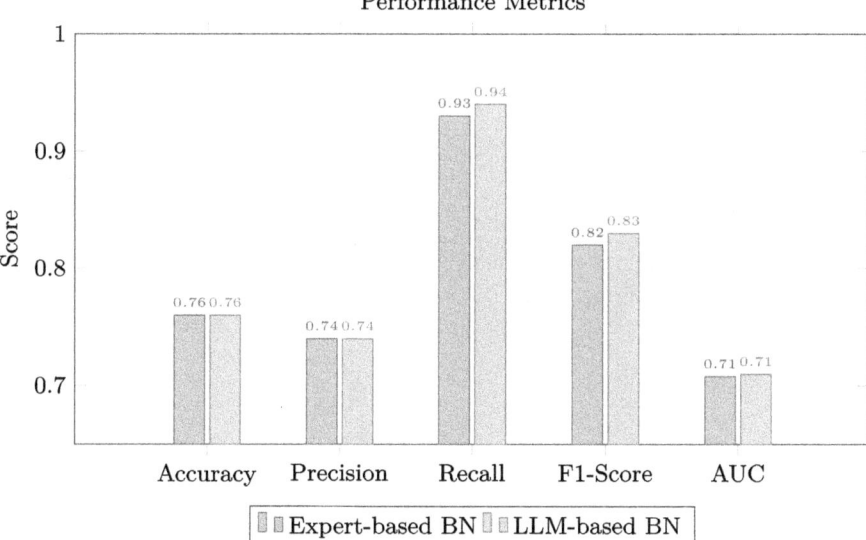

Fig. 3. BKT Model Performance Comparison

Bayesian network performed similarly to the expert-designed network. Furthermore, our analysis revealed that the AI-generated model captured dependencies similar to those identified by experts and produced nearly identical prior probability tables.

When integrated into our hybrid knowledge tracing model, which combines the Bayesian network with a Deep Neural Network (DNN) for knowledge tracing [14], both networks significantly enhanced the performance of the initial DKT (Deep Knowledge Tracing), as demonstrated in Fig. 4. Notably, in our hybrid approach, the Bayesian network is incorporated into the DKT through an attention mechanism, ensuring a more effective fusion of probabilistic inference and deep learning.

The use of generative AI for constructing Bayesian networks presents a promising alternative to traditional methods. The results demonstrate that the automatically generated model performs as effectively as an expert-designed one while significantly reducing development time and costs. This approach enables robust predictions for new learners with minimal to no initial data requirements. By leveraging generative AI, knowledge tracing becomes possible without training models on data, even in the absence of domain experts. Additionally, this solution helps mitigate the cold start problem, allowing adaptive systems to be operational immediately. While constructing a Bayesian network from available data is feasible, it is often time-consuming and resource-intensive [12]. Bayesian inference, particularly when exact and involving multiple nodes, is computationally complex and requires representative data. In contrast, a domain knowledge-based network can be deployed immediately, without prior data collection. How-

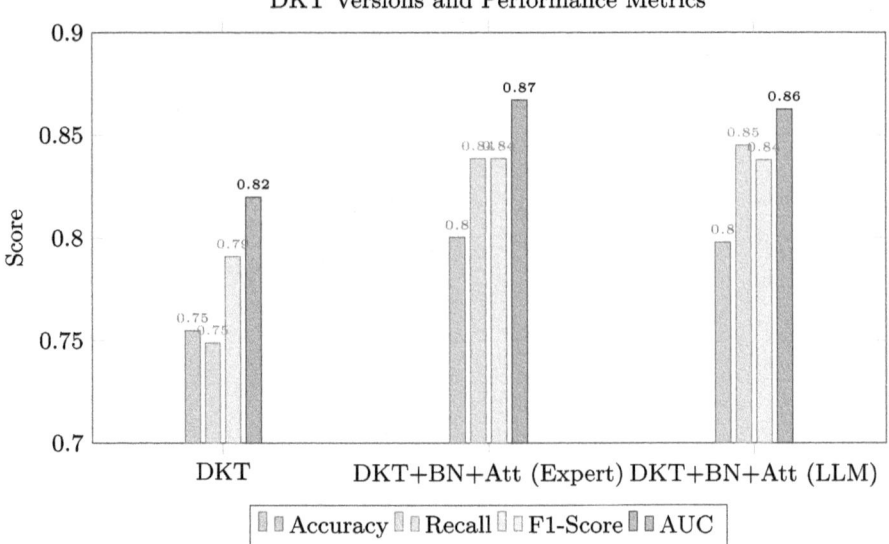

Fig. 4. DKT Model Comparison

ever, human oversight remains essential to refine specific relationships between variables.

It should be noted that the findings presented in this paper are derived from preliminary work and, due to the highly limited size of the dataset and the narrow application domain in which the study was conducted, it should not be interpreted as generalizable. In a subsequent phase, we conducted a more comprehensive investigation that encompassed a broader range of datasets and learning domains while also using multiple instances of LLMs. The findings from this subsequent study will be reported in [15].

References

1. Abdelrahman, G., Wang, Q., Nunes, B.: Knowledge tracing: a survey. ACM Comput. Surv. **55**(11), 1–37 (2023)
2. Byrne, R.M., Tasso, A.: Deductive reasoning with factual, possible, and counterfactual conditionals. Memory Cogn. **27**, 726–740 (1999)
3. Conati, C., Gertner, A.S., VanLehn, K., Druzdzel, M.J.: On-line student modeling for coached problem solving using Bayesian networks. In: User Modeling: Proceedings of the Sixth International Conference UM97 Chia Laguna, Sardinia, Italy June 2–5 1997, pp. 231–242. Springer, Cham (1997). https://doi.org/10.1007/978-3-7091-2670-7_24
4. Ge, Y., et al.: OpenAGI: When LLM meets domain experts. In: Advances in Neural Information Processing Systems, vol. 36 (2024)
5. Kopalle, P.K., Gangwar, M., Uppal, A.: Commentary on "ai is changing the world: For better or for worse?". J. Macromark. **44**(4), 886–891 (2024)

6. Markovits, H.: On the road toward formal reasoning: reasoning with factual causal and contrary-to-fact causal premises during early adolescence. J. Exp. Child Psychol. **128**, 37–51 (2014)
7. Neapolitan, E., Morris, S.: Probabilistic modelling with Bayesian networks. In: The SAGE Handbook of Quantitative Methodology for the Social Sciences, pp. 371–390 (2004)
8. Nkambou, R., Brisson, J., Tato, A., Robert, S.: Learning logical reasoning using an intelligent tutoring system: a hybrid approach to student modeling. In: Proceedings of the AAAI Conference on Artificial Intelligence, vol. 37, pp. 15930–15937 (2023)
9. Ramírez-Noriega, A., Juárez-Ramírez, R., Leyva-López, J.C., Jiménez, S., Figueroa-Pérez, J.F.: A method for building the quantitative and qualitative part of Bayesian networks for intelligent tutoring systems. Comput. J. **65**(12), 3035–3048 (2022)
10. Ray, P.P.: Stepping with caution: large language models for consulting infectious diseases. Clin. Infect. Diseases, ciae442 (2024)
11. Rowe, J., Lester, J.: Modeling user knowledge with dynamic Bayesian networks in interactive narrative environments. In: Proceedings of the AAAI Conference on Artificial Intelligence and Interactive Digital Entertainment, vol. 6, pp. 57–62 (2010)
12. Scanagatta, M., Salmerón, A., Stella, F.: A survey on Bayesian network structure learning from data. Progress Artif. Intell. **8**(4), 425–439 (2019)
13. Shen, S., et al.: A survey of knowledge tracing: models, variants, and applications. IEEE Trans. Learn. Technol. (2024)
14. Tato, A., Nkambou, R.: Infusing expert knowledge into a deep neural network using attention mechanism for personalized learning environments. Front. Artif. Intell. **5**, 921476 (2022)
15. Tato, A., Nkambou, R.: Can LLMs generate accurate Bayesian networks to enhance knowledge tracing? In: Proceedings of the 26th International Conference on Artificial Intelligence in Education: AIED 2025, Palermo, Italy, July 22–July 26, 2025. Springer. To appear (2025)
16. Tato, A., Nkambou, R., Brisson, J., Robert, S.: Predicting learner's deductive reasoning skills using a Bayesian network. In: Artificial Intelligence in Education: 18th International Conference, AIED 2017, Wuhan, China, June 28–July 1, 2017, Proceedings 18, pp. 381–392. Springer, Cham (2017). https://doi.org/10.1007/978-3-319-61425-0_32
17. Tsamardinos, I., Brown, L.E., Aliferis, C.F.: The max-min hill-climbing Bayesian network structure learning algorithm. Mach. Learn. **65**, 31–78 (2006)
18. Wu, X., Zhou, H., Shi, Y., Yao, W., Huang, X., Liu, N.: Could small language models serve as recommenders? Towards data-centric cold-start recommendation. In: Proceedings of the ACM on Web Conference 2024, pp. 3566–3575 (2024)

AI-Generated Code Detection: An Examination of Current Tools in Education

Juan Esteban Cuellar Argotty[✉] and Ruben Manrique

Department of Systems and Computing Engineering, Universidad de los Andes,
Bogotá, Colombia
{j.cuellara,rf.manrique}@uniandes.edu.co

Abstract. The increasing availability of large language models (LLMs) has raised significant concerns over academic integrity in introductory programming courses. Existing AI detectors, primarily developed for natural language, have shown limited efficacy when identifying AI-generated code, particularly after simple obfuscations. This study evaluates seven state-of-the-art detection tools on Python solutions collected from an educational platform (Senecode). We built a new dataset of 822 human-written and 822 AI-generated code samples, with the AI samples systematically modified using six prompt variants. Our findings reveal critical precision-recall tradeoffs and notable performance drops in the face of minor obfuscation. Our findings reveal that current AI-detection tools are unreliable for educational use and highlight the need to shift focus toward rethinking assessment practices in the age of generative AI.

Keywords: AI-generated code · Code detection · Academic integrity · Programming education · Large Language Models

1 Introduction

Recent advances in large language models (LLMs) have enabled the automated generation of code that is not only syntactically correct but often functionally effective [1,2]. While such capabilities can enhance productivity and facilitate learning, they also pose potential threats to academic integrity in formal educational contexts [3,5]. Students might submit AI-generated solutions without engaging in problem-solving, thereby undermining learning outcomes. Additionally, educators face difficulties in confirming code authenticity and maintaining a fair grading environment [5,6].

Although numerous AI-content detection tools exist, most were created for natural language and lack specialized mechanisms to handle the distinct syntax and structure of programming code [1,7]. Prior investigations signal that even minimal modifications, such as variable renaming or dead code insertion, can significantly degrade detection accuracy [2,3]. Pan et al. [5] showed that mainstream detectors frequently misclassify obfuscated code segments, reinforcing the idea that robust detection requires deeper structural analysis. Similarly, Wang et al. [10] found that AI-generated code produced by ChatGPT could successfully pass assessments designed for human students, highlighting the difficulty of distinguishing genuine student work from AI outputs. Moreover, Yang et al. [11] proposed a zero-shot detection method capable of identifying machine-generated code without extensive retraining, illustrating the growing sophistication of AI detection techniques but also the complexity of the underlying challenge.

In this work, we contribute to this ongoing discussion by conducting a systematic evaluation of seven AI-code detectors on both baseline and obfuscated AI-generated code. We highlight three primary contributions:

1. **Dataset Construction:** We curate a balanced dataset of 822 human-written solutions and 822 AI-generated solutions tied to 137 introductory Python problems, encompassing six prompt-based obfuscation variants.
2. **Comparative Evaluation:** We conduct a quantitative assessment of seven detectors on both baseline and obfuscated AI-generated code, reporting their respective performance tradeoffs.
3. **Educational Insights:** We discuss key implications for instructors and educational administrators, proposing multi-layered strategies that combine automated detection with pedagogical best practices.

2 Related Work

Most AI content detection methods rely on text-likelihood metrics, perplexity measures, or classifiers trained on known AI-generated text [3,7]. DetectGPT [3] exemplifies a zero-shot approach that leverages probability curvature, while GLTR [4] provides forensic analysis based on token distributions. Although these techniques often succeed in free-form text, they falter with source code due to the code's more rigid syntactic rules and context-specific patterns [5].

Recent research suggests that code-oriented detection can benefit from semantic features, such as abstract syntax trees (ASTs) or control-flow structures [5,8]. However, such methods remain in nascent stages and typically require large, labeled corpora for training. Pan et al. [5] showed that mainstream detectors frequently misclassify obfuscated code segments, reinforcing the idea that robust detection requires deeper structural analysis. Similarly, Yang et al. [11] proposed a zero-shot detection approach for machine-generated code that does not rely on retraining, highlighting the potential of leveraging structural patterns for better generalization across coding tasks.

Minimal code modifications often suffice to fool general-purpose detectors [2,3]. For instance, reordering lines, adding superfluous functions, or substituting variables with semantically equivalent synonyms can confuse token-based methods. These alterations pose unique challenges in academic contexts, where students can trivially apply them to evade detection. Additionally, Wang et al. [10] demonstrated that AI-generated code can achieve high success rates in introductory programming assessments, further complicating efforts to distinguish between authentic and AI-assisted submissions.

Collectively, these findings suggest some limitations of current detection approaches when applied to source code, motivating the need for more systematic evaluations like the one we present in this study.

3 Methods

3.1 Dataset Collection

We constructed our dataset by extracting human-written solutions from the Senecode platform, an educational environment used by first-semester students of Systems and Computing Engineering at Universidad de los Andes. Solutions were rigorously filtered based on two criteria: (1) submissions had to precede the public release of GPT-3.5 (November 2022) to avoid AI contamination, and (2) solutions were required to demonstrate substantial completion as indicated by the platform's internal progress metric, although complete correctness was not mandatory. This ensured authentic variability representative of introductory student programming. A total of 822 human-written solutions were collected, corresponding to 137 Python problems encompassing foundational programming concepts like loops, conditionals, and basic data structures.

Subsequently, we generated a matching set of 822 AI solutions using GPT-4o (Azure OpenAI). For each of the 137 problems, six systematically varied prompts were used to produce diverse AI solutions. Thus, our dataset maintains a deliberate 1:1 ratio between human and AI-generated code samples, facilitating rigorous comparisons.

3.2 AI-Generated Variants

To synthesize AI solutions for each of the 137 Python problems, we employed Azure OpenAI (GPT-4o). Along with a baseline variant (i.e., a direct prompt), we generated five additional variants, each designed to introduce specific modifications in the code. These included systematically renaming variables to random tokens (*Variable Name Substitution*), inserting or expanding explanatory logic (*Verbose*), reducing code to minimal statements (*Concise*), adding redundant or unused functions (*Dead Code Insertion*), and removing all inline comments (*No Comments*). Detailed descriptions of each prompt and specific examples of the resulting code transformations can be found in our repository[1].

For instance, the *Variable Name Substitution* variant systematically replaces meaningful variable names with random tokens to obfuscate code readability. A representative example from Problem 160 is shown below:

```
def trzn_cmlxps(initial_orientation, command):
    compass = {"N": 0, "E": 1, "S": 2, "W": 3}
    lkc_shp = {0: "N", 1: "E", 2: "S", 3: "W"}
    if command == "L":
```

---

[1] https://github.com/iGotty/AI-GCD-Appendices/blob/main/apendicces.md

```
        return lkc_shp[(compass[initial_orientation] - 1) %
↪ 4]
    elif command == "R":
        return lkc_shp[(compass[initial_orientation] + 1) %
↪ 4]
    elif command == "H":
        return lkc_shp[(compass[initial_orientation] + 2) %
↪ 4]
    elif command == ".":
        return initial_orientation
```

Using these methods, each problem ultimately had six variants (one baseline plus five additional transformations), producing a total of 822 AI-generated samples that closely mirrored the number of human-written solutions. This balanced dataset enabled a systematic comparison of detection effectiveness across multiple obfuscation styles, revealing how seemingly minor changes—such as renaming identifiers or deleting comments—can substantially affect AI identification rates.

3.3 Detectors Evaluated

We examined seven tools that are widely cited in the literature or commercially available.

1. **DetectGPT** [3]: Relies on probability curvature to assess AI likelihood.
2. **GLTR** [4]: Highlights likely versus unlikely token usage based on large LMs.
3. **X Detector**: Proprietary solution primarily targeting text but used here for code (no formal publication currently available)[2].
4. **Originality**: Commercial system integrating plagiarism checks and AI detection[3].
5. **ZeroGPT**: Web-based classifier specialized in GPT-series text detection[4].
6. **Sapling**: Writing assistant featuring grammar-checking and basic AI detection[5].
7. **GPTZero**: Dedicated GPT-based text detection platform[6].

Implementation Details. Whenever possible, we used each detector's most recent API or interface. For instance, Originality and ZeroGPT were accessed via their web portals, while DetectGPT and GLTR required local Python scripts. Output from each detector was consolidated into a unified CSV file containing the following fields: *sample_id*, *label (human or AI)*, *detector_prediction*, and *confidence_score* (if provided). Detectors that did not output confidence scores were simply recorded as AI or human classifications.

---

[2] https://xdetector.ai.
[3] https://originality.ai.
[4] https://zerogpt.com.
[5] https://sapling.ai.
[6] https://gptzero.me.

We then mapped the predictions to binary labels (AI vs. human). In ambiguous cases, we followed each tool's recommended threshold. For example, if a detector rated a sample as over 50% likely to be AI, we classified it as AI-generated. While these defaults might not be fully optimized, they reflect typical user experiences.

3.4 Evaluation Metrics

To compare detector outputs, we used the standard confusion matrix framework:

$$\text{Accuracy} = \frac{TP+TN}{TP+TN+FP+FN}, \tag{1}$$

$$\text{Precision} = \frac{TP}{TP+FP}, \tag{2}$$

$$\text{Recall} = \frac{TP}{TP+FN}, \tag{3}$$

$$F1 = 2 \cdot \frac{\text{Precision} \times \text{Recall}}{\text{Precision} + \text{Recall}}. \tag{4}$$

where TP = AI code correctly flagged, TN = human code correctly identified, FP = human code wrongly flagged, FN = AI code missed by the detector.

4 Results

4.1 Overall Detector Performance

Table 1 summarizes performance across both AI-generated and human-written samples. Notably, GPTZero and X Detector achieve near-perfect recall, indicating they rarely miss AI samples. However, these tools exhibit significantly higher false positive rates, thereby compromising precision and overall accuracy.

Table 1. Overall Performance Metrics

Detector	Accuracy (%)	Precision (%)	Recall (%)	F1 (%)
GPTZero	66.67	60.00	100.00	75.00
X Detector	50.18	50.09	100.00	66.75
Originality	62.59	83.28	31.51	45.72
DetectGPT	61.13	57.68	83.58	68.26
Sapling	44.71	46.96	81.75	59.65
GLTR	38.87	40.46	47.20	43.57
ZeroGPT	50.36	50.20	89.66	64.37

4.2 Confusion Matrix Insights

While Table 1 outlines summary metrics, a closer inspection of the confusion matrices (Fig. 1) reveals nuanced patterns. For instance, GPTZero's high recall is accompanied by a high false positive rate, indicating many human solutions are wrongly flagged as AI. In contrast, Originality's strategy yields fewer false positives but allows numerous AI solutions to slip undetected.

Qualitatively, we noticed certain "trivial" human solutions (e.g., single-line functions) were especially prone to false positives under detectors that heavily rely on surface tokens. These borderline cases reinforce the need for a balanced approach, where a deeper analysis of code structure or style could mitigate reliance on purely lexical features.

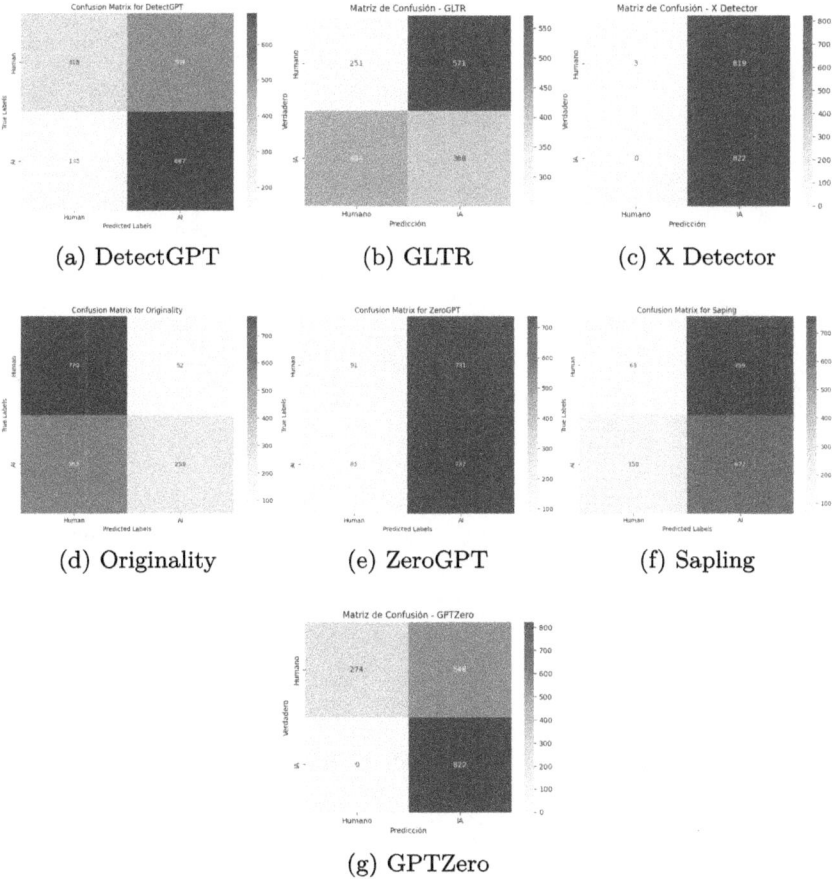

(a) DetectGPT   (b) GLTR   (c) X Detector

(d) Originality   (e) ZeroGPT   (f) Sapling

(g) GPTZero

Fig. 1. Confusion matrices for each detector, illustrating the distribution of true positives, false positives, true negatives, and false negatives.

4.3 Effects of Code Variants

We further examined each detector's robustness by applying six obfuscation variants to AI-generated code: *No Variants, Variable Name Substitution, Verbose Code, Concise Code, Dead Code Insertion,* and *No Comments* (Fig. 2). While some detectors, such as X Detector and GPTZero, maintained near-perfect detection rates, they also risked overclassifying human-written code as AI-generated. Others, notably Originality, saw detection rates drop from 44.53% in the baseline condition to 7.30% under *Dead Code Insertion*, indicating high sensitivity to structural modifications. This variability highlights the challenge of detecting intentionally altered AI-generated content.

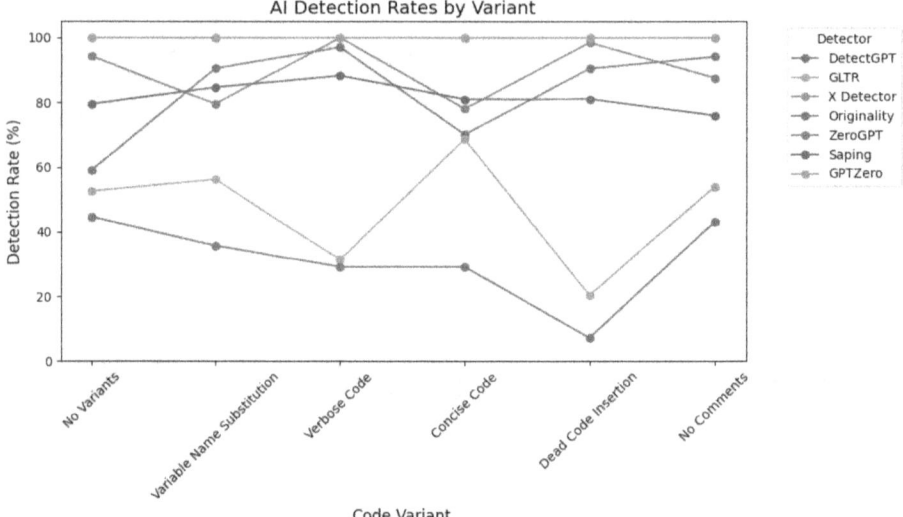

Fig. 2. AI detection rates across code variants for all detectors. Even minor obfuscations can severely degrade a tool's ability to identify AI-generated code.

5 Discussion

5.1 Precision-Recall Tradeoffs in Practice

The critical tension between high recall and high precision is evident in Table 1. GPTZero and X Detector rarely fail to detect AI but impose a large burden of false positives, potentially penalizing legitimate student work [8]. Meanwhile, Originality and DetectGPT minimize false accusations at the cost of missing a significant portion of AI submissions.

Given these findings, course instructors should be cautious when relying on these tools, as their high false positive rates can lead to over-penalization of legitimate student work. At the time of this evaluation, such limitations render these detectors unsuitable for practical use in academic settings. In contexts where academic integrity is paramount, the presumption of the student *good faith* must prevail over low-accuracy automated detection tools.

5.2 Obfuscation and Tool Limitations

Our variant-based evaluation shows that simple modifications can drastically reduce detection effectiveness. As noted by previous authors, approaches based solely on lexical features are insufficient when facing minor changes in code flow or variable names, and several studies have recommended adopting structurally informed methods to enhance robustness [5, 9].

In practical terms, these results imply that current plagiarism checks extended with a basic AI classifier may not suffice. Specialized methods that account for abstract syntax trees, dependency graphs, or typical style patterns of student-level code are more promising avenues for robust detection. In particular, access to a student's coding history—such as multiple past submissions—can enable the modeling of individual coding style, offering a more reliable basis for comparison and anomaly detection.

5.3 Educational Implications and Best Practices

Instructors face significant ethical and practical challenges when attempting to detect AI-generated code in the classroom. At present, the available tools are not sufficiently reliable for this task. Many exhibit high false positive rates that risk penalizing honest students, while others fail to detect AI-assisted submissions altogether. This lack of accuracy makes their use not only problematic but potentially harmful in academic contexts, where fairness and trust are fundamental. More broadly, in a world where AI tools are becoming increasingly integrated into programming workflows, the very goal of identifying whether code was generated by a human or an AI may become obsolete. Rather than focusing solely on detection, institutions may need to rethink evaluation strategies to emphasize process, understanding, and responsible use of AI, aligning assessments with the realities of modern software development.

6 Limitations and Future Directions

Limitations

While our study offers a thorough look at current AI detection tools, there are factors that limit the generalizability of our findings. First, the human-written solutions in our dataset were authored by first-semester students enrolled in the Systems and Computing Engineering program at Universidad de los Andes. Due to their introductory programming experience, the code exhibits a natural variability in terms of quality, complexity, and completeness. Second, the study was conducted specifically on Python assignments; performance may differ significantly with other languages or more advanced programming tasks. Third, the default confidence thresholds used by each detector may not be universally optimal for all educational contexts, and further fine-tuning might yield improved detection performance. Lastly, although our dataset is well-balanced and representative for introductory coursework, larger or more specialized datasets could potentially reveal additional performance trends or highlight new detection challenges not captured in this study.

Future Directions

Building on these observations, future research could expand to multiple programming languages and explore semantic or behavioral techniques, such as analyzing test coverage or runtime traces, to distinguish machine-generated logic from genuine human problem-solving. Efforts to construct larger labeled corpora with varied obfuscation methods may also drive more sophisticated evaluation of detection tools.

On the educational front, rather than reinforcing detection frameworks, future efforts might more fruitfully focus on rethinking how we assess learning in an era where AI tools are readily accessible. Qualitative investigations into how and why students use these tools can shed light on evolving learning behaviors and values. Such insights can guide educators not just in crafting clearer guidelines, but in redesigning assessments that prioritize understanding, creativity, and the responsible integration of AI into problem-solving—skills that will likely be more relevant than the ability to write code in isolation.

7 Conclusion

This study performed a systematic evaluation of seven AI-code detectors on a balanced dataset of human-written and AI-generated Python solutions derived from 137 introductory programming problems. Our variant-based approach revealed how even minor obfuscations (variable renaming, dead code insertion) can severely degrade detection accuracy. The results highlight an inherent tension: some detectors (e.g., GPTZero, X Detector) capture nearly all AI-generated code at the cost of excessive false positives, while others (e.g., Originality) favor lower false positives at the risk of missing most AI solutions.

According to our results, no single off-the-shelf tool currently provides a reliable solution for detecting AI-generated code in educational contexts. Rather than relying solely on detection, a more balanced and constructive path forward involves a multi-layered strategy that includes selective use of detection tools, thoughtful instructor review, and clear institutional guidelines on responsible AI use. In an educational landscape increasingly shaped by AI, rethinking assessment design to emphasize process, understanding, and ethical tool use may prove more effective than perfecting detection. Ultimately, sustained collaboration among educators, researchers, and developers will be essential to align pedagogical practices with the realities of an AI-integrated future.

Declarations

Data Availability. The dataset used in this study is available at our public repository.

Conflict of Interest. The authors declare no conflicts of interest.

References

1. Uchendu, A., Venkatraman, S., Le, T., Lee, D.: Catch Me If You GPT: tutorial on Deepfake texts. In: NAACL Tutorials (2024)
2. Weber-Wulff, D., Anohina-Naumeca, A., and Bjelobaba, S.: Testing of detection tools for AI-generated text. Int. J. Educ. Integrity (2023)
3. Mitchell, E., Lee, Y., Khazatsky, A., Manning, C.D., Finn, C.: DetectGPT: Zero-shot machine-generated text detection using probability curvature. OpenReview (2023)
4. Gehrmann, S., Strobelt, H., and Rush, A. M.: GLTR: statistical detection and visualization of generated text. ACL Anthology (2019)
5. Pan, W.H., Chok, M.J., Wong, J.L.S.: Assessing AI detectors in identifying AI-generated code: implications for education. IEEE Xplore (2023)
6. Li, Y., Li, Q., and Cui, L.: MAGE: machine-generated text detection in the wild. arXiv preprint arXiv:2305.13242 (2023)
7. Xu, Z., Sheng, V.S.: Detecting AI-generated code assignments using perplexity of large language models. In: AAAI Conference on Artificial Intelligence (2023)
8. New Era of AI in Education: towards a sustainable multifaceted revolution. Sustainability (2023)
9. The Role and Impact of ChatGPT in Educational Practices: insights from an Australian higher education case study. Educ. Inf. Technol. (2023)
10. Wang, K., Akins, S., Mohammed, A., Lawrence, R.: Student mastery or AI deception? Analyzing ChatGPT's assessment proficiency and evaluating detection strategies. arXiv preprint arXiv:2311.16292 (2023)
11. Yang, X., Zhang, K., Chen, H., Petzold, L., Wang, W.Y., Cheng, W.: Zero-shot detection of machine-generated codes. arXiv preprint arXiv:2310.05103 (2023)

Manchita: An AI-Powered Gamified Learning Environment

Nicolás Klopstock(✉), Ernesto José Duarte, Edier Becerra, and Rubén Manrique

Universidad de los Andes, Cra 1 #18A-12, Bogotá, Colombia
{n.klopstock,e.duartem,e.becerra1,rf.manrique}@uniandes.edu.co

Abstract. This paper introduces "Manchita", the first version of a gamified learning environment powered by Generative Artificial Intelligence (AI) to enhance engagement and participation in learning. The system integrates Large Language Models (LLMs) and Retrieval-Augmented Generation (RAG) techniques to automatically answer learners' questions in an interactive, conversational manner. Additionally, our environment enables educators to develop interactive questionnaires utilizing various gamified strategies. By incorporating elements such as narrative-driven challenges, scoring mechanisms, and streak-based games, our online learning environment fosters increased engagement. Initial testing with students and educators indicated a positive impact on learning participation and satisfaction.

Keywords: Large Language Models · Gamification · Learning Environment · Retrieval-Augmented Generation · Intelligent Agents · Multi-Agent System · Question & Answer Automatic Generation · Graph-orchestrated Agents

1 Introduction

In the age of digitalization and Artificial Intelligence (AI), Large Language Models (LLMs) have transformed the interaction humans have with information and knowledge. These language models are highly effective at generating textual content across a wide range of topics and in multiple languages, adapting to specific subjects. In the educational context, these technologies introduce a great opportunity to personalize learning, optimize the creation of educational materials, and facilitate access to knowledge dynamically and effectively [10].

A traditional method for evaluating students' progress in knowledge acquisition is through assessments, particularly using questionnaires with various question formats, such as multiple-choice questions (MCQs), true/false questions (TFQs), and open-ended questions (OEQs). This method, which has continued to have a safe place in the educational system, offers a means of measuring students' understanding of educational topics covered in class. However, with technological advancements, it is possible to enhance the effectiveness of these assessments by incorporating dynamism and interactivity, making the process more engaging for the student [10].

Gamification is identified as an important method for enhancing student motivation. By integrating game elements such as scores, rewards, difficulty levels, and narratives, the learning experience becomes more immersive and engaging, thereby encouraging active participation [8]. This methodology not only boosts student engagement with the material but also supports long-term knowledge retention [4]. Additionally, the feedback provided by the system plays a pivotal role, as it can reinforce concepts, clarify errors, and guide students toward a deeper comprehension of the subject matter.

This paper explores the integration of Large Language Models (LLMs) with gamification and Multi-Agent Systems to develop a gamified learning environment called "Manchita". The system is designed to interactively and conversationally answer learner questions based on materials selected by educators or instructional designers. Additionally, it can generate and deliver interactive questionnaires using external knowledge provided by educators. We also present an initial evaluation of the system, conducted with 22 students and two professors from an undergraduate Arts program at the Universidad de Bellas Artes in Cali, Colombia.

Although recent work has demonstrated that Large Language Models (LLMs) can automate the creation of pedagogically sound questions [2,9] and that gamified leverages learner motivation and retention [5,8], very few studies have integrated these two lines into a unified conversational environment that offers automatic question generation, dynamic feedback, and motivational mechanisms such as narratives or scoring. At the same time, emerging LLM-based multi-agent systems implementations, such as SimClass [11], show the pedagogical potential in the cooperation between agents, but those fail to connect said agents with gamified assessment workflows. Manchita faces this gap by unifying (i) question-generation agent based on retrieval augmented generation and (ii) a gamified evaluation agent within a modular graph-orchestrated architecture - thus offering a reproducible blueprint for AI-powered motivational learning experiences.

2 Related Work

Gamification has been widely recognized as a method to increase student motivation, engagement, and knowledge retention [5,8]. Educational systems frequently incorporate game elements—such as points, levels, or narratives—to create immersive and enjoyable learning experiences. Recent literature reviews highlight the growing trend of personalizing gamified elements to different learner profiles, showing positive effects on learning outcomes [6].

In parallel, Large Language Models (LLMs) have shown promise in educational settings, particularly for tasks such as automatic question generation (AQG) [2,9], tutoring [10], and content summarization. These models enable dynamic, real-time interactions and the scalable production of pedagogical content. However, most applications remain tool-centric and do not consider broader motivational or interactive dimensions.

While a few recent works have started to combine LLMs with gamified experiences—such as CareerSim, which uses role-playing games for career development [3]—these systems are narrowly focused and lack generalized frameworks for assessment and feedback. Multi-agent frameworks like SimClass [11] demonstrate how agents can simulate educational environments, yet they do not incorporate motivational design strategies or gamified feedback loops.

In contrast, our work introduces "Manchita", a gamified educational environment that blends retrieval-augmented question generation and gamified evaluation in a modular, graph-based architecture. Unlike prior efforts, our approach unifies content generation, learner interaction, and motivation in a coherent system designed for real-time educational deployment.

3 System Overview

The system consists of two agents that follow graph-oriented agent architectures developed in LangGraph [1]. The first, the **Q&A Generation Agent**, is responsible for creating questions and their corresponding answer. The second, the **Evaluative Agent with Integrated Gamification**, is in charge of presenting the questions to the user in an interactive manner and evaluating their answers, incorporating the gamified aspects that will be explained later (Fig. 1 shows Manchita's interface).

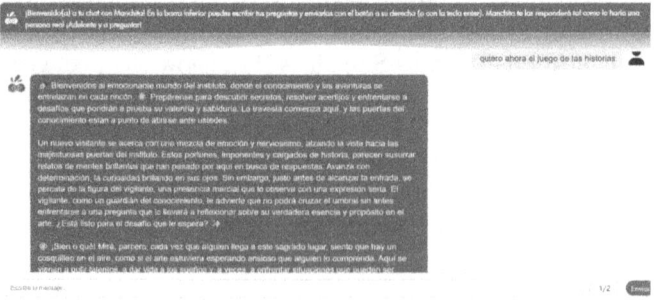

Fig. 1. Manchita's Story game introduction message.

3.1 Question and Answer (Q&A) Generation Agent

This agent is responsible for automatically generating questions and their corresponding answers, based solely on given external knowledge. The agent supports various question types, including multiple-choice (MCQ), true/false (TFQ), and open-ended (OEQ).

---

[1] https://www.langchain.com/langgraph.

The agent employs Retrieval-Augmented Generation (RAG) techniques to extract relevant external information based on a given prompt. Specifically, this approach generates initial question versions, ensuring that the LLM strictly relies on the retrieved content for its responses. The prompts are structured to include only the most relevant information, minimizing the risk of hallucinated knowledge. Additionally, the agent leverages key features of its graph-oriented architecture, including a self-evaluation node. This mechanism allows the system to assess the quality of generated questions based on human-defined criteria such as grammaticality, appropriateness, relevance, complexity, and novelty. If a question does not meet a predefined quality threshold, the agent initiates a self-evaluation loop to refine it.

We found this capability important in our experiments to avoid repetition issues. LLMs often generate duplicate questions within the same response. By incorporating self-evaluation, the system prevents previously generated questions from being mistakenly considered as new.

Below is a brief overview of each node in the agent graph (see Fig. 2):

- `context_generator`: Retrieve the necessary context for question generation by querying a vector database and retrieving up to k relevant results.
- `question_generator`: Generates ten questions based on the context given. The results depend on the type of difficulty desired.
- `question_seen_validator`: Calculates the cosine similarity between each of the previously generated ten questions and every *already-generated* question in earlier iterations, and finds the one question with the lowest similarity value.
- `question_evaluator`: Takes the previously validated question and lets an LLM agent evaluate its quality. This quality value is determined by five aspects used by Deroy et al. [2]: grammaticality, relevance, appropriateness, novelty, and complexity. The LLM returns a value between 0 and 1 for each metric following the same methodology proposed by Deroy et al. Then, we calculate the average rating and use this value to determine the quality of the question.
- `question_refiner`: Takes the previously evaluated question and lets a LLM refine it, so that it surpasses the established threshold. In the prompt, we include: the metrics obtained, the feedback given, and instructions to modify the question so that the metrics surpass the threshold.
- `messages_remover`: Removes messages from the `messages` list in the global state of the graph.
- `answer_generator`: Takes the evaluated and refined question, and does a RAG search using the question as the query. Then, it generates the corresponding answers to the type of the question.
- `qanda_saver`: Takes a JSON type structure that contains the question, the answer choices, the correct answer, the question type, and the question difficulty, and adds them to a JSON file, where all the questions and their answers are stored.

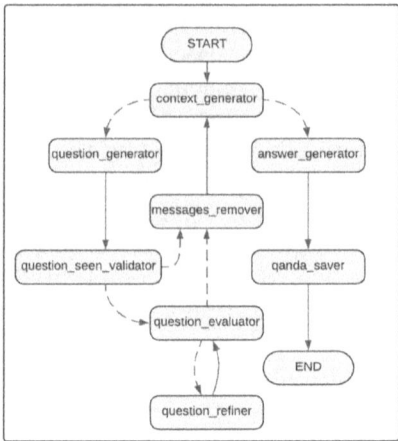

Fig. 2. Question & Answer Generation Agent graph arquitecture

3.2 Evaluative Agent with Integrated Gamification Elements

This agent is responsible for evaluating students' knowledge, while seamlessly incorporating some selected gamification techniques. It was designed to interact with students dynamically, presenting questions in an engaging manner and providing immediate, meaningful feedback on their responses.

The agent takes advantage of graph architecture capabilities. One of these is the ability to create loops. Given a node's response, a conditional edge can direct the graph's execution flow to one node or another. This is particularly used in the *Story Mode* in two instances: between attempts to answer a question correctly and during interactions with characters. Another graph capability employed is *human-in-the-loop*. This refers to an interruption in the graph's execution, allowing the user to input a message that will be taken into account throughout the rest of the execution. This is used to receive and evaluate user responses.

Gamification Elements. We identified three key gamification components: scoring systems, streak tracking, and narrative-driven interactions. These elements were chosen based on their ability to create a progressive learning experience, ensuring that students remain engaged while reinforcing their understanding of educational content. The implementation of these mechanics aligns with established gamification frameworks, particularly Octalysis [1], which categorizes game elements based on their motivational appeal. The scoring system activates extrinsic motivation by offering immediate rewards for correct answers and reinforcing learning through positive feedback. The streak tracker enhances long-term engagement by leveraging the psychological principle of consistency, encouraging students to sustain their efforts over time. Finally, narrative-driven interactions draw upon intrinsic motivation, incorporating elements of story-telling that transform learning into a compelling experience, making complex topics more approachable and memorable.

At this stage, three key gamification elements were selected. First, a scoring system to reward correct answers; second, a streak tracker to encourage consistent performance; and third, narrative-driven evaluations to immerse students in contextual stories. These elements were then integrated into three distinct games:

- Simple Questions Game: This game uses a point-based system. Users answer questions selected by the agent. Correct answers earn points and motivational feedback, while incorrect answers receive constructive guidance and the correct solution.
- Story Game: This game incorporates narratives to enhance engagement. Users solve riddles presented by characters in immersive storylines. Players start with three lives, losing one for each incorrect answer. Interactive elements allow users to chat with characters for hints.
- Tower Game: This game employs a streak mechanic. Each correct answer helps build a tower of blocks, while incorrect answers cause blocks to crash and potentially topple the tower. The goal is to maintain accuracy and build the tallest tower.

Based on the gamification elements the agent therefore has three main paths (see Fig. 3). First, in the Simple Questions mode, the agent selects a question, presents it to the student, and evaluates whether their response is correct. Second, in Story mode, users interact with three characters, each presenting a riddle. Correct answers allow them to progress in the narrative. Lastly, the Tower Game presents users with a series of questions that must be answered consecutively and correctly to maintain a streak and achieve the highest score. It is important to highlight that the agent constantly includes supportive, motivational, and congratulatory phrases in its messages, personalized to each student's performance. Additionally, the agent communicates using language and expressions familiar to students, creating a more relatable and engaging interaction [7]. A brief overview of each node and conditional edge in the agent can be found in the project's GitHub repository[2].

---

[2] https://github.com/Manchita-Assistant-Project/qag-se-system-backend/tree/main/app/agent.

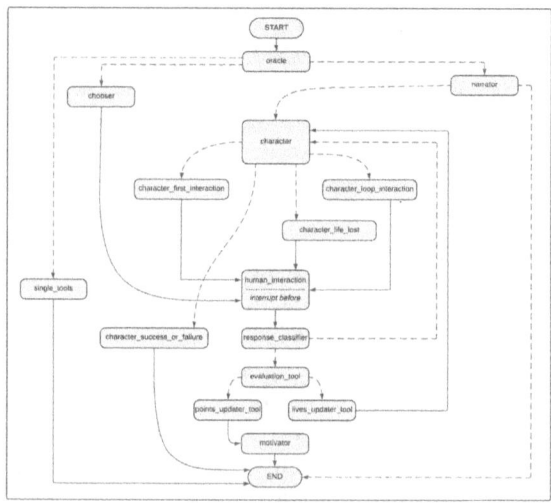

Fig. 3. Gamified Evaluation Agent graph architecture

4 Results

The system was tested on November 1st, 2024, with 22 first-year students and two professors. Students assessed usability and engagement, while professors evaluated the quality of the questions, answers and answer-evalutaion precision produced by the agents.

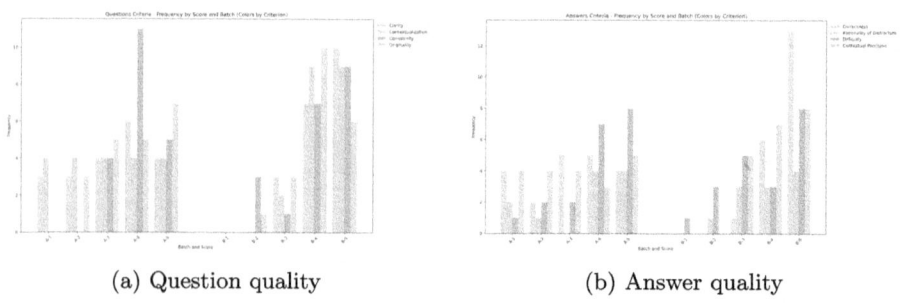

(a) Question quality (b) Answer quality

Fig. 4. Quality assessment of the generation pipeline. (a) Questions and (b) Answers.

4.1 Quality of Generated Questions

Thirty questions (ten MCQ, ten TFQ, ten OEQ) were randomly sampled from the Q&A Agent.

The first batch (**A**) utilized the proposed graph with a context containing over 6000 chunks. This context was provided by Universidad de Bellas Artes and unified files of various formats, each covering a wide range of topics across the entire degree program. The second batch (**B**) used the same graph but with a more specific and limited context, aligning with the criteria suggested by Deroy et al. [2]. This new context was also provided by Universidad de Bellas Artes, but with the difference that it was only a PDF document of between 10 and 15 pages, covering only the topic of the student regulations at Universidad de Bellas Artes.

The questions were evaluated by two professors based on four criteria: clarity, contextualization, complexity, and originality. These are some of the criteria used by Deroy et al. [2] in their feedback-based approach for evaluating human evaluation metrics. The scale is from 1 to 5, where 5 is the highest rating.

Limiting the context significantly enhances the quality of the generated questions (see Fig. 4a), particularly improving clarity and contextualization. Additionally, it leads to a notable increase in question originality, demonstrating that the proposed approach to context size and topic selection not only refines clarity and relevance but also ensures that questions are less generic and more tailored to the given context. Furthermore, the complexity of the questions in batch **B** achieved a better balance, suggesting that the experimental method effectively facilitated the generation of more challenging and well-structured questions.

4.2 Quality of Generated Answers

For each of the generated questions (ten of each type), corresponding answers were also produced (the batches **A** and **B** are the same as before, and the same rating scale is being used). It is noticeable that, similarly to the generated questions, using a more focused context significantly increases the quality of the generated answers (see Fig. 4b). The correctness and contextual precision have considerably improved. Remarkably, for the distractors in questions of type MCQ, there is an improved distribution of scores, achieving a balance where the distractors are similar to the correct answer but sufficiently distinct to create some level of confusion for the respondent. This finding suggests that the limited context not only improved the clarity and precision of correct answers but also led to more thoughtfully crafted distractors, enhancing the overall challenge and engagement level of the questions.

4.3 Evaluation of User Responses

The precision of user response evaluation refers to how accurate the agent's response was after the user entered their answer to a given question. This was assessed by using the evaluations made by two professors and experts in the field (see Fig. 5). The scale is from 1 to 5, where 5 is the highest rating.

In this evaluation, the bar-graph for batch **B** indicates that MCQ questions show a significant concentration of scores at level 5, highlighting a high level of correctness. This suggests that MCQs are consistently well-answered by the

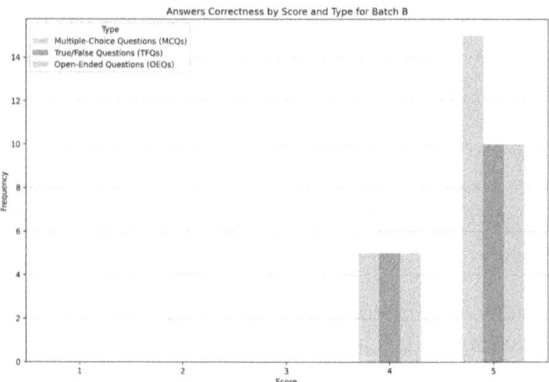

Fig. 5. Professor's assessment of the chatbot's input evaluation precision

internal agents of the generation graph. TFQ and OEQ questions also show a strong presence of scores at level 5, but their frequency at level 4 is similarly high. Overall, all question types have been evaluated positively, but MCQs demonstrate a slightly more stable correctness level, whereas TFQ and OEQ types exhibit high quality with a more even spread between the top two score levels.

4.4 System's Effect on Students

In this section, we present the results from student evaluations. The scores range from 3 to 5, with the majority clustering in the higher range (4 and 5), indicating an overall positive perception of the system's impact (see Fig. 6).

The highest-rated categories—**Usage Orientation**, **Satisfaction Level**, and **Learning Experience**—received a significant number of level 5 scores, suggesting that students find the system intuitive, easy to use, satisfying, and beneficial to their learning. Similarly, **Fun** and **Gamified Elements** were highly rated, predominantly at levels 4 and 5, reinforcing the system's engaging nature.

Contribution to the Program's Quality Processes and **Understanding of Universidad de Bellas Artes Regulations** exhibited more variation, with scores primarily between levels 3 and 4. While these aspects were generally well-received, the variability suggests opportunities for refinement and includes other learning strategies such as repetition and recapitulation.

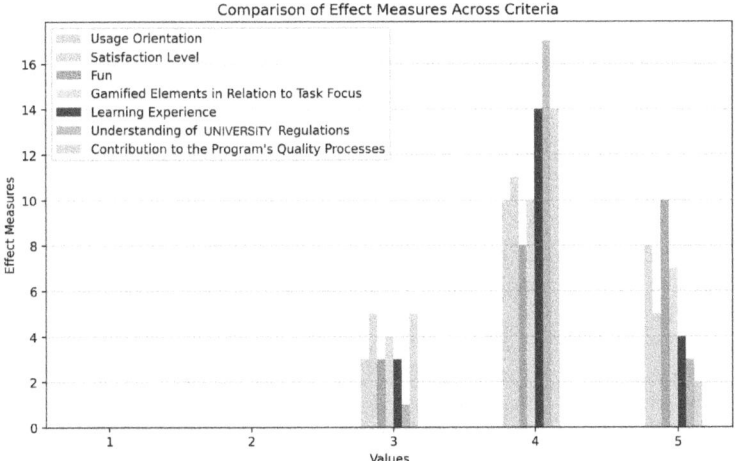

Fig. 6. Student's assessment of the system's effect

Limitations. One of the limitations of our results is the relatively small sample size. Moreover, the assessment was carried out in a controlled session where students were specifically instructed to evaluate the tool. Future work will incorporate larger samples, pre/post knowledge tests, asynchronous use, and a modular ablation study to isolate the contribution of each agent.

Reproducibility. To facilitate transparency and further development, all source code and prompt templates are openly available at: https://github.com/Manchita-Assistant-Project/qag-se-system-backend (backend) and https://github.com/Manchita-Assistant-Project/qag-se-system-frontend (frontend).

5 Conclusion

"Manchita" uses Large Language Models (LLMs), Retrieval-Augmented Generation (RAG) techniques, and gamification to enhance the educational experience. Testing with students and educators showed notable improvements in engagement, motivation, and knowledge retention, underscoring the relevance and quality of the generated content.

Findings also highlight the potential of generative technologies to provide personalized and scalable educational solutions. Gamification fostered a motivating and competitive learning environment, encouraging active participation and performance improvement. Students found interactions intuitive, reinforcing knowledge retention through a seamless, engaging approach.

Future research should explore structured gamification frameworks, such as Octalysis [1], to systematically assess the impact of different strategies on motivation and learning outcomes. A data-driven methodology would refine AI-driven education, ensuring adaptability and effectiveness across diverse learning contexts.

References

1. Chou, Y.K.: Actionable gamification, vol. 501. Packt Publishing (2019)
2. Deroy, A., Maity, S., Sarkar, S.: MIRROR: a novel approach for the automated evaluation of open-ended question generation. In: Proceedings of the NeurIPS 2024 Workshop on Foundation Models for Education (2024). https://arxiv.org/abs/2410.12893
3. Du, W., Zhu, Z., Xu, X., Che, H., Chen, S.: CareerSim: gamification design leveraging LLMs for career development reflection. In: CHI Extended Abstracts on Human Factors in Computing Systems, pp. 1–7 (2024). https://doi.org/10.1145/3611475.3622266
4. Jarnac de Freitas, M., Mira da Silva, M.: Systematic literature review about gamification in MOOCs, vol. 38, pp. 73–95 (2023)
5. Jarnac de Freitas, M., Mira da Silva, M.: Systematic literature review about gamification in MOOCs. Open Learn. J. Open, Distance E-Learning **38**(1), 73–95 (2023). https://doi.org/10.1080/02680513.2020.1798221
6. Hallifax, S., Serna, A., Marty, J., Lavoué,: Adaptive gamification in education: a literature review of current trends and developments. In: European Conference on Technology Enhanced Learning (EC-TEL), pp. 294–308 (2019). https://doi.org/10.1007/978-3-030-29736-7_22
7. Kuhail, M.A., Alturki, N., Alramlawi, S., Alhejori, K.: Interacting with educational chatbots: a systematic review. Educ. Inf. Technol. **28**, 973–1018 (2023)
8. Pastushenko, O., Hruška, T., Zendulka, J.: Increasing students' motivation by using virtual learning environments based on gamification mechanics: implementation and evaluation of gamified assignments for students. In: Proceedings of the Sixth International Conference on Technological Ecosystems for Enhancing Multiculturality, pp. 755–760 (2018)
9. Scaria, N., Chenna, S.D., Subramani, D.: Automated educational question generation at different bloom's skill levels using large language models: Strategies and evaluation (2024). https://arxiv.org/abs/2408.04394
10. Xu, H., Gan, W., Qi, Z., Wu, J., Yu, P.: Large language models for education: a survey (2024)
11. Zhang, Z., et al.: SimClass: simulating classroom education with LLM-empowered agents. In: Proceedings of the ACM Conference on Learning at Scale (L@S 2024) (2024). https://arxiv.org/abs/2406.19226

An Educational Virtual World System with Gamification Features and LLM Guided NPCs

Ariadni Barmpari, Eleni Voyiatzaki, and Ioannis Hatzilygeroudis(✉)

Department of Computer Engineering and Informatics, University of Patras, 26500 Patras, Greece
{evoyiatzaki,ihatz}@ceid.upatras.gr

Abstract. Existing Virtual World (VW) based curriculum oriented educational systems use conventional non-player characters (NPCs) to interact with users (players), represented as avatars, to guide and help them to accomplish learning activities. Also, few of them use some kind of gamification and keep data for user interactions and activities. In this paper, we present the design and implementation of an educational system based on VW technology, which employs gamification features, two types of NPCs, a conventional and an LLM based, and a Database that stores, apart from educational information, information about interactions of users with the NPCs. Evaluation of the system shows that both types of NPCs are useful for different reasons. LLM based ones offer more interesting dialogues, and conventional ones more targeted help.

Keywords: Virtual Worlds · Educational System · LLMs · NPCs · Gamification

1 Introduction

Virtual Reality (VR) is a simulated experience created through interaction with a computer-generated 3D environment that simulates reality, creating a virtual world. Non-immersive virtual reality is a virtual experience through a keyboard or a mouse of a desktop or a laptop. You can control characters or activities within the virtual world, but you do not really "feel" part of it. Immersive VR offers the highest level of realistic experience, completely immersing the user in a simulated 3D world, but requires the use of special devices, like helmets, gloves, and body connectors with sensors [1].

There has been extensive research into using VR in education and training [2]. In this paper, we focus on non-immersive VR based educational applications. More specifically, we refer to virtual worlds (VWs) used for educational purposes [3]. In VW, humanoid graphical characters, called *avatars*, represent users and allow interaction with objects in VW (e.g. displays, panels, machines etc.), or other artificial entities, like non-Player Characters (NPCs), and other avatars, to establish collaboration [4].

NPCs in VWs play a crucial role in enhancing interaction and engagement [5]. They can function as guides, leading students through activities, providing information, and helping them to pass to the next stages of a process. In most (if not all) of existing VW systems, NPCs are pre-programmed with pre-designed responses to pre-designed questions. This may create disappointment for users. Alongside NPCs, *notecards* are usually used, which are text blocks activated under specific conditions. They can contain links to web pages or to other notecards.

To make educational software more attractive to student-users, game-based features are added to a VW system. This methodology is called *gamification*. Gamification takes educationally interesting features from video games such as awards, badges, etc., and embeds them into purely educational systems, thus enhancing students' motivation and engagement [6]. In addition to gamification, serious games have also been developed for educational purposes but in a different way; they are more game-oriented [7].

On the other hand, for the tutor, it is essential to understand how students interact with the objects and personalities in the world and how the learning process unfolds. Monitoring students' behavior during educational activities, like movements, decisions, and interactions with NPCs, can provide valuable insights. This allows tutors to adjust their approach, identify the challenges students face, and provide targeted support, to create a more effective learning environment and experience. However, this is not possible in most existing systems, because avatars' behaviors are not properly recorded.

The objective of this work is to design and implement a VW based educational system that uses gamification and fulfills the above shortcomings. First, a new type of NPCs is introduced, called LLM-NPCs, which exploits the capabilities of ChatGPT to provide flexibility and some type of intelligence to NPCs. Second, the system is supported by a local database, where avatar (user) activities are recorded, so that the tutor can look at and analyze them to derive useful conclusions.

The structure of the paper is as follows. Section 2 presents related work, while Sect. 3 presents system design and architecture. Section 4 deals with the two types of NPCs employed in the application, whereas Sect. 5 presents the evaluation of the system. Finally, Sect. 6 concludes the paper.

2 Related Work

2.1 Educational Virtual Worlds and NPCs

In this paper, we focus on 3D Virtual Worlds that are used for educational purposes related to some kind of curriculum. Early, but even recent, such systems have not been as interactive as required, remaining at representations or simulations of real-world phenomena, processes of devices and their functionalities. In those cases, students were getting into the worlds as avatars to explore various items [8–10]. Later, interactive objects came into the scene, and also use of notecards and NPCs. As the time was progressing, the degree of interaction between the user-avatar and the NPCs was increased and improved. On the other hand, gamification features were gradually added. We focus here on the use of NPCs in such systems. Most of them have been implemented in OpenSim and the rest in Unity [11].

In [12], the authors present an innovative 3D virtual reality educational environment that aims to assist students in learning and teachers in explaining various processes of a physics course. In the 3D virtual reality environment laboratories facilitate students to carry out virtual experiments, explore procedures and get a deeper cognition and understanding of how procedures are conducted and physics processes work. In addition, pedagogical virtual agents, like the one looking like Albert Einstein, are designed to guide students in the virtual environment and assist them during the training activities, implemented as NPCs. No gamification is used.

In [13], a 3D virtual world, called VR4STEM is presented. It is proposed to assist young people to gain entrepreneurship skills. The virtual environment of VR4STEM is composed of several 3D islands. Each of them presents a specific subject in STEM (Science, Technology, Engineering and Mathematics) and ICT (Information and Communications Technology) domains, like e.g. "World of Lasers", "World of Unmanned Aerial Vehicles". Notecards and NPCs are used to inform users.

In [14], a 3D VW is used as the testbed for testing the "sense of presence", considered as attention and involvement of the student. The subject of the 3D VW is "Financial Management". The educational scene consists of a building simulating an accounting company, appropriately structured. Students are represented as avatars but there are also several NPCs distributed in the company's offices that guide and help them. The NPCs can "express themselves bodily and textually". The world embeds some features of gamification.

In [15], a 3D VW implemented in OpenSim is reported. Three different pedagogical agents, represented as NPCs, are used for making learning more attractive and improving engagement. Jella Delta has a humanoid form, resembling the role of the instructor or educator, and is a conversational agent (chatbot) with domain-specific question answering capabilities. Queen Kong is also a chatbot, though of a nonhuman type (ape). Its role is to disorientate students by providing incorrect or 'nonsense' answers to their queries in a 'ludicrous' way. Gizmo Gear has a robotlike form, operating as a vendor. The role of this agent is to provide, upon call, informational notecards, assign or suggest tasks and offer freebies (premade 3-D objects and scripts).

[16] presents the development of a 3D VW to be used as an educational tool for teaching a broad spectrum of energy education concepts, focusing on energy saving, through a wind farm management environment. Users are transported into an engaging virtual setting, where they encounter real-life energy threat scenarios. These scenarios are ingeniously presented as interactive games, allowing users to navigate through, engage with, and learn about various aspects, risks and threats associated with energy use. The game includes interactive elements such as discussions with Non-Player Characters (NPCs) experts, a quiz on wind energy, and tasks that require critical thinking and decision-making based on environmental impact and technical considerations.

[17] presents the development of a game-based VW, called "The Wonder land of IT", aiming at promoting a BSc degree curriculum, namely "Bachelor of Science in Information Technology". The scene of the game includes a real university environment, featuring authentic buildings, constructions, and computer labs. NPCs played a crucial role in the game by communicating with players, providing stage-related information, notifying them of missions to be completed, and posing questions to progress through the stages. Examples of missions include searching for objects and secret codes, answering questions based on presented information, interacting with non-player characters (NPCs), and collecting coins to get a larger score.

[18] refers to a 3D VW (called ENTREALITY) that concerns learning social entrepreneurship concepts in an expressive, entertaining, comprehensive and gamified way, implemented in OpenSim. An important proposed feature is the incorporation of mechanisms for monitoring user activity in the 3D world, analyzing and generating useful feedback in a personalized way through NPCs. To this end, learning analytics, like time spent, participation in the activities, score achieved, interactions with NPCs etc. will be recorded. Based on them, NPCs will provide personalized feedback.

2.2 NPCs and LLMS

To the best of our knowledge, there are no VW based educational systems of the above type that use NPCs driven by some LLM. One system that could be considered close to the above is [19], where a VW designed for brainstorming is presented. The main educational objects are two PCAs (Pedagogical Conversational Agents), called Rosie and Gigi. Rosie welcomes the user into the virtual world, provides an introduction to the environment, and explains the brainstorming setting. Gigi can act as a brainstorming supporter and moderator in the virtual world. It has been implemented with the "GPT Turbo Model", an AI-based language model. It helps learners develop ideas on their own, step by step. Gigi designed with the prompt for assessing learners' ideas and pointing out potential opportunities and challenges.

Of course, there are recent serious games and video games that use agents which are LLM driven. For example, in [20], an LLM is used to interact with players in a text-adventure game, empowering players to participate in the evolution of game narratives. Players can freely interact with non-player characters generated by GPT-4. In [21], the authors explore the problem of ways to communicate with LLM-based NPCs within a VR video game setting. Users can freely interact with ChatGPT-4 LLM-based NPCs, to solve a murder mystery. Furthermore, [22] presents a sophisticated architecture of integrating GPT in embodied agents for use in video games. The GPT-NPC agent can be split into 4 core modules: Perception, Situation, Conversation and Speech Synthesis, and 4 complementary modules: Memory, Thoughts, Emotions and Needs. Player agents communicate with speech, converted into text. The Situation module is GPT-powered. Its role is to aggregate perceived world events into a summary to provide a comprehensive overview of what is happening. GPT is also involved in the thought module, through its API, which takes in the internal agent state and generates new thoughts.

3 System Design and Implementation

3.1 System Objectives

Our main objective has been to improve the interaction between students-users and the NPCs in 3D VW systems like those presented in Sect. 2.1. We have used as basis the VW produced in the context of an Erasmus+ European project, called ENTREALITY (https://projectentreality.etcenter.eu/index.php/en/), which we participated in. That system was implemented in OpenSim and offered gamified scenarios for learning entrepreneurship concepts, where however no NPCs were used.

A first step in improving that system was [18], where NPCs were employed and designed to offer adaptive feedback to users. This required to register and store learning analytics measures and use them for providing personalized feedback. In this work, we go a step further by adding intelligence to NPCs via LLMs. Also, to improve graphics and simulation capabilities, we use Unity instead of OpenSim to implement it. Finally, we introduce a database for storing useful data and a tutor interface for handling things.

3.2 System Architecture and Implementation

The system consists of four modules: Unity environment, Backend, Frontend, and OpenAI-ChatGPT. The core Game (i.e. the VW) is built using Unity. It includes a set of entities that interact in the game environment to produce the desired outcome. Such entities are the Players and the NPCs (SCRIPT-NPCs and LLM-NPCs).

The Backend is the backbone of the entire system and consists mainly of the Database. The Database captures and stores extensive data on player activities during gameplay, like their movements and navigation, quiz performances, interaction with educational materials, as well as communication with NPCs.

The Backend is also responsible for communicating with the external service OpenAI ChatGPT to provide the answers for any of the Player's questions, through the LLM-NPCs. The Backend stores the history of all messages the player has sent and acts as proxy to the OpenAI ChatGPT LLM, that in turn answers the player's message.

To optimize and simplify the management of quizzes in the database, Frontend, a dedicated platform, has been developed, which is accessible exclusively from database administrators. Through this platform, administrators can view all quizzes stored in the database, each accompanied by its unique identifier (ID) used to link it with the game. Additionally, the platform enables administrators to easily delete or edit existing quizzes, as well as create new ones, streamlining content management and updates. Also, administrators have access to various statistical insights derived from the database logs, further enhancing their ability to oversee and analyze quiz-related activities.

3.3 Game-Based Learning Process

The educational content of VW is based on the content developed for the Entreality project (mentioned above), which was developed in the Opensim platform. In this study, a new world was developed in Unity with different characteristics, but on the same educational subject, which concerns basic issues of entrepreneurship. Unity allowed the use of more advanced implementation capabilities.

The virtual learning experience begins with user authentication, involving options to sign up or log in. The system accommodates both single-player and multiplayer modes. The scene of the game consists, at the moment, of five consecutive virtual rooms within a virtual building. Each room comprises either study material in the form of presentations on panels (study room) or one or more quizzes (quiz room). A student-player should go through all five rooms to be able to finish the game. There are two study rooms (first and third) and three quiz rooms (the rest). To go from a quiz room to the next study room, the player should pass the quiz(zes) in the room. In case of failure, a second try is allowed. The fifth room includes the final quiz. Each time the user gives the right answer to a question, gets a score. To pass a quiz, more than 50% of the total quiz score should be achieved. At the end, each player gets a total score of all quizzes, which represents his/her overall performance.

As soon as a player enters a room, a notecard pops-up at the lower right corner of the screen displaying information about the educational process to be followed in the room. Additionally, at the upper right corner, a box displaying the current player score and the highest score achieved so far from a player appears. During an intermediate quiz execution evolution, there are two NPCs the player can ask for help. The one at the right of the panel is a SCRIPT-NPC, while the one at the left is an LLM-NPC.

4 Types and Use of NPCs

NPCs act as helpers or guides within the game. They can provide advice, additional information, and facilitate the understanding of quiz questions, making the experience more interesting and interactive. To better guide and support players, NPCs with two different levels of support have been added: SCRIPT-NPC and LLM-NPC. An NPC is activated when a player approaches it, which triggers an action from the system.

4.1 Script-NPC

Approaching a SCRIPT-NPC triggers an interface displaying a set of predefined questions (see Fig. 1, left image), designed to align with the educational objectives of the game. The player can select a specific question of interest, and the NPC responds with detailed information or guidance tailored to the selected query.

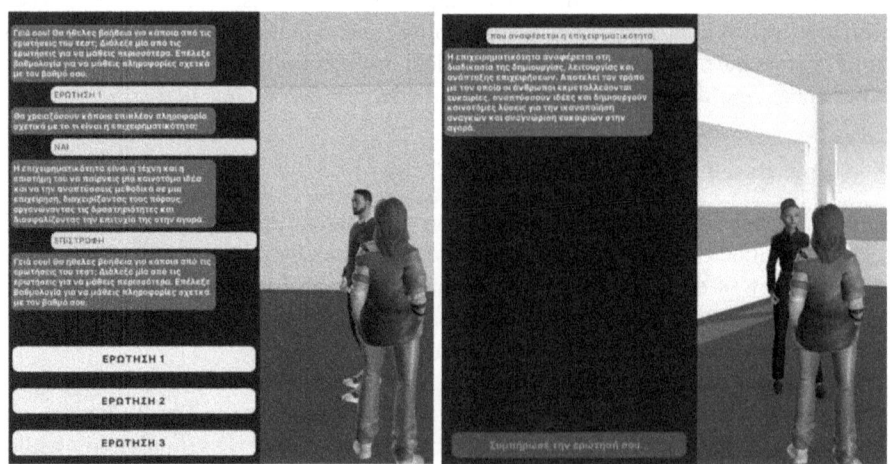

Fig. 1. Conversation panel of a player with SCRIPT-NPC (left) and LLM-NPC (right). The displayed language is Greek.

Incorporating an NPC with pre-defined questions and answers is a technique that offers significant benefits in educational games. It is particularly popular due to its ability to ensure consistency and provide clear guidance to players. The effectiveness of this type of NPC has been repeatedly proven. The main advantages are, a) using fixed questions and answers simplifies interaction, b) by providing help and hints keep players constantly active, and c) pre-defined questions and answers can ensure that specific educational concepts are systematically covered.

The SCRIPT-NPC plays a critical role in guiding players through quizzes and providing assistance for educational activities. By limiting its responses to predefined content, the NPC ensures consistency and clarity in delivering instructions. The interaction prioritizes usability, allowing players to easily navigate through questions and receive focused support.

Overall, an NPC with pre-defined questions and answers provides a simplified, yet effective solution to player interaction. Using this NPC ensures that players always have the necessary support available for the game's questions. This approach guarantees that every player can proceed with confidence and overcome any questions related to the quizzes. Functionality of a SCRIPT-NPC is defined via a Unity script.

4.2 LLM-NPC

The interaction with LLM-NPC is more dynamic and conversational. When the player approaches the NPC, a dialogue panel is activated, allowing free form communication (see Fig. 1, right image). The LLM-NPC, powered by the advanced language model ChatGPT, can understand and respond to a wide range of queries posed by the player. This feature enhances the immersive experience, as players can engage in natural language conversations, seek clarifications, and explore the subject matter in greater depth.

Unlike the SCRIPT-NPC, the LLM-NPC adapts its responses based on the context of the conversation and the player's individual needs. This flexibility allows it to address diverse learning styles and questions that may not be covered by structured NPCs. However, to maintain alignment with the educational objectives, the LLM-NPC has been trained to provide info relevant to the learning material and activities of the game.

For the LLM-NPC responses the following prompt was given to ChatGPT: "You behave like a human being. You are a tutor specializing in business. Avoid answering questions unrelated to business content. If you are asked about your performance, if it is up to 50% you will recommend repeating the theory and a test, if it is from 51–70% you will recommend only theory and if it is above 71% you will congratulate".

The integration of an AI-powered NPC offers significant advantages like, a) enhances realism, personalization and engagement, b) provides help and hints and keeps players constantly active, and c) acts as a knowledge source, offering clarifications and further explanations to questions related to both the quizzes and educational material.

5 Evaluation

Evaluation process took place in the presence of the researcher, so each participating user was in the same room (face-to-face). The game was successfully conducted thanks to the participation of 34 individuals, which allowed the collection of adequate number of answers and data to draw conclusions. At the start of the game, participants received both in-game instructions and verbal guidance. The verbal guidance focuses on the player's movement and the need to interact with both types of NPCs.

After the end of each user session, a questionnaire was completed by the participants. It was designed to obtain data on age of the participants, gender, levels of knowledge in virtual worlds and entrepreneurship and their evaluation of the different NPCs. From the 34 participants, 16 were men and 18 women. Half of the participants had prior experience with activities in virtual worlds. Also, 25 participants had limited knowledge of entrepreneurship, and only 9 reported having substantial knowledge in the field.

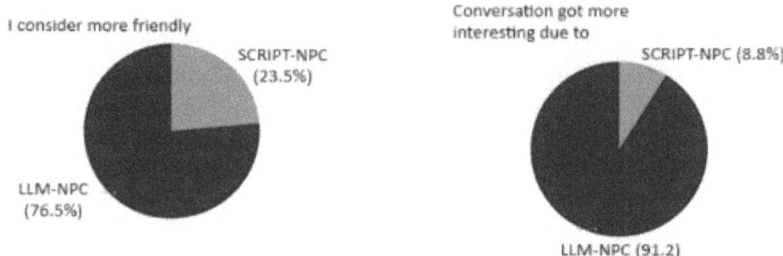

Fig. 2. Results on friendliness (left) and interestingness (right) of NPCs

The data reveal that most participants (94%) found the support provided by the environment and the NPCs to be either very or extremely helpful, with only two participants considering the support partially helpful. This indicates that the NPCs and the game environment were highly effective and positively received by most players.

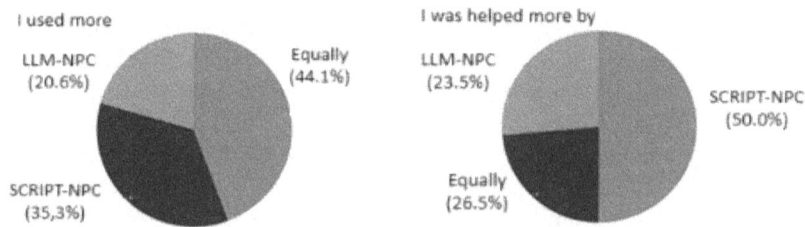

Fig. 3. Results on usage (left) and help (right) of NPCs

Furthermore, 97% of participants (33 participants) used both types of NPCs during their gameplay. Notable preference was observed for the NPC-LLM in terms of interestingness of conversation, with 91.2% (31 participants) (see Fig. 2-right pie), and friendliness, with 76.5% (26 participants) (see Fig. 2-left pie), appreciating its ability to enhance conversational engagement and interaction with the virtual world.

However, opinions were more divided when it came to assistance provision (see Fig. 3-right pie), with 50% (17 participants) declaring the SCRIPT-NPC more helpful, likely due to its targeted responses for quiz-related questions. Furthermore, 26.5% (9 participants) reported that both NPC types were equally helpful in supporting their learning experience. In terms of usage (see Fig. 3-left pie), 44.1% (15 participants) declared

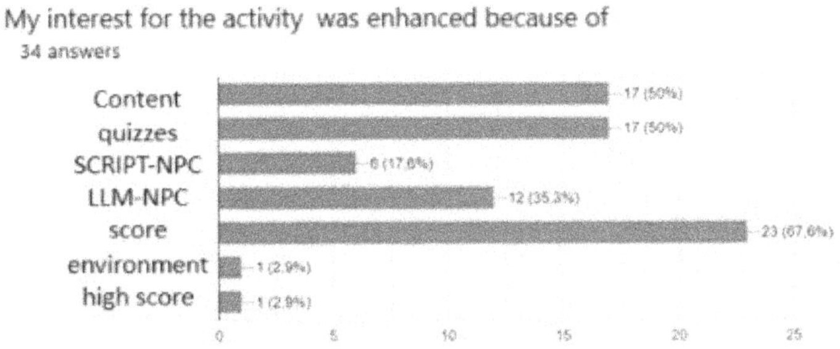

My interest for the activity was enhanced because of
34 answers

- Content — 17 (50%)
- quizzes — 17 (50%)
- SCRIPT-NPC — 6 (17.6%)
- LLM-NPC — 12 (35.3%)
- score — 23 (67.6%)
- environment — 1 (2.9%)
- high score — 1 (2.9%)

Fig. 4. Results on the reasons for enhancing interest

that equally used both NPCs, whereas 35.3% (12 participants) used only SCRIPT-NPCs and 20.6% (7 participants) only LLM-NPCs. Finally, regarding enhancement of interest during activity (see Fig. 4), it seems that score (a gamification feature) is the first reason, followed equally by content and quizzes.

On the other hand, data recorded in the database provides teachers with valuable information about players' interactions with NPCs. Specifically, it shows the total number of messages players sent to LLM-NPCs and the number of players who selected options from SCRIPT-NPCs. In addition, it tracks how many times specific questions were selected by SCRIPT-NPCs, allowing educators to identify which questions may have created challenges for the players. The average score of each quiz is also available, revealing that the two quizzes with the highest average scores were supported by both types of NPCs, not just LLM-NPCs as in the other two quizzes. This suggests that SCRIPT-NPCs significantly helped players to answer the quiz questions correctly, as confirmed by the questionnaire results, probably because the material focused specifically on quiz-related questions.

6 Conclusions

In this paper, we present the design and implementation of a curriculum related educational system based on 3D Virtual World technology. It uses some kind of gamification and, compared to existing similar systems, it uses, apart from traditional NPCs (called SCRIPT-NPCs), a kind of intelligent NPCs, called LLM-NPCs, which employ ChatGPT (free version) LLM to manifest more natural dialogues with avatars (players). Also, the system is provided with a database, which stores educational content and user transactions with the system entities and the NPCs, and a user interface for the teachers/tutors to manage the quizzes and gain insights from gathered statistics.

Evaluation of the system reveals that LLM-NPCs by providing personalized assistance to players, fosters a more engaging and friendly atmosphere that increases their involvement in the educational environment. On the other hand, SCRIPT-NPCs are more effective in addressing specific questions, such as those related to quizzes, offering targeted support. However, much more time is required for their development compared to that required for LLM-NPCs.

Additionally, progress tracking through the recording and analysis of students' movements and performance provides valuable data to educators, facilitating assessment and the adaptation of the learning process to meet students' needs.

Our future work will focus on a more detailed evaluation of the system, so that it will guide us to specify more appropriate prompts for the ChatGPT, which may lead to the introduction of other types of LLM-based NPCs (e.g. based on thematic training). Also, alternative LLMs, like Gemini, could be employed. Finally, an extra machine learning module exploiting data in the Database for user behavior recognition is another option.

References

1. Alqahtani, A.S., Daghestani, L.F., Ibrahim, L.F.: Environments and system types of virtual reality technology in STEM: a survey. Int. J. Adv. Comput. Sci. Appl. **8**(6), 77–89 (2017)
2. Makransky, G., Borre-Gude, S., Mayer, R.E.: Motivational and cognitive benefits of training in immersive virtual reality based on multiple assessments. J. Comput. Assist. Learn. **35**, 691–707 (2019)
3. Wikipedia. https://en.wikipedia.org/wiki/Virtual_world. Accessed 12 Feb 2025
4. Nowak, K.L., Fox, J.: Avatars and computer-mediated communication: a review of the definitions, uses, and effects of digital representations. Rev. Commun. Res. **6**(2), 201–232 (2018)
5. Grivokostopoulou, F., Kovas, K., Perikos, I.: The effectiveness of embodied pedagogical agents and their impact on students learning in virtual worlds. Appl. Sci. **10**, 1739 (2020). https://doi.org/10.3390/app10051739
6. Christopoulos, A., Mystakidis, S.: Gamification in education. Encyclopedia **3**, 1223–1243 (2023). https://doi.org/10.3390/encyclopedia3040089
7. Karagiorgas, D.N., Niemann, S.: Gamification and game-based learning. J. Educ. Technol. Syst. **45**(4), 499–519 (2017)
8. Grivokostopoulou, F., Perikos, I., Hatzilygeroudis, I.: An innovative educational environment based on virtual reality and gamification for learning search algorithms. In: Proceedings of 2016 IEEE Eighth International Conference on Technology for Education (T4E), Mumbai, India, pp. 110–115 (2016). https://doi.org/10.1109/T4E.2016.029
9. Kim, H., Ke, F.: Effects of game-based learning in an OpenSim-supported virtual environment on mathematical performance. Interact. Learn. Environ. **25**(4), 543–557 (2017). https://doi.org/10.1080/10494820.2016.1167744
10. Bai, J., Xia, C., Zhou, Z., Zhu, Y.: Design and implementation of a biological virtual display system based on 3DMax and Unity3D. In: Proceedings of the 2nd International Conference on Mechatronics, IoT and Industrial Informatics (ICMIII), pp. 641–646 (2024)
11. Maratou, V., Xenos, M., Vuckovic, D., GraniC, A., Drecun, A.: Enhancing learning on information security using 3D virtual world learning environment. In: Proceedings of 5th International Conference on Information Society and Technology, pp. 279–284 (2015)
12. Grivokostopoulou, F., Perikos, I., Kovas, K., Paraskevas, M., Hatzilygeroudis, I.: Utilizing virtual reality to assist students in learning physics. In: Proceedings of the 2017 IEEE International Conference on Teaching, Assessment, and Learning for Engineering (IEEE TALE 2017), pp. 486–489 (2017)
13. de Mattos, D.P., Popovici, D.: VR4STEM - a 3D virtual world for assisting young people to gain entrepreneurship skill in the STEM and ICT domains. In: Proceedings of the INTED 2018, pp. 9322–9330 (2018)

14. Krassmann, A.L., Nunes, F.B., Bessa, M., Tarouco, L.M.R., Bercht, M.: Virtual companions and 3D virtual worlds: investigating the sense of presence in distance education. In: Zaphiris, P., Ioannou, A. (eds.) HCII 2019. LNCS, vol. 11591, pp. 175–192 (2019). https://doi.org/10.1007/978-3-030-21817-1_14
15. Christopoulos, A., Conrad, M., Shukla, M.: Learner experience in hybrid virtual worlds: interacting with pedagogical agents. In: Proceedings of the 11th International Conference on Computer Supported Education (CSEDU 2019), pp. 488–495 (2019). https://doi.org/10.5220/0007758604880495
16. Guerra-Mota, M., Minas, D., Xenos, M., Sá, M.M.: Development of a 3D virtual world tool for sustainable energy education. In: Proceedings of the 1st International Conference on Sustainable Energy Education (SEED 2024), Valencia, Spain, 3–5 July, pp. 646–654 (2024)
17. Puttinaovarat, S., Pruitikanee, S., Kongcharoen, J., Saeliw, A., Inthong, P., Thippayamongkol, N.: The digital game for curriculum public relations (PR) and learning using Unity3D. Int. J. Interact. Mobile Technol. (iJIM) 17(14), 81–100 (2023)
18. Athanasiou, P., Voyiatzaki, E., Hatzilygeroudis, I.: Evolving non-player characters in educational games in virtual worlds. In: Proceedings of EDULEARN 2023, pp. 7053–7059 (2023)
19. Khosrawi-Rad, B., Shahda, F., Robra-Bissantz, S.: Towards pedagogical conversational agents as creativity drivers in virtual worlds. In: Proceedings of Mindtrek 2023, Tampere, Finland, 03–06 October 2023 (2023). https://doi.org/10.1145/3616961.3617807. ACM ISBN 979-8-4007-0874-9/23/10
20. Peng, X., et al.: Player-driven emergence in LLM-driven game narrative. In: Proceedings of the 2024 Conference on Games (CoG 2024) (2024). https://doi.org/10.1109/CoG60054.2024.10645607
21. Christiansen, F.R., Hollensberg, L.N., Jensen, N.B., Julsgaard, K., Jespersen, K.N., Nikolov, I.: Exploring presence in interactions with LLM-driven NPCs: a comparative study of speech recognition and dialogue options. In: Proceedings of VRST 2024, Trier, Germany, 09–11 October (2024). https://doi.org/10.1145/3641825.3687716
22. Ogunlesia, D., Wang, X.: GPT-NPC: enhancing NPC human-likeness and autonomy in video games. In: Proceedings of the ECAI 2024 Workshop on "eXtended Reality & Intelligent Agents" (XRIA 2024) (2024)

Using Minigames to Teach Computer Architecture

Reva Freedman[(✉)], Ian Sullivan, Annalise Brockmann, and Minhaz Patel

Northern Illinois University, DeKalb, IL 60115, USA
rfreedman@niu.edu

Abstract. In this paper we describe a minigame-based system that helps students master the basics of computer architecture for a required course in a large public university. The course contains a sequence of topics that work together to show students how a computer works. Due to resource limitations, the course is taught in a large lecture format without a lab. The purpose of the games is threefold: to help students master the material, to provide excitement and motivation to increase time-on-task, and to provide some of the hands-on experience that a lab would provide. The prototype covers topics from different sections of the course as proof of concept, including gates and circuits, the binary number system with two's complement format, and a simulation of a simple CPU. The purpose of the paper is to show how game mechanics can be employed to achieve these goals.

Keywords: intelligent tutoring system · teaching computer architecture · minigames

1 Introduction

This paper describes a minigame-based system to help students master the basics of computer architecture for a required course in a large public university. Topics covered include basic gates and circuits; the binary number system, including two's complement format; and a simulation of a simple CPU. These topics were chosen as prototypes for the different types of material covered in the course; our long-term plan is to build a game for every topic. There are three reasons for the minigame format: first, students like using cellphones, and we wish to take advantage of that fact; second, it is much simpler to write individual games than to write a complex system that covers all the topics; and third, to increase student interest and motivation, we want to take advantage of developer creativity to build novel games with different interfaces and game mechanics.

For efficient implementation, we have taken advantage of reusable design and gamification elements in earlier systems we have implemented [2,3]. Our goal is to improve student enjoyment, attention and performance in the course at a reasonable cost.

As in our previous work, the games are implemented with the Unity game engine [16], with user code written in C#. Unity contains many useful features, such as possible deployment on multiple platforms, a built-in event loop, handling of networking and concurrency issues, and useful underlying libraries for graphics and animation. However, we are not using the Unity screen design interface; instead, we are coding each interface that we need. Although the screen design interface allows developers to produce a rapid prototype, these prototypes are inflexible and do not allow game authors to implement all of the interactive elements that the games would benefit from.

In this paper we illustrate three games that we have implemented, their goals, and the game mechanics used to realize those goals. Section 2 describes the course for which the games are intended and examines related work. Then Sect. 3 describes Signal Seeker, a game to teach basic understanding of electronic gates. Section 4 describes Spin-to-Win, a game to teach basic binary and hexadecimal arithmetic. Section 5 describes CPU Simulator, where students can test their understanding of the central loop of instruction processing. Finally, Sect. 6 contains a brief summary and description of future work.

2 Context and Related Work

The course is a one-semester course on computer architecture intended for computer science majors. It covers Chaps. 2–4 of a standard textbook in the field [12] in detail and selected sections from Chaps. 5–8. In the first third of the course, students learn about gates and combinational and sequential circuits. In the central section of the course, students use this material to learn both hardwired and microcoded approaches to reading and interpreting binary instructions. The final section of the course consists of a discussion of higher-level components of a computer.

The first game, Signal Seeker, is intended to increase students' fluency with gates. The second game, Spin-to-Win, provides the practice with binary numbers, including two's complement notation, that students need to work problems in the key middle section of the course. The third game, CPU Simulator, is also relevant to the middle section of the course. That game relates directly to the core idea of the course, namely, how binary instructions are interpreted. These three topics were chosen as topics where students need additional practice and that were also suitable for gamification.

Although there are many recent survey articles on games in education, there is no consensus yet on the extent to which such games help students learn. Laine and Lindberg [8] give a useful literature review on motivators and design principles that we have tried to follow. Earlier surveys are provided by Hamari [4] and Battistella and von Wangenheim [1].

Oren et al. [13] study the extent to which engineering students benefit from playing Planet K, a game in which students design circuits. This game resembles typical homework in circuit design; while undoubtedly worthwhile, it is different from our project in that there is no intent to use game mechanics to make the game fun to play.

Tlili et al. [14] study the use of a game called Science Soldier, where the activities that students participate in, such as fighting an enemy, are unrelated to the topics in computer architecture that students need to learn. This is counter to the design principles of our games, where we always want the material to be relevant to game play.

Turing Tumble [15] is a mechanical game, similar to a Pachinko machine, that helps students learn to design circuits. While a tour de force as a game, due to its cost it is impractical for classroom use. There are several similar games available in software, including Nand2Tetris [9], Nandgame [7], and Turing Complete [11].

Nand2Tetris is based on the textbook by Nisan and Schocken [10] and includes material on programming that the others do not. It uses a VHDL-style language, while the others use a GUI with drag-and-drop wiring. The textbook by Nisan and Schocken is similar in spirit to our course, and these games are highly relevant.

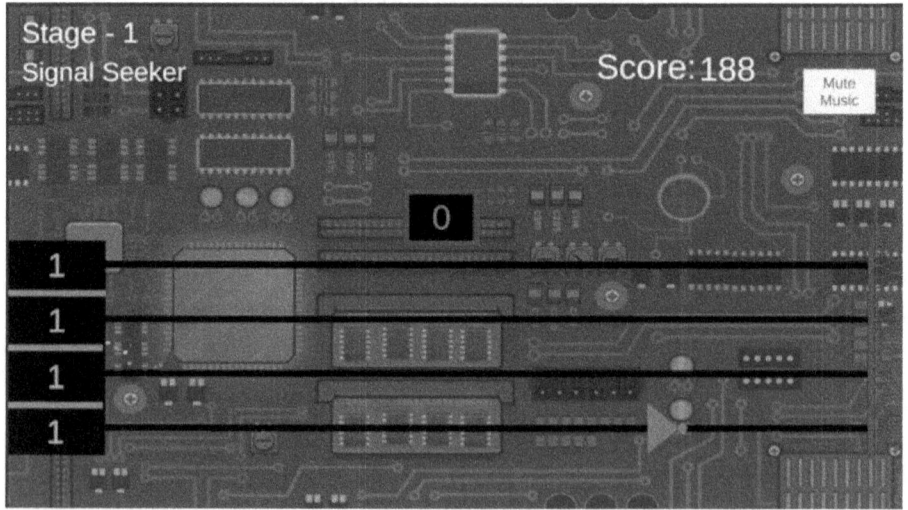

Fig. 1. Basic setup of the Signal Seeker game

3 Signal Seeker

Signal Seeker (Fig. 1) is an "endless runner" type game, i.e. a game similar to an older mobile game called Temple Run [5]. In Temple Run the player runs forever in a line steering left and right or making full turns in either direction. Characters get points by collecting optional gold coins and running for as long as they can without hitting an obstacle or failing to turn in time. The game speeds up over time, making it more difficult to keep running forever.

Signal Seeker is inspired by this concept. Instead of running away from the camera, as in Temple Run, the player is constantly running horizontal to the camera. The player does not have obstacles to avoid while running. They can run forever along randomly generated paths with various difficulties until they make a mistake. Instead of obstacles, we have implemented problems for the player to solve.

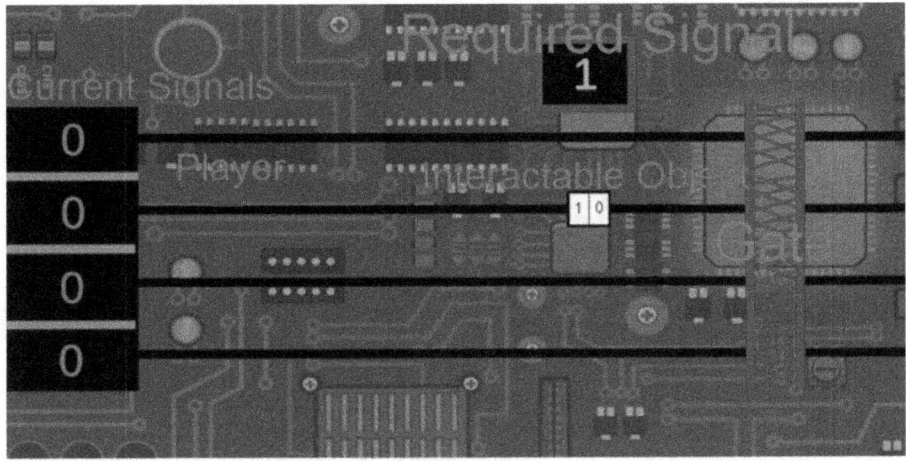

Fig. 2. Game view with objects labeled in pink (Color figure online)

In our game, the player must navigate four lines to be "riding" on a line that has the required signal as they cross the gate. Player experience themselves always moving to the right, although from the developers' point of view, the game is actually moving towards them. Players can speed up or slow down time to gain more points or take some extra time to think. Moving over interactive objects will automatically cause an interaction. As a result, players either need to touch or avoid these objects depending on what the situation calls for. In Fig. 2 the player needs to touch the switch object (the small white box) in order to change the signal to 1 before crossing the gate.

Figure 3 gives examples of the types of objects a player will meet that can affect the line signals. Players must interpret how these objects will affect the signals of the lines they are riding on, then choose to avoid or interact with them. Failing to do so will result in the player being on an incorrect signal as they cross the gate and having to restart the game.

The game is implemented as a set of tilesets, which are prewritten combinations of objects given to the player in a pseudo-random order. A tileset always includes some empty space for the player to reorient themselves after a previous task, a middle challenging area, and a signal gate at the end to check the player's actions. Although it is not visible in the game until the player crosses the signal gate, the tileset has a predetermined signal that it wants and it will always set the line signals to a predetermined starting signal as the player crosses the previous gate.

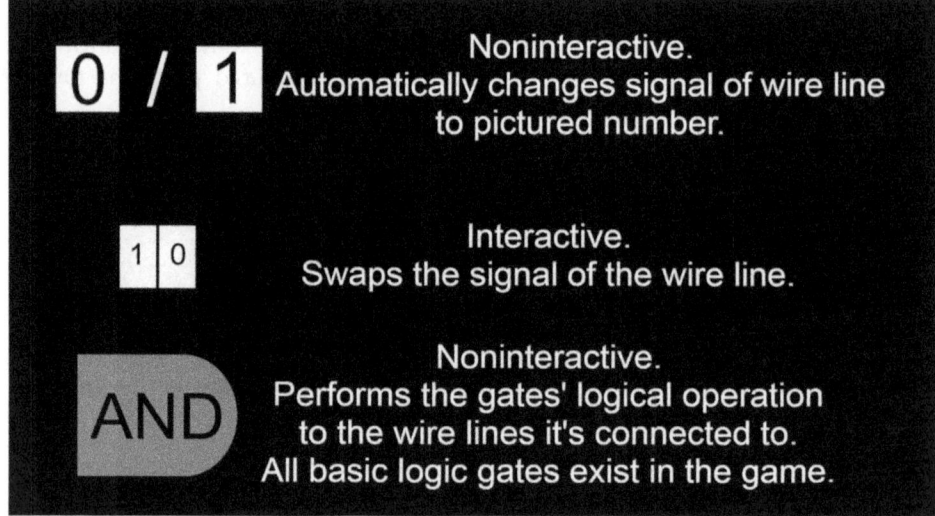

Fig. 3. Objects that a player will meet

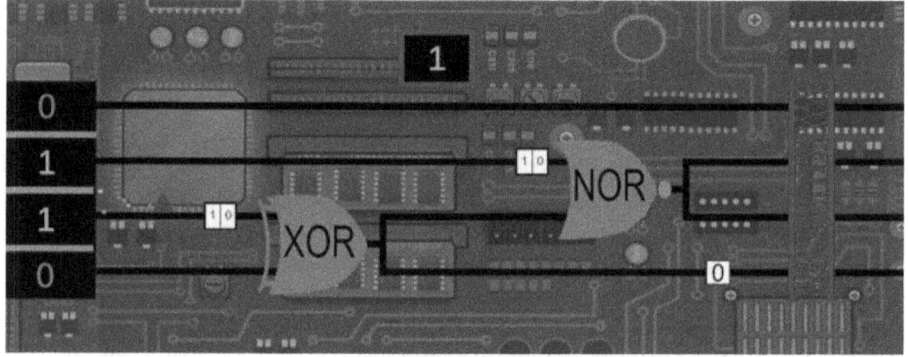

Fig. 4. Example of a harder tileset

The tilesets are sorted into difficulty categories based on their contents. The tilesets increase in difficulty based on the number of gates and objects included and whether the gates are simple ones like AND gates or more complex ones such as XOR. The game gradually ramps up the difficulty level by giving easier tilesets at the start and moving towards harder tilesets after the player has been playing for a while. Figure 4 contains an example of a harder tileset.

The overall goal of the game is to make learning how gates work more interesting and memorable. All the gates function as they would in real life, so concepts can be easily carried over to assignments, exams and actual circuit design. The game forces the player to encounter the material through a weighted randomization of the situations presented, so that the player cannot memorize the solution to previous scenarios. We want players to learn to interpret how the gates and other objects will interact with the signals to predict the results. Thus mastery of the material is required to get a truly high score.

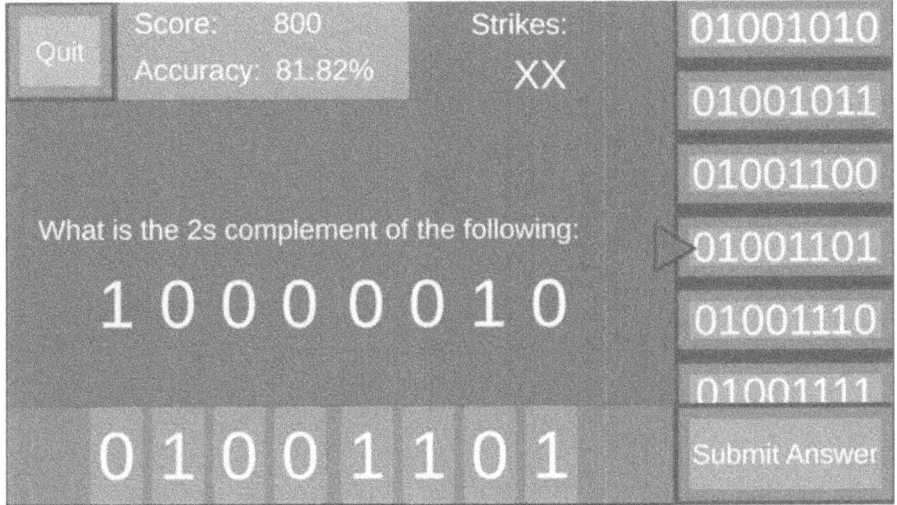

Fig. 5. Two's complement question in Math Marathon mode

4 Spin-to-Win

Spin-to-Win (Fig. 5) is an application designed to assist students in learning essentials of the binary and hexadecimal number systems that are fundamental to arithmetic in the ALU and memory address handling. In this game students are asked questions covering addition, subtraction, base conversion, and finding the two's complement of a number. The game accomplishes this through gamification of different math questions using an approach similar to the Math Blaster series of games for children [6], which was published in various versions for different platforms starting in 1983. The game challenges the user to solve as many problems as they can in a limited amount of time, going for as long as they can without incorrect answers, and allowing them to keep track and beat their own and others' high scores.

After opening the game, the user is welcomed and prompted to enter an ID. This ID is used to keep track of game results for active users, both for giving credit to students and for presenting a leaderboard of high scores at the conclusion of play. The options menu contains a switch allowing anonymous play, thus providing appropriate options both for more competitive players who enjoy public competition and for those who only want to track their personal best or not to play competitively at all.

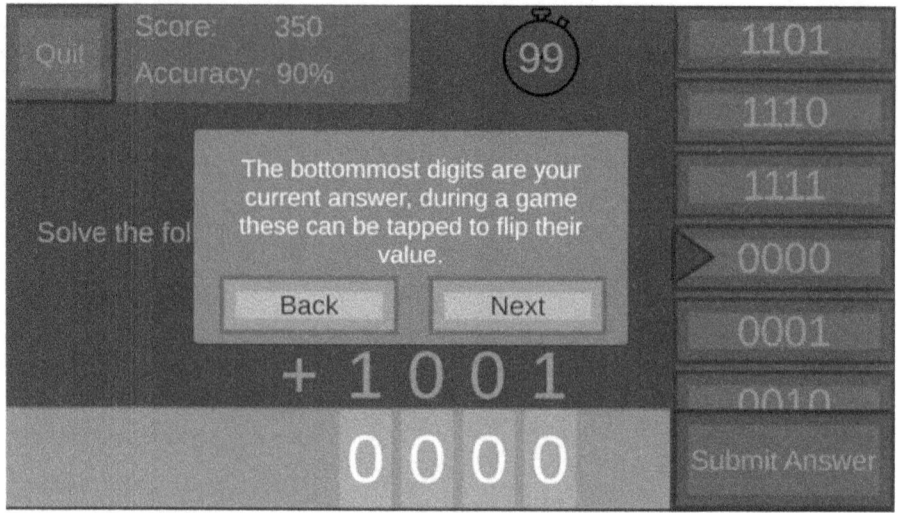

Fig. 6. Tutorial window describing the answer field

On the main menu, users can choose a tutorial that will walk them through the different parts of the GUI (Fig. 6) as well as one of two variants of the game, Binary Blitz or Math Marathon. Binary Blitz is a timed game, while Math Marathon uses a "three strikes, you're out" model. The two variants use the same GUI. The game also contains two difficulty levels. In easy mode, the questions are limited to 4-bit solutions, while in hard mode both 4- and 8-bit questions may be given. Which versions are more helpful to students is an empirical question that we are looking forward to investigating.

The game screen is built from a set of components, with the most prominent, in the center, being the problem to solve. At the top left there is a button to quit and end the round immediately, and a display for the current score and accuracy. To the right of this is a panel displaying either the number of strikes from incorrect answers the user has given in Math Marathon, or a timer showing a countdown to the end of the round in Binary Blitz. With mobile users in mind, the right-hand side of the screen includes a scrolling slide wheel showing sequential binary values that users can spin up or down using touch input or a mouse to alter the currently selected answer. For more exact adjustments, users may change individual digits of the answer by tapping them. Once a user is satisfied with their answer, they may check that it is correct by hitting the submit button in the bottom right, which is followed by an appropriate sound clip and an increase or decrease in the user's score and accuracy. After the user finishes a round, their final score is presented in a window which prompts the user to play the same round again or to exit back to the main menu to view the leaderboard or select another mode.

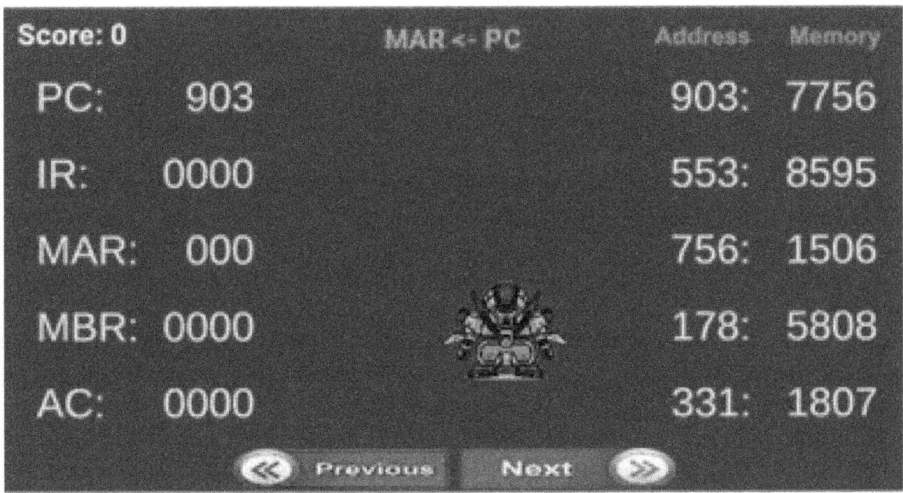

Fig. 7. Program and data memory

5 CPU Simulator

This game is designed to teach students the fundamental concepts of CPU operations using the MARIE assembly language. MARIE is a virtual machine invented by the authors of the course textbook. Although the authors of the book provide a simulator online for people who want to code in MARIE, our simulator runs at a lower level to ensure that students understand the internals of the machine.

Like many computers, the operations in the MARIE assembler are implemented in RTL, or Register Transfer Language. The purpose of this game is to give students a practical introduction to the RTL instructions and how the MARIE op codes are implemented in RTL.

MARIE contains five primary registers: the Instruction Register (IR), Program Counter (PC), Memory Address Register (MAR), Memory Buffer Register (MBR) and Accumulator (AC), where the MBR contains the data in the memory address pointed to by the MAR. The RTL instructions move values between these registers and between registers and memory. The game allows students to view and engage with these components, which helps them understand instruction execution, memory access, and register operations.

The game starts with a menu scene that presents users with a selection of MARIE op codes that they can study, including LOAD, ADD, STORE, and SUBT. Users choose one of these operations by clicking on it. Once an operation is selected, the game generates the appropriate RTL and initiates the simulation.

As shown in Fig. 7, the right-hand side of the screen displays a list of memory addresses along with their corresponding values, representing the program's data as stored in memory. The left side of the screen shows the registers used in MARIE, each initialized with a default value. At the top center of the screen, an instruction prompt, shown in green in the figure, guides the user on what action needs to be performed in the current step of the execution cycle. Additionally, a score counter is displayed in the top left corner, allowing users to track their progress as they successfully execute operations. Navigation controls are provided at the bottom of the screen, allowing users to move forward or backward through different stages of execution.

For the LOAD operation, the first RTL instruction displayed is MAR ← PC, which shows that the user must transfer the value from the PC register to the MAR. The game has a robot character that is used to simulate the execution of instructions by dragging data between registers or between a register and memory.

The user gets a reward of 100 points when they successfully perform the required operation. Upon completing a step correctly, the game automatically advances to the next phase of instruction execution.

If a user performs an incorrect operation, they receive a penalty of 20 points along with a hint in the center of the screen that explains the mistake, as shown in Fig. 8. This feature is designed to provide immediate feedback and help users to identify errors. After reviewing the hint, the user can click on the "got it" button below the hint to acknowledge the feedback and continue the game.

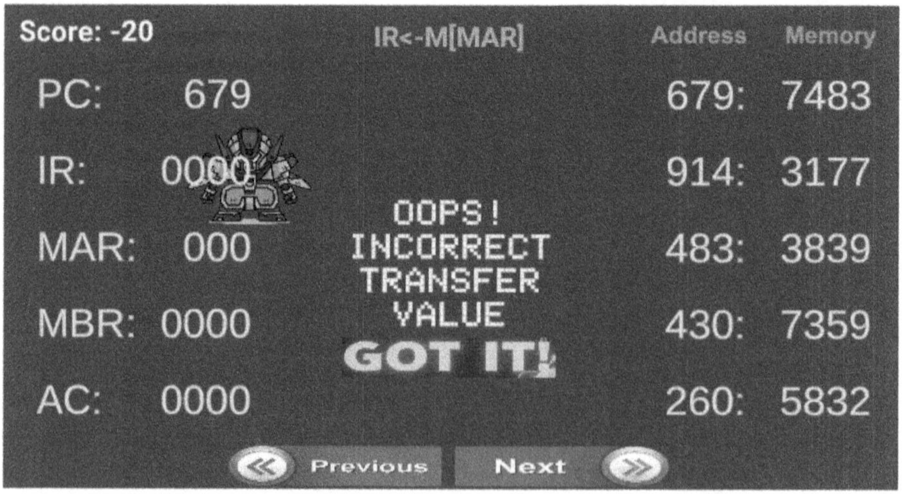

Fig. 8. User interface showing error message with hint

By correctly executing each line of RTL needed for the originally chosen op code, the user can progress through the game and complete the execution of the instruction. After practicing as many assembler instructions as the student chooses, the system displays the final score, summarizing the students's performance.

6 Conclusions and Future Work

In this paper we have described three minigames intended to increase fun and productivity in learning computer architecture through the use of game mechanics intended to appeal to college students. Two of the games are modeled on popular commercial games.

We have attempted to reuse popular game design elements wherever possible, both to reduce development cost and to provide a more entertaining experience for students. Each game was individually developed to increase the novelty value of the games.

All of our games can be made more challenging via time pressure and the use of a leaderboard, which allows both novices and competition-averse students to use the games in the way they find least stressful while also making the game more fun for experienced players. Students who learn better with less pressure, those who are novices to gaming, and students who find the course material difficult are free to turn off the timer and the leaderboard. By default, two of the games also come with music to increase the level of student involvement; again, students who do better with less distraction are free to silence the music.

The games have been set up to send information about student performance to a shared database so that we can analyze student behavior and provide an open learner model for students. We are looking forward to studying the relationship of game use, including specific gamification features, to student success in the course.

References

1. Battistella, P.E., von Wangenheim, C.G.: Games for teaching computing in higher education – a systematic review. IEEE Trans. Learn. Technol. **1**(3), 8–30 (2016)
2. Freedman, R., Edwards, L., Sullivan, I., Brockmann, A., LaBarbera, D., Naples, V.: Teaching cardiovascular physiology with a minigame-based ITS. In: Proceedings of the 19th International Conference on Intelligent Tutoring Systems, pp. 137–146 (2023)
3. Freedman, R., Naples, V., Sullivan, I., Edwards, L., LaBarbera, D.: Gamification, user-centered design and learning objectives as the basis for a minigame-based cardiovascular anatomy ITS. In: Proceedings of the 18th International Conference on Intelligent Tutoring Systems, pp. 336–342 (2022)
4. Hamari, J., Koivisto, J., Sarsa, H.: Does gamification work? — a literature review of empirical studies on gamification. In: Proceedings of the Forty-Seventh Annual Hawaii International Conference on System Sciences, pp. 3025–3034 (2014). https://doi.org/10.1109/HICSS.2014.377
5. Imangi Studios (2021). https://imangistudios.com/thegames/temple-run/
6. JumpStart (1983). https://www.mobygames.com/group/274/math-blaster-series/
7. Kjær, O.J. (nd). https://nandgame.com/
8. Laine, T.H., Lindberg, R.: Designing engaging games for education: a systematic literature review on game motivators and design principles. IEEE Trans. Learn. Technol. **13**(4), 804–821 (2020)
9. Nisan, N., et al. (nd). https://nandgame.com/

10. Nisan, N., Schocken, S.: The Elements of Computing Systems: Building a Modern Computer from First Principles, 2/e. MIT Press, Cambridge (2021)
11. NLN, S.: (2021). https://turingcomplete.game/
12. Null, L., Lobur, J.: Essentials of Computer Organization and Architecture, 5/e. Jones & Bartlett, Burlington (2018)
13. Oren, M., Pedersen, S., Butler-Purry, K.L.: Teaching digital circuit design with a 3-D video game: the impact of using in-game tools on students' performance. IEEE Trans. Educ. **64**(1), 24–31 (2021)
14. Tlili, A., Essalmi, F., Jemni, M.: Improving learning computer architecture through an educational mobile game. Smart Learn. Environ. **3**(7) (2016). https://doi.org/10.1186/s40561-016-0030-6
15. Turing Tumble (2018). https://upperstory.com/en/turingtumble/
16. Unity (2021). http://unity.com

Evaluating an AI-Driven Chatbot Tutor for Enhancing Introductory Programming Learning

Pablo Alejandro Guatibonza Briceño[✉], Daniel Osorio Cárdenas, Rubén Manrique Piramanrique, Edgar Eduardo Rosales Rosero, and Mario Eduardo Sánchez Puccini

Department of Systems and Computing Engineering, Universidad de los Andes, Bogotá D.C., Colombia
{p.guatibonza,d.osorioc2,rf.manrique,
ee.rosales24,mar-san1}@uniandes.edu.co

Abstract. Recent advancements in Artificial Intelligence and Natural Language Processing have catalyzed innovative educational tools, enhancing learning experiences across several domains. This paper investigates the development and evaluation of an AI-powered chatbot designed to support programming education in the Computer Science 1 course at University of the Andes. Addressing the limitations of traditional teaching assistants, the chatbot offers round-the-clock assistance, promotes problem-solving skills, and provides personalized feedback on students' Python exercises. A user study involving 45 participants, comprising students, teaching assistants, and professors, assessed the chatbot's effectiveness. Results indicate high satisfaction: 95.56% of participants reported clear communication, 91.11% found the chatbot's conversational flow effective, and 88.89% confirmed its ability to maintain context. Additionally, 97.78% found responses easy to understand, and 95.56% felt the chatbot contributed to their learning goals. While minor limitations were identified in handling ambiguous queries and response latency during peak usage, the chatbot demonstrated strong usability and pedagogical alignment. Future work will focus on optimizing response time, improving long-session context tracking, and evaluating the chatbot's impact on student performance at scale.

Keywords: AI · Agents · Education · RAG · LangGraph · Chatbot · CS1

1 Introduction

Recent advances in Artificial Intelligence (AI), particularly in Natural Language Processing (NLP) and Large Language Models (LLMs), have led to the widespread use of tools such as ChatGPT and Gemini [5]. These technologies power applications across diverse domains, including mental health support, financial planning, and product recommendations.

In programming education, AI offers opportunities to improve learning by delivering personalized tutorials, documentation, and coding challenges [4,10]. It also enables automation of grading and student progress tracking, allowing educators to focus on individual guidance. However, general-purpose chatbots often fail to align with the structure of introductory programming courses. Tools like ChatGPT may generate responses with advanced syntax or concepts not yet introduced, creating a mismatch that can hinder student learning.

At University of the Andes, the CS1 course enrolls over a thousand students per semester. Python is taught through a structured, incremental approach where foundational concepts precede more complex topics. While teaching assistants (TAs) help students, they often provide direct solutions that undermine problem-solving skills [6]. Their limited availability may also delay support [15], and the course's scale makes personalized assistance difficult.

To address these issues, this research develops and evaluates an AI-powered chatbot tailored to the CS1 curriculum. Unlike general chatbots, it is aligned with course content, offering stage-appropriate support without providing full solutions. The project proceeded in two phases: first, building the chatbot to answer questions and give code feedback on the Senecode platform; second, evaluating its effectiveness with real users to assess its impact on student learning.

2 Literature Review

The integration of AI into education has driven extensive research, mainly across three areas: general AI applications in education, AI-driven chatbots in personalized learning, and AI-assisted programming education. However, these studies often overlook targeted solutions for introductory programming courses, especially in large-scale CS1 settings. This section reviews prior work in these categories and outlines how our study advances the current understanding of AI's role in programming instruction.

Foundational studies explore AI's broad integration into educational contexts. Okonkwo et al. [10] highlight chatbots' versatility in teaching, assessment, and advising, while Wollny et al. [19] demonstrate their impact on knowledge acquisition and self-regulation. Tahiru [18] discusses AI adoption in developed nations, identifying both benefits and structural limitations. While these works underline AI's transformative potential, they primarily focus on administrative applications rather than subject-specific challenges.

Research on AI-driven chatbots shows their effectiveness in personalized learning. Perez et al. [12] demonstrate improvements in engagement and learning outcomes, and Crompton [3] emphasizes enhanced accessibility and affordability. Kuhail [7] explores adaptive web-based chatbots supporting collaborative learning. However, these studies do not tackle the specific problem-solving challenges of programming education. Our work extends this line by designing an AI assistant tailored to CS1 course objectives and student needs.

In programming education, AI-driven tools have shown promise. CodeHelp, evaluated by Liffiton [8], improves engagement, while Sheese et al. [13] find

AI tool usage correlates with better performance, albeit dependent on effective query formulation. Pankiewicz [11] reports positive outcomes from GPT-3.5 feedback, despite adaptation challenges. Existing solutions mainly provide general-purpose coding assistance; in contrast, our chatbot addresses course-specific alignment, structured guidance, and balanced support to promote independent problem-solving.

Overall, while AI-driven educational tools offer considerable promise, applying them effectively in introductory programming remains challenging, particularly at scale. Our research builds on successful AI interventions, adapting them to CS1's pedagogical needs to foster meaningful, scalable, and effective support.

3 CS1 Course

The *CS1* course is a foundational class designed for undergraduate students at University of the Andes. It introduces students to core programming concepts and problem-solving strategies using Python. The course covers fundamental topics such as variables, control structures, functions, and data structures, aiming to develop computational thinking and algorithmic problem-solving skills.

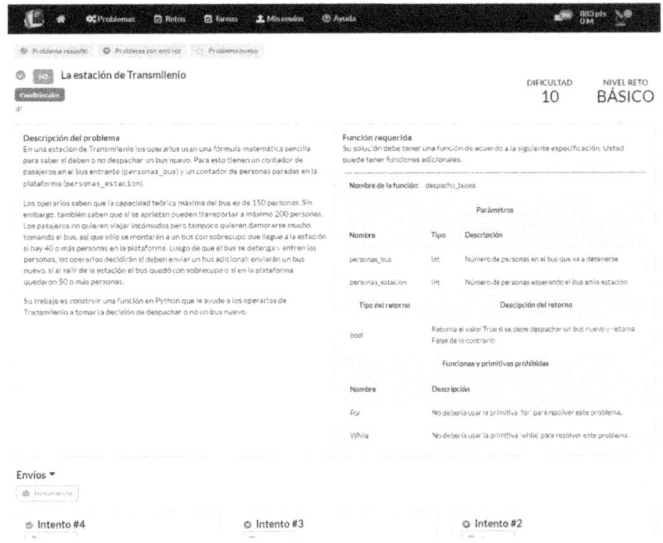

Fig. 1. Overview of the Senecode platform.

With over 1,000 students enrolled each semester, providing personalized assistance is a significant challenge. Students often struggle with understanding abstract programming concepts, debugging code, and applying theoretical knowledge to practical exercises. To support their learning, the course incorporates Senecode (Fig. 1), an educational platform that allows students to submit exercises, receive automated feedback, and track their learning progress.

Senecode plays a crucial role in structuring course assignments and assessments. It enables automated testing of student submissions against predefined test cases, streamlining grading for professors. However, while Senecode provides feedback on correctness, it lacks interactive support to guide students through problem-solving processes. This gap creates an opportunity for a chatbot-based intelligent tutoring system.

To address these challenges, the chatbot was designed with the following core functionalities, identified in collaboration with the course coordinators:

1. **Problem Analysis:** Helping students break down problems into inputs, outputs, and constraints.
2. **Concept Mastery:** Reinforcing fundamental programming concepts such as variables, loops, and conditionals.
3. **Code Implementation and Testing:** Assisting in Python coding, debugging, and validating solutions against expected outputs.

By integrating with Senecode, the chatbot aims to enhance the learning experience by offering on-demand, interactive assistance at scale, addressing the needs of a large student population.

4 System Overview

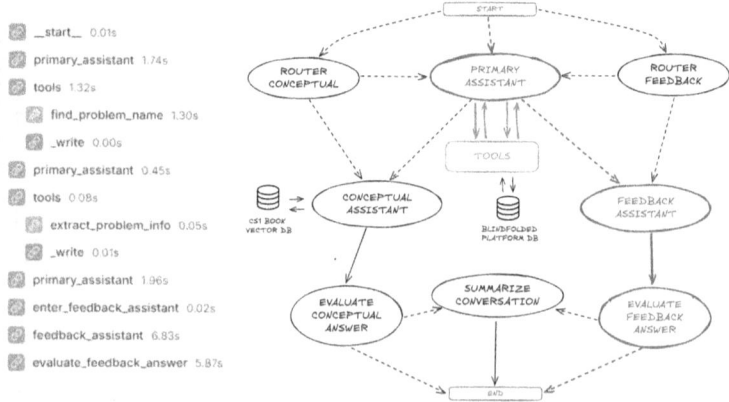

Fig. 2. The figure shows the graph execution for a feedback request on a Senecode exercise. A user asks for help with a specific problem. Since no prior conversation exists, the primary assistant retrieves the problem name and description from the database. The request is then passed to the feedback assistant, which prompts the user for their code. The response is evaluated to avoid providing a direct solution before being shown to the user.

The architecture was built using LangGraph's framework [1], following a modular design where nodes update the system state based on connections or LLM outputs. GPT-4o serves as the core LLM for all components.

The system features two specialized agents: the feedback assistant and the conceptual assistant. Based on user input, the primary assistant delegates tasks to the appropriate agent, ensuring targeted support.

The feedback assistant analyzes student code for Senecode exercises. It retrieves the problem description from the database, requests the user's code, and generates personalized feedback while avoiding direct solutions. The conceptual assistant addresses theoretical questions using a Retrieval Augmented Generation (RAG) setup. Relevant course material, stored in a Supabase vector store [17], is retrieved to provide contextually aligned responses with code examples and explanations.

Router nodes determine whether queries remain within the current agent or require escalation. A summarization node condenses conversations after twelve messages to maintain context and improve efficiency. Figure 2 shows the full LangGraph implementation, detailing nodes, tools, and connections activated during a feedback request.

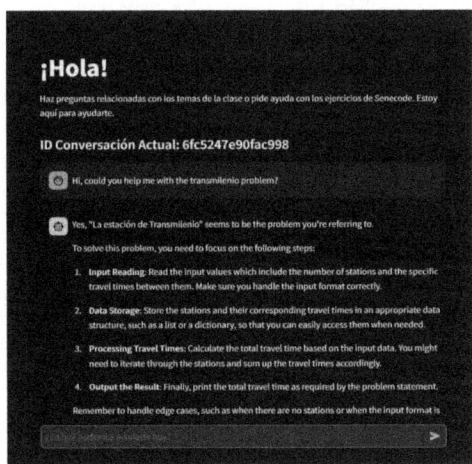

Fig. 3. Chatbot User Interface made with Streamlit

The virtual assistant's interface was developed using Streamlit [16], as shown in Fig. 3. The system was deployed on a university virtual machine and made remotely accessible via ngrok [9], allowing professors and students access. To monitor the language model's performance and graph execution, we used LangSmith tracking [2].

5 User Evaluation

This evaluation aimed to answer the following research question:

How effectively does the AI-powered chatbot assist students in understanding programming concepts and improving their problem-solving skills while upholding academic integrity?

To address this, an experiment was designed in which participants had free access to the chatbot and interacted with it through predefined scenarios.

5.1 Experiment Design

The study included 45 participants: 4 CS1 professors, 7 active TAs, and 34 students who had completed the course. This composition ensured diverse perspectives from educators, support staff, and learners familiar with common programming challenges. Participants interacted with the chatbot through predefined scenarios, each designed to assess a specific aspect of the chatbot's performance.

A scenario consists of a user request, the chatbot's response strategy and an expected interaction flow. For example, in the Conceptual Question scenario, a student asks about a programming concept, and the assistant either requests clarification or provides a targeted explanation. In the Feedback Request scenario, the chatbot retrieves the problem description, evaluates the student's submitted code, and offers suggestions without directly providing the solution. The eight scenarios designed for the experiment are: answering conceptual questions, providing code feedback, detecting logical errors, handling ambiguous input, adapting to changes in user requests, managing off-topic queries, and maintaining academic integrity when responding to direct solution requests. These scenarios were designed to simulate realistic interactions and assess how effectively the chatbot supports learning.

The complete examples of interaction scenarios for each case are available in a supplementary file[1].

5.2 Methodology

Participants completed a survey after interacting with the chatbot across predefined scenarios, each illustrated with example conversations. Usability and pedagogical alignment were assessed using the *Bot Usability Scale (BUS)* [14], with twelve Likert-scale (1–5) items available in a supplementary file[2].

In addition to quantitative ratings, participants could provide qualitative feedback on each scenario, highlighting strengths and areas for improvement. Each conversation was assigned a unique ID to link user feedback with interactions while preserving anonymity.

Potential biases were considered. Professors and TAs might approach interactions from a teaching rather than a learning perspective, while students' with prior CS1 experience may have found the explanations clearer than first-time learners. Predefined scenarios, while ensuring consistent evaluation, may

---

[1] Complete interaction scenarios.
[2] Complete BUS questions.

not fully capture natural usage patterns. To mitigate these effects, the sample included balanced representation across groups, and interaction guidance was minimized.

6 Results

6.1 User Experience and Usability

Overall, communication clarity was rated highly, with 86.67% strongly agreeing and 8.89% agreeing that the chatbot communicated clearly. Similarly, 82.22% strongly agreed and 8.89% agreed they were immediately aware of the chatbot's capabilities. The majority (80% strongly agreed, 11.11% agreed) also felt interactions resembled an ongoing conversation, and 77.78% strongly agreed that context was maintained (Fig. 4).

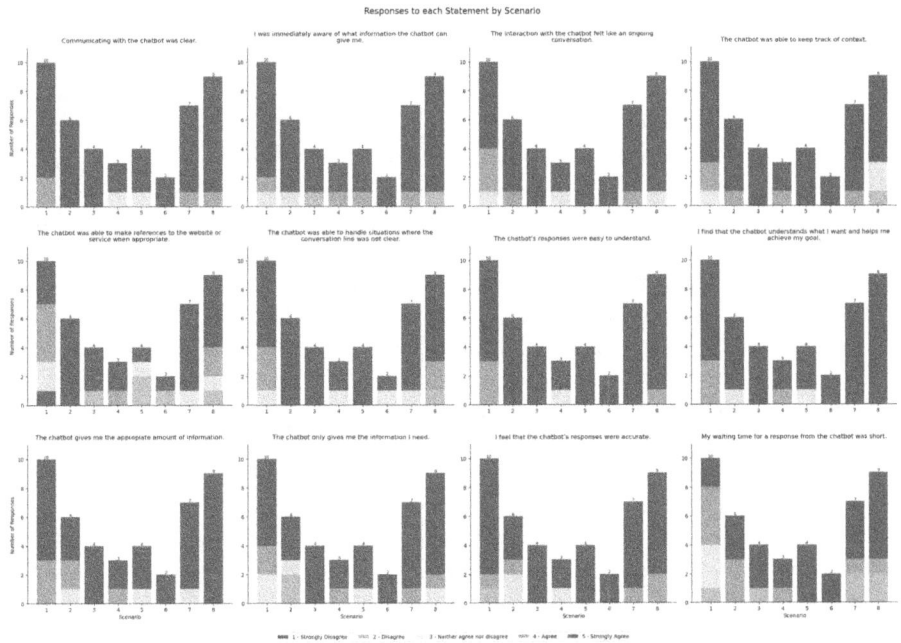

Fig. 4. Answers to each statement by scenario.

Regarding content quality, 88.89% strongly agreed that responses were easy to understand, while 86.67% strongly agreed the chatbot helped them achieve their goals. Information provision was also rated positively, with 80% strongly agreeing that the amount of information was appropriate and 73.33% affirming that only relevant details were provided.

Performance on more complex tasks showed greater variability. For handling unclear conversations, 75.56% strongly agreed that the chatbot managed ambiguity effectively. However, website and service references were slightly lower, with 60% strongly agreeing on relevance. In terms of response accuracy, 77.78% strongly agreed the answers were accurate. Response time satisfaction was lower, with 57.78% strongly agreeing and 22.22% agreeing, but 13.33% expressed dissatisfaction.

Scenario-specific analysis revealed that Scenario 1 (Conceptual Question) and Scenario 4 (Logical Errors) achieved the highest agreement across metrics. In contrast, Scenario 5 (Ambiguous Input) exposed challenges in context tracking and ambiguity management, while Scenario 8 (Direct Code Solution) showed mixed evaluations, particularly regarding response time and information sufficiency.

6.2 Performance in Specific Scenarios

Participants had the option to provide qualitative feedback for each scenario. Below are the results:

1. **Conceptual Question**
   Overall, participants found the chatbot's explanations of fundamental programming concepts clear, with most in strong agreement. However, a few users noted that it missed providing references to external sources and lacked detail in more advanced topics.
2. **Request for Feedback on a Specific Problem**
   The chatbot effectively provided constructive feedback. However, one-third of participants disagreed that it offered only necessary information, due to a bug that caused the tool to repeat problem descriptions. This bug was fixed soon afterwards. Some users also reported that the chatbot failed to detect incorrect code and that it recommended methods outside the course curriculum.
3. **Provide Correct Code**
   Feedback was mostly positive, with the majority agreeing that the chatbot provided correct code solutions. However, one user reported dissatisfaction with the chatbot's response time and handling of incomplete code input, which led to irrelevant feedback.
4. **Provide Code with Logical Errors**
   The chatbot performed well in identifying and explaining logical errors in code, with no negative feedback. Most users appreciated the chatbot's hints that directed them to problematic areas, promoting independent debugging.
5. **Ambiguous Input from the User**
   The chatbot struggled with ambiguous input in some cases. One user strongly disagreed with its ability to maintain context and handle unclear inputs. The chatbot also failed to cite sources when answering conceptual questions, which led to dissatisfaction.

6. **Change of Request by the User**
   The chatbot adapted well when the user changed requests. However, one participant disagreed with its lack of source references, which affected trust in the responses.
7. **Off-Topic Question**
   The chatbot effectively redirected off-topic questions in most cases, but some users mentioned delays in response times. One user noted that the chatbot provided information irrelevant to the course content.
8. **Direct Request for the Code Solution**
   When users requested direct solutions, the chatbot adhered to academic integrity standards, offering guidance instead of providing the solution. However, some users were dissatisfied with its response time and the chatbot's ability to maintain context across different queries.

6.3 Insights from User Feedback

The qualitative feedback from participants provided valuable insights into areas for improvement, with several key themes emerging. Firstly, there was a request for simpler explanations. While the majority of students found the chatbot's responses helpful, some suggested that certain explanations could be further simplified, especially for less experienced learners. Secondly, context management was highlighted as an area needing enhancement, as a few participants observed that the chatbot sometimes lost context during lengthy conversations, resulting in a decline in response quality. Improving the mechanisms for context-tracking could enhance consistency in prolonged interactions. Lastly, response time was identified as another area for enhancement. Although the chatbot generally performed well, a few students noticed delays during peak server traffic times. Optimizing response time during high-traffic periods could improve user satisfaction.

7 Conclusion and Future Work

This paper presented the development and evaluation of an AI-powered chatbot designed to support CS1 students at the University of the Andes. Results show the chatbot effectively maintains conversational flow, provides clear and accurate responses, and facilitates learning. User evaluations reflected high satisfaction, highlighting the system's potential to deliver scalable, personalized educational support.

However, improvements are needed. Some participants noted inconsistencies in context tracking during prolonged interactions. Future work will focus on enhancing context management and optimizing response times, particularly under peak loads, to ensure seamless user experiences.

We also plan a quantitative evaluation of the chatbot's impact, including analyzing Senecode score improvements, comparing course grades between users and non-users, and assessing correlations with dropout or failure rates to provide empirical validation.

Another direction involves categorizing Senecode problems based on chatbot interaction volume, helping identify ambiguous or misclassified exercises and informing both chatbot refinement and course improvements. Insights could also guide professors in adjusting instruction.

A broader evaluation involving the full CS1 population would strengthen our findings by capturing diverse perspectives across multiple teaching approaches.

Currently, the chatbot handles every query with LLM calls and direct database access, a potentially inefficient approach at scale. Future work will explore a hybrid architecture that uses a structured knowledge base for frequent queries, reserving LLM use for complex interactions. This could significantly reduce computational costs and improve response times. Furthermore, evaluating the impact of such optimizations on user experience and system efficiency would be essential to justify their adoption.

Disclosure of Interests. The authors have no competing interests to declare that are relevant to the content of this article.

References

1. Langgraph framework. https://www.langgraph.dev/. Accessed 28 Apr 2025
2. Langsmith debugging and tracing platform. https://smith.langchain.com/. Accessed 28 Apr 2025
3. Crompton, H., Burke, D.: Artificial intelligence in higher education: the state of the field. Int. J. Educ. Technol. High. Educ. **20**(1), 22 (2023). https://doi.org/10.1186/s41239-023-00392-8
4. Fariani, R.I., Junus, K., Santoso, H.B.: A Systematic literature review on personalised learning in the higher education context. Technol. Knowl. Learn. **28**(2), 449–476 (2023). https://doi.org/10.1007/s10758-022-09628-4
5. Kasneci, E., et al.: ChatGPT for good? On opportunities and challenges of large language models for education. Learn. Individ. Differ. **103**, 102274 (2023). https://doi.org/10.1016/j.lindif.2023.102274. https://www.sciencedirect.com/science/article/pii/S1041608023000195
6. Krause-Levy, S., Lim, R.S., Villegas Molina, I., Cao, Y., Porter, L.: An exploration of student-tutor interactions in computing. In: Proceedings of the 27th ACM Conference on on Innovation and Technology in Computer Science Education, ITiCSE 2022, vol. 1, pp. 435–441. Association for Computing Machinery, New York (2022). https://doi.org/10.1145/3502718.3524786. https://dl.acm.org/doi/10.1145/3502718.3524786
7. Kuhail, M.A., Alturki, N., Alramlawi, S., Alhejori, K.: Interacting with educational chatbots: a systematic review. Educ. Inf. Technol. **28**(1), 973–1018 (2023). https://doi.org/10.1007/s10639-022-11177-3
8. Liffiton, M., Sheese, B., Savelka, J., Denny, P.: CodeHelp: using large language models with guardrails for scalable support in programming classes (2023). arXiv:2308.06921 [cs]
9. ngrok, Inc.: ngrok: secure tunnels to localhost (2024). https://ngrok.com. Accessed 28 Apr 2025

10. Okonkwo, C.W., Ade-Ibijola, A.: Chatbots applications in education: a systematic review. Comput. Educ. Artif. Intell. **2**, 100033 (2021). https://doi.org/10.1016/j.caeai.2021.100033. https://linkinghub.elsevier.com/retrieve/pii/S2666920X21000278
11. Pankiewicz, M., Baker, R.S.: Large language models (GPT) for automating feedback on programming assignments. arXiv preprint arXiv:2307.00150 (2023). https://doi.org/10.48550/arXiv.2307.00150
12. Pérez, J.Q., Daradoumis, T., Puig, J.: Rediscovering the use of chatbots in education: asystematic literature review. Comput. Appl. Eng. Educ. **28**(6), 1549–1565 (2020). https://doi.org/10.1002/cae.22326. https://onlinelibrary.wiley.com/doi/abs/10.1002/cae.22326
13. Sheese, B., Liffiton, M., Savelka, J., Denny, P.: Patterns of student help-seeking when using a large language model-powered programming assistant. In: Proceedings of the 26th Australasian Computing Education Conference, pp. 49–57 (2024). https://doi.org/10.1145/3636243.3636249. arXiv:2310.16984 [cs]
14. Simone, B., et al.: The chatbot usability scale: the design and pilot of a usability scale for interaction with AI-based conversational agents. Pers. Ubiquit. Comput. **26**(1), 95–119 (2022). https://doi.org/10.1007/s00779-021-01582-9. https://www.proquest.com/docview/2618384175/abstract/81B2B36CDF5944B6PQ/1
15. Smith, A.J., Boyer, K.E., Forbes, J., Heckman, S., Mayer-Patel, K.: My digital hand: a tool for scaling up one-to-one peer teaching in support of computer science learning (2017). https://doi.org/10.1145/3017680.3017800. https://dl.acm.org/doi/10.1145/3017680.3017800
16. Streamlit Inc.: Streamlit (2024). https://streamlit.io. Accessed 28 Apr 2025
17. Supabase Inc.: Supabase: the open source firebase alternative (2024). https://supabase.com. Accessed 28 Apr 2025
18. Tahiru, F.: AI in education: a systematic literature review. J. Cases Inf. Technol. (JCIT) **23**(1), 1–20 (2021). https://doi.org/10.4018/JCIT.2021010101. https://www.igi-global.com/article/ai-in-education/www.igi-global.com/article/ai-in-education/266434
19. Wollny, S., Schneider, J., Di Mitri, D., Weidlich, J., Rittberger, M., Drachsler, H.: Are we there yet? - a systematic literature review on chatbots in education. Front. Artif. Intell. **4** (2021). https://doi.org/10.3389/frai.2021.654924. https://www.frontiersin.org/journals/artificial-intelligence/articles/10.3389/frai.2021.654924/full

A Comprehensive Survey and Taxonomy on Large Language Model-Based Knowledge Tracing

Sunwoo Park🆔 and Hyeoncheol Kim(✉)🆔

Korea University, Seoul, Republic of Korea
{sunwoosan,harrykim}@korea.ac.kr

Abstract. Large language models (LLMs) have significant potential for intelligent tutoring systems (ITS), particularly in knowledge tracing (KT). Many current studies exhibit diverse approaches to LLM-based KT. However, despite the growing body of research, there is a lack of a consistent taxonomy for integrating LLMs into KT. In response, this study proposes a systematic taxonomy that categorizes the various roles LLMs can play in KT into three categories: LLM-enhanced, LLM-integrated, and LLM-standalone. Using this taxonomy, we systematically review and analyze studies published over the past three years that incorporate LLMs into knowledge tracing. Our analysis reveals that the role of LLMs, their strengths and weaknesses, and the type of data used, metrics vary across these categories. We also discuss the major challenges faced by each taxonomy, including optimizing feature fusion, handling real-time and unstructured inputs, designing effective prompts, and ensuring explainability. This comprehensive review provides a conceptual foundation and directions for future research in ITS driven by generative AI.

Keywords: knowledge tracing · Large Language Models · Intelligent tutoring system · Taxonomy · Personalized Education

1 Introduction

1.1 Knowledge Tracing and Large Language Models

Knowledge tracing (KT) is a key technique in intelligent tutoring systems (ITS) that continuously tracks and predicts learners' knowledge states [21,36]. Although early KT research often simplified knowledge into binary states, more recent methods capture nuanced representations of each concept and leverage advanced AI for enhanced predictive accuracy [23,30,31,34,37,44].

In particular, the recent development of LLMs, which shows excellent performance in the understanding and generation of natural languages, provides new opportunities for KT. This is because it supports integration of narrative answers, activity logs, and conversation data beyond the existing binary answer input method, and can reflect complex learning states through finetuning [2,7,8,10,12,25,48]. Many researchers have hypothesized and experimentally verified that LLMs can improve KT models by interpreting students' open-ended answers, predicting question difficulty, and identifying misunderstandings in answers, and published related papers [11,13–15,17,27,35,45].

1.2 Motivation and Contributions for a Taxonomy of LLM-Based KT

Motivation. The convergence of LLMs and KT is a critical turning point in the evolution of ITSs. In recent studies, various KT methodologies using LLMs have been attempted, which can be broadly divided into several categories. Some studies focus on the use of LLMs as a feature extractor to improve the performance of existing KT models [19,22,28,42]. Other studies integrate existing KT models into LLMs to directly manage and update learners' knowledge states [16,20,24,43]. Another study does not use traditional KT, but uses LLMs as a standalone KT model that directly predicts student status [15,17,27].

This variety of roles for LLMs has created ambiguity in defining their function within systematic KT research. Because there is no clear consensus for the researcher, it becomes difficult to compare methods or accumulate findings between studies. Now, researchers usually use interchangeable terms like "LLM-based KT," "GPT-based tutoring," or "knowledge tracking with LLMs" to describe similar concepts.

In other domains, researchers have introduced taxonomies to bring order to such ambiguity [1,4,9,33,40,41]. For example, in reinforcement learning, a recent review proposes a taxonomy of LLM-based RL integrations to categorize how the two techniques interact [32]. Similarly, in software engineering, researchers have outlined a taxonomy for LLM-integrated applications to establish common terminology and design dimensions [47]. Given the ongoing development of KT research, there is a pressing need for a clear and standardized taxonomy to guide the integration of LLMs. Without such a classification, the diverse streams and categories of research become difficult to delineate, leading to fragmentation and a lack of clarity regarding the contribution of each study.

To address this issue, we propose a comprehensive taxonomy that systematically categorizes LLM-based KT approaches, specifying the ways in which LLMs can be incorporated into existing KT models and the specific roles they can fulfill. By offering precise definitions and well-defined categories, our taxonomy facilitates meaningful comparisons across different methods, standardizes the terminology used in the field, and promotes more effective communication and collaboration among researchers.

Objectives and Contributions. The primary goal of this study is to present a taxonomy that positions diverse LLM-based KT approaches within three integration levels: LLM-Enhanced, LLM-Integrated, and LLM-Standalone. We also compare datasets, domain contexts, and performance metrics across LLM-based KT models to establish a coherent basis for assessing disparate studies.

Through the introduction of standardized terminology and a unified taxonomy, we address existing ambiguities in naming conventions, thereby promoting consistency, reproducibility, and methodological clarity. Ultimately, this taxonomy is designed to deepen theoretical understanding, streamline model development, and enhance the effective integration of LLMs into KT research and practice.

2 Survey Methodology

2.1 Literature Search and Scope

For this study, we conducted a systematic search in IEEE Xplore, ACM Digital Library, Scopus, and Google Scholar using keywords, such as "LLMs," "GPT," "LLaMA," with "KT" or "LLMs and student modeling," "student prediction," and so on. The search period was set from 2022 to 2024. The primary search resulted in 39 papers, and after excluding duplicates and short workshop abstracts, we further filtered out papers that did not explicitly integrate LLMs into KT work or lacked empirical evaluation of KT performance.

Additionally, we did not define LLMs as studies that used simple language models such as BERT, Transformer, or Attention structures. In this study, LLMs refers to a large, resource-consuming language model that can process prompts based on fine-tuning. Therefore, we excluded KT-related studies that utilized simple language model structures. This reflects our intention to identify recent trends by analyzing the surge of related research since the emergence of ChatGPT in November 2022. Ultimately, 25 studies met the above criteria and were included. The 25 selected studies have a small literature size, but this should be taken into account the fact that LLM-based KT is a recently formed research field and practical factors such as data accessibility and implementation complexity.

2.2 Classification Scheme

To systematically analyze the key dimensions of LLM-based KT, we propose a taxonomy that centers on the extent and manner in which LLMs are incorporated into traditional KT pipelines. Building on this classification, we further consider how various studies utilize different data modalities and evaluate model performance via commonly used metrics such as AUC (Area Under the Curve), ACC (Accuracy) and F1-Score. By comparing these elements holistically, our taxonomy highlights distinct methodological strengths, weaknesses, and domain-specific characteristics, providing a coherent basis for both quantitative assessment and the identification of emerging trends in LLM-based KT research.

3 Results

3.1 A New Taxonomy: LLM-Enhanced KT, LLM-Integrated KT, LLM-Standalone KT

As shown in Fig. 1, building on the diverse body of work reviewed for LLM-Enhanced, LLM-Integrated, and LLM-Standalone KT, this section provides a detailed analysis that emphasizes how each approach is implemented, why certain studies are categorized in each manner, and where the boundaries of these categories may become blurred. We further discuss cases where existing studies do not perfectly fit into a single category, thus underscoring the need for flexibility in applying this taxonomy.

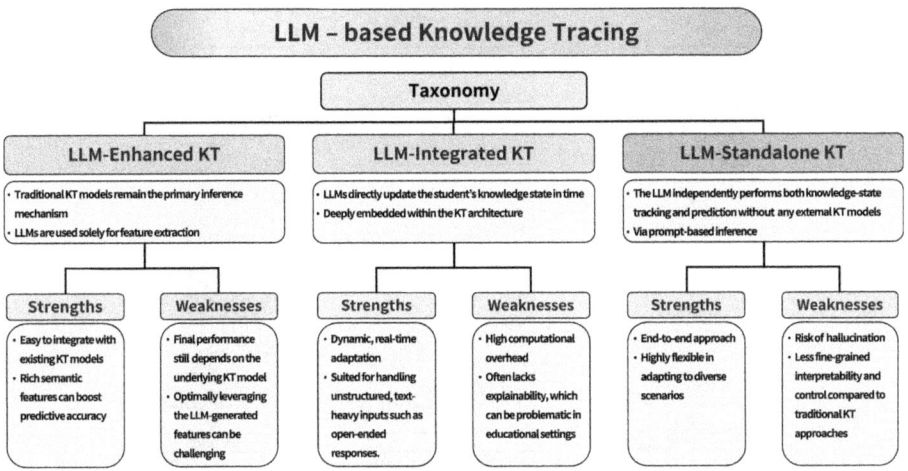

Fig. 1. Three Taxonomies for LLM-Based Knowledge Tracing.

LLM-Enhanced KT: Leveraging LLMs as Feature Generators. As depicted in Fig. 2, the LLM-Enhanced approach retains traditional KT models as the core inference engine while incorporating LLMs to augment feature extraction. In this taxonomy, LLMs primarily serve as feature generators, transforming unstructured data, such as open-ended student responses or problem text, into structured representations like semantic embeddings or difficulty estimates. These enriched features are subsequently fed into the existing KT pipeline, enhancing predictive accuracy without altering the core structure of traditional KT models.

The distinguishing feature of LLM-Enhanced KT, in contrast to the other categories, is that LLMs are used only in the initial phase of feature extraction. The generated text embeddings or semantic vectors are then processed by the existing KT models to update the student's knowledge state. This integration boosts prediction accuracy with minimal modifications to the existing algorithms, as shown in Fig. 1 [6,19,22,26,28,29,42,46].

However, this model's performance is intrinsically tied to the quality of the underlying KT model. If the base KT model is inadequately tuned, the features generated by the LLMs may not be fully leveraged, thus limiting the model's capacity to enhance predictive accuracy. Future research in this domain could explore incorporating multimodal data, such as audio, video, or sensor data, to further expand the feature extraction capabilities of LLMs, thereby enabling richer and more robust representations of student behavior.

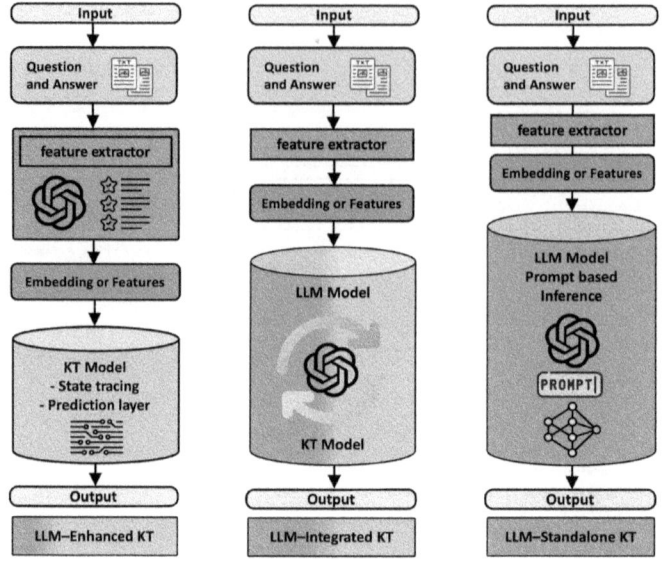

Fig. 2. Overview of LLM-based KT Architectures.

LLM-Integrated KT: Dynamic Knowledge State Updates. Figure 2 illustrates the more sophisticated nature of the LLM-Integrated approach, where LLMs play a central role in dynamically updating the student's knowledge state [3,5,16,18,20,24,38,39,43].

LLMs in this taxonomy are not merely employed as feature extractors; instead, they are deeply embedded into the KT architecture, directly influencing the student's knowledge state based interactions. In this model, LLMs continuously analyze incoming student responses and update the knowledge state. This process is dynamic, with LLMs evaluating the student's current knowledge and adjusting predictions based on their evolving performance.

However, the dynamic processing requirements of LLMs present significant computational challenges. The need to process large volumes of student interaction data rapidly can result in performance bottlenecks, especially in large-scale applications. Furthermore, LLM-based models often suffer from opacity, with limited interpretability of their decision-making processes. This lack of transparency is a critical issue in educational settings, where understanding the rationale behind feedback is crucial for both educators and students.

To address these challenges, future research should focus on optimizing the efficiency of LLMs for dynamic applications. Techniques such as model distillation, pruning, or quantization could be explored to reduce computational overhead while preserving performance. Additionally, improving the transparency and explainability of LLM-based predictions will be essential to enhance user trust and facilitate the broader adoption of these models in educational contexts.

LLM-Standalone KT: Autonomous Knowledge State Prediction. As shown in Fig. 2, the LLM-Standalone approach represents a significant departure from traditional KT models by completely removing the need for external KT components. Instead, LLMs autonomously track and predict the student's knowledge state via prompt-based inference. This model leverages LLMs to handle both knowledge state tracking and performance prediction, offering a fully integrated, end-to-end solution. By processing immediate student input, the LLMs can provide real-time feedback and predictions, making this model particularly effective in dynamic and fast-paced educational environments. Unlike traditional KT models, the LLM-Standalone approach does not rely on external modules but instead employs self-supervised learning techniques to predict outcomes based on previous interactions. The model benefits from LLMs' ability to generalize knowledge from extensive pre-trained corpora [11,13–15,17,27,35,45].

However, one of the significant challenges with LLM-Standalone KT is the phenomenon of hallucinations, where the model generates predictions or feedback that are not grounded in the provided input, leading to inaccurate or misleading outputs. Additionally, unlike traditional KT models, which offer explicit control over specific knowledge components, such as skill-level estimation, LLM-Standalone KT lacks the same level of granularity and interpretability. This limitation can hinder the model's ability to provide fine-grained, skill-specific tracking of student progress.

Therefore, future research should focus on mitigating the hallucination problem by incorporating techniques such as calibration or confidence scoring, which could ensure more reliable predictions. Additionally, exploring methods to enhance control over specific competencies within the LLMs would allow for more precise tracking of student knowledge, making it possible to achieve a finer level of granularity in performance prediction and analysis.

3.2 Cross-Comparative Analysis

Datasets and Domains. Datasets are fundamental to the architecture and performance of KT models, as they define the input features and the scope of inference. Figure 3 provides a comparative analysis of the three LLM-based KT approaches based on the datasets used and the domains they target. The choice of dataset influences the model's ability to generalize and accurately predict learners' knowledge states.

In the LLM-Enhanced KT model, LLMs are incorporated into existing KT architectures to augment prediction capabilities by adding semantic features

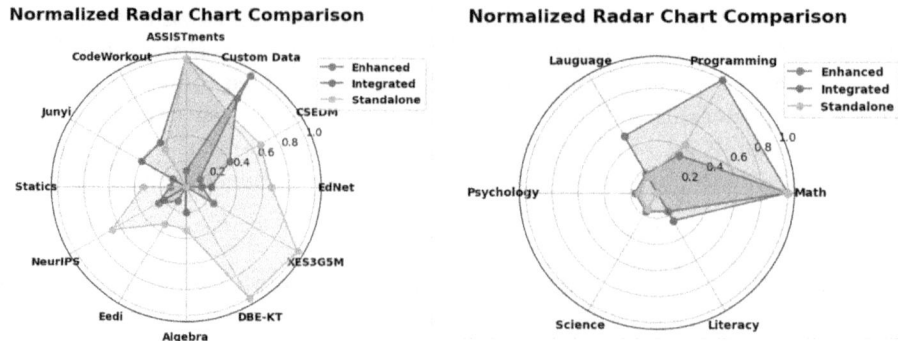

Fig. 3. Comparative Evaluation of LLM-Enhanced, Integrated, and Standalone KT Models Across Datasets and Domains. The left panel illustrates datasets, and the right panel illustrates targeted domains for each model type.

extracted from unstructured data. Given the nature of this model, it typically utilizes custom datasets, which may be collected from diverse sources or tailored to specific domains. The richness of the dataset plays a critical role in ensuring that the LLM can effectively capture nuanced semantic information, thus enhancing the model's performance.

LLM-Integrated KT, in contrast, relies heavily on its rich, domain-specific datasets, as LLMs are highly adept at understanding text. However, because LLMs directly interact with the KT model, handling noisy or unbalanced data becomes a key challenge. Consequently, pre-processing and balancing of the data are crucial steps for achieving optimal model performance. This approach often leverages large, structured educational datasets such as ASSISTments and EdNet, which are designed to provide detailed and diverse learning data.

The LLM-Standalone KT model operates independently of traditional KT modules, relying solely on LLMs for both tracking and prediction. This approach typically uses structured datasets, such as ASSISTments or XES3GSM, which could be prompt-based learning. The structured nature of these datasets helps stabilize model performance by simplifying the underlying complexity and making it easier to interpret the predictions. By using these well-organized datasets, LLM-Standalone systems can focus on leveraging prompt-based inference without being overwhelmed by the intricacies of unstructured data.

As illustrated on the right side of Fig. 3, all three approaches are commonly applied to math and programming data, which feature well-defined question-answer structures. These domains are heavily studied within KT due to their clarity and predictable response patterns. However, for domains rich in text, the LLM-Integrated model proves to be more versatile, offering the flexibility to handle diverse and less structured inputs. On the other hand, the LLM-Enhanced and LLM-Standalone models tend to focus on more structured, question-oriented datasets, which are better suited to their inherent design.

Performance Metrics. The increasing reliance on LLMs in KT models necessitates the use of appropriate performance metrics to evaluate the effectiveness and accuracy of these models. Figure 4 compares the performance metrics commonly used to assess LLM-based KT approaches.

In the LLM-Enhanced KT model, traditional metrics such as AUC and ACC are frequently used to evaluate the prediction accuracy of the enhanced system. These metrics are commonly employed in KT models to assess their ability to rank and predict learner responses. Since LLM-Enhanced models focus on improving the predictions of existing KT frameworks, they rely on these conventional metrics to measure their performance in comparison to baseline models.

For LLM-Integrated KT, the dynamic and interactive nature of the model requires additional evaluation metrics beyond traditional ones. In particular, CodeBLEU and Dist-1 are used to assess the performance of these models. CodeBLEU is designed to evaluate the accuracy and semantic consistency of generated code, which is especially useful when the KT model interacts with code-related data. Dist-1, on the other hand, evaluates the diversity of the generated output, which is important for assessing the model's ability to capture and predict a variety of learner solutions. These metrics ensure that the LLM-Integrated model can handle complex, varied learner inputs and track their progress effectively.

The LLM-Standalone KT model, relying solely on LLMs for inference, employs a combination of AUC, ACC, and F1-Score. The inclusion of the F1-Score is particularly important, as it balances precision and recall, making it ideal for evaluating performance in contexts where predictions may be imbalanced, such as when dealing with unstructured text data. F1-Score helps determine how well the model can detect incorrect answers, especially in cases where misclassifications may have significant consequences. Given that prompt design plays a crucial role in the reliability of LLM-Standalone models, balancing precision and recall is essential for ensuring that predictions are both accurate and reliable.

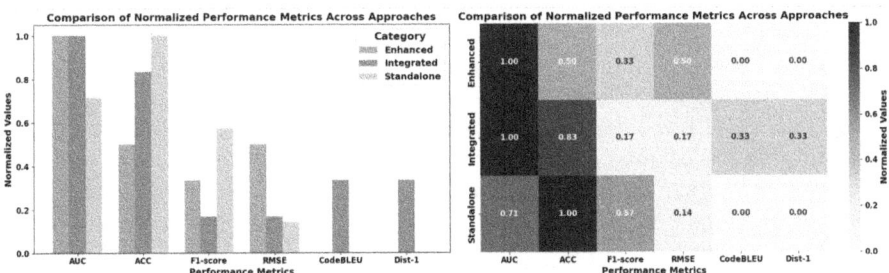

Fig. 4. Comparison of Performance Metrics Used to Evaluate LLM-based KT. The left chart shows the frequency of metric usage, while the right chart visualizes the metric values normalized by frequency.

The comparative evaluation of these performance metrics highlights the nuanced differences between the three approaches. While AUC and ACC remain the most commonly used metrics across all approaches, LLM-Integrated models require more specialized metrics to handle the complexities of interactive, dynamic learning environments. The addition of metrics like CodeBLEU and Dist-1 reflects the need for a more granular understanding of the model's performance in diverse and open-ended contexts. Conversely, LLM-Standalone models prioritize balance metrics, such as F1-Score, to address issues of imbalance and ensure that predictions maintain high reliability across a variety of learner inputs. This comprehensive evaluation underscores the importance of selecting the appropriate metrics to capture the full range of model performance, depending on the specific design and use case of the LLM-based KT system.

4 Discussion

The taxonomy introduced in this study aims to address a critical gap in the evolving landscape of KT research, particularly with respect to the integration of LLMs. While previous research has explored LLMs applications across a variety of domains, there remains a lack of a standardized taxonomy to systematically categorize these applications within KT. Our taxonomy, consisting of LLM-Enhanced, LLM-Integrated, and LLM-Standalone approaches, provides a structured way to assess and understand the various strategies for embedding LLMs into KT systems. This classification offers both theoretical insights and practical guidance for future implementations of LLM-based solutions in educational technology.

LLM-Enhanced systems primarily augment existing KT pipelines by integrating LLMs as additional feature extractors. These systems leverage the semantic power of LLMs to extract meaningful insights from unstructured data such as textual feedback or open-ended responses. This augmentation is particularly valuable in scenarios where traditional KT models are effective at tracking overall learner mastery but may struggle to capture subtle semantic cues embedded in learners' interactions. By enhancing these models with LLM-derived features, the system can capture more nuanced information, potentially improving prediction accuracy and learner modeling.

In contrast, LLM-Integrated systems rely on dynamic adaptation, making them suitable for learning environments that require constant updates and interpretations of learner data. These models are particularly effective in contexts where interactions are frequent and rich, such as in dialogue-based learning or interactive simulations. However, their reliance on dynamic data also makes them susceptible to noise and inconsistencies, such as unbalanced inputs in conversations or feedback loops that may distort learning assessments. This vulnerability highlights the challenge of managing and filtering noisy data in systems that depend on continuous feedback from learners.

On the other hand, LLM-Standalone approaches propose a more autonomous solution, where the LLM itself drives the entire knowledge tracing process without reliance on traditional KT models. This approach offers the potential for a unified, prompt-driven solution capable of independently extracting both semantic and predictive signals from learner data. However, the scalability of this approach is limited when dealing with complex, nuanced, or domain-specific content. As such, LLM-Standalone models may work well in well-defined domains with clear, structured input but struggle in environments where content is more ambiguous or not sufficiently predefined.

Despite the promise of these approaches, there is a clear lack of standardized benchmark datasets tailored to LLM-based KT. The scattered nature of existing datasets across various domains complicates direct comparisons of model performance. The development of domain-specific benchmarks is crucial not only for evaluating the effectiveness of LLM-based solutions but also for enabling fair, consistent comparisons between different LLM-KT models. These benchmarks should also include fixed performance metrics to ensure the reliability and reproducibility of results, offering a foundation for further research and refinement.

The ambiguity surrounding the roles of LLMs in some hybrid systems further complicates the landscape. In cases where LLMs serve dual roles—both enhancing feature extraction and directly updating knowledge states—there is potential overlap between the categories of LLM-Enhanced and LLM-Integrated models. This gray area suggests the need for more fine-grained sub-classifications as the field matures, allowing for a more precise understanding of how LLMs can be utilized in different KT contexts.

Looking forward, further research is needed to empirically test the effectiveness of each category under controlled experimental conditions. Standardized experiments could assess the relative contributions of LLM-driven features versus traditional KT representations, thereby clarifying when LLM-Enhanced methods are sufficient and when more integrated or standalone approaches are warranted. Additionally, exploring the compatibility of different LLM architectures, such as GPT-based systems versus other model classes, could yield insights into the optimal use of LLMs in real-time feedback loops and structured item-response data. By situating these investigations within the taxonomy framework, researchers can gain a deeper understanding of how LLMs can be best integrated into KT systems, ultimately leading to the advancement of intelligent tutoring technologies.

5 Conclusion

Each of the three approaches to LLM-based Knowledge Tracing presents distinct benefits and challenges. The LLM-Enhanced model excels in augmenting existing systems by incorporating richer semantic features, improving the overall prediction accuracy of traditional KT methods. On the other hand, the LLM-Integrated model introduces a higher level of adaptability by enabling dynamic updates to learners' knowledge states, making it well-suited for interactive environments that require constant feedback. However, its reliance on continuous data inputs also introduces potential vulnerabilities, particularly in noisy or unbalanced learning contexts. Meanwhile, the LLM-Standalone approach offers a more simplified, autonomous solution that reduces the dependency on traditional KT systems. Despite its potential for scalability and real-time predictions, it faces limitations when applied to complex or undefined content areas.

To fully harness the potential of LLMs in educational contexts, future research must address several key challenges. Optimizing computational efficiency will be crucial, particularly for real-time systems that need to handle large volumes of dynamic data. Additionally, improving model interpretability will help bridge the gap between the complex inner workings of LLMs and the practical needs of educators and learners. Finally, ensuring the reliability and scalability of LLM-based KT models will be vital for their widespread adoption and effectiveness across diverse educational environments. By tackling these challenges, future work can unlock the full promise of LLMs, advancing the field of intelligent tutoring systems and personalized learning.

References

1. Cao, Y., et al.: Survey on large language model-enhanced reinforcement learning: concept, taxonomy, and methods. IEEE Trans. Neural Netw. Learn. Syst., 1–21 (2024). https://doi.org/10.1109/tnnls.2024.3497992. http://dx.doi.org/10.1109/TNNLS.2024.3497992
2. Chowdhery, A., et al.: PaLM: scaling language modeling with pathways. J. Mach. Learn. Res. **24**(240), 1–113 (2023)
3. Duan, Z., Fernandez, N., Hicks, A., Lan, A.: Test case-informed knowledge tracing for open-ended coding tasks. In: Proceedings of the 15th International Learning Analytics and Knowledge Conference, pp. 238–248 (2025)
4. Feng, Z., et al.: Trends in integration of knowledge and large language models: a survey and taxonomy of methods, benchmarks, and applications (2024). https://arxiv.org/abs/2311.05876
5. Fu, L., et al.: SINKT: a structure-aware inductive knowledge tracing model with large language model. In: Proceedings of the 33rd ACM International Conference on Information and Knowledge Management, pp. 632–642 (2024)
6. Guo, Y., et al.: Mitigating cold-start problems in knowledge tracing with large language models: an attribute-aware approach. In: Proceedings of the 33rd ACM International Conference on Information and Knowledge Management, pp. 727–736 (2024)
7. Han, Z., Gao, C., Liu, J., Zhang, J., Zhang, S.Q.: Parameter-efficient fine-tuning for large models: a comprehensive survey. arXiv preprint arXiv:2403.14608 (2024)
8. Hasan, S.M.: Multidimensional human activity recognition with large language model: a conceptual framework. arXiv preprint arXiv:2410.03546 (2024)
9. Jin, H., Huang, L., Cai, H., Yan, J., Li, B., Chen, H.: From LLMs to LLM-based agents for software engineering: a survey of current, challenges and future (2024). https://arxiv.org/abs/2408.02479
10. Jin, M., et al.: Time-LLM: time series forecasting by reprogramming large language models. arXiv preprint arXiv:2310.01728 (2023)
11. Jung, H., Yoo, J., Yoon, Y., Jang, Y.: CLST: cold-start mitigation in knowledge tracing by aligning a generative language model as a students' knowledge tracer. arXiv preprint arXiv:2406.10296 (2024)

12. Jyothy, S.N., Kolil, V.K., Raman, R., Achuthan, K.: Exploring large language models as an integrated tool for learning, teaching, and research through the fogg behavior model: a comprehensive mixed-methods analysis. Cogent Eng. **11**(1) (2024)
13. Kim, J., Chu, S., Wong, B., Yi, M.: Beyond right and wrong: mitigating cold start in knowledge tracing using large language model and option weight. arXiv preprint arXiv:2410.12872 (2024)
14. Lee, U., et al.: From prediction to application: language model-based code knowledge tracing with domain adaptive pre-training and automatic feedback system with pedagogical prompting for comprehensive programming education. arXiv preprint arXiv:2409.00323 (2024)
15. Lee, U., et al.: Language model can do knowledge tracing: simple but effective method to integrate language model and knowledge tracing task. arXiv preprint arXiv:2406.02893 (2024)
16. Lee, U., et al.: Difficulty-focused contrastive learning for knowledge tracing with a large language model-based difficulty prediction. arXiv preprint arXiv:2312.11890 (2023)
17. Li, H., et al.: Explainable few-shot knowledge tracing. arXiv preprint arXiv:2405.14391 (2024)
18. Li, Z., et al.: TutorLLM: customizing learning recommendations with knowledge tracing and retrieval-augmented generation. arXiv preprint arXiv:2502.15709 (2025)
19. Liang, Z., Yu, W., Rajpurohit, T., Clark, P., Zhang, X., Kaylan, A.: Let GPT be a math tutor: Teaching math word problem solvers with customized exercise generation. arXiv preprint arXiv:2305.14386 (2023)
20. Liu, N., Wang, Z., Baraniuk, R., Lan, A.: Open-ended knowledge tracing for computer science education. In: Proceedings of the 2022 Conference on Empirical Methods in Natural Language Processing (2022)
21. Liu, Q., Shen, S., Huang, Z., Chen, E., Zheng, Y.: A survey of knowledge tracing. arXiv preprint arXiv:2105.15106 (2021)
22. Liu, Z.: XES3G5M: a knowledge tracing benchmark dataset with auxiliary information. Adv. Neural. Inf. Process. Syst. **36**, 32958–32970 (2023)
23. Long, T., et al.: Automatical graph-based knowledge tracing. In: EDM (2022)
24. Makharia, R., et al.: AI tutor enhanced with prompt engineering and deep knowledge tracing. In: 2024 IEEE International Conference on Interdisciplinary Approaches in Technology and Management for Social Innovation (IATMSI), vol. 2, pp. 1–6. IEEE (2024)
25. Mirchandani, S., et al.: Large language models as general pattern machines. arXiv preprint arXiv:2307.04721 (2023)
26. Moon, H., Davis, R., Neshaei, S.P., Dillenbourg, P.: Using large multimodal models to extract knowledge components for knowledge tracing from multimedia question information. arXiv preprint arXiv:2409.20167 (2024)
27. Neshaei, S.P., Davis, R.L., Hazimeh, A., Lazarevski, B., Dillenbourg, P., Käser, T.: Towards modeling learner performance with large language models. arXiv preprint arXiv:2403.14661 (2024)
28. Ni, L., et al.: Enhancing student performance prediction on learner sourced questions with SGNN-LLM synergy. In: Proceedings of the AAAI Conference on Artificial Intelligence, vol. 38, pp. 23232–23240 (2024)
29. Ozyurt, Y., Feuerriegel, S., Sachan, M.: Automated knowledge concept annotation and question representation learning for knowledge tracing. arXiv preprint arXiv:2410.01727 (2024)

30. Pandey, S., Karypis, G.: A self-attentive model for knowledge tracing. arXiv preprint arXiv:1907.06837 (2019)
31. Piech, C., et al.: Deep knowledge tracing. In: Advances in Neural Information Processing Systems, vol. 28 (2015)
32. Pternea, M., et al.: The RL/LLM taxonomy tree: Reviewing synergies between reinforcement learning and large language models. J. Artif. Intell. Res. **80**, 1525–1573 (2024). https://doi.org/10.1613/jair.1.15960. http://dx.doi.org/10.1613/jair.1.15960
33. Qu, G., Chen, Q., Wei, W., Lin, Z., Chen, X., Huang, K.: Mobile edge intelligence for large language models: a contemporary survey (2024). https://arxiv.org/abs/2407.18921
34. Salomons, N., Scassellati, B.: Time-dependant Bayesian knowledge tracing–robots that model user skills over time. Front. Robot. AI **10** (2024)
35. Scarlatos, A., Baker, R.S., Lan, A.: Exploring knowledge tracing in tutor-student dialogues using LLMs. In: Proceedings of the 15th International Learning Analytics and Knowledge Conference, pp. 249–259 (2025)
36. Shen, S., et al.: A survey of knowledge tracing: models, variants, and applications. IEEE Trans. Learn. Technol. (2024)
37. Wang, C., Sahebi, S.: Continuous personalized knowledge tracing: modeling long-term learning in online environments. In: Proceedings of the 32nd ACM International Conference on Information and Knowledge Management, pp. 2616–2625 (2023)
38. Wang, D., Zhang, L., Zhao, Y., Zhang, Y., Yan, S., Hou, M.: Deep knowledge tracking integrating programming exercise difficulty and forgetting factors. In: International Conference on Intelligent Computing, pp. 192–203. Springer (2024)
39. Wang, Z., et al.: LLM-KT: aligning large language models with knowledge tracing using a plug-and-play instruction. arXiv preprint arXiv:2502.02945 (2025)
40. Weber, I.: Large language models as software components: a taxonomy for LLM-integrated applications (2024). https://arxiv.org/abs/2406.10300
41. Xi, Z., et al.: The rise and potential of large language model based agents: a survey (2023). https://arxiv.org/abs/2309.07864
42. Xia, J., Wang, H., Zhuge, Q., Sha, E.: Knowledge tracing model and student profile based on clustering-neural-network. Appl. Sci. **13**(9), 5220 (2023)
43. Yu, Y., Zhou, Y., Zhu, Y., Ye, Y., Chen, L., Chen, M.: ECKT: enhancing code knowledge tracing via large language models. In: Proceedings of the Annual Meeting of the Cognitive Science Society, vol. 46 (2024)
44. Zanellati, A., Di Mitri, D., Gabbrielli, M., Levrini, O.: Hybrid models for knowledge tracing: a systematic literature review. IEEE Trans. Learn. Technol. (2024)
45. Zhan, B., et al.: Knowledge tracing as language processing: a large-scale autoregressive paradigm. In: International Conference on Artificial Intelligence in Education, pp. 177–191. Springer (2024)
46. Zhang, L., et al.: Predicting learning performance with large language models: a study in adult literacy. In: International Conference on Human-Computer Interaction, pp. 333–353. Springer (2024)
47. Zhang, Q., et al.: A survey on large language models for software engineering (2024). https://arxiv.org/abs/2312.15223
48. Zhao, W.X., et al.: A survey of large language models. arXiv preprint arXiv:2303.18223 (2023)

Improving Feedback Generation in a Drawing-Based ITS

Islam Barchouch[1(✉)], Nathalie Girard[2], Eric Anquetil[1], Laura Leconte[3], and Eric Jamet[3]

[1] Univ Rennes, INSA Rennes, CNRS, IRISA - UMR 6074, 35000 Rennes, France
{islam.barchouch,eric.anquetil}@irisa.fr
[2] Univ Rennes, CNRS, IRISA - UMR 6074, 35000 Rennes, France
nathalie.girard@irisa.fr
[3] Univ Rennes, CNRS, LP3C, 35000 Rennes, France
{laura.leconte,eric.jamet}@univ-rennes2.fr

Abstract. This paper presents a significant extension of the architecture of IntuiSketch, an Intelligent Tutoring System (ITS), conceived to help students learn in the field of anatomy. This ITS is specifically developed to support learning by drawing using pen-based tablets by analyzing semi-structured sketches on the fly and providing real-time feedback to students. The original system, conceived to process structured drawings, was improved to handle semi-structured sketches based on new recognition and supervision engines.

The proposed improvement consists in defining a flexible recognition engine by introducing different types of constraints into the Context-Driven Constraint Multiset Grammar (CD-CMG) formalism. The idea is to categorize constraints into primary and secondary constraints: primary constraints ensure essential accuracy by suspending the recognition process until critical errors have been corrected, while secondary constraints allow minor inaccuracies so that students can continue working without interruption. Based on these new categories of constraints we propose to adapt the production of feedback, i.e. depending on the type of unsatisfied constraints, feedback will be produced in real-time and/or deferred to better adapt to individual learning needs.

The system is evaluated on a database of student-drawn anatomical sketches, measuring both recognition accuracy and the relevance of immediate and deferred feedback.

Keywords: ITS · Constraint-Based Tutors · Real-Time and Deferred Feedback · Online Sketch Recognition · Generative Drawing

1 Introduction

Active learning strategies, such as drawing, are particularly effective, especially in complex learning contexts such as anatomy [1]. Many studies show that students perceive this approach positively, and that it seems to stimulate their motivation [1,2]. Drawing is also a strategy that has been widely studied in cognitive psychology, demonstrating beneficial effects on learning. Cognitive processes mobilized by learners when creating a drawing involve selecting and organizing relevant information, as well as active retrieval of knowledge, thereby promoting effective memory consolidation and enhancing conceptual understanding [3,4]. Although early studies involving mouse-based interaction showed no overall effect of drawing on learning [5], more recent studies based on drawing with pen-based tablets have shown positive effects [6], particularly when learners benefit from support during the learning process [7]. Yet anatomy education is particularly advanced in the integration of digital technologies [7], and these tools offer considerable advantages by allowing environments to be personalized and learning to be adaptive. Digital supports, such as pen-based tablets, replicate traditional paper-and-pencil drawing experience with interactive advantages [8,9]. These devices encourage greater flexibility and can be adapted to the individual needs of learners. In addition, intelligent tutorial systems (ITS) have shown benefits for learning by offering personalized support and feedback adapted to the difficulties encountered by students. Integrating drawing into these interactive environments could therefore offer a new approach combining active engagement, interactivity and adaptability. ITS that enable students to draw figures on pen-based tablets already exist. As an example IntuiGeo is an ITS developed to learn geometry by drawing. It is based on the CD-CMG formalism [13] to interpret structured geometric sketches on the fly by applying spatial and geometric constraints [14]. This allows it to accurately analyze sketches and provide real-time feedback, helping students to develop fundamental geometry skills in an interactive learning environment.

Inspired by IntuiGeo's architecture [14], we aimed to address a new challenge: developing an ITS adapted to semi-structured sketches, named IntuiSketch. It allows students to draw anatomical sketches on pen-based tablets (Fig. 1a) and receive real-time feedback in student mode based on their progress when they are completing an exercise, created by the teacher in author mode, step by step (Fig. 1b). Unlike geometric drawings, anatomical drawings present a unique challenge due to their semi-structured nature. They cannot be interpreted using geometric and spatial constraints only, and often include complex shapes and spatial relationships between elements. Consequently, a high degree of freedom is allowed in the drawing process, making real-time recognition and feedback generation more difficult than in well-defined domains such as geometry.

Initial work on IntuiSketch focused on adapting the CD-CMG formalism to accurately recognize semi-structured sketches on the fly and developing an ITS capable of generating real-time feedback based on student progress. IntuiSketch operates through two main engines: recognition and supervision engines (See blocks highlighted in grey in Fig. 3). The recognition engine combines the CD-CMG formalism [13] with an incremental classifier [15] and fuzzy logic [16] to interpret semi-structured sketches on the fly using domain-specific knowledge encoded in CD-CMG rules with shape, geometric, and spatial constraints. Meanwhile, the supervision engine, based on a constraint-based model [17], evaluates student sketches using a Knowledge Graph (KG) that represents the teacher's solution and provides corrective, real-time feedback tailored to learning progress.

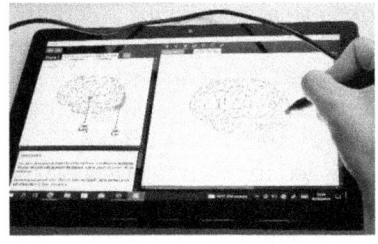

(a) Pen-based tablets

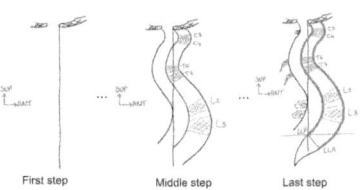

(b) An anatomy exercise created step by step (Ex. a spine exercise)

Fig. 1. Using pen-based tablets to create and solve anatomy exercises step by step

One of the challenges IntuiSketch faces is the rigidity of the CD-CMG formalism, which applies its constraints equally, despite the severity of errors made by students during the drawing process. Moreover, while the positive effect of feedback on learning is widely recognized in the scientific literature [10], there are conflicting results on the most effective timing for feedback (i.e. during or after the task) [11,12]. Indeed, while immediate feedback may help correct errors quickly, it can also interrupt the task and increase cognitive load. To address this challenge, we propose to extend the CD-CMG formalism by introducing two-level constraints that control the interpretation of sketches on the fly. The first level, known as primary constraints, focuses on the essential structural context and spatial relationships required for basic recognition of sketches. The second level, secondary constraints, is used to evaluate the more refined aspects of the drawings and to provide detailed qualitative feedback. By making this fundamental distinction between constraints, we want the system to provide immediate feedback when primary constraints are not satisfied, ensuring that major errors are immediately corrected, and deferred feedback when secondary constraints are not satisfied, providing more granular feedback to refine the drawing. This avoids interrupting the drawing process too often and allows the student to stay focused while receiving feedback at appropriate time intervals.

The rest of the paper details related work (Sect. 2), IntuiSketch's existing architecture and its limitations (Sect. 3), the proposed contributions (Sect. 4), experimental evaluation (Sect. 5), and conclusion (Sect. 6).

2 Related Work

ITS based on learning by drawing have progressed considerably in recent years, addressing challenges from well-structured sketches to complex semi-structured drawings [14,18]. This section explores the tutoring and recognition approaches used to address these challenges.

2.1 ITS Overview

ITS are computer-based pedagogical tools conceived to mimic certain functions of a human tutor by providing personalized feedback and helping students to learn independently [19,20]. Initially, these systems were principally rule-based, with each student action compared against predefined rules. Although effective for rigid domains, they were limited when confronted with diverse or unpredictable learning paths [19,21,22]. To address these limitations, constraint-based tutoring (CBT) has been developed, a more flexible system where valid solutions are defined by essential constraints that can be satisfied in multiple ways [23,24]. This adaptability is particularly beneficial for semi-structured tasks, where students can draw or solve problems in different ways. Example-based tutors [25,26] have also been developed to map student steps to a variety of possible solutions, but enumerating all solution paths can be challenging. Data-driven ITS and machine learning [27,28] use large datasets to provide adaptive feedback for a variety of learning styles, but they often require extensive annotated data and are not always adapted to online sketch recognition. Since IntuiSketch aims to interpret semi-structured sketches on the fly, the constraint-based ITS approach seems to be the most suitable, allowing flexibility while ensuring accuracy. IntuiGeo [14], uses this approach for structured drawings, and we therefore take inspiration from it for semi-structured anatomy drawings.

2.2 Handwriting Recognition Approaches Overview

Handwriting recognition approaches are generally divided into statistical and structural approaches [29]. Statistical approaches including Hidden Markov Models (HMMs) [30], Gaussian Mixture Models (GMMs) [31] and Dynamic Time Warping (DTW) [32] have been widely implemented for handwriting recognition, particularly for tasks requiring sequence analysis or probability distributions of shape features. Convolutional neural networks (CNNs) often perform well when large amounts of data are available [33]. However, these approaches struggle to generate contextual real-time feedback, as they tend to behave like "black boxes", complicating eager interpretation in educational contexts. Structural approaches focus on the spatial and geometric relationships between drawn elements [14,30,34]. They are suitable for well-defined domains as in geometry, but their rigid application can fail when shapes are complex and vary considerably. Graph-based models [35] also rely on predefined relationships, which poses problems for highly variable drawings. Consequently, hybrid approaches combining statistical shape recognition with structural modeling have been more successful, accommodating both shape variability and strict domain relationships [36].

Using a hybrid recognition approach combined with a constraint-based tutoring model, IntuiSketch can analyze each stroke on the fly, checking whether domain constraints are satisfied and providing corrective feedback if they are not. This maintains the flexibility required to recognize a wide range of complex shapes, while preserving the consistency essential for learning anatomy.

3 Architecture of the Existing IntuiSketch System

In this section, we describe the existing architecture of IntuiSketch, based on two engines: a recognition engine, using CD-CMG to recognize semi-structured sketches on the fly, and a supervision engine, generating a Knowledge Graph (KG) to provide real-time corrective feedback. These engines operate together in the system's two modes: author mode, which allows teachers to create exercises, and student mode, which allows students to solve predefined exercises while receiving feedback in real time (See blocks highlighted in grey in Fig. 3).

3.1 Recognition Engine

IntuiSketch's recognition engine uses the CD-CMG formalism [13] combined with an incremental classifier [15] that learns from few examples and fuzzy logic [16] to represent domain-specific knowledge. CD-CMG is composed of production rules used to interpret strokes based on spatial, geometric, and shape constraints. The production rules can be divided into three stages: preconditions, constraints and postconditions (See blocks highlighted in grey in Fig. 2). Each stage helps the system to determine if a new stroke can be recognized, and how the following elements should be interpreted according to the evolving context of the document. Firstly, the preconditions provide the global vision required for the application of a rule. They model the spatial relationships and relative positions of elements using fuzzy logic [16]. Secondly, the constraints block defines shape and geometric properties that are locally applied and must be respected by the element in the drawing. In IntuiGeo [14], constraints were rigorous, requiring precise adherence to geometric properties. In IntuiSketch, they allow flexibility to accommodate the variability of semi-structured drawings, which require a shape classifier such as Evolve. Students usually follow the teacher's step-by-step exercise, drawing elements one by one. To accommodate different drawing behaviors, the system can enforce a specific order when elements are geometrically related, but allows flexibility otherwise. Finally, postconditions determine how the system should treat the following elements of the drawing after the constraints have been satisfied. They update the overall context of the document by indicating which new elements can now be added and interpreted based on the recognized elements.

However, a key challenge is handling student errors when drawing. Even minor errors can lead to recognition failures, as constraints may not be satisfied despite the system's flexibility (See contributions in Sect. 4).

3.2 Supervision Engine

The supervision engine generates feedback based on KG, which represents domain knowledge extracted from CD-CMG rules modeled using expert tutorials.

The KG is central to IntuiSketch's ability to evaluate and interpret the student's drawing. The process begins when the student loads the exercise, previously recognized using the CD-CMG formalism to generate the KG. In this graph, each node corresponds to a recognized element of the teacher's solution, while the edges encode the constraints between these elements. These constraints reflect CD-CMG rules, capturing shape, geometric, and spatial relationships in a structured form. Once created, the KG serves as a benchmark to compare the student's drawing with the teacher's solution. While the student is drawing, the system evaluates each stroke by trying to match it to a node in the KG. If a stroke matches a node, the system checks its associated constraints. If the student's drawing does not respect any of these constraints, the system generates immediate feedback to inform the student of the specific error and highlights the areas where the student's drawing does not match the expected solution.

In the existing model, all constraint violations are treated equally, which means that the system generates immediate feedback for every error, whatever its severity. However, the errors made by the students themselves can vary considerably in terms of severity, which is why IntuiSketch's supervision engine, based on the KG, needs to be adapted to take this into account, in order to avoid interrupting the student's work excessively.

4 Contributions

To address the severity of students' errors and adapt the system to correctly recognize strokes and provide feedback at the appropriate time, we propose two contributions: (1) the extension of the CD-CMG formalism to improve the flexibility of the recognition engine by categorizing constraints, and (2) a new feedback mechanism that differentiates feedback into immediate and deferred feedback. These contributions improve IntuiSketch's robustness and ensure adaptability to various learning scenarios.

4.1 Extension of CD-CMG: Primary and Secondary Constraints

To improve IntuiSketch's recognition flexibility, we extended CD-CMG by introducing constraint-level validation into its rules, defining two levels: **primary and secondary constraints** (See red constraints blocks in Fig. 2).

The introduction of primary and secondary operators in the grammar changes the way rules are addressed, allowing a more tailored treatment of constraints depending on the severity of student errors. These operators are manually added to CD-CMG rules by the developer, based on information provided by the domain expert. They are implemented as attributes integrated into the constraints and restrict recognition to primary constraints only. During constraint verification, CD-CMG evaluates each label: if a constraint is labeled as primary, standard behavior is applied, ensuring that the constraint is strictly validated to maintain the essential context and accuracy required for recognition. However, if a constraint is labeled as secondary, it is excluded from the recognition process and considered only for deferred feedback either at the end of a particular step in the exercise, or upon the student's request for more details on how to improve their drawing, allowing the system to proceed despite minor inaccuracies.

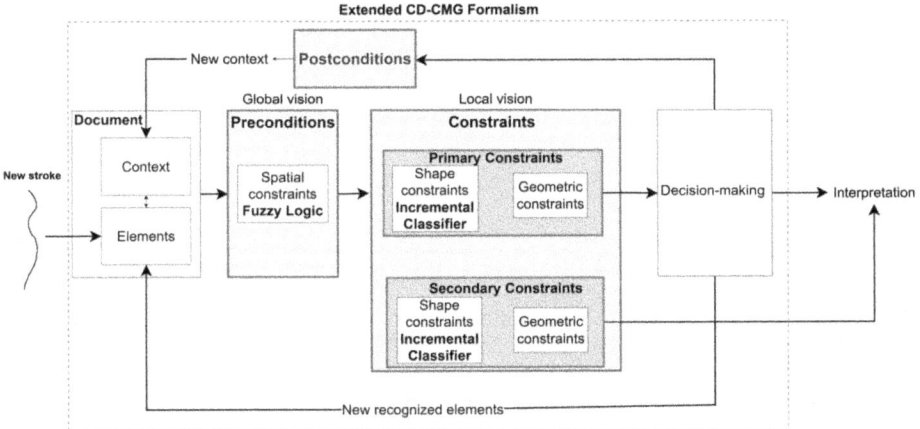

Fig. 2. Extended CD-CMG formalism using primary and secondary constraints (Color figure online)

This extension enhances the system's flexibility to handle errors while preserving recognition accuracy. Both operators contribute to the generation of a more informative KG, which is then used to generate feedback based on the type of unsatisfied constraints and the student's error.

4.2 Categorization of Feedback: Immediate and Deferred Feedback

Categorized constraints in the extended KG improve feedback generation in IntuiSketch. Primary and secondary constraints enable the system to differentiate between **immediate and deferred feedback**, ensuring a more tailored learning experience. If a student does not respect a primary constraint, this would indicates a significant problem in the drawing. In this case, the system generates immediate feedback, alerting the students to the error and inciting them to correct it. This ensures that critical errors are corrected early, avoiding the propagation of errors to subsequent elements. Secondary constraints, on the other hand, allow minor deviations without preventing recognition. When these constraints are not respected, the system provides deferred feedback. As shown in Fig. 4, feedback is provided both through textual instructions and visual overlays on the student's drawing, making corrections more intuitive.

In conclusion, constraint categorization has been integrated into IntuiSketch, directly impacting recognition and feedback. As illustrated in red in Fig. 3, what distinguishes the extended architecture is the interaction with the supervision engine, which manages constraint categorization. When a new stroke is recognized, the supervision engine checks both structural aspects and whether the relevant constraints are primary or secondary. The key innovation lies in the system's ability to identify the type of constraint that is not respected and adjust the feedback process accordingly, ensuring a smoother learning experience with minimal disruptions when providing feedback.

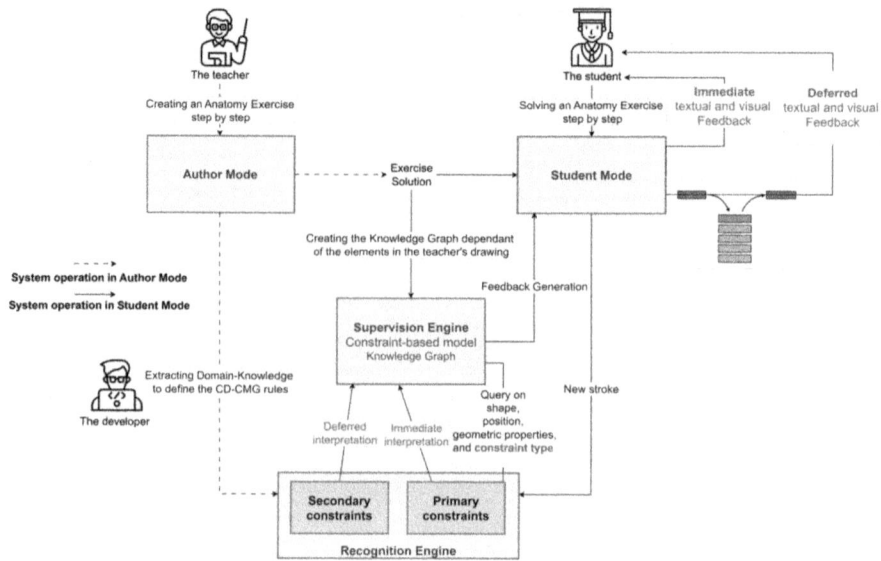

Fig. 3. The extended architecture of IntuiSketch

5 Results

We developed a test protocol to evaluate recognition and feedback accuracy based on student realizations, covering the entire process from data collection to evaluation. We focus on the "Spine Exercise", created in collaboration with anatomy experts to test students' ability to draw anatomical elements step by step, guided by the exercise instructions. Each student's participation is recorded in real time and strokes are collected using pen-based tablets (Fig. 4).

Once students have completed the exercise, their drawings are saved and serve as the raw data for the next evaluation stages. We define a ground truth file for each student's realization based on evaluation grids completed by domain experts. This process enables evaluation of both recognition accuracy (whether the system correctly identifies anatomical elements) and feedback efficiency (whether it generates appropriate guidance according to the student's errors).

To assess IntuiSketch's performance, we report Recognition and Feedback metrics: Precision ($\frac{TP}{TP+FP}$), Recall ($\frac{TP}{TP+FN}$), and Error Rate ($\frac{FP+FN}{TP+TN+FP+FN}$). Table 1 reports results from **10 student realizations**, with **466 strokes** and **463 feedback** (345 positive, 63 immediate and 55 deferred).

Table 1 shows that the system achieves high performance, with a recognition precision of 0.993 and recall of 0.931, confirming its ability to identify anatomical elements with minimal omissions. A feedback precision of 0.897 and recall of 0.926 indicate effective error detection and relevant guidance. Among the 463 feedback, 55 (12%) concerned secondary constraints, allowing the system to avoid

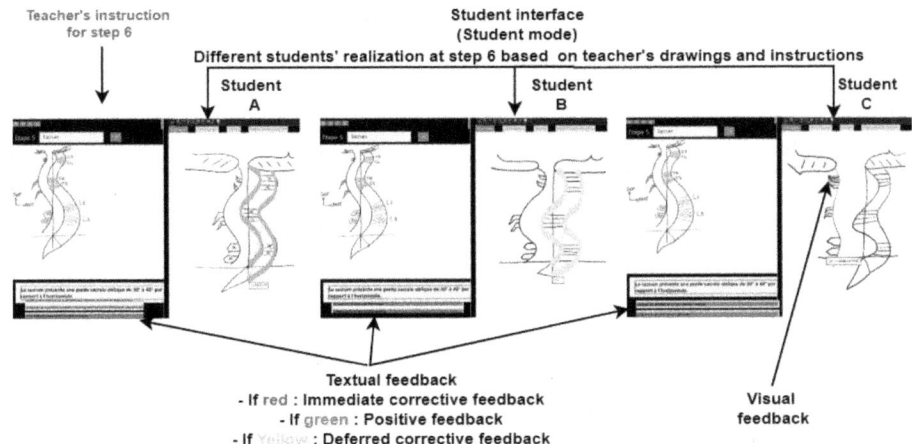

Fig. 4. Examples of students' drawings with immediate or deferred feedback at step 6

frequent interruptions of the student's work and to defer feedback until step completion or student request, without interrupting the recognition process.

Table 1. Performance Metrics for System Evaluation

Metrics	Precision	Recall	Error Rate
Recognition	0.993	0.931	0.074
Feedback	0.897	0.926	0.156

6 Conclusion and Future Work

This paper presented key improvements to IntuiSketch, a pen-based ITS conceived to recognize semi-structured sketches on the fly and provide corrective feedback. Using the CD-CMG formalism, the system interprets sketches with complex shapes and spatial relationships. Although CD-CMG is effective, student errors sometimes block recognition due to unsatisfied constraints, even if the sketch remains structurally valid, and generate excessive feedback that interrupts the student's work. To address this, we extended CD-CMG to distinguish major and minor errors, providing deferred feedback for minor errors and reserving immediate feedback for major errors. These improvements reduce interruptions and enhance learning by providing feedback at the right time.

Based on tests elaborated with domain experts, results demonstrated that IntuiSketch provides effective feedback and improves the recognition of semi-structured sketches. The system performed well on complex anatomical sketches, proving its potential in anatomy education.

Future work includes testing IntuiSketch in university lectures, extending our approach to other anatomy exercises, expanding our dataset with new exercises and student realizations, and making it available to the research community.

Acknowledgments. This work was supported by ANR under Project number 21-CE38-0009. We extend our gratitude to our collaborators and the domain experts from IFSI and IFPEK for their essential assistance.

References

1. Peart, D.J.: Hand drawing as a tool to facilitate understanding in undergraduate human biology: a critical review of the literature and future perspectives. Stud. Sci. Educ. **58**, 81–93 (2022)
2. Borrelli, M., Leung, B., Morgan, M., Saxena, S., Hunter, A.: Should drawing be incorporated into the teaching of anatomy? J. Contemp. Med. Educ. **1** (2018)
3. Fiorella, L., Zhang, Q.: Drawing boundary conditions for learning by drawing. Educ. Psychol. Rev. **30**, 1115–1137 (2018)
4. Van Meter, P., Firetto, C.: Cognitive model of drawing construction. In: Learning and Visual Displays, pp. 247–280 (2013)
5. Cromley, J.G., Du, Y., Dane, A.P.: Drawing-to-learn: does meta-analysis show differences between technology-based drawing and paper-and-pencil drawing? J. Sci. Educ. Technol. **29**, 216–229 (2020)
6. Styn, A., et al.: Effects of tablet-based drawing and paper-based methods on medical students' learning of gross anatomy. Anat. Sci. Educ. **16**, 266–279 (2023)
7. Jamet, E., Michinov, E.: Effects of verbal and visual support on learning by tablet-based drawing. Comput. Educ. **181**, 104460 (2022)
8. Clunie, L., Morris, N.P., Joynes, V., Pickering, J.D.: How comprehensive are research studies investigating the efficacy of technology-enhanced learning resources in anatomy education? A systematic review. Anat. Sci. Educ. **11**, 303–319 (2018)
9. Haßler, B., Major, L., Hennessy, S.: Tablet use in schools: a critical review of the evidence for learning outcomes. J. Comput. Assist. Learn. **32**, 139–156 (2016)
10. Mousavinasab, E., Zarifsanaiey, N., Niakan Kalhori, S.R., Rakhshan, M., Keikha, L., Ghazi Saeedi, M.: Intelligent tutoring systems: a systematic review of characteristics, applications, and evaluation methods. Interact. Learn. Environ. **29**, 142–163 (2021)
11. Wisniewski, B., Zierer, K., Hattie, J.: The power of feedback revisited: a meta-analysis of educational feedback research. Front. Psychol. **10**, 3087 (2020)
12. Shute, V.J.: Focus on formative feedback. Rev. Educ. Res. **78**, 153–189 (2008)
13. Macé, S., Anquetil, E.: Eager interpretation of on-line hand-drawn structured documents: the DALI methodology. Pattern Recogn. **42**(12), 3202–3214 (2009)
14. Krichen, O., Anquetil, E., Girard, N.: IntuiGeo: interactive tutor for online geometry problems resolution on pen-based tablets. In: ECAI 2020, pp. 1842–1849. IOS Press (2020)
15. Almaksour, A., Anquetil, E.: Improving premise structure in evolving Takagi-Sugeno neuro-fuzzy classifiers. Evol. Syst. **2**, 25–33 (2011)
16. Zadeh, L.A.: Fuzzy sets. Inf. Control (1965)

17. Ohlsson, S.: Constraint-based student modeling. In: Student Modelling: The Key to Individualized Knowledge-Based Instruction, pp. 167–189. Springer (1994)
18. Williford, B., Runyon, M., Li, W., Linsey, J., Hammond, T.: Exploring the potential of an intelligent tutoring system for sketching fundamentals. In: Proceedings of the 2020 CHI Conference on Human Factors in Computing Systems, pp. 1–13 (2020)
19. Carbonell, J.R.: AI in CAI: an artificial-intelligence approach to computer-assisted instruction. IEEE Trans. Man-Mach. Syst. **11**(4), 190–202 (1970)
20. Farr, M.J., Psotka, J.: Intelligent Instruction Computer: Theory and Practice. Routledge (2013)
21. Ashley, M.I.K.D., Chan, T.-W.: Intelligent Tutoring Systems. Springer (1982)
22. Noh, N.M., Ahmad, A., Halim, S.A., Ali, A.M.: Intelligent tutoring system using rule-based and case-based: a comparison. Procedia Soc. Behav. Sci. **67**, 454–463 (2012)
23. Mitrovic, A.: Fifteen years of constraint-based tutors: what we have achieved and where we are going. User Model. User-Adap. Inter. **22**, 39–72 (2012)
24. Karaci, A.: Intelligent tutoring system model based on fuzzy logic and constraint-based student model. Neural Comput. Appl. **31**(8), 3619–3628 (2019)
25. Davidovic, A., Warren, J., Trichina, E.: Learning benefits of structural example-based adaptive tutoring systems. IEEE Trans. Educ. **46**(2), 241–251 (2003)
26. Aleven, V., McLaren, B.M., Sewall, J., Koedinger, K.R.: A new paradigm for intelligent tutoring systems: example-tracing tutors. Int. J. Artif. Intell. Educ. **19**(2), 105–154 (2009)
27. Kochmar, E., Vu, D.D., Belfer, R., Gupta, V., Serban, I.V., Pineau, J.: Automated data-driven generation of personalized pedagogical interventions in intelligent tutoring systems. Int. J. Artif. Intell. Educ. **32**(2), 323–349 (2022)
28. Chang, M., D'Aniello, G., Gaeta, M., Orciuoli, F., Sampson, D., Simonelli, C.: Building ontology-driven tutoring models for intelligent tutoring systems using data mining. IEEE Access **8**, 48151–48162 (2020)
29. Agrawal, V., Jagtap, J., Kantipudi, M.V.V.P.: An overview of hand-drawn diagram recognition methods and applications. IEEE Access (2024)
30. Sezgin, T.M., Davis, R.: HMM-based efficient sketch recognition. In: Proceedings of the 10th International Conference on Intelligent User Interfaces, pp. 281–283 (2005)
31. Al-Habian, G., Assaleh, K.: Online Arabic handwriting recognition using continuous Gaussian mixture HMMs. In: 2007 International Conference on Intelligent and Advanced Systems, pp. 1183–1186. IEEE (2007)
32. Hsu, Y.-L., Chu, C.-L., Tsai, Y.-J., Wang, J.-S.: An inertial pen with dynamic time warping recognizer for handwriting and gesture recognition. IEEE Sens. J. **15**(1), 154–163 (2014)
33. Li, L., Zou, C., Zheng, Y., Su, Q., Fu, H., Tai, C.-L.: Sketch-R2CNN: an RNN-rasterization-CNN architecture for vector sketch recognition. IEEE Trans. Visual Comput. Graphics **27**(9), 3745–3754 (2020)
34. Delaye, A.: Structured prediction models for online sketch recognition. Interpretation **1**(3), 4–16 (2014)
35. Lee, W., Kara, L.B., Stahovich, T.F.: An efficient graph-based recognizer for hand-drawn symbols. Comput. Graph. **31**(4), 554–567 (2007)
36. Alvarado, C., Davis, R.: SketchREAD: a multi-domain sketch recognition engine. In: ACM SIGGRAPH 2007 Courses, pp. 34–es (2007)

A Unified Ontological Approach for Modeling Domain Theory and Procedures: Applications, Issues and Prospects

Marc-Antoine Courtemanche[1](✉), Roger Nkambou[1](✉), and Psyché Valéry[2]

[1] Université du Québec à Montréal, Montréal, Canada
courtemanchem.marc-antoine@courrier.uqam.ca, nkambou.roger@uqam.ca
[2] Université TELUQ, Quebec City, Canada
valery.psyche@teluq.ca

Abstract. This paper explores the use of ontological engineering as a solution for solving complex problems in real-world applications. More specifically, ontology engineering is suggested as a unified approach to problem solving in areas where procedural knowledge is complex and dynamic. The ontological formalism enables the establishment of robust semantic relationships between declarative knowledge and procedural rules, facilitating automated reasoning processes that yield promising results for intelligent tutoring systems. To demonstrate the framework's effectiveness, we present an aeronautical case study involving the development and implementation of comprehensive task and domain ontologies for Airbus A320 piloting procedures. Furthermore, we illustrate two significant extensions of this framework: (1) its adaptation for cognitive agent development, and (2) its application in cognitive-load management during aircraft piloting tasks.

Keywords: Ontology · Task Ontology · Domain Ontology · Intelligent Tutoring Systems · Piloting procedures · Knowledge representation

1 Introduction

Ontologies have often been regarded as purely declarative structures lacking procedural expression capabilities. It is therefore not surprising that they have primarily been used to declaratively specify the conceptualization of a domain, resulting in a semantic memory of that domain. In the context of intelligent tutoring systems and artificial intelligence in education more broadly, ontologies have been employed to create a declarative model of the domain, encompassing concepts and the relationships between them, with varying levels of expressiveness depending on the domain's complexity and requirements [1,24,27,28]. In this context, the ontology is often indexed by an additional structure that supports the procedural aspects of activities, such as production rules, task graphs, or spaces defined by problem-solving constraints. This hybrid approach, which combines two distinct methodologies for modeling domain theory and procedures, limits the flexibility of indexing or linking the two, which in turn complicates the direct reasoning mechanisms on these structures. Consequently, it is often necessary to rely on intermediate structures to actively implement these relationships. An example of this is the Q-Matrix or the competency matrix, which links domain skills with tasks [2].

Our hypothesis posits that it may be possible to unify these two levels of representation by utilizing ontologies to model both domain theory and procedural memory. This approach would create a unified framework that facilitates knowledge tracking and tutoring through a strong link between domain theory and procedures.

This paper introduces such a unified framework, enabling the integration of ontologies in both their declarative and procedural dimensions. The goal is to establish a strong semantic grounding between problem-solving activities and domain theory, thus offering greater flexibility in tracking learner activities and supporting human actions during task execution.

This paper is structured as follows. In Sect. 2, we begin by defining the concept of ontology and examining its various applications in the field of informatics. Section 3 investigates the potential of ontologies for addressing complex problems, with an emphasis on their use as tools to leverage knowledge within problem spaces and facilitate solution-finding in dynamic environments. In Sect. 4, we present our unified ontological approach, where ontologies are employed to construct a reference model for aircraft piloting, integrating both domain theory and piloting procedures. This section also provides a detailed description of the architectural components, including the interpreter designed to automate the execution of scenarios within the reference model. In Sect. 5, we explore two distinct contexts where our framework was used: 1) the implementation of a cognitive agent serving as a synthetic pilot, and 2) the extension of the framework to incorporate mechanisms for evaluating cognitive load during task execution. The paper concludes with a summary of our contributions and a discussion of open research questions.

2 Ontology

Ontology, as an artifact of artificial intelligence, holds epistemological significance rooted in philosophy. Traditionally, ontology refers to the theory or conception of reality— it concerns the study of being and its representation in the world [3,23]. When applied more specifically to informatics and artificial intelligence, ontology serves as a means of declaratively representing consensual knowledge through various formal representation languages. In this context, Gruber defines ontology as "an explicit specification of a conceptualization [...] In such ontology, definitions associate the names of entities in the universe of discourse (e.g., class relations, functions, or other objects) with human-readable text describing what the names are meant to denote, and formal axioms that constrain the interpretation and well-formed use of these terms" [9]. From a problem-solving perspective, a more targeted definition is offered by Lin et al.: "Ontologies are consensus-based controlled vocabularies of terms and relations with associated definitions, which are logically formulated to promote automated reasoning" [16].

By using ontology as a representation formalism, we can declaratively decompose tasks into a highly detailed structure that closely aligns with domain theory. Task ontologies, in particular, provide a framework for representing the structure of problem-solving processes in a domain-independent manner. As defined by Mizoguchi, "Task ontology is a system of vocabulary for describing the problem-solving structure of all the existing task domain-independently. It is obtained by analyzing task structures of real-world problems. The design of the task ontology is done in order to overcome the shortcomings of generic tasks and half weak methods while preserving their basic philosophies. The ultimate goal of task ontology research includes providing vocabulary necessary and sufficient for building a model of human problem-solving processes." [22].

3 Ontology for Problem Solving

In a context of problem resolution, the ontology is a good alternative that is flexible enough to formulate highly ambiguous knowledge. Some domain has a lot of elements that have an influence on the problem-solving solution. With this perspective, Mitrovic et al. [18] see this problem solving context with procedural knowledge that has to be linked to declarative knowledge. The procedural knowledge is represented as a set of production rules specific to the problem solving. On the other hand, we have the declarative knowledge that is associated with the domain of the application. Once both knowledge are liked, production rules, as procedural knowledge, are the solution that can be applied in the problem space (declarative knowledge).

In addition to this problem solving architecture, some tracing strategies, also known as *Model Tracing* can be used to follow a real problem solving scenario by a human and compare the resolution with the one in the resolution model [18,25]. With that perspective in mind, some research has shown the possibility of using *Knowledge Tracing* for evaluating the performance of a human execution in a real-world application [14,25]. With this approach, production rules are used by the architecture to represent the resolution specified by domain theory. The rules are then compared to the real execution and different mechanisms are used to evaluate the performance of execution.

To build an architecture that is flexible enough for our need, we choose to use the ontology. Mizoguchi and Bourdeau [20] also selected ontologies for its possibility to semantically link the procedural knowledge to the declarative knowledge that is highly factual. Other production rules used to support the cognitive tutor in the perspective of problem solving [4,5]. An interesting approach has been proposed by Mizoguchi [19] where problem-solving knowledge is contained in multiple sets of rules. Those rules are called PROLOG and are then used by the intelligent tutor who has the objective of understanding the knowledge that the learner has mastered or does not mastered. A complex mechanism of inference is used to make these assertions about the state of knowledge of the learner and its evolution. This can help to make a detailed profile of a learner and its evolution of learning with effort and time. From a pedagogical perspective, the SMARTIES authoring system uses the OMNIBUS ontology, which is specific to learning scenarios [12,21]. Using the OMNIBUS ontology, the authoring system can exploit procedural knowledge about pedagogical strategies, making the authoring system *Theory aware, ch22hayashi2008structurization, ch22hayashi2009using*. Currently, many existing approaches suffer from low quality, particularly in their inability to effectively leverage the domain knowledge. By employing ontologies, we aim to address these limitations, enabling more structured and efficient use of domain theory in problem-solving systems.

Another major advantage of using ontologies is their support for interoperability. By adhering to standards such as the Web Ontology Language (OWL) [30], it becomes possible to exploit richly structured, formalized domain knowledge that is widely shared and reused. Numerous ontologies across various domains are readily available and can be integrated into problem-solving architectures. This allows systems to access valuable, pre-existing knowledge at low cost, significantly enhancing their ability to address complex problems. In our case, with a focus on problem-solving within the aviation domain, we employ the Air Traffic Management Ontology (ATMONTO), which encompasses comprehensive domain knowledge related to airspace, flight parameters, and standard airline operations [13,17]. Many other ontologies relevant to diverse fields are also available for reuse in a range of applications. The key benefit lies in enabling developers to concentrate on building the problem-solving architecture itself, while leveraging detailed, domain-specific ontologies that are already established and readily exploitable. This approach greatly facilitates the development and testing of robust resolution systems.

4 A Case Study of the Ontology-Driven Problem Solving Model for Aircraft Piloting

The unified ontological approach entails the use of ontologies not only to specify domain theory but also to address both the declarative and procedural dimensions of a task. In collaboration with our industrial partner, we applied this approach to develop an ontological reference model for problem-solving. Specifically, the goal was to construct a reference model for aircraft piloting tasks, with a focus on the critical take-off phase of the Airbus A320. The framework architecture includes a domain ontology that captures and formalizes the theoretical foundations of piloting tasks, alongside a task ontology that precisely specifies the steps, actions, and constraints associated with piloting procedures, with strong references to the terminological concepts within the domain ontology. Detailed information regarding this reference model can be found in Courtemanche et al. [6]. Upon completion of this reference model, we developed a solution enabling the automatic execution of the model, as well as its integration into a flight simulation device for training purposes [7].

4.1 The Domain Ontology: Semantic Grounding of Piloting Actions

To build the reference model, it was necessary to select and integrate a method to describe the underlying theory of piloting of aircraft, including concepts, roles, interactions, and other relevant elements. This required defining a representation of the knowledge specific to the terminological terms of the aviation domain. More specifically, the domain ontology consists of a set of terminological terms with formal representation that can later be used as a reference for the task ontology, and to link execution parameters to a given simulation environment. For example, a key parameter in piloting of aircraft is the aircraft speed. This speed is represented by a terminological term in the domain ontology, which serves as a reference. Since the speed within a simulation environment is constantly changing, the reference term is stored in the terminology library and used to track the real-time value of speed within the simulation. This allows the reference model to easily access the live speed data during the problem-solving process (piloting). Given the extensive volume of terminological entries that must be referenced, the domain ontology was subdivided into subcategories to improve the organization of knowledge representation and to facilitate the retrieval of specific parameters. The concept of **Environment** serves as the overarching category within the domain ontology, providing a unifying structure that connects all environmental subcategories. Within this framework, the **Aircraft Inside Environment** is defined as a specialization that focuses on the interior of the aircraft, including the cockpit and its associated instruments. In contrast, the **Aircraft Outside Environment** represents another specialization of the general environment, capturing parameters related to the external conditions surrounding the aircraft—such as position, weather, and other relevant external factors. Additionally, the **Aircraft Systems** category formalizes the internal systems of the aircraft that lie outside the scope of the cockpit. This includes components such as engines and other mechanical or electronic subsystems essential to aircraft operation.

4.2 The Task Ontology: Reference Model for Piloting Procedures

The aim of this part of our work was to formalize both normal and abnormal piloting procedures for the Airbus A320 aircraft. A key challenge in this domain is the high complexity of the reference knowledge and the associated problem-solving approach. By adopting ontology as a unified framework, we were able to decompose and formally represent the knowledge in detail, with input from domain experts and leveraging the reference manual for the Airbus A320 [6]. The formal representation of these procedures was visually decomposed using the Unified Modeling Language. The use of a straightforward visualization tool was intended to enable the involvement of domain experts (pilots and flight engineers), who lacked expertise in ontology engineering. Through this visual representation, expert pilots were invited to provide feedback on the quality and accuracy of the knowledge representation of the piloting procedures. These experts participated at multiple stages of the process, contributing to the validation and refinement of the reference model.

As previously mentioned, the elements of the task ontology and the implemented procedures are semantically anchored in the domain ontology. The domain ontology encompasses parameters related to the aircraft and the environment in which it operates. Thus, when procedures are developed, semantic links are created between the steps and the states of the parameters involved, implementing the semantic anchoring of the task into the components of the piloting environment as represented in the domain ontology [7]. Instantiations of the task ontology (defining specific procedures) in accordance with the proposed model allow for the materialization of their executions based on the current state of the environment. For example, performing the taxiing step in preparation for takeoff under certain weather conditions (e.g., wind speed). It should be noted that the implementation of the domain and task ontologies was made possible by the high level of semantic detail offered by the Web Ontology Language (OWL).

4.3 Automated Execution of Task Ontology

The ontology is fundamentally based on description logic, which provides it with computational (reasoning or inference) capabilities. Therefore, given a reference model such as the one presented in the previous sections, the key question is whether it is possible to reason automatically over this model. In the case of the task ontology, reasoning means executing a partial or complete task (e.g., preparing the aircraft for takeoff, executing the takeoff procedure, etc.). To address this, we developed a framework for the automatic execution of the reference model [7]. This framework consists of an interpreter that leverages the Semantic Web Rule Language (SWRL) to execute given tasks. The additional semantics provided by SWRL were sufficient to automate our model, allowing for the execution of various elements of the task ontology without human intervention.

5 Potential Uses of the Proposed Approach

To illustrate the significance of our unified approach, which integrates both the declarative and procedural perspectives of ontology, we collaborated with other researchers to apply it in two distinct scenarios. First, we leveraged this approach to support the implementation of semantic and procedural memory within an ACT-R-based cognitive architecture. The goal was to create a cognitive agent capable of supervising or executing a pilot task. Thus, a synthetic pilot was developed for the take-off phase of an Airbus A320 aircraft, with further details provided in Sect. 5.1. Subsequently, we applied our unified approach to incorporate information aimed at managing the cognitive load associated with task execution. This is a critical concern, especially in complex task scenarios such as take-off of aircrafts, where it is essential to monitor the cognitive load of the pilot to prevent overload and potential incapacitation. In Sect. 5.2, we describe how the unified ontological model was used to integrate elements that allow estimation of cognitive load.

5.1 Cognitive Architecture

Working with a colleague developing a cognitive agent as a synthetic pilot, we explored grounding this agent in our ontological reference model. We first opted for using ACT-R-based agent for many good reasons. The ACT family of architectures, developed by Anderson and his colleagues, is the oldest (since 1973) and best known, with the highest number of scientific articles devoted to it [15]. The aim of ACT-R (Adaptive Control of Thought - Rational) is to model the human mind, exploring the four dimensions of artificial intelligence: thinking like a human, thinking rationally, acting like a human and acting rationally. ACT-R is a production system that consists of a declarative memory that contains facts and a procedural memory that contains production rules. The declarative module recognizes what is presented to the model and calculates the activation of rules, while the procedural module calculates the utility of each activated rule and triggers the most appropriate one. Cognition emerges from the interaction between procedural and declarative structures. We then investigated the possibility of basing this agent on our ontological reference model. Figure 1 shows how domain and task ontologies have been integrated in an ACT-R-based cognitive agent, enabling it to act as a synthetic pilot.

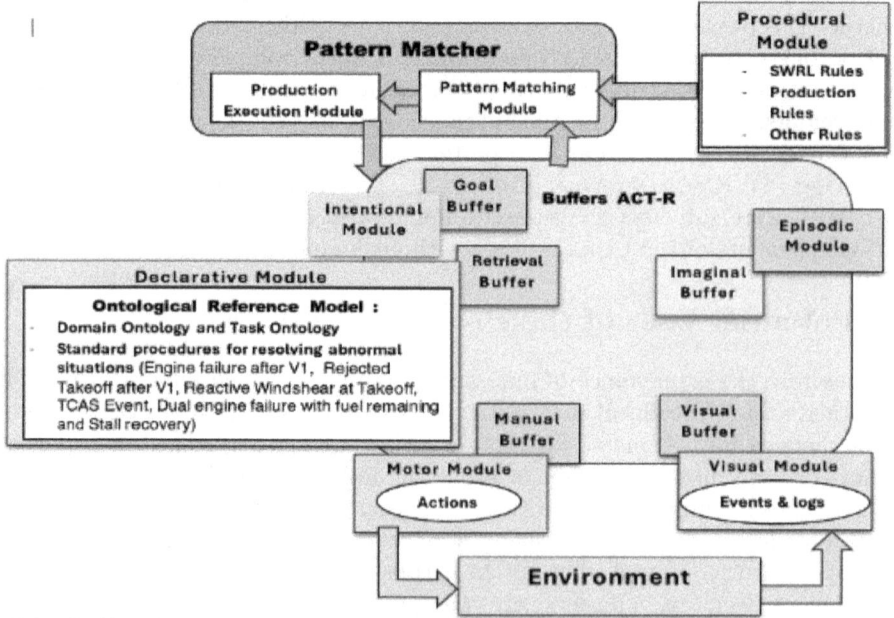

Fig. 1. The ACT-R-based Synthetic Pilot built using our Unified Ontology Model

The cognitive agent is capable of perceiving relevant information from the operational environment. Through its Visual Module, it accesses various flight parameters in real time, enabling it to accurately determine the current state of the aircraft. The Pattern Matcher processes this incoming data—collected and stored in different buffers—and compares it against a set of production rules derived from the task ontology. This allows the agent to identify the appropriate action, which is then dispatched to the execution environment via the Motor Module.

Crucially, the ontological reference model is employed as an integral framework within the cognitive architecture. The flexibility of the ontology allows the ACT-R modules to interpret input from the piloting system, reason about the incoming data, and generate contextually appropriate responses for the piloting environment. The ontology informs each stage of the problem-solving process—for instance, by providing a formalized and comprehensive sequence of actions necessary for managing both normal and abnormal takeoff procedures, along with the specific conditions under which these actions should be triggered. This seamless integration enables the cognitive agent to offer real-time assistance to the human pilot as needed. Further details of this work are available in Tamkodjou, Coutermanche et al. [29].

5.2 Cognitive Load Management

In another significant study, we focused on determining the cognitive load associated with each phase of flight and its corresponding tasks, with the objective of extending the reference model to support cognitive load estimation during problem-solving. To achieve this, we conducted a focus group experiment involving experienced A320 pilots, who provided detailed feedback on their perceived cognitive load during various stages of flight. Each piloting procedure was broken down into blocks of subtasks—for instance, the takeoff procedure was decomposed into several discrete segments. Participants were asked to reflect on their experiences and respond to targeted questions concerning each specific subtask.

These questions addressed the workload involved in task execution, and the pilots were encouraged to discuss their responses collectively. To standardize the evaluation of expert responses, we developed a hybrid workload assessment scale by combining elements of the NASA Task Load Index (NASA-TLX) [10] and the Bedford Rating Scale [26], both of which have been previously validated in the context of aviation. Our adapted survey assessed five key dimensions of workload: mental demand, physical demand, effort, stress, and available time. Experts rated each item on a six-point scale ranging from "not existing" to "extreme existence."

Additionally, participants were asked to identify the primary contributing factors to workload during each phase of flight. These included task difficulty, time pressure, number of concurrent tasks, task interruptions, external disturbances, frustration, boredom, and the precision required. The primary aim of the study was to collect qualitative and quantitative insights into the attentional demands throughout the entire flight cycle, thereby enabling the modeling of pilot attention and establishing a baseline for expected workload levels.

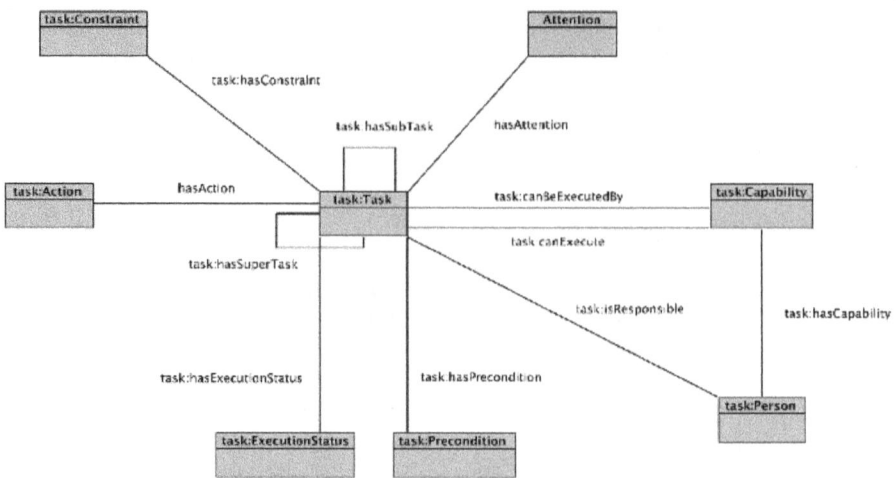

Fig. 2. Attention integration in the Reference Model

Based on the collected data, we were able to associate specific cognitive load scores with each task in the flight model. As illustrated in Fig. 2, the reference model has been enhanced with an attention component, enabling the computation and integration of cognitive load values directly into the task decomposition structure. This enriched model facilitates reuse by other researchers or system designers, providing a semantically grounded framework that is tightly linked to both the operational environment and the problem-solving process. By embedding cognitive load data into the model, we significantly increase its value for future studies on cognitive load management and its impact on task execution and complexity. Further details on this research can be found in Ghaderi, Courtemanche et al. [8].

6 Conclusion and Discussion

In this paper, we proposed ontology as a unified-framework for addressing automation of complex real-world problem solving. Grounded in epistemological foundations, we demonstrate how ontologies serve as formal structures for representing and manipulating complex knowledge. Specifically, we introduced a task ontology architecture to decompose knowledge in a way that captures the problem-solving process. A key advantage of this approach is its ability to establish robust semantic connections between declarative and procedural knowledge. We applied this unified framework to develop domain and task ontologies for aircraft piloting, showcasing its adaptability in two distinct contexts: (1) supporting cognitive aspects and (2) serving as a semantic and procedural memory for cognitive agents. The ontology-based reference model successfully captured knowledge decomposition and execution dynamics, enabling rapid environmental evaluation and task selection in highly dynamic settings.

However, a major limitation of our approach is its reliance on expert-driven ontology development. While our aviation case study benefited from direct access to subject matter experts and comprehensive technical documentation, such ideal conditions are often unavailable in practice. Current literature shows extensive research on automated domain ontology generation from textual corpora (e.g., [31]), yet comparable advances in task ontology construction remain notably lacking. Recent work by [4], which extracts rule-based ontologies from tutoring interactions, could complement our framework. Future research will investigate automating the creation of both domain and task ontologies from data to reduce reliance on expert input.

Acknowledgements. This work was supported by the NSERC Alliance program [grant number ALLRP 549083-19]. We are thankful to CRIAQ, Bombardier, CAE and BMU for their financial support.

References

1. Ahmed, G., Alshboul, J., Kovács, L.: Development of ontology-based domain knowledge model for it domain in e-tutor systems. Int. J. Adv. Comput. Sci. Appl. **13**(5), 28–34 (2022)
2. Aleven, V., Rowe, J., Huang, Y., A., M.: Domain modeling for AIED systems with connections to modeling student knowledge. In: Handbook of Artificial Intelligence in Education, pp. 127–169 (2023)
3. Bihan, G.: Lexique de philosophie. Éditions du Seuil, Paris (1996)
4. Chang, M., D'Aniello, G., Gaeta, M., Orciuoli, F., Sampson, D., Simonelli, C.: Building ontology-driven tutoring models for intelligent tutoring systems using data mining. IEEE Access **8**, 48151–48162 (2020)
5. Corbett, A., Kauffman, L., Maclaren, B., Wagner, A., Jones, E.: A cognitive tutor for genetics problem solving: learning gains and student modeling. J. Educ. Comput. Res. **42**(2), 219–239 (2010)
6. Courtemanche, M.A., Tato, A., Nkambou, R.: Ontological reference model for piloting procedures. In: International Conference on Intelligent Tutoring Systems, pp. 95–104. Springer (2022)
7. Courtemanche, M.A., Tato, A., Nkambou, R.: Automatic execution of the ontological piloting procedures. In: International Conference on Intelligent Tutoring Systems, pp. 29–41. Springer (2023)
8. Ghaderi, M., Khalaj, A.B., Ben Abdessalem, H., Frasson, C.: Attention assessment of aircraft pilots using eye tracking. In: International Conference on Intelligent Tutoring Systems, pp. 209–219. Springer (2023)
9. Gruber, T.R.: A translation approach to portable ontology specifications. Knowl. Acquis. **5**(2), 199–220 (1993)
10. Hart, S.: Development of NASA-TLX (task load index): results of empirical and theoretical research. Human Mental Workload/Elsevier (1988)
11. Hayashi, Y., Bourdeau, J., Mizoguchi, R.: Structurization of learning/instructional design knowledge for theory-aware authoring systems. In: International Conference on Intelligent Tutoring Systems, pp. 573–582. Springer (2008)

12. Hayashi, Y., Bourdeau, J., Mizoguchi, R.: Using ontological engineering to organize learning/instructional theories and build a theory-aware authoring system. Int. J. Artif. Intell. Educ. **19**(2), 211–252 (2009)
13. Keller, R.M.: Ontologies for aviation data management. In: 2016 IEEE/AIAA 35th Digital Avionics Systems Conference (DASC), pp. 1–9. IEEE (2016)
14. Koedinger, K.R., Anderson, J.R., Hadley, W.H., Mark, M.A., et al.: Intelligent tutoring goes to school in the big city. Int. J. AI Educ. **8**(1), 30–43 (1997)
15. Kotseruba, I., Tsotsos, J.: 40 years of cognitive architectures: core cognitive abilities and practical applications. Artif. Intell. Rev. 17–94 (2020)
16. Lin, Y., Xiang, Z., He, Y.: Towards a semantic web application: ontology-driven ortholog clustering analysis. In: Biomedical Ontology, pp. 33–40 (2011)
17. M. Keller, R.: Building a knowledge graph for the air traffic management community. In: Companion Proceedings of the 2019 World Wide Web Conference, pp. 700–704 (2019)
18. Mitrovic, A., Koedinger, K.R., Martin, B.: A comparative analysis of cognitive tutoring and constraint-based modeling. In: International Conference on User Modeling, pp. 313–322. Springer (2003)
19. Mizoguchi, F.: Prolog based expert system. N. Gener. Comput. **1**(1), 99–104 (1983)
20. Mizoguchi, R., Bourdeau, J.: Using ontological engineering to overcome common AI-ED problems. J. Artif. Intell. Educ. **11**, 107–121 (2000)
21. Mizoguchi, R., Hayashi, Y., Bourdeau, J.: Inside a theory-aware authoring system. In: Semantic Web Technologies for e-Learning, pp. 59–76. IOS Press (2009)
22. Mizoguchi, R., Vanwelkenhuysen, J., Ikeda, M.: Task ontology for reuse of problem solving knowledge. Towards Very Large Knowledge Bases, pp. 46–59. IOS Press (1995)
23. Psyché, V., Mendes, O., Bourdeau, J.: Apport de l'ingénierie ontologique aux environnements de formation à distance. Sciences et Technologies de l'Information et de la Communication pour l'Éducation et la Formation **10**, 89–126 (2003)
24. Ramírez-Noriega, A.e.a.: Towards the automatic construction of an intelligent tutoring system: domain module. Adv. Intell. Syst. Comput. **930**(3), 293–302 (2019)
25. Roll, I., Aleven, V., Koedinger, K.: The invention lab: using a hybrid of model tracing and constraint-based modeling to offer intelligent support in inquiry environments. In: Proceedings of the 10th International Conference on ITS, pp. 115–124. Springer (2010)
26. Roscoe, A.H., Ellis, G.A.: A subjective rating scale for assessing pilot workload in flight: a decade of practical use (1990)
27. Sun, Y., Li, Z.: Ontology-based domain knowledge representation. In: 4th International Conference on Computer Science & Education, pp. 174–177 (2009)
28. Suraweera, P., Mitrovic, A., Martin, B.: The role of domain ontology in knowledge acquisition for ITSS. In: ITS. LNCS, vol. 3220, pp. 207–216 (2004)
29. Tamkodjou Tchio, G.C., Courtemanche, M.A., Tato, A.A.N., Nkambou, R., Psyché, V.: Integrating an ontological reference model of piloting procedures in act-r cognitive architecture to simulate piloting tasks (2023)
30. W3C: OWL 2 web ontology language: structural specification and functional-style syntax (second edition) (2012)
31. Zouaq, A., Nkambou, R.: Building domain ontologies from text for educational purposes. EEE Trans. Learn. Technol. **1**(1), 49–62 (2008)

Designing an AI Coaching System for Interactive Video-Based Skill Learning

Cherie Lum(✉), Erin Deye, Grace Brazil, Tim Bydlon, Shashank Verma, Rochan Madhusudhana, Rahul Dass, and Ashok Goel

Georgia Institute of Technology, Atlanta, GA 30332, USA
{clum7,edeye3,gbrazil2,tbydlon3,sverma342,rochan.hm, rdass7,ag25}@gatech.edu

Abstract. Achieving deeper understanding in online learning requires adaptive support that evolves with learner needs. This paper traces the iterative design of Ivy, a generative AI coach that combines structured knowledge representations with large language models to deliver pedagogically aligned responses. Across three versions: pre-Ivy, Ivy 1.0, and Ivy 2.0, we analyzed learner interactions and preferences. Expert users consistently favored Ivy's structured, example-driven responses, while novices often preferred the more conversational tone of a ChatGPT-powered assistant. These insights shaped Ivy's refinement and suggest its potential to support novices in developing conceptual understanding and progressing toward expertise.

Keywords: Generative AI · Knowledge-Based AI · Skill Acquisition · Video-based Learning

1 Introduction

Online courses often lack immediate, context-aware instructional support. Teaching assistants (TAs) are limited in availability, and traditional AI tutors typically do not adapt to learners' knowledge levels. To address these challenges, we designed Ivy, a generative AI coaching system that integrates structured knowledge representations with language generation to deliver tailored, pedagogically aligned explanations.

This paper presents an exploratory study comparing Ivy [5,6] to Jill Watson [8,10,21], a virtual teaching assistant powered by ChatGPT and trained on class content. We ask: How do learners at different levels of expertise respond to structured AI coaching versus more general, conversational assistance? Although we do not measure learning outcomes, we examine usage patterns, user preferences, and implications for AI-based instructional support.

2 Related Work

Recent advances in generative AI have enabled new forms of interactive learning support. Systems such as Tutorly [14], RAGMan [16], and lecture-aware tutoring agents [15] combine retrieval-augmented generation [13] with large language models like GPT-3 and GPT-4 [2] to provide real-time, context-aware explanations. These systems demonstrate strong fluency and adaptability, making them appealing to novice learners. However, their responses can sometimes lack alignment with instructional goals or domain structure. Many AI tutors offer structured feedback, but may fall short of the depth required for skill-based learning environments [18]. Ivy extends this line of work by combining generative AI with Task-Method-Knowledge (TMK) models [9,17], which encode the goal, process, and domain-specific knowledge associated with a skill. This integration supports deeper, example-driven explanations aligned with instructional reasoning.

Unlike prior systems, Ivy is embedded alongside interactive instructional videos, promoting learners to ask questions in real time during both concept explanations and practice exercises. Ivy was developed by domain experts with extensive experience in TMK modeling. This study builds on earlier research that introduced Ivy as a prototype QA system [5,6], extending it into a production-ready AI coach for classroom deployment.

Learner preferences often depend on prior knowledge. Novices tend to prefer brief, conversational answers, while experts value deeper conceptual structure [24]. This is consistent with constructivist learning theories [19,22], which emphasize the importance of existing knowledge, and with cognitive load theory [20]. Kirschner, Sweller, and Clark [12] argue that minimal guidance overwhelms novices, who benefit more from worked examples and structured support. As learners gain experience, however, this guidance may become redundant—a phenomenon known as the expertise reversal effect [11].

3 Methodology

3.1 TMK Modeling for Structured Reasoning

TMK models provide the structured representation that enables Ivy to generate reasoned and explanatory responses. Each model consists of three interconnected components. The *Task* component defines the goal of the skill, and the *Method* component outlines the procedural steps for achieving the goal by decomposing tasks into subtasks and modeling states and transitions using a finite-state machine. Finally, the *Knowledge* component encodes the domain-specific concepts, relationships, and properties required for reasoning. These components collectively form a unified model that supports causal, goal-oriented, and structured explanations. Figure 1 is an illustration of the partial TMK model representing the *Classification* skill taught as part of the KBAI course.

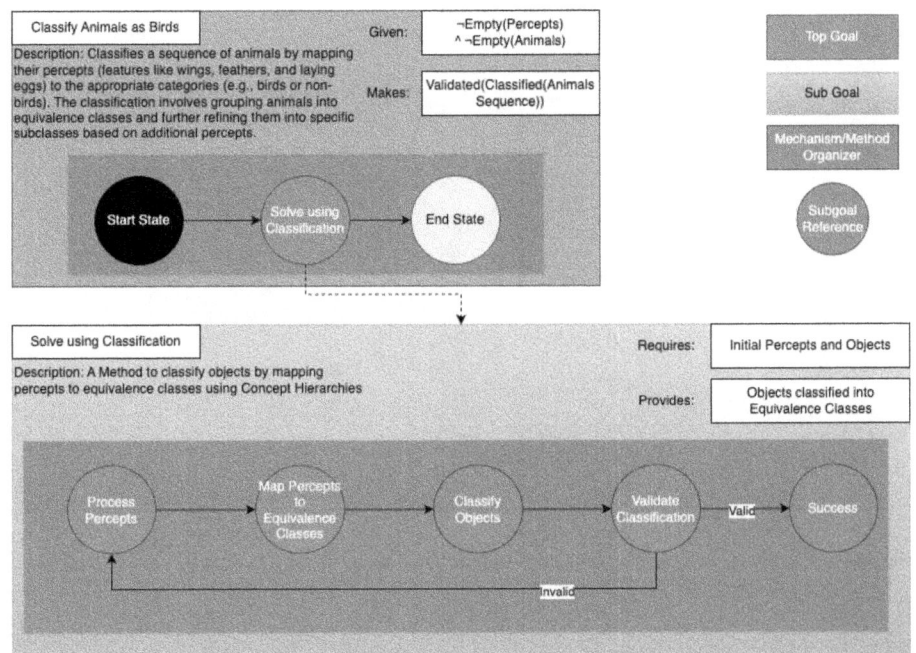

Fig. 1. Diagram of a TMK model segment for the 'Classification' skill

3.2 Interactive Video Integration and System Architecture

Ivy is embedded alongside HTML5-based videos that use the H5P framework to support interactive exercises. This system supports both instruction and comprehension checks, allowing learners to engage actively with the material. Learners can pause the video at any point to ask questions about the course content. Ivy responds in real time by generating explanations that preserve content integrity and extend instructional presence, an element often diminished in online learning [7]. Interactive elements, such as multiple-choice questions, fill-in-the-blank prompts, and drag-and-drop exercises, are embedded directly in the videos to promote active learning [3,4]. This design transforms passive video consumption into an interactive coaching experience.

The interactive videos are hosted on the EdStem learning platform and integrated with the Canvas Learning Management System (LMS) via the Learning Tools Interoperability (LTI) standard (see Fig. 2). Ivy operates within a secure, scalable, cloud-based infrastructure hosted on AWS. Its system architecture supports real-time learner interaction by coordinating question processing, TMK-based retrieval, and LLM response generation through a modular backend service. Learner interactions are logged in DynamoDB to enable analysis of engagement patterns. While a detailed discussion of Ivy's cloud deployment, database schema, and monitoring infrastructure is beyond the scope of this paper, the

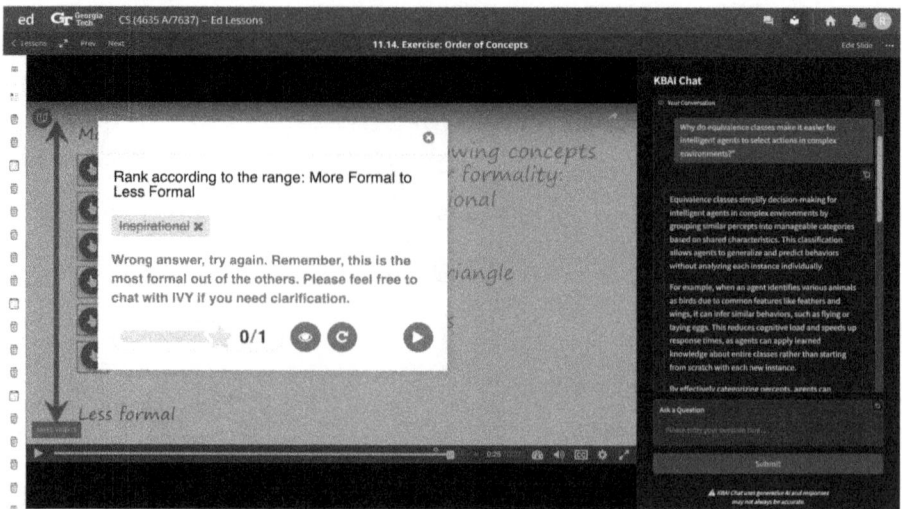

Fig. 2. Ivy embedded in interactive videos within the Ed Stem online learning platform for a Knowledge-based AI (KBAI) course taught at Georgia Tech

architecture enables Ivy to function as a production-ready AI coaching system suitable for supporting real-world classroom deployment.

3.3 Use Cases: Interactive Coaching

Ivy supports two key learning interactions. First, learners can pose procedural questions regarding course skills (e.g., Classification) while watching instructional videos. Ivy determines whether a learner's question is relevant to the skill being taught, retrieves the corresponding components from the skill's TMK model, and generates a response which provides reasoned explanation grounded in course pedagogy. For a detailed description of Ivy's question-answering pipeline, see our previous work [5,6]. Second, learners complete interactive exercises embedded within the videos. By combining ground-truth-based real-time explanations with in-video practice, Ivy transforms passive video viewing into a reliable interactive coaching experience.

3.4 Process of Designing Ivy

Ivy has undergone several iterations, and the experimental studies that informed its development are described in Sect. 4. When we understood what types of questions students might ask pre-ivy or Ivy 0.0, such as a lot of concept and fact-based (Knowledge) questions, and procedural (Method) questions, it helped validate going in the right direction for Ivy (Table 1).

Ivy 1.0 employed Chain-of-Thought (CoT) prompting [23] to generate final responses, which often produced overly complex responses. It's question type

Table 1. Timeline of Ivy Evaluation Stages

Version	Dates	Key Updates and Observations
Ivy 0.0	November 2023	Pre-product. Noted questions five students asked from watching a skill-based lesson
Ivy 1.0	November 2024	Initial deployment. Improved responses. Strict filtering led to many unanswered queries
Ivy 2.0	January 2025	Improved relevance classifier. Answered 96.8% of student questions

classifier mapped each learner question to a specific TMK (Task, Method, Knowledge) component or a fixed combination of components. For example, if a learner posed a "Knowledge" question, Ivy 0.0 retrieved information exclusively from the Knowledge component. It's question relevance classifier was unfortunately too strict resulting in Ivy 1.0 successfully answering only 59% of learner questions.

Ivy 2.0 introduced two key improvements. First, Ivy shifted from strict question relevance classification based retrieval to similarity-based retrieval across all TMK components. It now retrieves the top-k most relevant Task, Method, and Knowledge documents to construct a structured response. Secondly, Ivy 2.0 now employed a two-step response generation pipeline: an initial response was generated using the standard process and then refined by a response optimizer agent to enhance clarity and conciseness. These enhancements significantly improved both the quality and coverage of Ivy's responses, making it more reliable for use for instructional use.

4 Experiment Design

4.1 Pilot Study

We conducted a pilot study in early 2025 using course materials from an AI course with eight students. Each participant interacted with both Ivy and Jill Watson across two lessons. To avoid bias, both systems were labeled simply as "Ivy". Learners could ask questions freely during video lessons and received system responses in real time.

When there was an interview, a research scientist from the team was always present to facilitate smooth execution, while one or no developers shadowed the session. The scientist's role included reminding participants to ask "how" and "why" questions or questions that helped them learn best when learning new concepts, and to provide feedback by liking or disliking Ivy's responses.

Ivy logs all activity on the page. This includes user question, coach's response, user interactions on the interactive quizzes like correct answer, supplied answer, etc. This allows Ivy developers to create a user journey and monitor metrics like number of successful responses from Ivy, number of retries on interactive quiz, average response latency, etc.

Two versions of Ivy were evaluated. In the initial deployment or Ivy 1.0, only 59% of learner questions received answers due to overly strict question relevance filtering. After iterative refinement, Ivy 2.0, achieved a 96.8% answerability rate. Student feedback, question logs, and system response ratings were collected and analyzed qualitatively to understand engagement patterns and user preferences.

5 Results

In the pilot study for Ivy 2.0, learners were told they were interacting with Ivy the entire time but they unbeknownst to them were engaging with Ivy for their first lesson and Jill Watson for the second lesson.

Our analysis of student inquiries reveals distinct patterns in the types of questions posed to Ivy and Jill Watson. Both systems received a majority of K-based (knowledge) questions, but Ivy received significantly more (34 vs. 24). Questions such as "How would DeMorgan's Law apply to formal logic for implication?" or "What are specialization and generalization" as seen in Fig. 4 were asked to better understand concepts being shown in the videos. This suggests that users perhaps appreciated Ivy's conceptual and factual clarifications.

Interestingly, while M-questions (method-based) were less frequent overall, Jill Watson received nearly twice as many. In fact, no M-questions were asked by novice users to Ivy as seen in Fig. 4. This may indicate that students sought procedural guidance more often in the second lesson, either due to the nature of the content or because Jill Watson's response style encouraged follow-up inquiries in this category.

T-questions (task-oriented) showed a smaller disparity, with Ivy receiving slightly more (6 vs. 4), suggesting that students posed practical, application-based questions consistently across both lessons.

Analysis as shown in Fig. 3 revealed a clear distinction in learner preferences based on prior expertise. Expert users preferred Ivy's structured, conceptually aligned responses in 75% of comparisons, whereas novices favored Jill Watson's conversational style in 67% of comparisons. Experts tended to ask conceptual or problem-solving questions that aligned with Ivy's structured explanations, while novices more often asked for definitions or procedural clarifications better suited to Jill Watson's fluent replies.

5.1 Types of Learner Questions

Learners posed a wide variety of questions to Ivy and Jill Watson during the pilot study sessions. These questions generally fell into four categories: *conceptual understanding* (e.g., asking about underlying principles), *procedural knowledge* (e.g., asking how to perform a specific task), *definitional clarity* (e.g., asking for terminology explanations), and *causal reasoning* (e.g., asking why a certain step or method is needed).

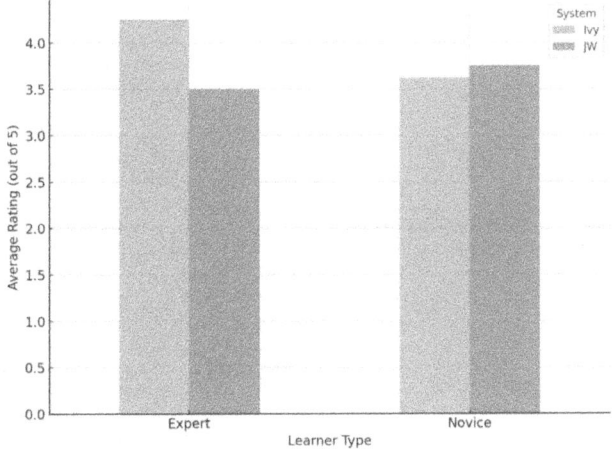

Fig. 3. Preference Ivy vs. Jill Watson

Expert learners tended to ask *conceptual* and *causal* questions, seeking to deepen their understanding of underlying mechanisms or implications of methods. For instance, an expert asked, "Is incremental concept learning a subcategory of case-based reasoning?" and "Why shouldn't we have negative terms in preconditions?" These questions required nuanced, structured responses.

In contrast, novice learners primarily asked *definitional* and *procedural* questions, often seeking surface-level clarifications. Examples include, "What is propositional logic?" and "How would you select which animals are birds?" These questions required accessible, fluent explanations without overwhelming cognitive load.

Across both groups, learners appreciated responses that provided *concrete examples* rather than purely abstract definitions.

5.2 Examples of Ivy and Jill Watson Responses

As can be seen in Fig. 4 and Fig. 5 there are examples of questions asked by learners, what types of questions they were (T, M, or K), along with a condensed version of answers provided by Ivy or Jill Watson. Green shading depicts user liking the answer provided and red shading depicting user disliking the it. These examples illustrate how Ivy's responses emphasized structured, conceptually grounded reasoning aligned with course models while, Jill Watson often provided more conversational, general-purpose answers.

Overall, Ivy's answers demonstrated deeper alignment with structured skill models, which expert users particularly appreciated. Jill Watson's answers, while fluent and conversational, were often less aligned with the instructional content, making them easier for novices to digest but less precise for conceptual learning.

	Type	Question	Answer
Expert	T	Why are there 2^n percepts and 2^m actions?	"The expressions 2^n percepts and 2^m actions refer to the combinatorial possibilities in classification tasks... Here, 'n' is the number of distinct percepts (features) that can be observed. Each percept can have multiple states (e.g., True, False, Maybe, Undefined)..."
	M	Does incremental concept learning deal with the idea of abstraction?	"Yes, incremental concept learning (ICL) involves abstraction. It includes variabilization, which is the process of identifying key features and relationships from examples to form a general understanding of a concept. This allows the system to create abstract representations applicable to similar instances...."
	K	What are specialization and generalization?	"Specialization and generalization are processes in concept formation... Generalization expands a concept to include a broader range of examples. For instance, if ""bird"" includes only ""sparrow"" and ""eagle,"" generalization would add ""penguin"" and ""ostrich,"" thus encompassing flightless birds...Specialization narrows a concept by excluding examples that do not fit..."
Novice	T	Can you calculate the euclidean distances between the following pairs of points? \n1. (0.8, 0.8) and (0.5, 0.5)\n2. (0.8,0.8) and (1.5, 0.5)\n3. (0.8, 0.8) and (1, 1.5)?	"Sure! Let's calculate the Euclidean distances for the given pairs of points using the formula:...{Distance} = \sqrt{(x_2 - x_1)^2 + (y_2 - y_1)^2}\n\}..So the distances are approximately:\n1. \(0.424\)\n2. \(0.761\)\n3. \(0.728\)..."
	M	N/A	N/A
	K	How would DeMorgan's Law apply to formal logic for implication?	"De Morgan's Law relates to the negation of conjunctions and disjunctions in formal logic. It can be applied to implications by first rewriting the implication \(A \rightarrow B \) as \(\neg A \lor B \)....Therefore, an implication is false only when \(A \) is true and \(B \) is false, clarifying the conditions under which implications hold true or false. This application is useful in logical proofs and reasoning..."

Fig. 4. Questions Answered by Ivy 2.0

	Type	Question	Answer
Novice	T	Generate the answers for these questions	"It seems that your query may not be directly related to the course material. I suggest that you try rephrasing your question or asking another question that is more relevant to the course..."
	M	Context matters for reasoning, how would we formulate frames for words that have multiple meanings?	"To formulate frames for words that have multiple meanings, you can follow these steps: ..1. Identify the Word*...2. Determine Contexts...3. Define Each Meaning...4. Create Frame Structures...By creating these frames, you can effectively represent the different meanings of a word and how they function in various contexts..."
	K	Give me some possible exam questions about learning by recording cases	"Here are some possible exam questions about learning by recording cases: 1. Define learning by recording cases and explain its significance in artificial intelligence. 2. What are the key assumptions of case-based reasoning? ...10. Discuss the importance of patterns in problems and how they influence the effectiveness of case-based reasoning...Feel free to modify these questions to better fit your exam format or focus!"

Fig. 5. Questions Answered by Jill Watson

5.3 Other Insights

From a user engagement perspective, a key trend that emerged was impatience with response time. Many learners expressed frustration over delays, highlighting the need for efficiency optimizations in Ivy's answer generation.

Students also exhibited misconceptions about Ivy's capabilities; several assumed Ivy could interpret visual elements within the videos, leading to occasional misalignment between question intent and response content. Some users also reported minor frustration with system response delays. Despite these challenges, learners broadly appreciated responses that incorporated concrete examples, suggesting the value of example-driven feedback even for novice users.

These findings suggest that structured AI coaching aligned with course pedagogy is especially valuable for learners with stronger prior knowledge, while novices may initially benefit from more accessible, conversational scaffolding.

6 Discussion

6.1 Verifying Key Claims

Our findings highlight the tension between structured reasoning and conversational fluency in AI coaching. Ivy's TMK-based responses provided conceptual depth but may have exceeded the needs or expectations of novice learners. Jill Watson's conversational style, while less aligned with pedagogy, was more accessible to beginners. Future AI coaches should consider dynamically adapting the response depth based on the learning background.

6.2 Role of Example-Driven Feedback

The study emphasizes the importance of transparent, example-rich answers in fostering conceptual understanding and engagement. Experts preferred Ivy's structured responses in 75% of cases, a preference that reflects their ability to recognize and benefit from detailed, domain-aligned explanations. They consistently noted that responses grounded in specific examples enhanced their understanding by connecting abstract principles to concrete applications. This aligns with research showing that contextualized explanations can reduce cognitive load [20] and support deeper inquiry and facilitate skill acquisition, but their effectiveness depends on the coherence and accuracy of the responses they generate.

Experts also asked more procedural and explanatory questions, aligned with higher-order thinking in Bloom's taxonomy [1]. Ivy's TMK-driven responses effectively addressed these queries, while novice learners, who favored Jill Watson in 67% of cases, focused on definitional questions. Their preference for conversational fluency suggests accessibility took precedence over depth. However, their partial acceptance of Ivy's answers suggests growing utility as their understanding matures.

Ivy's responses were refined over time through this feedback loop, improving both relevance and clarity. The inclusion of examples not only aided learner understanding but also increased trust in the system's expertise, further encouraging question-asking behavior. These findings underscore the importance of balancing structured reasoning with accessible delivery when designing for diverse learner needs.

7 Conclusion

This study introduced Ivy, an AI coach that blends generative AI and structured reasoning with interactive videos. While novices often preferred the conversational tone of Jill Watson, most TAs and expert users favored Ivy's structured responses, highlighting Ivy's potential to scaffold novice understanding and support their progression toward expertise. These findings underscore the importance of evolving the design of Ivy to meet the diverse needs of learners at different stages of what they feel they need or want when in a skill-based class. As a next step, we plan to deploy Ivy in a classroom setting to further evaluate its impact on student learning outcomes and instructional practices.

Acknowledgments. We are grateful to Dr. Spencer Rugaber at Georgia Tech's Design Intelligence Laboratory for his invaluable insights into TMK models and modeling. This research has been supported by NSF Grants #2112532 and #2247790 awarded to the National AI Institute for Adult Learning and Online Education.

References

1. Bloom, B.S., Krathwohl, D.R.: Taxonomy of Educational Objectives: The Classification of Educational Goals, Volume Handbook I: Cognitive Domain. Longmans, Green, New York (1956)
2. Brown, T., et al.: Language models are few-shot learners. Adv. Neural. Inf. Process. Syst. **33**, 1877–1901 (2020)
3. Chi, M.T., et al.: Translating the ICAP theory of cognitive engagement into practice. Cogn. Sci. **42**(6), 1777–1832 (2018)
4. Chi, M.T., Wylie, R.: The ICAP framework: linking cognitive engagement to active learning outcomes. Educ. Psychol. **49**(4), 219–243 (2014)
5. Dass, R., et al.: Enhanced question-answering for skill-based learning using knowledge-based AI and generative AI. arXiv preprint arXiv:2504.07463 (2025). Presented at the AI4ED Workshop, AAAI 2025
6. Dass, R., et al.: Ivy: a hybrid knowledge-based and generative AI coach for explaining procedural skills. In: Proceedings of the 26th International Conference on Artificial Intelligence in Education (AIED 2025). Lecture Notes in Artificial Intelligence. Springer (2025, to appear)
7. Garrison, D.R., Anderson, T., Archer, W.: Critical inquiry in a text-based environment: computer conferencing in higher education. Internet High. Educ. **2**(2–3), 87–105 (2000)
8. Goel, A.K., Polepeddi, L.: Jill watson: a virtual teaching assistant for online education. In: Learning Engineering for Online Education, pp. 120–143. Routledge (2018)

9. Goel, A.K., Rugaber, S.: Gaia: a cad-like environment for designing game-playing agents. IEEE Intell. Syst. **32**(3), 60–67 (2017)
10. Kakar, S., et al.: Jill watson: scaling and deploying an AI conversational agent in online classrooms. In: International Conference on Intelligent Tutoring Systems, pp. 78–90. Springer (2024)
11. Kalyuga, S., Ayres, P., Chandler, P., Sweller, J.: The expertise reversal effect. Educ. Psychol. **38**(1), 23–31 (2003)
12. Kirschner, P.A., Sweller, J., Clark, R.E.: Why minimal guidance during instruction does not work: an analysis of the failure of constructivist, discovery, problem-based, experiential, and inquiry-based teaching. Educ. Psychol. **41**(2), 75–86 (2006)
13. Lewis, P., et al.: Retrieval-augmented generation for knowledge-intensive NLP tasks. In: Advances in Neural Information Processing Systems, vol. 33, pp. 9459–9474 (2020)
14. Li, F., Xu, K., Smith, J.: Tutorly: AI-powered interactive video tutoring. In: Proceedings of the 2024 International Conference on Artificial Intelligence in Education (AIED) (2024)
15. Liu, F., Chen, D., Moore, S.: AI-driven lecture augmentation for context-sensitive tutoring. In: Proceedings of the 2024 International Conference on Artificial Intelligence in Education (AIED) (2024)
16. Ma, I., Krone-Martins, A., Lopes, C.V.: Ragman: a retrieval-augmented AI tutor for programming courses. J. AI Educ. (2024). arxiv:2407.15718
17. Murdock, J.W., Goel, A.K.: Meta-case-based reasoning: self-improvement through self-understanding. J. Exp. Theor. Artif. Intell. **20**(1), 1–36 (2008)
18. Park, F., Wang, R.E., Ribeiro, A.T., Robinson, C.D., Loeb, S., Demszky, D.: Scalable AI tutoring for skill-based learning. In: Proceedings of the AI in Education Conference (2024). arxiv:2410.03017
19. Piaget, J.: The Origins of Intelligence in Children. WW Norton & Company (1952)
20. Sweller, J.: Cognitive load during problem solving: effects on learning. Cogn. Sci. **12**(2), 257–285 (1988)
21. Taneja, K., Maiti, P., Kakar, S., Guruprasad, P., Rao, S., Goel, A.K.: Jill watson: a virtual teaching assistant powered by chatgpt. In: International Conference on Artificial Intelligence in Education, pp. 324–337. Springer (2024)
22. Vygotsky, L.S.: Mind in Society: The Development of Higher Psychological Processes. Harvard University Press (1978)
23. Wei, J., et al.: Chain-of-thought prompting elicits reasoning in large language models. arXiv preprint arXiv:2201.11903 (2023)
24. Zhang, F., Feng, T., Liu, S., Ghosal, D.: Adaptive AI tutoring: balancing structure and flexibility for different learners. J. Learn. Sci. (2024). arxiv:2407.10246

Large Language Models Performance in Propositional Logic Proofs: Solving and Evaluating Argument Validity

Evandro de Barros Costa[1]($\boxtimes$), Jean Felipe Duarte Tenório[1], Alison Bruno Martires Soares[1], Rian Américo Brito da Silva[1], Wallace Lins Casado de Sousa[1], Davi Silva de Melo Lins[1], and Dante de Araújo Costa[2]

[1] Computing Institute, Federal University of Alagoas (UFAL), Maceió, AL 57072-970, Brazil
{evandro,jfdt,abms,rabs,wlcs,dsml}@ic.ufal.br
[2] Centro de Inovação EDGE, Maceió, AL 57072-970, Brazil
https://ic.ufal.br/ , https://www.edge.ufal.br/

Abstract. The present study investigates the ability of Large Language Models (LLMs) in generating and evaluating formal proofs within propositional logic. Specifically, we examine whether an LLM can accurately construct formal proofs to determine the validity of logical arguments and if other independent LLMs can reliably assess the correctness of such proofs. That is, when a LLM plays the problem solver role, the other involved LLMs play the role of evaluator. The evaluation comprises 12 diverse propositional logic proof problems, classified into distinct characteristics. Experimental scenarios were designed such that one model, exemplified by DeepSeek, performed the solver role by generating formal proofs, while three other models, represented by Qwen, GPT, and Gemini, independently evaluated the validity of these proofs. Our findings for each different configuration are described in this article, revealing positive results in favor of the LLMs used.

Keywords: Argument validity via natural deduction · Large Language Models · Propositional Logic · Computing Education

1 Introduction

Logical reasoning is a foundational skill within STEM (Science, Technology, Engineering, and Math) disciplines, relevant for effective problem-solving and critical thinking. Intelligent tutoring systems (ITS) [2] have been developed as important software tools to support students in improving these abilities, particularly problem-solving activities in formal domains like propositional logic [1]. This includes assist students in reasoning activities, particularly in learning to construct and verify formal logic proofs, where solutions follow well-defined steps, but can be combined in various ways to reach a correct conclusion. However, despite their structured nature, formal proof construction remains challenging for many students, who frequently experience difficulties in selecting appropriate inference rules, applying these rules correctly, and systematically organizing proof steps. How might a software agent be playing the problem solver and evaluator role for logical proof tasks?

Recent advances in Large Language Models (LLMs) capabilities [4] present an opportunity to explore their potential in automating and enhancing problem-solving tasks in logic, due to their ability to process and generate complex symbolic manipulations make them promising tools for both proof generation and evaluation. However, the extent to which LLMs can effectively perform these tasks remain uncertain. While prior studies have explored LLMs' individual capabilities in either proof generation or evaluation, a comprehensive analysis of their performance in both roles, particularly in a comparative setting, remains lacking. This study aims to bridge this gap. To the best of our knowledge, no study has yet explored the extent to which LLMs can aid simultaneously in proof generation and evaluation.

The present study aims to investigate how well LLMs works on logic problem solving aspects, systematically evaluating their effectiveness in both generating and assessing formal proofs in propositional logic, that is, addressing the problem of verification of argument validity using Natural Deduction method. Specifically, we investigated whether a LLM, by using a well-specified prompt, acting as a problem solver, can construct a correct formal proof for a given logic proof problem, while two other LLMs, acting as evaluators, assess the validity and correctness of the generated proof.

To conduct this analysis, we use a total of 12 logic proof problems, manually selected. We then examine three different solver-evaluator configurations:

DeepSeek as the solver, with Qwen, ChatGPT, and Gemini as evaluators;
Qwen as the solver, with DeepSeek, ChatGPT, and Gemini as evaluators;
Gemini as the solver, with DeepSeek, ChatGPT, and Qwen as evaluators;
ChatGPT as the solver, with DeepSeek, Gemini, and Qwen as evaluators.

To guide our investigation, we address the following research questions:

RQ1: To what extent can LLMs generate correct formal proofs in propositional logic across different types of proof problems?
RQ2: What are the comparative strengths and weaknesses of different LLMs when performing the roles of solver and evaluator in logic proof problems?

In summary, the main contributions of this paper include:

1. A systematic evaluation of LLMs in both proof generation and evaluation within propositional logic;
2. A comparative analysis of different LLMs (DeepSeek, Qwen, GPT, and Gemini) in the roles of problem solver and proof evaluator;
3. Empirical insights into the strengths, limitations, and potential for LLM-based ITS integration in formal logic learning.

2 Background and Related Work

In this section, we briefly provide an overview of some concepts on propositional logic relevant to our study, as well as we discuss some related work with respect to the use of LLMs for Logic Introductory courses in computing education, more specifically for logic problem solving related proof problems linked to argument validity. Specifically, we explore to construct formal proofs using the natural deduction method, a structured approach for determining the validity of arguments by systematically applying inference rules. Furthermore, we discuss some related work.

Constructing logical proofs for checking of argument validity within classical logic has been identified as an important and yet challenging topic for students in computing education and mathematics education [6]. There are different methods to accomplish proof construction to the task of verifying argument validity within propositional classic logic, like Natural Deduction, Sequent Calculus [5]. This work uses Natural Deduction method, using inference rules that can be applied to derive proofs. Inference rules are patterns of sound inference.

In propositional logic, an argument is considered valid if its conclusion logically follows from its premises. Natural Deduction is a proof system designed to mirror the way humans naturally reason, using a set of inference rules and replacement laws to derive conclusions from premises. This involves constructing each step of the proof themselves, using natural deduction method, where students repeatedly apply inference rules to deduce a target proposition (conclusion) from the premises provided. More formally, an argument in propositional logic consists of a non-empty set of sentences in a formal language, where one sentence is designated as the conclusion, and the others serve as premises, if any. The aim is to determine whether a conclusion can be logically derived from the premises using a sequence of deductive steps. Among the inference rules that can be used by the agent, are: Modus Ponens, Modus Tollens, Hypothetical Syllogism, Disjunctive Syllogism, Simplification, Conjunction. Furthermore, there are also rules for replacement or Standard logical equivalences, such as Morgan's Law, Double Negation, etc. These rules enable agents to construct valid proofs by linking premises to the desired conclusion in a logically sound manner.

Regarding related work, previous researches on the use of LLMs for Intelligent Tutoring Systems or similar Interactive Learning Environments, we have observed the increase investment in tools using generative artificial intelligence. Several research teams have explored the use of LLMs in some domains of education computing, including programming, mainly to create content and generate questions [3]. However, to the best of our knowledge, no study has yet explored the extent to which LLMs can aid simultaneously in proof generation and evaluation.

3 Methodology

In this section, we present our pipeline for generating and evaluating solutions by using LLMs, using the Fig. 1 with pipeline for solving problem and for solution evaluation.

3.1 Method

The main aim of this study is to assess the ability of LLMs to play problem solving roles, particularly the logic proof solver and solution evaluator, considering a benchmark dataset containing a collection of logic proof problems with different levels of difficulties, including 12 problems.

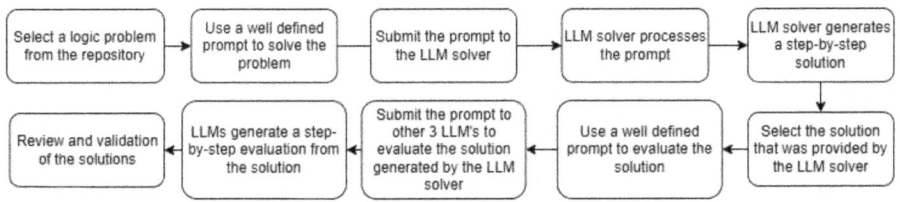

Fig. 1. Adopted Pipeline

We selected 12 problems from a constructed database across three difficulty levels (easy, average, and hard) with four per level. Each LLM (DeepSeek, Qwen, GPT, and Gemini) solved three problems, one from each difficulty level, and evaluated nine solutions produced by the other three models. This cross-evaluation design ensured each solution received assessments from three different LLMs, none of which had generated that particular solution. Problems within the same difficulty level tested similar logical concepts while maintaining comparable complexity, enabling meaningful assessment of each model's reasoning capabilities. To solve each problem, as illustrated in Fig. 1, we defined a well-defined prompt, where each LLM was assigned one problem from each difficulty level and generated a solution. The output from the solver LLMs was then submitted to three other LLMs, which acted as evaluators to assess the correctness and quality of the solutions. After obtaining the evaluation outputs from the evaluator LLMs, we reviewed and validated the assessments to conduct further analysis. We carefully balanced the distribution of problems across all models so that each LLM encountered tasks of equivalent difficulty and structure. This deliberate arrangement prevented any information leakage or cross-contamination during evaluation, thereby minimizing potential biases. At the same time, it allowed us to probe each model's reasoning skills independently, preserving the rigor of our comparative study. Importantly, we did not supply the models with extensive collections of inference rules. Instead, we relied on concise, task-specific prompts that encouraged the LLMs to demonstrate their natural capacity for logical reasoning. By avoiding large rule sets, we reduced the likelihood of superficial shortcuts and prompted the models to engage more deeply with each problem. Once all solutions and evaluations were collected, we conducted a detailed manual validation. First, we checked that every solution adhered to valid inference steps and did not omit critical reasoning or substitute informal arguments. Then, we compared the LLMs' assessments with our own analyses, marking any discrepancies as incorrect evaluations.

To define our easy, average, and hard categories, we drew upon our own experience in formal logic. We then classified each problem based on criteria such as the length of derivations, the complexity of premises, the inference rules required, and the clarity of each reasoning chain. This approach ensured that our selection was both fair and relevant to the experiences of our primary audience.

3.2 Prompt Design

We developed two prompt templates adhering to Schulhoff et al.'s taxonomy to facilitate logical proof tasks. Our first template employs a zero-shot instructional approach augmented with Chain-of-Thought reasoning and role specification:

Solve the following logic proof problem and provide a detailed, step-by-step explanation (step-by-step proof construction) using the natural deduction method using logical inference rules like Modus Ponens, Modus Tollens, Hypothetical Sylogism, as well as rules for replacement (like De Morgan's Law, Double Negation). The explanation should be tailored for undergraduate students in introductory logic courses, meaning you should define any technical terms and explain each step clearly (step-by-step proof construction). Problem: [Insert the problem here].

This template avoids providing examples while explicitly requesting step-by-step reasoning and accessibility at the undergraduate level.

Our second template focuses on critical assessment of logical proofs:

Evaluate the following logical proof resolution and provide a detailed explanation, evaluating the method of natural deduction using logical inference rules such as Modus Ponens, Modus Tollens, Hypothetical Syllogism, as well as rules for substitution (such as De Morgan's Law, Double Negation). The evaluation should be adapted for undergraduate students in introductory logic courses, which means you should evaluate any technical terms and explain each step clearly if it is correct or not.

This template similarly operates in the zero-shot regime while directing the model to produce validity judgments for each step in the proof.

By positioning both templates in the zero-shot paradigm and incorporating Chain-of-Thought and role prompting techniques, we elicit comprehensive reasoning traces and accessible explanations without the confounding effects introduced by few-shot examples. This approach enables us to isolate and examine the models' intrinsic reasoning capabilities in formal logical proof construction and evaluation.

4 Results and Discussion

In this section, we present the results of our study, considering each LLM and discuss them, as well as we compared the four large language models: Deepseek, Gemini, GPT, and Qwen, as illustrated in Fig. 1 and Fig. 2, consider the answers and discussions about the following three research questions.

Concerning the results of our RQ1: To what extent can LLMs generate correct formal proofs in propositional logic across different types of proof problems?

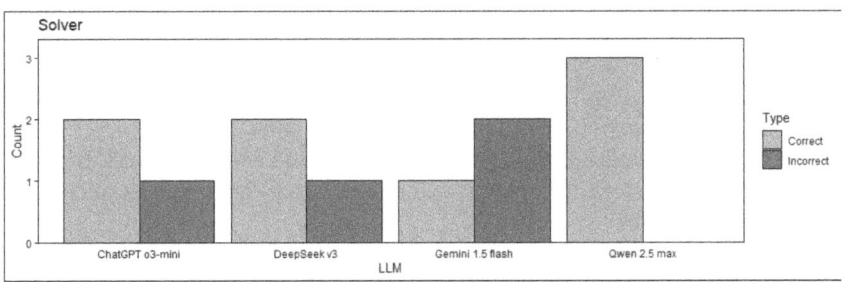

Fig. 2. Comparison among LLM solver

In order to answer this question, we performed experimental activities focused on problem solving with all the four LLMs. The LLMs exhibited satisfactory problem-solving capabilities, delivering appropriate solutions for 12 of the problems. The results of the evaluation are presented in Table 1.

Table 1. Overall Performance of LLMs

Overall Performance		
LLM	Solver Accuracy	Evaluator Accuracy
Gemini	33%	55.55%
Qwen	100%	55.55%
DeepSeek	66%	55.55%
GPT	66%	88.88%

The results presented by the Solver provide insight into how well the used different LLMs can generate formal proofs in propositional logic. The data shows that model performance varies significantly, suggesting differences in their ability to construct valid logical arguments.

Among the four models tested, Qwen 2.5 Max demonstrated the highest accuracy, producing 3 correct proofs and 0 error. This suggests that Qwen was able to handle the proof-generation task with a high degree of reliability, at least for the types of problems included in the evaluation. In contrast, Gemini 1.5 Flash struggled the most, with only 1 correct proof and 2 errors. This indicates that Gemini encountered difficulties in consistently applying logical inference rules to construct valid proofs. ChatGPT o3-mini and DeepSeek v3 performed at an intermediate level, each generating 2 correct proofs and 1 error. This suggests that while they can construct valid proofs in many cases, they are not immune to make mistakes. These errors could be due to misapplication of inference rules or replacement rules.

Overall, the results indicate that LLMs can generate correct formal proofs to some extent, but their accuracy is not uniform across models. The fact that none of the models achieved perfect accuracy across all proof problems suggests that relying on LLMs for formal proof generation requires caution, as errors may still occur. However, the performance of Qwen 2.5 Max demonstrates that at least some models can achieve a high level of reliability in this task.

Concerning the results of our RQ2: What are the comparative strengths and weaknesses of different LLMs when performing the roles of solver and evaluator in logic proof problems?

To compare the strengths and weaknesses of different LLMs in both the Solver and Evaluator roles, we need to analyze their performance in generating formal proofs and in assessing the validity of proofs generated by others. The results from the two bar charts, as illustrated in Fig. 2 and Fig. 3, provide a clear view of how each model performed in these distinct tasks. In summary, we find the following information related to comparative performance in the solver role, where the LLMs were tested on their ability to construct correct formal proofs. The results were as follows:

- Qwen 2.5 Max performed the best, achieving a very relevant score with 3 correct proofs and 0 errors. This suggests that Qwen 2.5 Max is highly effective at applying logical inference rules correctly and structuring valid proofs.
- ChatGPT o3-mini and DeepSeek v3 both performed well, each achieving 2 correct proofs and 1 error. This indicates that while they can solve formal logic problems, they are not flawless and may occasionally make mistakes in reasoning or inference.
- Gemini 1.5 Flash struggled the most in this role, with only 1 correct proof and 2 errors. This suggests that Gemini had more difficulty correctly structuring formal proofs or may have misapplied logical rules more frequently than the other models.

With respect to Strengths and Weaknesses as Solvers, we can observe:

- Strengths: Qwen 2.5 Max showed a significant advantage in proof generation, suggesting a well-developed logical reasoning capability. ChatGPT o3-mini and DeepSeek v3 also demonstrated strong performance, making them reliable for constructing proofs in most cases.
- Weaknesses: Gemini 1.5 Flash had difficulty generating correct proofs, which could indicate issues with handling formal logic structures, correctly applying inference rules, or maintaining consistency in reasoning.

Regarding to Comparative Performance in the Evaluator Role, the obtained results were as follows:

In the evaluator role, the models were tested on their ability to distinguish between correct and incorrect reasoning steps in given proofs. The results were as follows.

- ChatGPT o3-mini was the strongest performer, achieving 8 correct evaluations and only 1 error. This suggests that it has a strong ability to critically analyze proofs and identify errors.
- Qwen 2.5 Max, DeepSeek v3, and Gemini 1.5 Flash all had similar performance, with 5 correct evaluations and 4 errors each. This means that they correctly classified proofs just over half the time, but struggled with accuracy, frequently misidentifying correct or incorrect proofs.

About Strengths and Weaknesses as Evaluators, the obtained results were:

- Strengths: ChatGPT o3-mini was the most reliable evaluator, showing a strong ability to accurately judge the proofs. This suggests that it has better developed skills for assessing logical structures and detecting flaws in reasoning.
- Weaknesses: The other three models (Qwen 2.5 Max, DeepSeek v3, and Gemini 1.5 Flash) had moderate accuracy, indicating inconsistency in their evaluation abilities. Their high error rates suggest that they might not recognize logical errors or incorrectly flag valid proofs as incorrect.

This preliminary analysis highlights how different LLMs have varying strengths and weaknesses when applied to logical reasoning in propositional logic.

5 Conclusion and Future Work

In this paper, our general goal was to assess the feasibility of using LLMs to solve logic proof problems, as well as to evaluate developed solutions. To achieve this goal, we compared four different LLMs with respect to these two problem solving activities. Our preliminary findings suggest that LLMs achieved reasonable success for the two problem solving activities examined, providing somehow appropriate answers, but some uncertainty remains regarding the quality or even the correctness of the solution.

Of course, we are aware of some important limitations related to our approach. In an immediate future work, for instance, we intend to perform a more qualitative analysis and to improve our quantitative evaluation with statistical analysis to apply our experimental approach to larger LLMs, running more experiments with a vast number of problems.

References

1. de Barros Costa, E., et al.: An agent-based tutoring system for learning propositional logic using multiple linked representations. In: 2014 IEEE Frontiers in Education Conference (FIE) Proceedings, pp. 1–7 (2014). https://doi.org/10.1109/FIE.2014.7044342
2. du Boulay, B.: Artificial intelligence as an effective classroom assistant. IEEE Intell. Syst. **31**(6), 76–81 (2016). https://doi.org/10.1109/MIS.2016.93
3. Doughty, J., et al.: A comparative study of AI-generated (GPT-4) and human-crafted MCQs in programming education. In: Proceedings of the 26th Australasian Computing Education Conference, ACE 2024, pp. 114–123. Association for Computing Machinery, New York (2024). https://doi.org/10.1145/3636243.3636256
4. Hellas, A., Leinonen, J., Sarsa, S., Koutcheme, C., Kujanpää, L., Sorva, J.: Exploring the responses of large language models to beginner programmers' help requests. In: Proceedings of the 2023 ACM Conference on International Computing Education Research - Volume 1, ICER 2023, pp. 93–105. Association for Computing Machinery, New York (2023). https://doi.org/10.1145/3568813.3600139
5. Lesta, L., Yacef, K.: An intelligent teaching assistant system for logic. In: Cerri, S.A., Gouardères, G., Paraguaçu, F. (eds.) ITS 2002. LNCS, vol. 2363, pp. 421–431. Springer, Heidelberg (2002). https://doi.org/10.1007/3-540-47987-2_45
6. Yacef, K.: The Logic-ITA in the classroom: a medium scale experiment. Int. J. Artif. Intell. Educ. **15**, 41–62 (2005). https://telearn.hal.science/hal-00257107

Generative AI Agents for Instructional Co-design: A Sequential Agent-Based Approach Using a Low-Code/No-Code Platform

Dimitrios Tolis[1]($^{\boxtimes}$), Stylianos Mystakidis[2], Ioannis Hatzilygeroudis[3], and Konstantinos Siozopoulos[4]

[1] Faculty of Technology, University of Turku, Turku, Finland
`dimitrios.tolis@utu.fi`
[2] School of Natural Sciences, University of Patras, Patras, Greece
`smyst@upatras.gr`
[3] Department of Computer Engineering and Informatics, University of Patras, Patras, Greece
`ihatz@ceid.upatras.gr`
[4] Department of Applied Informatics, University of Macedonia, Thessaloniki, Greece
`aid24006@uom.edu.gr`

Abstract. This paper explores how a Low-Code/No-Code (LCNC) platform can be used by non-technical users, such as educators, to design and deploy a Sequential Agent-Based Generative AI System to facilitate instructional design. The system deploys an LLM-based sequential workflow of AI agents to support educators in the first three stages of the ADDIE instructional design model: Analysis, Design, and Development. It follows a co-design, Human-In-The-Loop (HITL) approach, where AI agents guide instructional designers on needs analysis, content validation and generation, while allowing user intervention. The system also explores the role of self-checking agents for fact-checking, bias detection, and instructional quality review, based on specific prompts. However, the identified potential remains theoretical, requiring empirical validation through user testing to assess usability, effectiveness, and adoption by non-IT users.

Keywords: Generative AI · AI Agents · Low-Code/No-Code · Instructional Design · Citizen Development · Human-In-The-Loop · AI in Education · Flowise · LangChain · LangGraph · Fact-checking · Bias detection

1 Introduction

The integration of Artificial Intelligence (AI) in education, especially after the advancement of LLMs in recent years, has the potential to transform education, as it offers new ways to explore how to create, optimize and personalize learning experiences. Emerging educational technologies can be used to facilitate new conceptual models to improve the effectiveness of education [1]. However, it is evident that many educators without technical background lack programming skills to develop sophisticated and complex AI-driven applications to fulfill their educational needs and ideas [2].

This paper explores how a Low-Code/No-Code platform can be used to create a Sequential Agent-Based Generative AI System. Although the system was not designed and implemented by educators, using LCNC tools requires minimal programming skills, making it possible for educators to understand and adjust its behavior through visual interfaces and editable prompt templates.

The system novelties are that it employs a structure of sequential AI agents that guide instructional designers using the ADDIE instructional design process as an example modular methodology [3]. The Analysis, Design and Development steps are implemented, incorporating automated learning needs analysis, learning outcomes and content generation, fact-checking, bias detection and instructional design quality check following a Human-In-The-Loop approach (HITL) [4].

2 Literature Review

In the past classic intelligent tutoring systems, such as AutoTutor, have demonstrated the potential of AI in education by engaging learners in natural language dialogues to enhance deep learning [5]. However, these models focused on knowledge modeling but required more technical expertise. Our approach uses generative AI and LCNC to reduce technical barriers following the increasing trend internationally regarding Citizen Developers [6], who are users with minimal or no programming skills to design and develop their own software solutions using user-friendly LCNC platforms and tools. Low-Code/No-Code (LCNC) platforms create an easy to understand and use environment where users can build applications using visual interfaces, like drag-and-drop tools, with minimal or no programming code, instead of relying heavily on traditional coding [7]. Our proposed system brings co-design of AI flows within reach of educators as non-programmers.

ChatGPT has been used extensively in education and in Instructional Design with impressive results [8]. However, AI agents are significantly more capable—and more complex to design and deploy—than simple chains of LLM prompts. This increases the design complexity, which can be mitigated with the ease of use provided by LCNC platforms. Although there are benefits of AI in education, concerns remain regarding the accuracy, bias, and ethical implications of AI-generated content. In response to these concerns, Fact-Checking & Bias Detection self-checking agents may play a crucial role in verifying content accuracy, detecting biases, and mitigating hallucinations in Large Language Models (LLMs) [9].

3 System Architecture

3.1 Frameworks, Platforms and Tools

For the design and implementation of the system, Flowise is an open-source LCNC platform which allows non-IT users to use both LangChain and LangGraph frameworks with a drag-and-drop GUI [10]. LangChain [11] is an open-source framework for developing applications powered by LLMs. LangGraph framework [9] is more suitable for more complex agent-based applications.

3.2 System Overview

The developed system called AiHub [12] is structured into three main components (see Fig. 1), the User Management & Interface, the Flowise LCNC Platform & Agent Flow (Sequential Agents) and the Course Generation & Delivery Subsystem.

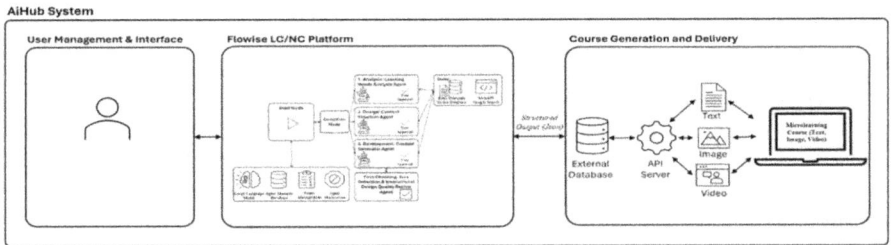

Fig. 1. The AiHub Architecture Overview

This paper focuses on the Sequential Agent-Based Co-Design Process using Flowise LCNC platform (see Fig. 2); User Management & Interface and Course Generation & Delivery components are beyond the scope of this study.

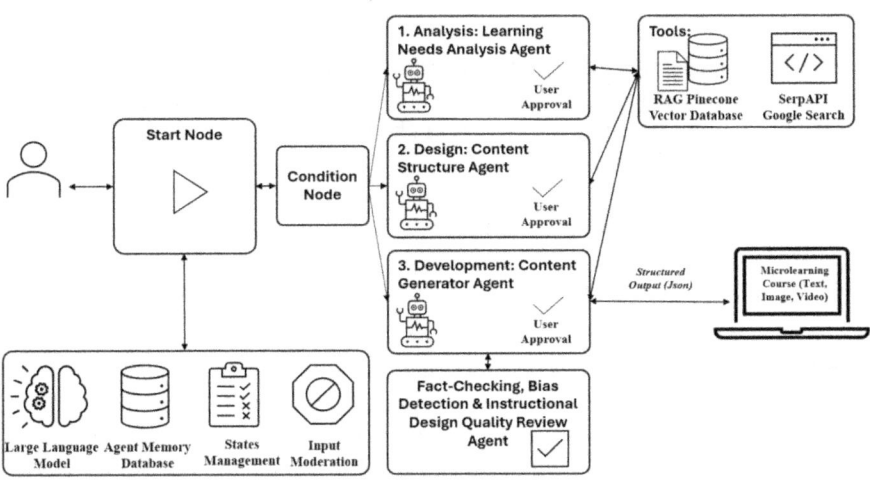

Fig. 2. The Agent Flow (LangGraph-Based Sequential Agents)

3.3 Agent Workflow Description

The Sequential Agent-Based Co-Design Process using Flowise LCNC platform (see Fig. 2) is based on an architecture that enables multiple autonomous agents to collaborate, reason, and make collective decisions. Choi et al. [13] argue that AI is efficient at generating course maps, but human expertise is required to validate the quality and accuracy of the content that is produced. To address this, we have applied a Human In-The-Loop (HITL) approach in every step of the content generation process to add credibility and accountability of the designer. Also, Agents are designed to align with instructional design best practices such as scaffolding and feedback loops.

Start Node: In Sequential Agent architecture, the Start Node is the initial point where the workflow begins. It receives the user's initial query and passes it to subsequent nodes and agents for processing. The Start Node is connected to a Chat Model in our case GPT-4o as an example and to an Agent Memory Node providing a mechanism for persistent memory storage. The Start Node is further connected to the State Node which plays a crucial role in managing and preserving the workflow's states, ensuring that the context is preserved throughout the interaction. Finally, the Start Node is connected to a prompt-based Input Moderation Node that analyzes user inputs to prevent potentially harmful or inappropriate content from being processed by the language model and the flow in general.

LLM Node and Condition Node: The routing function is executed jointly by the LLM Node and the Condition Node. The LLM Node analyzes the conversations with the user, using the connected LLM, and determines where we are in the process and what needs to happen next. The LLM Node is linked to the Condition Node, which evaluates the predefined logical expressions or rules based on the current state or input data, and when the conditions are met, it directs the workflow along different branches of connected Agents in the sequence.

Learning Needs Analysis Agent: The Learning Needs Analysis Agent goal is to collect from the Instructional Designer the key learning needs analysis data, such as target audience, curriculum requirements, needs or challenges that have been identified by the user and need to be addressed. The steps the agent must follow based on the prompt given are: a. Introduce the Agent Persona and System's Goals, b. Gather Key Learning Needs Analysis Information, c. Customize the design with user specific data, d. Extend the search to the web for more context, e. Summarize and get approval, f. Generate proposes Title, Training Overview and Learning Outcomes, g. Seek User's Final Approval (HITL).

Content Structure Design Agent: Based on the Title, an Overview and the Learning outcomes, and with the RAG or web information, if available, this agent, responsible for generating microlearning content, will design the proposed Content Structure for the user to approve (HITL). The content structure may be generated by the agent prompt and the user's resources, for example the custom RAG implementation or a web search.

Content Generator Development Agent: Based on all the previous information (Title, Overview, Learning Outcomes and Content Structure Design) the Content Generator Agent will develop the actual content using also custom RAG and the Web search engine tool for more content if needed.

Fact-Checking, Bias Detection and Instructional Design Quality Review Agent: Before the user receives the outcome of the content generator design, to increase trustworthiness, avoid biases and hallucinations [9] a Fact-Checking, Bias Detection and Instructional Design Quality Review Agent structure has been implemented.

4 Scenario-Based Evaluation: Corporate Training Use Case

We have tried the system with a sample scenario from the hospitality industry. A corporate training firm in the Hospitality Industry seeks to develop a micro-learning course on "Guest Experience". The instructional designer uses the agent-based workflow to co-design structured content efficiently.

Step 1: The discussion starts with the needs analysis process, where this first agent collects all the information that it needs, from 3 sources: The text input from the user, the RAG documents they might upload and the web search for further context. Based on this information the agent produces a summary of the needs and asks for approval or refinement by the user.

Step 2: Upon approval, corresponding states are updated with the new information and results are sent to the next agent, the Content Structure Agent, whose task is to propose the content structure for approval or refinement by the user.

Step 3: Upon approval, the Content Generator Agent develops the actual material which is processed by Fact, Bias, and Quality Checking mechanisms with multiple passes to ensure accuracy, fairness, and engagement.

5 Conclusions and Future Research

This paper presents a proposed Sequential Agent-Based Generative AI System designed and deployed using LCNC tools, without the need for advanced programming skills, making it accessible to non-technical Citizen Developers, like educators. Unlike static AI chatbots, which primarily serve as conversational assistants, AI agents can show advanced reasoning capabilities, decision-making, and external tool integration to perform complex instructional tasks, including content generation, verification, and loops of iterative refinement.

The sequential agent-based workflow introduces a structured semi-automated process, with HITL approvals in every step, in which agents work collaboratively, moving sequentially from learning needs analysis to content generation, fact-checking, bias detection, and quality validation, before final content production. Their ability to retrieve and analyze external knowledge, through prompt engineering, web search, Retrieval-Augmented Generation (RAG) and self-checking agents, ensures that the generated instructional content is factually accurate, pedagogically sound, and contextually relevant.

Despite the proposed system's potential, it remains theoretical, as it relies on scenario-based evaluation rather than empirical evidence. To address this limitation, future research is proposed to focus on empirical validation with educators designing, using, adjusting the system, testing it in real-world educational settings and measurement of the system's effectiveness, usability and impact on the instructional design process.

References

1. Mystakidis, S., Lympouridis, V.: Immersive learning design in the metaverse: a theoretical literature review synthesis. In: Liu, D., Huang, R., Hosny Saleh Metwally, A., Tlili, A., Fan Lin, E. (eds.) Application of the Metaverse in Education, pp. 55–71. Springer, Cham (2024). https://doi.org/10.1007/978-981-97-1298-4_4
2. Celik, I., Dindar, M., Muukkonen, H., Järvelä, S.: The promises and challenges of artificial intelligence for teachers: a systematic review of research. TechTrends **66**, 616–630 (2022). https://doi.org/10.1007/s11528-022-00715-y
3. Spatioti, A.G., Kazanidis, I., Pange, J.: A comparative study of the ADDIE instructional design model in distance education. Information **13**, 402 (2022). https://doi.org/10.3390/info13090402
4. Mosqueira-Rey, E., Hernández-Pereira, E., Alonso-Ríos, D., Bobes-Bascarán, J., Fernández-Leal, Á.: Human-in-the-loop machine learning: a state of the art. Artif. Intell. Rev. **56**, 3005–3054 (2023). https://doi.org/10.1007/s10462-022-10246-w
5. Graesser, A.C., Chipman, P., Haynes, B.C., Olney, A.: AutoTutor: an intelligent tutoring system with mixed-initiative dialogue. IEEE Trans. Educ. **48** (2005). https://doi.org/10.1109/TE.2005.856149
6. Binzer, B., Winkler, T.J.: Democratizing software development: a systematic multivocal literature review and research agenda on citizen development. In: Lecture Notes in Business Information Processing, pp. 244–259. Springer (2022). https://doi.org/10.1007/978-3-031-20706-8_17
7. Viljoen, A., Altın, E.N., Hein, A., Krcmar, H.: Beyond Citizen Development: Exploring Low-Code Platform Adoption by Professional Software Developers (2024)
8. Madunić, J., Sovulj, M.: Application of ChatGPT in information literacy instructional design. Publications **12**, 11 (2024). https://doi.org/10.3390/publications12020011
9. Wang, J., Duan, Z.: Controlling Large Language Model Hallucination Based on Agent AI with LangGraph (2025). https://www.cambridge.org/engage/coe/article-details/677c7fbafa469535b905cace. https://doi.org/10.33774/coe-2025-xkwl5
10. Flowise: Flowise Documentation. https://docs.flowiseai.com. Accessed 08 Feb 2025
11. LangChain Documentation. https://python.langchain.com/docs/introduction/. Accessed 07 Feb 2025
12. Tolis, D., Mystakidis, S., Christopoulos, A.: Generative AI applications in education: a Low-Code/No-Code approach. In: Geroimenko, V. (ed.) Human-Computer Creativity: Generative AI in Education, Art, and Healthcare, pp. 135–151. Springer, Cham (2025). https://doi.org/10.1007/978-3-031-86551-0_8
13. Choi, G.W., Kim, S.H., Lee, D., Moon, J.: Utilizing generative AI for instructional design: exploring strengths, weaknesses, opportunities, and threats. TechTrends **68**, 832–844 (2024). https://doi.org/10.1007/s11528-024-00967-w

Author Index

A

Abdessalem, Hamdi Ben   II-47, II-181
Ahn, Taekyung   II-259
Akrida, Eleni   II-229
Al Saqaabi, Arwa   II-229
Al-Barazie, Ray   II-32
Alexe, Vasile Paul   I-32
Anquetil, Eric   I-259
Antoniou, Sarantis   II-302

B

Bae, Jiyeong   II-259
Balaska, Vasiliki   II-64, II-302
Balyan, Renu   II-17
Barchouch, Islam   I-259
Barmpari, Ariadni   I-213
Becerra, Edier   I-202
Belpaeme, Tony   I-3
Ben Ayed, Yassine   II-197
Bernard, Jason   I-144
Betbeder, Marie-Laure   I-17
Bold, Nicolae   II-114
Bonyad, Amin   II-47, II-181
Born, Seanghort   II-244
Bouaziz, Bassem   II-3
Bratanov, Daniel   II-64
Brazil, Grace   I-281
Brockmann, Annalise   I-224
Bydlon, Tim   I-281
Byun, Gyuri   II-213, II-287

C

Caramihai, Simona Iuliana   II-104
Chang, Daniel   I-88
Choi, Haemin   II-73
Choi, Seongyune   II-169
Costa, Dante   I-159
Costa, Evandro   I-159
Courtemanche, Marc-Antoine   I-270
Cristea, Alexandra I.   II-229

D

D.Vologiannidis, Stavros   II-152
da Silva Neo, Alana Viana Borges   II-274
da Silva Neo, Giseldo   II-274
da Silva, Leandro   I-159
da Silva, Rian Américo Brito   I-292
Dass, Rahul   I-281
de Araújo Costa, Dante   I-292
de Barros Costa, Evandro   I-292, II-274
de Melo Lins, Davi Silva   I-292
de Sousa, Wallace Lins Casado   I-292
Dewan, M. Ali Akber   II-159
Deye, Erin   I-281
Dittel, Jeffrey S.   I-171
Duarte, Ernesto José   I-202
Dumitran, Adrian Marius   I-32

E

Efstathiou, Dimitrios E.   II-152
Eom, Juhong   II-287
Esteban Cuellar Argotty, Juan   I-192

F

Frasson, Claude   II-47, II-181
Freedman, Reva   I-224

G

Garcés, Kelly   I-131
Gargouri, Faiez   II-3
Gasteratos, Antonios C.   II-152
Gasteratos, Antonios   II-64, II-302
Girard, Nathalie   I-259
Goel, Ashok   I-281

Graf, Sabine I-144
Guatibonza Briceño, Pablo Alejandro I-235
Gustafson, Jerry Ryan David II-159
Gutierrez, Carlos Enrique II-159

H
Hamza, Sihem II-197
Hatzilygeroudis, Ioannis I-213, I-301
Henriet, Julien I-17

I
Iacobelli, Francisco II-17
Iksal, Sébastien II-244
Ionita, Anca Daniela II-104

J
Jamet, Eric I-259
Jang, Yeonju II-169
Jeon, Minji II-213
Jeong, Hyeonseo II-287
Jhajj, Gaganpreet II-159
Johnson, Benny G. I-171
Jung, Heeseok II-169

K
Kadri, Rahma II-3
Kang, Minji II-287
Kansizoglou, Ioannis II-64, II-302
Karakatsanis, Theoklitos S. II-152
Karakatsanis, Theoklitos II-302
Kawulok, Mateusz I-116
Kim, Dohee II-259
Kim, Gospel II-287
Kim, Hansung II-287
Kim, Hyeoncheol I-246, II-88, II-137, II-169, II-213, II-259, II-287
Kim, Woojin II-88
Klopstock, Nicolás I-202
Koh, Junbo II-213
Kosmidis, Michail II-64

L
Leconte, Laura I-259
Lee, Gunho II-259
Lee, Seungyeon II-287
Lee, Sookbun II-259
Lee, Unggi II-213, II-259, II-287
Lee, Yunseo II-213, II-287
Li, Xiaoyan I-102

Lin, Fuhua II-159
Lin, Michael Pin-Chuan I-88, II-159
Liu, Arita Li I-88
Lugo Sánchez, Juan Diego I-131
Lum, Cherie I-281

M
Maćkowski, Michał I-116
Madhusudhana, Rochan I-281
Malinao, Jasmine A. II-125
Manrique Piramanrique, Rubén I-235
Manrique, Rubén I-131
Manrique, Ruben I-192
Manrique, Rubén I-202
May, Madeth II-244
Meftah, Leila Haj II-313
Mnejja, Sirine II-313
Mocanu, Stefan Alexandru II-104
Mohamed, Azza II-32
Moon, Jewoong II-287
Morland, Raymond II-159
Moroianu, Theodor-Pierre I-32
Moskalenko, Nikita I-74
Moura, J. Antão B. II-274
Mystakidis, Stylianos I-301

N
Na, Jihoi II-287
Nadarajan, Gayathri II-73
Nedelcu, Irina-Gabriela II-104
Nkambou, Roger I-59, I-182, I-270
Nyamen Tato, Ange Adrienne I-59

O
Osorio Cárdenas, Daniel I-235

P
Park, Jaekwon II-259
Park, Sunwoo I-246, II-137
Patel, Minhaz I-224
Piau-Toffolon, Claudine II-244
Popescu, Doru Anastasiu II-114
Popescu, Ion Alexandru II-114
Psomoulis, Athanasios II-64
Psyché, Valéry I-59

R
Ribeiro, Brena Marques I-131
Roca, Therese Nuelle II-125

Rosales Rosero, Edgar Eduardo I-235
Rosiak, Maria I-116
Rutatola, Edger P. I-3
Ryoo, Jeeho I-88

S

Saffari, Saeed I-88
Sánchez Puccini, Mario Eduardo I-235
Saru, Daniela II-104
Shin, Jaeyoon II-213
Sidor, Andrey I-74
Silva, Emanuele I-159
Silva, Marlos I-159
Silva, Priscylla I-159
Siozopoulos, Konstantinos I-301
Soares, Alison Bruno Martires I-292
Son, Yoorim II-213
Sotiropoulou, Anna II-114
Soto-Forero, Daniel I-17
Stefanidakis, Michalis II-114
Stewart, Craig II-229
Stroeken, Koen I-3
Sullivan, Ian I-224

Sychev, Oleg I-74
Symeonidis, Symeon II-302

T

Tamkodjou Tchio, Guy Carlos I-59
Tato, Ange I-182
Tenório, Jean Felipe Duarte I-292
Thompson, Kayla II-17
Tmar, Mohamed II-3
Tolis, Dimitrios I-301

U

Uglev, Viktor I-47

V

Valéry, Psyché I-270
Van Campenhout, Rachel I-171
Verma, Shashank I-281
Vlachou, Eftychios I. II-152
Vlachou, Vasileios I. II-152
Voyiatzaki, Eleni I-213

W

Wang, Jingyun I-102
Wynn, Adam I-102

GPSR Compliance
The European Union's (EU) General Product Safety Regulation (GPSR) is a set of rules that requires consumer products to be safe and our obligations to ensure this.

If you have any concerns about our products, you can contact us on

ProductSafety@springernature.com

In case Publisher is established outside the EU, the EU authorized representative is:

Springer Nature Customer Service Center GmbH
Europaplatz 3
69115 Heidelberg, Germany

www.ingramcontent.com/pod-product-compliance
Lightning Source LLC
Chambersburg PA
CBHW052119040825
30594CB00029B/651